Diaries of

compiled and edited by

David J. Hogg

Published by David J. Hogg, 2009.

For Georgina, Ella, Charlie, Eve, George and Megan.

ISBN 978-0-9554457-3-6

Printed and bound in Great Britain by
CPI Antony Rowe, Chippenham and Eastbourne

Figure 1. Tyntesfield in 1870.

DIARIES OF TYNTESFIELD

CONTENTS

Introduction

This book is a response to a challenge. When the National Trust purchased Tyntesfield, it was thought that the late Lord Wraxall's archive would be accessible for research purposes. Sadly this was not to be the case. Since Lord Wraxall's demise the family archive has remained closed. However there are other resources available. Luckily Henry Hucks Gibbs, the first Lord Aldenham and William Gibbs' nephew, was very interested in the history of his family. He collected family letters, and wrote diaries which cover most of the period between 1846 and 1907, when he died. He also assembled and published a Pedigree of the Family of Gibbs. The current Lord Aldenham very kindly gave me access to the diaries and the books on the history of his family in his possession. These included the diaries of Henry Hucks Gibbs, the diaries of George Gibbs of Belmont, married to William Gibbs' sister Harriett, and the diary of George Henry Gibbs, William's elder brother. The Aldenham letters are kept in the Antony Gibbs and Sons Archive in the Guildhall Library in London and I spent many hours there looking through the thirty or more large folios of family letters dating from 1744 to 1905. Ideally this book would have included the diaries of William Gibbs and his son Antony, but these are held in the closed family archive. However Henry Hucks Gibbs was such a frequent visitor to Tyntesfield and such a close friend to William and Blanche Gibbs, that his diaries give a unique insight into the Tyntesfield family during the nineteenth century.

Dr Denis Gibbs, also descended from George Henry Gibbs, and his wife Rachel were exceedingly helpful and hospitable and gave me access to the "Reminiscences" of the Rev. John Lomax Gibbs, William Gibbs' nephew and Henry Hucks Gibbs' brother. Rachel Gibbs produced the most recent edition of the Pedigree of Gibbs in 1981 and it is a scholarly and most informative resource on the Gibbs family. Denis showed me family photograph albums from the nineteenth century and allowed me to digitally photograph the relevant pictures from these albums.

The Rev. John Lomax Gibbs' eldest son, John Arthur Gibbs, wrote "The History of Antony and Dorothea Gibbs and their Contemporary Relatives including the History of the Origin and Early Years of the House of Antony Gibbs and Sons", which was published in 1922. It is a very lengthy and detailed study of which I have made a concise summary, which forms the first chapter of this book. This will enable the reader to trace the background of many of the people and families mentioned in the diaries. It also provides the historical context in which some of the events took place.

The Victorians were great letter writers and hence I have included the names of many of the correspondents of Henry Hucks Gibbs, although not all the names mentioned in his diaries are given since some have little or no relevance to Tyntesfield. It may well be that local readers will recognise the names of past family members or friends. Readers from the Gibbs family may also be able to throw light on some of the characters in this drama.

I have concluded the book with a description of what happened to the family firm after the end of their involvement in the guano trade. It is a tale of the rise and decline of a great merchant house – Antony Gibbs and Sons. For this I consulted Charles Maude's book, "Antony Gibbs and Sons Limited, Merchants and Bankers, 1808 to 1958", which commemorated 150 years of the House of Gibbs. The firm was taken over by the Hong Kong and Shanghai Bank in 1980, which for the Gibbs family marked the end of an era.

David J. Hogg, December 2008.

The Author and Editor

David Hogg was educated at Dulwich College. He is a graduate of University College London and has a Diploma in Education from Oxford University and a Master's Degree from the University of Bath. His career in teaching included posts in London, Gloucestershire and Cardiff, but he spent much of his working life abroad in the Federation of Rhodesia and Nyasaland, Singapore, Canada, Uganda and eventually in Belgium, where for fourteen years he taught Geography and History at the European School of Brussels. He is the author of numerous articles in various journals and wrote "Sir Arthur Lawley, Eloquent Knight Errant", the biography of Lady Wraxall's father. The "Diaries of Tyntesfield" is his second book on the history of Tyntesfield.

Acknowledgements

The National Trust at Tyntesfield is to be thanked for permitting the use of the pictures in Figures 1, 5, 6 and 7 and in Plates 5, 7, 8, 9, 10, 12, 17, 18 and 20. I should like to thank too Lord Aldenham and Denis and Rachel Gibbs for permitting me to use their Diaries and Reminiscences and their family portraits and photographs. My thanks are also due to the staff of the Guildhall Library's Manuscripts Section in the City of London, where the Archive of Antony Gibbs and Sons is held, for all their help, patience and understanding.

The Story of Antony and Dorothea Gibbs and their family.[i]

Early Days

George Abraham Gibbs was born in 1718 and died on November 17th 1794. He inherited the 100 acre Estate of Pytte at Clyst St George in 1744. Well educated, in 1747 he was appointed Surgeon at the Royal Devon and Exeter Hospital. On December 22nd 1747, he married Anne Vicary, the daughter of Anthony and Elizabeth Vicary of Exeter. Anthony Vicary was a wealthy man, who kept a grocer's shop in combination with a linen draper's. On his marriage George Abraham took a house near the Bishop's Palace in the Cathedral Close in Exeter. George Abraham was brought up a Presbyterian, but later joined the Church of England.

George and Anne had eleven children, one of whom, their first son George, died in infancy. They had four other boys – Vicary, George, Abraham and Antony – and they all went to Exeter Grammar School. Vicary obtained a King's Scholarship at Eton, and was there from 1764 to 1770. In 1770 he was elected a scholar of King's College Cambridge of which he was a Fellow from 1774 to 1784. He was a very distinguished Greek Scholar. In August 1778 he was admitted as a student at Lincoln's Inn and was called to the Bar in 1783. George Gibbs was apprenticed to his cousin, Samuel Munckley, West India Merchant and in 1768 Master of the Merchant Venturers of Bristol. In January 1789 he was taken into partnership by Munckley. The fourth son, Abraham Gibbs, was sent by his father to Genoa to work with a firm importing Devon cloth. Four of George and Anne's daughters married – Elizabeth to Dr Robert B. Remmett, a physician in Plymouth, Anne to Samuel Banfill of Exwick, Mary to the Rev. Charles Crawley of Flaxley Abbey and Catherine to Bellett Burroughs of Taunton. Their two other daughters, Sibella and Sarah did not marry. Sarah died at the age of 21, but Sibella lived to the ripe old age of 81 and died in Long Ashton on Christmas day 1841. She was buried at Wraxall.

Captain John Gibbs of Topsham also had a son called Abraham who founded the mercantile houses of Abraham Gibbs and Co. of Palermo, and with Edmund and George Noble – Falconnet, Gibbs and Co. of Naples and Palermo.[ii] This Abraham Gibbs became banker to the Court of Naples, agent for Lord Nelson in the management of his Estate at Bronte, and Consul at Palermo for the United States of America. The fifth son, Lyle, went out to Italy in 1778 and became a partner with John and Charles Heath in the firm of Heath and Co. of Genoa. After the death of Charles Heath and the retirement of John Heath, Lyle changed the name of the firm to Gibbs and Co.[iii]

1774 – 1784: Exeter and Exwick

Antony Gibbs was born 3rd March 1756 in Exeter. He was educated at Exeter Grammar School. In 1774 he was apprenticed to Mr. Brook of Exeter whose firm was trading with Spain. Here he learned Spanish. From 1778 to 1789 Antony ran his own enterprise as a merchant exporting woollen cloth to Spain and elsewhere and he was also a partner in Gibbs, Granger and Banfill, a firm manufacturing woollen cloth at Exwick. His father George Abraham Gibbs financed him and was also a partner in the woollen mill. In January 1784, Antony became engaged to Dorothea Barnetta Hucks. She had previously been engaged to his brother, Abraham, who died in 1782. Her father William Hucks was a wine merchant from Knaresborough in Yorkshire. The Knaresborough family was a branch of the family of wealthy London Brewer, Robert Hucks, whose estates at Aldenham in Hertfordshire and at Clifton Hampden and Wallingford in Oxfordshire and elsewhere were eventually inherited by Antony's eldest son George Henry Gibbs (always known as Henry). In 1774, Dorothea's eldest sister Eleanor had married the wealthy London Solicitor Henry Townley Ward, and between 1777 and 1779, Dorothea had lived with them in their house in Soho in London. Eleanor had no children, but was very sociable and had many influential friends. She and Dorothea were very close.

In 1784 three of George Abraham Gibbs children got married. On 12th April, Antony's sister Mary married the Rev Charles Crawley, the son of Thomas Crawley Boevey of Flaxley Abbey in Gloucestershire.

On 8th July 1784, Vicary Gibbs married June Frances Mackenzie (born in 1755) at St Marylebone Church in London. She was the eldest daughter of Major William Mackenzie and his wife Mary. They set up home at Red Lion Square in London where their only child Mary Elizabeth was born in 1785. They later resided in Bloomsbury Square (1792), 42 Bedford Square (1806), 35 Russell Square (1811) and Baltimore House, 67 Russell Square (1814). From 1802 they also had a country house, Hayes Grove, on Hayes Common in Kent.

On 3rd October 1784, Antony Gibbs married Dorothea Barnetta Hucks in the Church of St Margaret and St Andrew in Littleham near Exmouth. They moved into a house on the Town Walls in Exeter where their eldest son George Henry Gibbs was born on 24th August 1785.

7

They then moved into Exwick House, which they could ill afford, where their eldest daughter Harriett was born on 8th October 1786

In 1786, a woollen cloth factory was established at Exwick in which Antony was seemingly the senior partner with Edmund Granger of Rougemont Castle, Exeter, and Samuel Banfill. Gibbs, Granger and Banfill bought cloth in Exeter which they finished and died in the Exwick factory. The factory had a water wheel which furnished the power for the machinery. Later the factory was to become a fully fledged woollen mill. Over ambitious expansion had resulted in the company being very heavily indebted.

1785 – 1789: Exeter and Exwick

On August 11th 1788, Antony Gibbs embarked for Calais. His business took him to Amiens, Beauvais, Paris, Orléans, Tours, Limoges, Lyons, Montpelier, Toulouse and Bayonne in France. Thence he continued into Spain stopping at Guipuzcoa, Castille, Asturias and Galicia en route to Madrid. He had intended returning by sea, but decided instead to return by the same overland route to settle unfinished business. He did not reach home until May 1789. He was seeking new orders for woollen goods and endeavouring to obtain money outstanding from previous deals. The serious financial crisis in France and Spain prior to the French Revolution meant that Antony was unable to obtain all the monies owed for cloth exports and further orders were at risk.

Over-optimistic endeavours at a time when events in France were disturbing the markets across Europe had led Antony into financial peril. His liabilities far exceeded his assets and he was ruined. Not only had he lost all his own money and the little money his wife had from her father, but also the money his father had borrowed to put into his son's business. His father's failure was involved in his, compelling the sale of Pytte and the land at Clyst St Mary. The family home of Pytte was purchased by the Rev Charles Crawley, Antony's brother in law, in May 1790 for £3,250.

On 16th July 1789, an advertisement appeared in 'Trewman's Exeter Flying Post' announcing that Messrs Collyns and Waymouth had been appointed Commissioners to administer the financial affairs of the indebted Antony Gibbs[iv]. There is also a record of George Abraham Gibbs having to undergo bankruptcy proceedings on July 28th 1789. After the bankruptcy both Antony's and his father's unpaid debts were obligations of honour not legal debts. By arrangement with the Commissioners, the firm of Granger and Banfill continued to produce woollen cloth at the Exwick Mill. Edmund Granger was a wealthy man in his own right and the Banfills moved into Exwick House and lived there until 1830.

Antony, who was now 33 years of age, wasted no time in starting a new career. His journeys abroad and experience of selling by direct personal contact with buyers pointed the way. He decided to establish himself in business in Madrid and take his family there with him, and he arranged to have the Spanish agency for Granger and Banfill and also for other manufacturers. Antony set himself the duty of repaying not just his own but also his father's debts and after his father's death undertook to support his mother and unmarried sisters. Although Antony did not complete the task, his sons, George Henry and William, through the family firm of Antony Gibbs and Sons repaid the last debt with interest in 1840.

1789 – 1791: Madrid

Antony Gibbs was loaned £500 by his brother George, by Granger and Banfill and by his mother in law, Mrs Hucks, to equip and outfit his journey to Spain. His travelling party consisted of himself, his wife and their two children, a nurse, a maid, William Branscombe (a young man he engaged in Exeter) and Elizabeth Gibbs, the daughter of Captain John Gibbs of Topsham.

The party set off by sea for Corunna in the middle of August 1789. On arrival in Madrid they were well received by Antony's friend James O'Connor and they took a furnished house at 22 Calle De La Regna for £60 a year. In May 1790, they took an apartment at 6 Calle de Cantarranas at a rent of £30 a year plus £50 for furnishings. In that apartment William Gibbs was born on May 22nd, and in spite of a bout of smallpox soon seemed to be a strong and healthy infant. Cervantes used to live at 2 Calle de Cantarranas. The street, which has since been renamed "Calle Lope de Vega", is near the Prado.

Antony's business took him all over Spain and Portugal, and Dorothea was often left on her own in Madrid sometimes for months. The textile manufacturers who had given him their business were Granger and Banfill of Exwick, from whom he received a yearly salary of £250, William Taylor and Son and Casenave from Norwich who gave him £250 per annum and 2 per cent on orders over £8000 a year, Alexander Turner and Co of Leeds, and Benjamin Smith of Rochdale. Other firms for whom he acted included Baulaine Loserre and Co., muslin manufacturers of Geneva, Vaughan Baugh and Co. of Bristol who dealt in Irish linens, and the woollen firm of Amadé Duscher and Gendre Ainé of Schmiedenburg in Prussian Silesia. Antony worked to obtain orders in Madrid, Andalusia (Cadiz, Seville and Malaga), where he was from December 1789 to February 1790, from December 1790 to January 1791, and during January and February 1792. He also worked in Zaragossa, Barcelona and Valencia during August 1790, October and November 1791 and June 1792. From March to May 1791 he was in Lisbon, Oporto and Santiago. In 1790 Antony Gibbs earned nearly £1000 and in 1791 he estimated he would earn £1500.

The heat of the Madrid summer was not good for Dorothea's health and the cost of living in Madrid was much higher than in England. Therefore Antony resolved to take his family back to England. However William was taken ill and so for the summer of 1791 Dorothea and the children went to San Ildefonso, a town in the Sierra de Guadarrama, where there was a summer palace of the Kings of Spain at La Granja. The family rented a good house with a garden for £12 from July to October.

In October 1791, Dorothea wrote to Sibella Gibbs about the children:-
"William is a fine little fellow, a sad little pet. Henry and Harriett like much more to speak English than Spanish; they are quiet and shy as ever before strangers and Henry as stiff as a Quaker when he has any compliments to make; he can talk Spanish as quickly as English to Harriett and his master and with great propriety and good pronunciation, and reads it better than English for when he is reading to me he spanishes all his words."

It was then agreed that Antony would take all his party home to England in the summer of 1792. He was to join a partnership from 1st July 1793 with Juan Pomar of Malaga, a firm whose business was the export of Spanish wines and fruit.

The Gibbs family started homewards on July 18th. They travelled in the diligence (stage coach) for six days to Bayonne and then continued overland to Bordeaux and arrived in Paris on August 18th. This was a hazardous time to arrive in Paris. On August 10th the mob had stormed the Tuileries Palace and massacred the Swiss Guards defending the King and Queen. The monarch and his wife were taken prisoner and the monarchy was abolished. The following month saw the notorious September Massacres.

Antony Gibbs and his party eventually, on August 20th, obtained passports from the British Ambassador. Having spent a week in revolutionary Paris, they then left for England. On September 13th they arrived at the town of Stowe Nine Churches in Northamptonshire where Antony's parents were staying with the Crawleys. Thence they journeyed on to George Gibbs home in Bristol and then on to Exeter.

10

1792 – 1796: Malaga and Exeter

Antony stayed for three months in England visiting London, Norwich, Birmingham, Leeds, Rochdale, Litchfield, Newcastle, Manchester, Southampton, Bristol and Exeter. He was received by his manufacturing friends and was able to renew his agreements with them satisfactorily. On November 1st 1792 Antony travelled to Falmouth to take the government packet ship for Lisbon. This was in future his regular route to and from the Iberian peninsular. Antony took £20,000 of orders to Lisbon.

On February 1st 1793, Antony Gibbs was badly injured in a coach accident while en route to Seville. There were serious head injuries but in March he was moved to Cadiz where he stayed with friends and gradually recovered. On June 8th the news came through that he was out of danger. His right arm had been badly hurt and in his first letter home of May 25th 1793, the handwriting was unrecognisable. Sailing home via Lisbon and Falmouth he rejoined his wife and family in Exeter in late August and early September. The family lived in Cowick Barton until October 1794 and then moved to Town Walls, Exeter.

During all his trials and tribulations Antony had the constant support of his brother Vicary whose legal career was flourishing. He was counsel for the defence in the celebrated trials for high treason of Thomas Hardy and Horne Tooke. "His masterly performance at once raised Mr Gibbs to the front rank of his profession." His speeches in the two trials were published separately in 1795. Following his success he was made a K.C. and in 1795 Solicitor-General to the Prince of Wales. He then became Attorney-General to the Prince from 1799 to 1804.

At the end of August 1794, Antony set off again for Spain and, after visiting Madrid, reached Malaga early in October. At this stage England and Spain were at war with France. By the end of October, Juan Pomar, Gibbs and Co. had despatched all their cargoes to England. Antony then went on business to Seville, Xeres and Cadiz. He was back in Malaga in December where he heard the news that his father had died on November 10th 1794. George Abraham Gibbs was buried at Clyst St George, where, in 1860, William Gibbs installed a stained glass window dedicated to his memory. Antony then went on an extensive journey to Madrid, Valencia and Barcelona returning to Madrid in May 1795. Antony's business was developing so well that in 1795 he expected to make not less than £2000. In February he sent £1000 to his brother George for various purposes and wrote that he was now in credit with him instead of being many hundreds of pounds in his debt. In May,

Antony and Dorothea's son Francis died, and in July 1795, the Malaga business also requiring a visit to England, he went home to Exeter.

At that time Antony and his family seem to have moved house to St David's Hill. Antony made his usual visit to the northern counties, but was later delayed a long time at Falmouth. He arrived in Lisbon in October and then proceeded to Madrid in December. Returning from Madrid he then went on to Malaga, Cadiz and Seville. At the end of March 1796, he was back in Lisbon, whence he set sail for England arriving in Exeter on April 25th 1796.

After a visit with his wife and family to see George Gibbs and his family in Bristol, Antony set out on his annual journey through Lancashire and Yorkshire to Edinburgh and Glasgow returning home on July 14th. He met with considerable success, but the shadow of the coming war between England and Spain was already affecting business – the war actually breaking out in October. Juan Pomar, Gibbs and Co. continued to exist throughout the war which ended in 1801, but business was severely curtailed by the hostilities.

In June 1796, Dorothea moved with her mother, her children and Joseph Hucks into a new house – Lower Cleave, Exwick – rented from Thomas Northmore of Cleave.

1797 – 1801: Exeter and Lisbon

Cut off from his work in Spain by war, Antony rejoined his family at Lower Cleave in March 1797. He had settled his account with his brother George and had paid Granger and Banfill what he owed them. In May 1797, his daughter Anne was born at Lower Cleave. Antony had enough money for six months only. In August Vicary Gibbs sent Antony a gift of £100 and George Gibbs also helped with advances.

In September 1798 Antony set out for Lisbon and arrived there at the beginning of October to be met with the good news of Nelson's victory at the Battle of the Nile on August 1st. On November 1st, Antony wrote to his wife to say that two of Nelson's ships of the line had come into Lisbon with five of the nine prizes taken in the battle. Antony had dined with the two British captains on board ship.

Very soon after his arrival in Lisbon, Antony found that a large amount of business was open to him. He was engaged in getting orders for Amadé Duscher and Co of Schmiedenburg and by March 1799 had earned as much as £800 from them. He then began receiving and selling from stock large quantities of woollen goods sent to him on consignment from England. At one time he had £15,000 worth of these goods on the water coming to him. By October 1799 he had already earned no less than £2000.

After the war with Spain had begun at the end of 1796, Antony Gibbs had considered trading through Guernsey where Spanish ships were still admitted, but Vicary Gibbs advised against this. At that time Granger and Banfill found themselves with £10,000 of goods on hand at Exwick prepared for the Spanish market. In July 1797 Antony had entered into an agreement with them under which he was to dispose of these good in Spain as soon as peace was declared. Antony found that there already was a market for them in Lisbon with Spanish merchants coming into Portugal to purchase the goods and then smuggling them back into Spain.

Barings factory in Exeter, and John and Robert Holt of Rochdale also sold through Antony in Lisbon. Other business came from Norwich and Leeds. In June 1800, Antony returned to England to see his family and visit his business friends and associates. By August 1800 fewer Spaniards were coming to Lisbon because of troops guarding the border between Spain and Portugal. In the autumn of 1800, an epidemic of yellow fever hit Andalusia with many people dying in the cities of Seville and Cadiz. By December this had subsided and so in January 1801, Antony decided to travel back to Lisbon with his eldest son Henry aged just 15. Henry was with his brother William at Charles Lloyd's School in Exeter.

Frances Jackson wrote to Antony at the end of 1799, "Lloyd gives the boys excellent characters. Henry for his attention to business and the progress that he has made in the Classics, William for his quickness of talent and perception which so far gets the better of his volatile spirits as to place him at the head of the class of sixteen, many older than himself. Harriett is no less improved in her own way, and little Anne is one of the most interesting children I have met." William was sent in September 1800 to Blundell's Grammar School at Tiverton.

1801 – 1805: Cadiz, Exeter and Cowley.

At the end of November 1801, Antony set off with his eldest son Henry for Lisbon. They travelled overland by terrible roads to Ayamonte and thence by boat to Cadiz. Peace with Spain resulted in the Lisbon establishment being completely broken up and transferred to Cadiz, where in January 1802 Antony set himself up with a house, an office and a warehouse. Antony's profit for 1802 came to over £5000.

The plan for the future which Antony set himself was to retire altogether from residence in Spain in 1804, and live in or near Exeter, making arrangements with his partner in Malaga and with Branscombe, whom he would leave in charge of the Cadiz office. He wanted a nice establishment for himself and the boys in England while keeping his business in Spain as something handsome to pass on to William and Henry.

By August 1802, Antony and his son Henry were home again, having left Branscombe in charge in Cadiz. Antony and Dorothea gave up the little house at St David's Hill for a more commodious residence in the same part of Exeter. Antony then withdrew William from school and on September 5th 1802 set off for Spain with Henry and William in a carriage specially purchased for the journey. They sailed from Southampton to Le Havre on September 7th and continued their journey via Honfleur, Pont Eveque, Lisieux, St Aubin, Falaise, Alençon (12 Sept.), Tours (13 Sept.) and Bordeaux (17 Sept.), reaching Bayonne on September 21st. They crossed into Spain and journeyed on via Vitoria and Burgos to Madrid, which they reached on October 1st, and Cadiz where they arrived on October 9th 1802.

During March 1803, Antony Gibbs remitted no less than £13,500 to British manufacturers as the proceeds from sales. He sent some of his goods in Cadiz to Spanish friends in Seville and Malaga for safekeeping in the event of war. Antony sent Henry and William home by sea and he followed later after a 31 day passage on a merchant ship arriving in England on April 2nd 1803.

Antony set out again in May 1803 with his son William for Seville. From Seville they travelled overland to Lisbon where they arrived on June 4th. Thence they sailed home to Exeter where they arrived on June 19th.

Now that finances were improving, Dorothea decided to rent Cowley Cottage near the bridge over the River Exe above Exeter for which William Jackson asked a rental of £30 a year. This house was a well loved home for them for the remaining years of their residence in Devonshire. They soon rented an additional small farm from John Merivale of Barton Place, and kept two horses, cows and other livestock.

In July 1803, Antony visited George Gibbs in Bristol and then went on to Rochdale and Wakefield to see textile manufacturing associates. Henry was sent back to Madrid alone at the end of September 1803, reaching Cadiz by Lisbon on October 21st. He joined Antony's agents Branscombe and Mardon. By giving up his father's house, he was able to save £300 to £400 a year in rent. He left Cadiz in a merchant ship in May 1804 arriving back in Exeter at the beginning of July. Branscombe left soon after, having put all the stock in Madrid in the hands of Antonio Vallarino of Cadiz to protect it from embargo or confiscation.

Towards the end of 1803, Anna Maria, the daughter of Abraham Gibbs of Palermo, was nine years old. Abraham, whose wife Mary had died in March 1797, was a widower. He wished to send Anna Maria, called Mary after her mother, to England for her education. Lord Nelson agreed to take her home on his flag ship, the HMS Vanguard, and in Christmas week entertained her and four young midshipmen of her own age aboard ship.[v]

On August 23rd 1804, Antony set off for Lisbon with his son William. Henry followed a week later sailing from Falmouth. On December 12th 1804, Spain declared war against England. An embargo was put on all English goods in Spain. In April 1805, Antony sent his sons, Henry and William, back to England. He stayed on in Lisbon where he received between £3000 and £4000 remittances from Spain. Antony wished to complete a scheme for selling all his goods in Spain, valued at £25,000.

At the end of January 1806, William Gibbs was sent to Bristol to work as a clerk in the office of his Uncle, George Gibbs of Redland. He lived with his cousin George Gibbs junior at Stapleton.

1806 – 1807: The "Hermosa Mexicana".

Antony Gibbs devised a scheme with his Spanish associate Antonio Vallarino to procure an English Government Licence for a Spanish merchant vessel to take the greater part of his stock in Spain from Cadiz to South America. George Gibbs of Bristol and Sir Vicary Gibbs took the request to the relevant authorities in London. On December 14th 1805, the Privy Council gave its assent to the request.

Antony was undecided whether to send the goods to Lima, Vera Cruz or Buenos Aires. Eventually he decided on Lima. In December 1805, Antony and his eldest son, Henry, taking their licence with them, sailed out to meet Vallarino. This was Antony's twelfth and last expedition abroad. They arrived in Lisbon on January 6th 1806. Because of the delays, Henry had to return to England to get the licence extended until December 1807. Their ship, the "Hermosa Mexicana" sailed on December 24th 1806 and Admiral Lord Collingwood arranged for her to sail in convoy with a British frigate bound for Buenos Aires, which the British had taken in June 1806.

News came through in October that the "Hermosa Mexicana" had arrived in Lima on 27th April 1807. Vallarino had already paid Antony for his goods, but there were profits to be reaped too. The return cargo was to be sent to Antony Gibbs in England. However the ship with Vallarino on board returned to Vigo in Spain. Despite fears to the contrary Antony was in due course paid his 12 per cent of the profits by Vallarino.

Sir Vicary Gibbs resigned his office of Solicitor General on the death of William Pitt in January 1806. He became Attorney General in the Duke of Portland's government, a post he retained for five years. In April 1807, he was elected M.P. for Great Bedwyn, and in the succeeding General Election of May 1807, he was elected as one of the two Members of Parliament for the University of Cambridge.

1807 – 1808: Napoleon invades Portugal and Spain.

In October 1807, a French army under Marshal Junot invaded Portugal and occupied much of the country. The Prince Regent of Portugal set sail for Rio de Janiero in the Portuguese territory of Brazil. That same month Antony employed an agent in Gibraltar – Peter Belloti – soon replaced by Josias Weeks. The English Orders in Council of January and November 1807 and Napoleon's Continental System inhibited trade with Spain. In February 1808, Antony's eldest son, Henry, sailed with the Royal Navy, on H.M.S. Amphion, for Gibraltar with a letter of credit for £500 to collect remittances and revenues and to negotiate for George Gibbs of Bristol the possibility of sending West Indian or American produce to Spain through Gibraltar. He was also to look at the possibility of importing silver dollars from Spanish America into England.

In January 1808, with help from Sir Vicary Gibbs, Antony was named one of four Commissioners appointed by Order in Council to look after and dispose of Portuguese property sent to England since the departure of the Prince Regent to Brazil. It was not until March 1811 that the Government paid him anything, and then only £2500.

In January 1808, Antony moved to London and took up residence at 24, Russell Street where he had two rooms at a guinea a week. In March 1808, his son William left the office of Gibbs, Richards and Gibbs in Bristol and came to join his father in London. He became one of the clerks to the Portuguese Commissioners. William also assisted his father in his own business. By September 1808, William had risen to be Head Clerk to the Commission with seven or eight clerks under him.

On September 9th 1809, Antony wrote of his son, "William has been the life and soul of the immense business we have had at the Commissioners' Office". Writing to his brother, Sir Vicary Gibbs, he said, "My expectations of William were fully answered and all at the Commission were much pleased with his services. At Christmas 1808, Mr Burn desired William to accept 100 guineas as a mark of the

16

Commissioners' approbation and as I wished exceedingly for him to remain on the best terms with them, I did not object to this Christmas compliment".

In April 1808, Antony heard that Juan Kiddell, who held his goods in Seville, had received £3500 from the sale of these goods, but had been declared bankrupt due to the failure of a Paris Merchant House with which he was associated. Antony believed that he still had £5000 of goods in Spain, but because the sale of British goods had been prohibited there, his creditors – J. and R. Holt, J. and J. Naylor, Benjamin Smith and Granger and Banfill – would have to wait until the prohibition was lifted.

1808 – 1812: Spain and Britain at war with France.

On June 6th 1808, the Spanish through the Junta of Seville declared war against France, and proclaimed Peace with England on July 4th. On July 19th, the French under General Dupont were defeated by General Francisco de Castanos at Baylen in Andalusia. Then on August 21st Marshal Junot was defeated at Vimiero in Portugal by a British army commanded by General Sir Arthur Wellesley.

Henry Gibbs was able to visit Cadiz and Seville to try to settle matters with Kiddell and Vallarino. He could recover only a small proportion of Kiddell's debt – Malaga wines shipped to England to a value of £400. Over three thousand pounds was still outstanding in 1815. From Vallarino Henry recovered about £1100 mainly in Spanish wines which were shipped to his father in England. Henry then attended to the sale of Antony's other goods in Spain – mainly English woollen textiles – to the value of £3000.

In July 1808, George Henry Gibbs opened the Cadiz office of Antony Gibbs and Son. That September he was joined by William Branscombe as a partner in the Cadiz firm. On October 28th, Henry wrote that he had taken a whole house and warehouses for the Cadiz establishment at a rental of £165 per annum.

Meanwhile family circumstances in England were changing. In April 1808, it was decided that the cottage at Cowley would be given up and the whole family moved to London. Dorothea wrote, "We shall give up our cottage with a heavy heart". She sold up the livestock and all that would not be needed in London. William came down to help her. Dorothea and the children who were with her – Harriett (aged 22), Anne (aged 11) and Joseph (aged 7) came to London on October 22nd and found Antony and William in larger furnished lodgings at 34, Great Russell Street. In January 1809, they went to live at Denmark Hill and in

May 1810 they moved to a house on Dulwich Common where they stayed until May 1812.

On September 8th 1808, the firm of Antony Gibbs and Son was founded. By 9th January 1809 the stock of goods in Spain was nearly all sold and winding up old business could even have produced a surplus. Antony was able to pay his debts to John and Robert Holt of Rochdale, John and Jeremiah Naylor of Wakefield, Benjamin Smith of Rochdale and Granger and Banfill of Exwick.

Napoleon's Continental System enabled English merchants to make significant profits. Wool sent to Antony Gibbs and Son from Seville invoiced at £1600 fetched £4600 in England. Similarly British goods sold for a handsome profit in Spain.

On August 8th 1809, Henry Gibbs wrote from Cadiz to his brother William in England: "What a day of rejoicing this has been for us, what embraces, what ringing of bells, what salutes, what madness of joy. The news of the glorious battle of Talavera reached us this morning about five minutes after the "Donegal", with the Marquis of Wellesley on board, had cast anchor in the bay. Everyone began to ask questions of those they met and soon after a paper was stuck up saying that Marshal Victor had been completely routed. Congratulations and embraces ceased when it was time to go to the quay and see the Marquis land. A salute was fired and all the bells of the town were ringing. When the Marquis stepped from the ship into the boat every ship of war in the bay manned their yards and saluted. The town saluted likewise. The people received him with the wildest acclamations of joy. The horses were immediately taken from the carriage and their places supplied by as many people as could get near enough to touch the traces. In this way he was conducted amidst the "Vivas" of the people to the house prepared for his reception. On passing under the gates the English and Spanish flags were waved over their heads, while the French flags formed a carpet over which the coaches and the mob passed – a good idea on such a day".

After the victory of General Sir Arthur Wellesley at Talavera on 27th July 1809, the failure of the Spaniards to support the British left uncertainty. October's British exports to Spain were only £500, but in November these rose to £3900, in December to £5800, and in January stood at £2900. Antony Gibbs and Son's share of these exports amounted to £7500. Antonio Vallarino and other clients in Spain asked Antony Gibbs to insure cargo voyages to and from Latin America, and by the end of November 1809, the firm had earned £500 in commission.

On 19th November 1809, a French army under Marshal Soult defeated the Spaniards under General Juan Carlos Areizaga at the Battle of Ocana. The French crossed the Sierra Morena in January 1810. In February they attacked and plundered Seville and were soon in possession of all of Andalusia except for Cadiz. They then began the Siege of Cadiz which lasted uninterruptedly until August 1812. The English, having command of the sea and with Gibraltar and Lisbon as bases, were always able to keep a strong force in Cadiz.

Henry Gibbs arrived home from Cadiz in March 1810. By the end of January 1810, Antony Gibbs and Son had sent out to their Cadiz House goods costing nearly £70,000 of which £30,000 was on their own account and the rest from various merchant venturers. In the same period they had sent goods ordered by Spanish clients to the value of £15,000. The siege reduced trade and in 1810 the firm only sent £1000 worth of their own goods and £4000 ordered by clients. In 1811 and 1812 their own ventures came to about £17,000 with a further £10,000 in 1811 and £16,000 in 1812 ordered by clients. The balance sheets showed £13,500 on July 31st 1810, £14,500 on December 31st 1811 and £18,000 on December 31st 1812, mainly in unsold stock in Cadiz. The Siege of Cadiz was finally lifted on August 12th 1812, and a strong demand for Gibbs' goods in Spain soon followed.

From early in 1809, Antony and Henry wished to open up in Brazil and Spanish America. In 1811 and 1812, Antony Gibbs and Son sent £5000 of goods to Rio de Janiero and Buenos Aires on joint account with a Buenos Aires firm and John Edwards and Sons, textile manufacturers of Halifax. Correspondence opened with Vera Cruz, and Antonio Bares in Lima began to give the firm some business.

1808 – 1812: Family Life in England.

Dorothea Gibbs' mother, Mrs Eleanor Hucks, died on May 23rd 1807, and Dorothea and her children benefitted to the extent of £1850 from her legacy. Then Henry Townley Ward, the widower of Dorothea's sister Eleanor, died in February 1810. He left £20,700 of which £9,510 was bequeathed to Dorothea. These bequests improved the family's finances considerably.

In April 1810, Mary Elizabeth, the only child of Abraham Gibbs of Palermo, came to live with Antony and Dorothea's family in their house on Dulwich Common. Mary was then 16 years old. Her mother was the youngest daughter of Sir James Douglas, British Consul General in Naples. She had died in 1797. Abraham Gibbs was banker to the British Mediterranean fleet and managed Nelson's estates at Bronte in Sicily.

In December 1803, George Henry Gibbs had met Mary in Cadiz during her voyage home on board Nelson's flagship. Her grandfather, Sir James Douglas of Farringdon, had died in 1795 leaving her a legacy in his will.

After Nelson's death at Trafalgar in October 1805, Mary had spent nearly two years living with her Uncle James and Aunt Betsy Richards in Abbots Leigh near Bristol. Aunt Betsy was her father's sister. Young William Gibbs met Mary there and was captivated. Early in 1808, she returned to London to complete her education under the supervision of Lady Hamilton. Mary had been much under the influence of Emma Hamilton and it was to remove her from that influence that Antony and Dorothea Gibbs offered to take her into their own family and attend to her education. Sir Vicary Gibbs and his wife, Kenny, also took a great interest in her educational development. Mary became a great favourite with the family and stayed with them for about a year. Antony managed to settle Sir James Douglas's legacy to Mary, and after living for a while with Uncle James and Aunt Betsy in Ilfracombe, Mary went in January 1812 to stay with her uncle, Captain William Gibbs of Topsham. Later that year she sailed with her uncle back to Sicily and in 1815 married Colonel Charles Ashe à Court in Palermo.[vi] In July of the following year her father, Abraham Gibbs, committed suicide, bankrupted after the failure of his company due to the recession in Sicily, which followed the withdrawal of British troops in 1814, and the return of the Neapolitan Royal Family to Naples. The War of 1812 between Britain and the United States had eliminated his profitable American trade and in 1814 he ceased to be the American Consul in Sicily.[vii]

Meanwhile the lull in business caused by the Siege of Cadiz allowed William to visit his uncle and cousins in Bristol in April 1810, and in June that year he and his brother Henry went to visit Charles Crawley, who was a student at University College, Oxford. The family took the opportunity to visit their friends and relations in Stowe in Northamptonshire, in Bristol and in Exeter. In May 1811, Antony, Dorothea and their daughters went to Cheltenham to take the waters.

In November 1809, George Gibbs Junior's wife Salvina had died in London. In 1811, George had gone to stay with his Aunt Sibella in Exeter while Dorothea and her daughters were staying there too. In August 1811, he proposed to Harriett, who would have none of it and summarily declined his offer.

On May 11th 1812, the Prime Minister, the Rt. Hon. Spencer Percival was murdered by John Bellingham. Sir Vicary Gibbs as Attorney General prosecuted Bellingham, who was found guilty and hanged at Newgate on May 18th. Spencer Perceval was a personal friend of Sir Vicary, who was so devastated by the murder that he gave up his post of Attorney General, his seat in Parliament and his private business. On May 29th he accepted a puisine judgeship in the Court of Common Pleas and was made a Sergeant at Law. He told Antony that he would still have £7000 a year. Sir Vicary became Lord Chief Baron of the

Exchequer on 8th November 1813, a Privy Councillor on November 30th, and Lord Chief Justice of the Common Pleas on 24th February 1814.

In May 1812, the family gave up the house on Dulwich Common and, in November, Antony took a six year lease on a house at 2, Powis Place, Great Ormonde Street, and purchased the £550 of furniture that went with it. This house was Antony and Dorothea's home for the rest of their lives. During the summer of 1812, Dorothea and her daughters stayed with the Rev. Charles Crawley and his family at Stowe and they spent the weeks between August 28th and October 9th at Leamington Spa.

1812 - 1813: The French retreat in Spain.

Sir Arthur Wellesley's army of British and Portuguese allies won an important victory at Salamanca on July 22nd 1812, and then entered Madrid. The French forces abandoned the Siege of Cadiz and withdrew from Andalusia, Extremadura and La Mancha. Henry and William Gibbs travelled to Falmouth at the beginning of January 1813 and took the packet ship "Swiftsure" to Cadiz.

Henry, William and Mr and Mrs William Branscombe took a furnished house at 131 Calle del Calvaro at the corner of Calle Uncello. The ground floor had the office and a bedroom for William and Henry. William was to live in this house for seven years. The two brothers spent the days of Carnival in Seville where they went on business. On July 4th, Henry sailed home to Falmouth where he arrived on July 21st. William, who had become a partner in the firm on January 1st, remained in charge of the Cadiz office and of the firm's business in Spain. William Branscombe resigned at the end of 1813.

In the new company of Antony Gibbs and Sons, Antony had one half share and William and Henry one quarter share each. William resisted attempts to lure him home to England and insisted on the importance of building up the business in Cadiz and possibly of opening a branch in duty free Gibraltar. The business now prospered. The profits of the London House were £5,000 in 1813 and £5,000 plus £4,200 put in reserve for 1814. The Cadiz House made £2,600 in 1813 and broke even in 1814. In 1814 the firm was too sanguine and sent no less than £96,000 of goods on their own account which was added to the £29,000 remaining at the end of 1813. At the end of 1814 they still had £105,000 stock in hand, and it was not until 1816 that William cleared the backlog. In addition, in 1813, £50,000 and in 1814, £150,000 worth of goods were sent by the London House to Spain to meet Spanish orders.

At the decisive battle Battle of Vitoria, 21 June 1813, British forces under General Arthur Wellesley defeated the French army of

Marshal Jean-Baptiste Jourdain at Vitoria in northern Spain, forcing Joseph Bonaparte – who had been made king of Spain by Napoleon – to flee back to France.

In 1778, Captain John Gibbs of Topsham's fifth son, Lyle, was apprenticed to the Genoese office of a French firm under the care of John Heath, who established his own firm of John Heath and Company in 1789.[viii] In 1814, Lyle established his own Counting House in Genoa called initially Lyle, Gibbs and Company, and after 1820 Gibbs and Company. He transacted business with Antony Gibbs and Sons in London. His nephew Charles, Captain William Gibbs' son, became a partner in the business in 1828. When he retired in 1837, Charles took over the company, and when he died in 1839, was his principal heir.[ix] Charles Gibbs died in Genoa in 1857.

In June 1813, Dorothea who had been unwell went to stay in the lodgings of David Cox, the water colour artist, in Dulwich. It was thought that the country air would be good for her health. David Cox had given art lessons to both Harriett and Anne, joined occasionally during 1812 by William and Joseph. Towards the end of August, Dorothea went with Mrs Cox to Hastings, where she stayed until May 1814. Antony wrote to Henry from Hastings, on 15th September 1813, saying that Dorothea was constantly coughing and spitting blood and the assumption was that she was suffering from consumption (tuberculosis).

On December 18th 1813, Harriett finally accepted George Gibbs' proposal of marriage. In her letter she wrote, "Sincerely I return your affection in consenting to a union with you". George had moved from Stapleton in the spring of 1813 to a house which he bought at the bottom of his father's garden in Redland. George and Harriett were married on August 8th 1814 at Cheltenham. Their families settled £4000 on the young couple. On August 26th 1814, William Gibbs wrote from Cadiz, "The circumstances of my having considered and loved George as a brother would not fail to have made the connection particularly gratifying to me. You have the satisfaction my dear sister of not only having satisfied your own choice but also that of your friends".

1815 – The death of Antony Gibbs.

When Sir Vicary Gibbs became Chief Justice of the Common Pleas in 1814, he moved his residence to Baltimore House, 67 Russell Square, London. Dorothea went to see the house in September and wrote, "I never saw such a house in a town in my life, not only handsome, but comfortable in every respect".

Dorothea and her daughter Anne left London early in October 1815 to go to a house at Redland, Bristol, near the houses of George Gibbs father and son. Antony was to follow them. He stayed in Bristol until December 4th when he travelled back to London. Arrived at his house, he was seized that night in bed with a stroke and died five days later on December 10th. Henry had already written to George Gibbs (junior) to ask him to break the news to Dorothea of Antony's stroke. She, her daughters, Joseph and George came to London and were present at the end.

Henry wrote to William in Cadiz, "The letter which I was obliged to write you by the last post gave me more pain than I can express knowing full well the shock you would receive on reading its contents. I did not tell you that we had lost our dearest father, but everything I said will have led you to this certain and afflicting conclusion. In fact he had already ceased to exist having died on Sunday last, the 10th, at half past ten at night."

Antony was buried in the churchyard of the Parish Church of St Mary the Virgin at Hayes, where also in the same grave his widow, and in a separate tomb his brother Vicary were afterwards interred.

The family remained all together in London until March 1816 when Harriett took her mother and her sister Anne to her own house in Redland. In the event they stayed there until June 1817, and were joined by Joseph who attended the school run by George's friend, the Rev John Parsons.

Antony Gibbs and Sons had made speculative purchases in 1815 and though their stocks had been reduced they still stood at £60,000 at the end of the year. The result was a loss to the London business of £390, while the Cadiz House made a profit of only £360. The £4,200 set aside from 1814 was kept as a provision against losses in 1816. That year turned out to be a very difficult one and Antony Gibbs and Sons was helped by significant loans from George Gibbs and Son in Bristol. William was able to make large forced sales in Spain and remittances arrived from Lima in Peru. Nonetheless the loss for 1816 turned out to be £15,110 or £10,910 after the reserve funds had been used. In 1817 and 1818, when the London firm's business was growing large, George Gibbs and Son were more ready than ever to help them increase it by placing funds with them.

In 1816, Antony's remaining debts of honour amounted to £7,000 on his own account and £9,000 on the account of his father, George Abraham Gibbs. In 1818, William suggested to Henry that they should gradually form a fund, which would be kept on deposit with Antony Gibbs and Sons, from which the debts should be paid. The account was to be called the "D.S. account", the letters standing for "deudas sagradas" (sacred debts). On January 1st 1819, the two brothers deposited £1,000 in this account.

In December 1815, Henry Gibbs became engaged to Caroline Crawley. Her mother, Mary Crawley, wrote to Dorothea, "I cannot think of anyone to whom I should have so well liked to give her. She will be surrounded by those she has always loved, and will be (which I consider a great advantage as does she) an inmate of your house". The marriage took place at Stowe the Nine Churches on July 7th 1817, and Henry and Caroline went to the Isle of Wight for their honeymoon. William returned from Spain on August 18th and so missed the wedding. In September, William went on holiday with his sister Harriett and their mother to Bognor Regis and then to the Isle of Wight, where they joined Anne Gibbs, Charles Crawley and his sister Mary.

Dorothea had all her children and George Gibbs (junior) with her in London for Christmas 1817. Then William departed for Cadiz again on 5th January 1818. He took with him Charles Crawley who was to learn something of the business in Spain and to perfect himself in the language. They travelled overland for William suffered terribly from sea sickness.

George Gibbs (senior) of Redland retired in April 1818. He went to Bath for his health without the hoped for benefit, and returned home where he became seriously ill. Dorothea, hearing this news, left London on July 3rd to join her daughter Anne who was already staying at the house in Redland. Sadly George died the following month. Dorothea wrote in her diary, "16th August 1818. At 2 o'clock this morning our dear brother breathed his last and we have lost a most dear and valued friend".

George Gibbs' funeral took place on August 22nd 1818 in the parish church of Redland. Henry and Joseph came down from London to attend it. In his will, he left £1,000 to his sister Sibella, £500 to Harriett Gibbs, his house in Redland to his widow with ample provision for her maintenance, and his compting house in Bristol to his son George with the rest of the estate being divide between George and his sister Joanna. His widow, Anne Gibbs, lived in Redland until her death in 1832.

Early in 1820, George and Harriett Gibbs took up residence at Knole Park, a delightful old house belonging to the Chester family near the village of Almondsbury about six miles north of Bristol.

Henry and Caroline Gibbs' second child and eldest son, Henry Hucks Gibbs, was born at 2, Powis Place on 31st August 1819. Caroline went to her parents at Stowe soon after and remained there till the end of the year. Their first child Anne had also been born at 2, Powis Place, on 27th May 1818, but she died on 10th May 1820 at Redland in Bristol.

Sir Vicary Gibbs was ailing during most of 1817 and much away at health resorts, and in June 1818 Dorothea described him as being "dreadfully broken, so pale and feeble". He formally resigned his office of Chief Justice of the Common Pleas on November 5th 1818, and was granted a pension of £3,300 a year.

Now returned to Cadiz, William Gibbs and Charles Crawley were enjoying the social life there. In a letter to Harriett dated 7th July 1818, William wrote, "For about a month or six weeks in the spring we went every Saturday into the country, but during the summer Cadiz is cooler than any place in the neighbourhood, so that our country excursions are at an end. The heat of the sun prevents us taking any exercise until the evening, when about sun-set we generally take a walk in the Alameda, where many people assemble for the same purpose. After we have taken a proper review of the ladies we come home and take a warm bath (and a cup of tea) after which we devote ourselves to the service of the fair sex. Sometimes they order us to stay at home with them and listen to their singing, playing or chatting, but generally we sally forth with them to walk." It is recorded that William gave a ball in Cadiz in April 1818.

In October 1818, William opened a house for the company in Gibraltar with John Lee Casson as manager. The house of Gibbs, Casson and Company continued trading until 1833. In March 1819, William Branscombe returned to Cadiz as a partner with a one third holding in the company there. In the autumn of 1819, Cadiz was struck by an epidemic of yellow fever and William moved to stay with friends in Seville and then to the Hacienda de las Caleras in the countryside near Cadiz. William Branscombe died of yellow fever in Cadiz that November. José Maria Boom was chosen to replace Branscombe as a partner in Cadiz, but he was subject to supervision by Casson and both had a one third share in the Cadiz firm with Antony Gibbs and Sons holding the other third. William Gibbs was to be the principal manager of Cadiz with optional residence, while residence was obligatory for Boom, and when William was absent Casson was in overall control. The new partnership began on March 1st 1820 and ended when the firm closed in 1827.

On January 1st 1820, Charles Crawley was taken on as a partner in Antony Gibbs and sons with a one ninth share in the company. On the retirement of George Gibbs (senior) in Bristol on May 1st 1818, Robert Bright took up the partnership in the Bristol firm with a one third share of the company to the two thirds allocated to George Gibbs (junior). The firm was renamed Gibbs Son & Bright. Robert Bright's younger brother, Samuel, became a partner in the Liverpool branch of this company in 1825.

On 8th February 1820, Sir Vicary Gibbs died at his house in Russell Square. He was buried on the 15th in the church yard of the parish church of St Mary the Virgin in Hayes, Kent, where he is commemorated by an inscription on his raised tomb and another on a

25

mural tablet in the church. Dorothea died on February 24th 1820. She had expressed her earnest wish to be buried with her husband at Hayes. The funeral took place on March 10th. At 8 a.m. on the day of the funeral Henry and Joseph Gibbs, Charles and George Crawley, Robert Remmett and Hannah White set off in postchaises to Croydon, where they met the coffin and the mourning coaches. They reached Hayes Church at 12.30. William Gibbs was in Cadiz in the process of acquiring a new house with an office and a warehouse for the firm at 79 Calle del Camino. Henry wrote to his sisters, "The Rev. Till, the Rector of Hayes, performed the service in a very impressive manner. I saw the coffin placed close by the side of my dearest father and there they now rest together awaiting for the hour when they shall be raised incorruptible."

In September, George Henry Gibbs gave up his residence at Powis Place, moving to 11, Bedford Square which was his home for the rest of his life. From 1822, he was a Director of the London Assurance Corporation. He and George Gibbs and Robert Bright were among the chief promoters of the Great Western Railway from its inception at the offices of Antony Gibbs and Sons in 1833. He was a London director of the Great Western Railway Company and Chairman of Antony Gibbs and Sons until his death in Venice in August 1842 at the age of 56.

William, after coming home from Spain in the autumn of 1820, set out again for Cadiz in April 1821 and took his brother Joseph with him. He had heard that Lord Cochrane, in command of the Chilean fleet transporting the "Liberating Army of Peru" had sailed from Valparaiso on August 20th 1820 and had, on November 6th, cut out the Spanish frigate Esmeralda from under the guns of Callao. The firm of Antony Gibbs and Sons was waiting for Peruvian independence before establishing an office there. Joseph, after spending some time in Madrid and Granada, rejoined William at Cadiz, and, when William returned home in the spring of 1822, he entered the Gibraltar office.

During this visit to Spain, William became engaged to be married to Doña Francisca de la Peña from Chiclana near Cadiz. "She was a charming woman, very clever and cultivated and of excellent family, great friends of his. Her letters are admirable. The question of religion stood in their way: both her family and his were averse to a mixed marriage and neither of them would leave the faith of their fathers."

William went again to Spain in January 1824, accompanied on that occasion by his sisters Harriett and Anne and by George Gibbs, and returned home that same year. He did not visit Spain again until 1831. In 1853 he journeyed one last time to Spain, where he visited Doña Francisca at Chiclana in the company of two of his nephews, Henry Hucks Gibbs and John Lomax Gibbs. Francisca never married. William resided with his brother George Henry Gibbs, at 11 Bedford Square, London until his marriage to Matilda Blanche Crawley Boevey in 1839.

In 1828, George and Harriett Gibbs moved from Knole Park to Belmont which was leased initially from the Rev Turner Seymour. In 1832, on the death of his mother, George purchased the house together with half of Turner Seymour's estate. George bequeathed Belmont to go after Harriett's death to Joseph and Emily Gibbs for their lives, and after them to their eldest surviving son, George Louis Monck Gibbs.

Antony Gibbs and Sons 1815 to 1840.

After their risky speculative ventures into Spain, Antony Gibbs and Sons took the lesson to heart and by the end of 1816 their stocks of goods in Spain had reduced to £7000. The introduction of heavy import duties in Spain made it impossible for the firm to make money by sending out goods on its own account without evading duties. Hence in 1815 the shipment was only £4000, and in 1816 and 1817 only £4500 for the two years together. Between 1818 and 1820, now including the new duty free house in Gibraltar, the average shipments were still only £6000 per annum. The factor which revived their trade was the placing of orders on commission by merchants who knew their goods and reputation. Accordingly the firm shipped £60,000 per annum in 1815 and 1816, which rose to £130,000 in 1817 and 1818. In 1819 this declined to £110,000, and in 1820 to £90,000. The produce and bullion sent to the London House for sale came to £14,000 in 1815, £28,000 in each of 1816 and 1817, and in 1818 to nearly £50,000, reducing to £35,000 a year in 1819 and 1820.

The net profits for the London and Spanish Houses were £6200 in 1817, £8100 in 1818, £4500 in 1819, and £4700 in 1820 with the London House accounting for the lion's share. Between 1817 and 1820, the Cadiz House made altogether £4000 and the Gibraltar House from 1818 to 1820, £3700. For the next three years the Cadiz House, with William Gibbs in charge, made £2000 a year, but after William left the profits fell off rapidly and in 1827 the House was closed. The Gibraltar House made an average of £5000 a year between 1821 and 1827, but only an average of £520 a year in the next six years and so the House there was closed in 1833. Both the Cadiz and Gibraltar Houses were able to transact a fair amount of import and export business with Peru on behalf of Spanish merchants during the War of Liberation in Peru.

The French occupation of Spain by Napoleon's armies dealt a death blow to the Spanish Empire in Latin America and there were rebellions all over South America with the exception of Peru. By 1816,

Argentina had freed itself from Spanish rule, and in 1817, their General San Martin crossed the Andes with an army of Chileans and Argentinians. The Spanish forces were defeated and Bernardo O'Higgins was established as Supreme Director of Chile. Having broken the Spanish blockade of Valparaiso, the Chileans gathered together a navy with 13 ships and in 1818 recruited Lord Cochrane, famous for his naval exploits during the Napoleonic wars, to become its commander.

In 1819, Cochrane twice took part of the Chilean fleet out from Valparaiso for raids on the coast of Peru, captured Spanish treasure and stores, blockaded Callao, and spread revolutionary ideas among the people. He attacked the Spanish Arsenal in Guayaquil, and in January 1820 with just one warship captured Valdivia, the last significant Spanish base in Chile. In August 1820, a convoy commanded by Admiral Lord Cochrane conveyed San Martin and an army of 4000 men north towards Peru. In November, Cochrane, having captured the Spanish frigate Esmeralda from beneath the guns of the forts of Callao, landed San Martin's army at Huacho, ninety miles north of the port of Callao. By the end of the year all the north of the Viceroyalty of Peru was in the hands of the Peruvian Patriots.

John Moens, a son of the Dutch Consul in Bristol, was engaged by Antony Gibbs and Sons early in 1820 to represent the firm in Lima. When Moens arrived in Callao in December 1820, it was still under Spanish control and it was only Gibbs' Royalist friends in Lima that gained him permission to land. In July 1821, John Moens shipped $150,000 in gold and silver coin and bars to Antony Gibbs and Sons in H.M.S. Conway on behalf of Spanish Royalist friends. In November he shipped a further $130,000 in bullion and specie and some produce in H.M.S. Superb and in December $40,000 in H.M.S. Creole.

John Moens had to contend with the war between on the one side the Patriot and Chilean army led by General San Martin, supported by Simon Bolivar, and on the other side the Spanish armies with their Royalist supporters. At sea Admiral Lord Cochrane and the Chilean Navy were a force to be reckoned with. Two ships sent by Gibbs, Casson and Company from Gibraltar were impounded by Cochrane, who suspected the firm of having sympathies with the Royalists. It was only after the intervention of Sir Thomas Hardy, the Commodore of the Royal Navy's squadron along the Pacific coast of South America, that the ships were eventually released. The two ships, the "Edward Ellis" and the "Lord Suffield", were escorted by Sir Thomas Hardy to Callao, but due to the hazard of the ships being seized again, Moens and the Lima consignee decided to send the ships with their cargoes back to Gibraltar under Hardy's protection along the Pacific coast.

In December 1821, Samuel Mardon and the cargo ship "Bristol" with goods for two Spanish exporters, Marco and Ibanez, and goods for George Gibbs, Antony Gibbs and Sons and another British firm set sail for South America. The ship arrived in Valparaiso on May 11th to the news that the Peruvian port of Callao had fallen to the Patriots. The ship was still at Valparaiso in November, but the following year was able to unload at Quilca and the goods were shipped up to Arequipa for sale. It wasn't until November 1823 that Mardon could get a British warship to take the money home. Goods remained unsold in Arequipa and it wasn't until 1832 that the account was finally closed with a loss of £12,000. By 1839 further recoveries of money reduced the actual loss to £6000. During the War between the Patriots and the Royalists, several other ships encountered similar problems. Antony Gibbs and Sons' earlier contacts with the Royalists in Callao and Lima led Admiral Lord Cochrane and others to think that the firm may have had Royalist sympathies.

As soon as Callao and Lima had fallen to the Patriots, the Peruvians gave foreigners leave to establish Commercial Houses in these two cities. Peru established its freedom of trade with the entire World in 1824 when the war ended. John Moens founded the Lima branch of Antony Gibbs and Sons on January 1st 1822. The firm opened Houses in Arequipa and Callao in 1823 and Valparaiso in 1826, where George Thomas Davy was put in charge. Sadly John Moens took unnecessary risks and was too sanguine for commercial success. He was involved in several questionable ventures. These deficiencies reduced the effectiveness of the firm. When in 1826 John Hayne joined the Lima House as a partner in Gibbs, Crawley and Company, conditions improved. That same year the British Foreign Secretary George Canning, Victoria de Burgh Gibbs' great-great-grandfather, in a celebrated speech in Parliament said, "I called the New World into existence, to redress the balance of the Old". Britain was committed to opening up trade with Latin America. By the time John Hayne went on leave in 1829, the firm had been established on sound principles. In January 1829, Charles Crawley arrived from England and persuaded George Davy in Valparaiso to become a partner in the company too. The South American branch of the firm was now importing British and Spanish goods and exporting cocoa, tropical hardwoods, alpaca wool, copper, silver and gold from Peru and Chile.

After 1831 the firm's difficult times were at an end and in the years between 1832 and 1840, the London partners – George Henry and William Gibbs and Charles Crawley divided among themselves an average of £20,000 a year. In 1838, Charles Crawley retired to his new home, "The Lawns" at Littlemore near Oxford, to live near to his

Tractarian friend the Rev. John Henry Newman. He had had a one seventh interest in the partnership. By 1840, George Henry and William Gibbs had the satisfaction of paying off the last of their father's debts.

Antony Gibbs and Sons and the Trade in Guano from Peru.

John Hayne and the South American partners entered into contracts to export guano from Peru in 1841 and 1842. This caused some alarm in London where William Gibbs feared the trade might bring heavy losses. Initially Gibbs encountered many difficulties establishing the company in the guano business between 1842 and 1847. They broke even, but did not become rich over night. Gibbs, Crawley and Company shared the contract to export Peruvian guano to Britain and Europe from 1842 to 1847 with William Joseph Myers and Company of Liverpool. Other interested parties were Quiros Allier and Company of Lima and Puymerol Poumarroux and Company of France. The import of guano from Ichaboe Island off South West Africa in the mid 1840s depressed the market for Peruvian guano. Here the Cold Benguela Current and Kalahari Desert created conditions similar to coastal Peru with the Cold Humboldt Current and Atacama Desert. The African guano was however inferior in quality and far less plentiful.

William Gibbs obtained the guano monopoly in 1847, when W.J. Myers and Company withdrew from the contract, and was able to retain this against considerable opposition and political intrigue until 1861, when the company left the business for good. The Gibbs monopoly for the European market began on December 22nd 1847 and ended in December 31st 1861, when Antony Gibbs and Sons completed their final contract. The really good years were from 1851 to 1864. In the last three years Antony Gibbs and Sons were selling off stock piles and moving into new trading enterprises, which in due course included trading in nitrates mined in the Atacama Desert in Northern Chile and coastal Bolivia (annexed by Chile in 1884 after the War of the Pacific). They were becoming merchant bankers as well as merchants. The initial monopoly was for Britain and Continental Europe excluding France and Spain. In 1854 Australia and the West Indies were added and in 1858, Spain, France and the French colonies were granted to Gibbs because of malpractice by Michel Montané in France and Murrieta in Spain. The only large market never given to Gibbs was North America.

Antony Gibbs and Sons received a commission on sales which varied from 3.5 to 5 per cent. They made a 2.5 per cent charge for charters of shipping on some earlier contracts. When this was discontinued after 1851, they charged a brokerage fee of 2.5 per cent. The effect was the same – profit for Antony Gibbs and Sons. They also made advances of money to the Peruvian Government at 5% interest, guaranteed by exports of guano. After the due date for the loan the interest rate became 1% per month. Gibbs was lending the money, shipping the guano, selling the guano and then lending more money. They were also charging exchange commission on monies sent back to Peru. If all these transactions are considered together, they were making in total a profit of from 5 to 7.5 percent on each ton of guano sold. On exports to Europe a 2 per cent commission was paid by the importers to Antony Gibbs and Sons. In 1855, 161,852 tons of guano were sold in the U.K., and 71,167 tons in Continental Europe. Commission and brokerage brought in £100,609. Total profits were £115,530. (U.S. $577,650 at the exchange rate which was then £1 = $5).

Figure 2. The Great Pier for loading guano, Chincha Islands, Peru.

Under the Gibbs monopoly, the price of guano had started at £10 ($50) a ton in 1847 and dropped to a minimum of £9.5s in 1849. In April 1854 the price rose to £10, in July 1855 to £11, in July 1856 to £12, and in December 1856 to £13. Between 1856 and 1858 the price peaked at £13 ($65) a ton. The depletion of the guano reserves and the possibility of the fertiliser companies in Britain, Continental Europe and America developing alternative and improved fertilisers were not yet fully

31

considered. The Peruvian Government and Treasury wanted to maximise their income.

Half the money earned by the Peruvian Government through the sale of guano was used to pay interest to holders of Peruvian Government bonds and to redeem bonds due for repayment. The other half was remitted back to Peru. Gibbs traded very profitably in Peruvian Government bonds.

The Peruvian dictator Grand Marshall Castilla ruled Peru for most of the period during which Gibbs had the guano monopoly (1845 to 1851 and 1855 to 1862) with an interval of democratic rule under General Echenique from 1851 to 1854. Gibbs could offer the Peruvian Treasury what it needed most, loans of ready cash in large sums. Most of the money loaned by Gibbs was squandered by the Peruvian government on arms in wars against Bolivia and Ecuador and against Spain, who attempted to seize the Chincha guano islands. When Gibbs withdrew from the guano trade, he called in the Peruvian government's debts and sold the guano stocks for any debt unpaid by Peru. During the period 1860 to 1864, when Tyntesfield was being built, the average annual profits of Antony Gibbs and Sons were £137,244.

There were frequent complaints by farmers about the price of guano and the Peruvian Monopoly. For example Sir Robert Peel wrote to the Prime Minister Palmerston on the subject in July 1849 advising him that the system of guano importing and the high prices ensuing from it were damaging the agricultural interest. He alleged that if the Gibbs monopoly were scrapped, prices would fall to £6 a ton and consumption greatly increase. This complaint was sent to the British chargé d'affaires in Lima, but was regarded by President Castilla as being uninformed and likely to create more problems than it solved. It was even suggested by some that Britain should lay claim the Lobos Islands with their large guano reserves and annex them. This idea was taken up in a sustained political campaign. Francisco de Rivero, Peruvian Minister in London for most of the duration of the Gibbs' monopoly, protested strongly. On May 31st 1852, Lord Malmesbury, the Foreign Secretary, declared that no British warships could be sent to Lobos to protect any illegal British traders there.

"The campaign reached its peak on 11 June when 'a deputation of the most influential character' met the prime minister, Lord Derby, 'to impress on him the great importance of using every possible means to obtain a cheap and abundant supply of guano' and to raise once again the specific question of the Lobos Islands. Thomas Wentworth-Buller represented the Royal Agricultural Society of England and the Duke of Buccleuch spoke for the Highland and Agricultural Society of Scotland. The Duke of Richmond brought a memorial from Banffshire. John

Hudson of Castleacre in Norfolk was the representative of the tenant farmers of England. Robert Hildyard, the protectionist M.P. for Whitehaven, was there on behalf of the shipping interest. A number of other individuals representing local farming and shipping associations also presented memorials. All the well-practised arguments were produced: some spoke in moderate terms, others more vehemently. John Hudson asserted that guano at £6 would give more benefit to the farmers than any fair duty that might be placed on corn imports. This, according to the Times, 'was received with loud cries of "hear, hear", and produced a marked sensation.' Derby listened and then gave the deputation an account of the history and organisation of the trade and of British negotiations with Peru on guano. He insisted that Peru was the sole and rightful owner of the Lobos Islands and that this had been accepted by a Law Officer of the Crown as far back as 1834. The British, whether they liked it or not, were entirely in Peru's hands as far as guano was concerned: she exercised a monopoly and knew that farmers were still eager to buy the fertilizer, high prices not withstanding."

After 1856 the market in guano slumped and in 1857, only 110,490 tons were sold by Gibbs in Britain. This was a fall of 48 per cent from the previous year. The average for the five years 1857 to 1861 was 36 percent down on the 1856 figure. Imports exceeded sales by almost 200,000 tons between 1857 and 1861. In Gibbs' Continental European market, the sales slumped from 105,019 tons in 1855-56 to 86,348 tons in 1856-57 and to 70,179 tons in 1857-58. There was a small recovery to 84,808 in 1858-59. What is beyond doubt is that Peru's guano trade with Britain had reached and passed its peak. Peruvian gross earnings from guano sold in Britain were halved between the late 1850s and the late 1870s. In early December 1858, 459,805 tons of guano lay unsold in Gibbs' various depots around the world. There was enough guano lying in the Victoria Docks in London to fill the Crystal Palace. New fertilisers were being manufactured in competition with guano. By March 1860 Gibbs still had 258,266 tons lying in its warehouses.

It seemed likely that Gibbs' contract would not be renewed after December 1861, and so the company decided to charter as much shipping as possible and build up stocks for future sales at a high price. William Gibbs and John Hayne did not approve of this policy and Henry Hucks Gibbs agreed, at the end 1860, that he had been in error. In November 1861, just before the end of Gibbs' contract, stocks stood at 230,000 tons. These were sold in 1862 at £13 a ton and 1863 at £12 a ton. This enabled Antony Gibbs and Sons to recoup the monies loaned to Peru, to be paid their commission and loan interest in full, and to leave the business in a most satisfactory fashion.

The Diary of George Gibbs of Belmont

GEORGE GIBBS OF BELMONT [x] was born in Bristol on the 27th December 1779. He was trained in his father's West Indian business in Bristol from 12 years old, and became a partner in it with him from 1802 to April 1818 and thereafter head of the firm till he died in 1863. His partner in Bristol from April 1818 was Robert Bright, and the style of their firm there was Gibbs Son & Bright from 1818 to 1839, and Gibbs Bright & Co. from 1839 to 1881 when it was absorbed by Anthony Gibbs & Sons of London together with its Liverpool Branch (founded in 1805) and its Australian Branch (founded in 1853).

George Gibbs was Warden for 1804, and Master for 1820, of the Society of Merchant Venturers of Bristol. With Robert Bright he was on the Bristol Committee (1832 to 1835) which in conjunction with the London Committee promoted the Great Western Railway Company of which company Robert Bright was an original director and vice-chairman (1835 to 1843). He was Patron of the living of Hutton, in Somerset, and in his will nominated for it his nephew the Rev. George Henry Gibbs. He resided in Stapleton, near Bristol, from 1802 to 1813, in Redland from 1813 to 1820, at Knole Park in Almondsbury, Gloucestershire, from 1820 to 1828 and, from 1828 until he died, at Belmont in Wraxall, Somerset, a house which he at first leased, but in 1832 bought from the Rev. George Turner Seymour together with a portion of the estate in which it lay. Seymour had built Tyntesfield on his remaining larger portion and was his own architect. In 1850 Gibbs Bright and Company purchased the S.S. Great Britain, designed by Isambard Kingdom Brunel and completed in 1843 for the Great Western Railway Company for their New York service. She was the first screw steamer to cross the Atlantic. After Gibbs Bright & Company bought her, she was employed for many years in the Australian trade and was very popular with passengers. She was also the first privately owned ship to be chartered for troop carrying both in the Crimean War and the Indian Mutiny.

The Diary
Wednesday 10th December 1828.
Wrote to Mr Seymour declining the purchase of Belmont.
Tuesday 3rd January 1832.
William left Belmont by the Mail.
Wednesday 11th February 1835.
Heard from William of his election to the Athenaeum.

Tuesday 2nd January 1838.

William left Belmont.

Monday 29th July 1839.

Left Belmont at half past twelve and went with our own horses to Nicholls. Took luncheon there and stayed an hour. Reached Flaxley at half past ten.

Thursday 1st August 1839

William and Blanche married – Most delightful and admirably arranged. Spent the *rest of the* day in a long drive to Tintern – a most agreeable excursion – the ruins looked to great advantage from the highland of the area – seen to advantage from the churchyard behind.

Thursday 3rd October 1839.

At home. Called at church, and Mr Vaughan and Merilee, William and his wife came to Belmont in the evening.

Monday 31st August 1840.

The Great Western to Bath opened. Went with Joseph and Harrison to Nightingale Valley and saw the first train pass. William, Blanche and Susan came to Belmont.

Monday 13th June 1842.

Went to church in the morning yesterday. Went with Mrs Gibbs, William and Blanche and Mr L. Crawley to Aldenham House and Church, Merry Hill and Hart's Bourne.

Thursday 14th July 1842.

At Exhibition Yard and Pavilion Dinner with Lloyd, William, Mr and Mrs Newton, Harriett and Blanche.

Friday 15th July 1842.

At sale of stock and "Great Britain" with Mr Newton, William and Joseph.

Saturday 16th July 1842.

Edward Vaughan called. Bright spent the greatest part of the morning at Belmont. Joseph and Charles left Belmont in the afternoon. The "Great Western" sailed.

Monday 18th July 1842.

Went with William, Blanche and some of the children to Cheddar Cliffs.

Wednesday 20th July 1842.

Heard from Venice on the 9th. Henry (*George Henry, William Gibbs' elder brother*) very unwell with an attack like that which he had in Pavia last year.

Friday 22nd July 1842.

At home. Drove with William and Blanche after dinner to Portbury and then through Charlton.

Monday 25th July 1842.

William went to London by the 7 o'clock train.

Tuesday 26th July 1842.

Went to Bristol with Mrs Gibbs to the Flower Show. Brought home William who returned from London.

Friday 29th July 1842.

William went to London in consequence of dispatches from Lima and we all went to Clevedon in his carriage. The "Great Western" took on the children and nurses.

Monday 1st August 1842.

In the afternoon went to Weston with William, Blanche and Harriett. William returned from London at 2 o'clock on Sunday morning.

Tuesday 2nd August 1842.

Very bad news from Venice (*of William Gibbs' brother, George Henry*).

Monday 8th August 1842.

Mrs Gibbs, Blanche and the children went to Bristol.

Friday 16th September 1842.

Took a long walk with William to Tyntesfield.

Saturday 17th September 1842.

Called with William and Blanche on Mr Edward Vaughan.

Saturday 8th October 1842.

Mr Seymour spent the morning at Belmont and offered Tyntesfield to William. Joseph went to Clifton Hampden.

Monday 26th December 1842.

Left Belmont by train for Clifton Hampden. 13 in out party.

Tuesday 27th December 1842.

The funeral took place (*of George Henry Gibbs*) this day. All the expected attendants together with R. and S. Bright attended.

Monday 16th January 1843.

William and Blanche came in on their way to London.

Saturday 4th March 1843.

William and Blanche came from London in the evening.

Tuesday 7th March 1843.

William and Blanche returned home.

Thursday 6th April 1843.

William came quite late at night

Friday 7th April 1843.

Preparing guano to be strewn to manure our grass.

Saturday 8th April 1843.

Wind too high to put on guano.

Monday 10th April 1843.

Guano on 8 acres covering eight twelfths of the Field.

Tuesday 11th April 1842.

William went to London by the 9.40 train.

Tuesday 20th June 1843.

At Bristol. William came from Flaxley.

Wednesday 21st June 1843

Mr Seymour came to Belmont and William agreed to purchase Tyntesfield. He and Seymour exchanged memos to this effect. Fine day for hay on the whole, but cold in the evening.

Thursday 22nd June 1843

Went with William to Bristol and saw him off to Swindon. The five half acres – with four different kinds guano and without any manure – put on waggons previously to their being taken tomorrow to be weighed at Nailsea. Wrote to Mr Seymour about the expense of looking after Tyntesfield before the conveyance was made.

Friday 28th July 1843.

William, Blanche and their two children came to Belmont at about two o'clock.

Saturday 29th July 1843.

Went with William and Blanche to Tyntesfield in the afternoon.

Monday 28th August 1843.

Went to Tyntesfield and heard that Seymour had settled with them up to Saturday. I wrote to William that I should pay the five shillings a week from that time.

Thursday 31st August 1843.

William, Blanche and the children came to Belmont together with Joseph and Harry.

Saturday 2nd September 1843

William Blanche and the children together with Joseph and Harry left Belmont. We went into Bristol with William and Blanche.

Friday 27th October 1843.

Settled with Holbrook that from Monday morning next he should take charge of the grounds generally at Tyntesfield receiving his present advantages.

Saturday 6th January 1844.

Went to Tyntesfield with Nicholls. Wrote to William.

Friday 19th January 1844.

The Fosters came to Belmont with plans for Tyntesfield where I went with them. They stayed measuring the field for the road. (*This is probably the firm of John Foster and Son of Bristol who designed Queen Elizabeth's Hospital, completed in 1847.*)

Thursday 25th January 1844.

William came to Belmont. Blanche and Anne prevented by the illness of little Antony.

Monday 29th January 1844.

Daubeny came to Belmont just after we had dined at Tyntesfield with

Foster.

Tuesday 30th January 1844.

At Wraxall Lodge and afterwards at Tyntesfield with things about the road.

Wednesday 31st January 1844.

William left us – went into Bristol with him and Daubeny.

Friday 8th March 1844

William, and their children with Anne came to Belmont by the 5 o'clock train to Nailsea.

Thursday 4th April 1844.

William came to Belmont.

Saturday 6th April 1844.

Walked to Tyntesfield with William and in the evening went to the Watercress and drank tea there.

Tuesday 9th April 1844.

William, Blanche and their children and servants left Belmont.

Friday 19th April 1844

At Bristol. Mr Lucas came from London to make a final settlement of the purchase of Tyntesfield. William went with him to Bristol and paid the money to Mr Turner Seymour. (*£21,295 and 3 shillings paid to Mrs Louisa Seymour and Mr G.T. Seymour – Title Deeds*). Lucas was to return to London tomorrow with the deeds for the whole.

Saturday 20th April 1844

At home. Went to Tyntesfield. Mr Lucas came to Belmont again with two deeds for me to sign. I gave him a note which I was writing to him as to effect payment of 4 percent interest on purchase.

Saturday 27th April 1844

Mr and Mrs Seymour came to Belmont. They dined with us and I went with him to Tyntesfield.

Wednesday 19th June 1844

Wrote again to William. Went to Tyntesfield. Building going satisfactorily. Expect to get ready for the roof in about 6 weeks.

Thursday 20th June 1844

Went to Tyntesfield and the Water Cress with Chesterman and Foster.

Friday 21st June 1844

With Chesterman at Belmont and Tyntesfield about water the greater part of the morning.

Wednesday 26th June 1844.

Walked to Tyntesfield. In the afternoon went with Mrs. Branscombe and Miss Gibbs to Cadbury Camp….Wrote to William.

Thursday 18th July 1844

William left London with Blanche for the Continent. Saw the Fosters about the farm. Told them that I did not much like it.

Monday 22nd July 1844.

Work at Tyntesfield going on very slowly. I spoke to Davis very shortly about it. He admitted that the masons had been waiting for flour – but said that the roof would be on in a week.

Wednesday 24th July 1844.

Men at Tyntesfield doing better – Davis says the whole building will be finished by the March after Xmas,

Saturday 27th July 1844.

Met Foster and went over to Tyntesfield with him – settled about Ice House.

Thursday 12th September 1844.

Walked to Tyntesfield – work at the house very backward.

Friday 13th September 1844.

Spent a great deal of time with Foster at Tyntesfield…and determined to have a porch at Tyntesfield.

Friday 4th October 1844

Went to Tyntesfield and Watercress. Water running at both springs.

Friday 18th October 1844.

Walked with William to Tyntesfield.

Wednesday 23rd October 1844.

At Tyntesfield with William and Blanche about private ledger.

Saturday 7th December 1844.

Ice House at Tyntesfield made fit to receive ice – 20 tons taken from our ponds hauled there – men working without intermission – Bread, cheese and beer sent to them….Porch at Tyntesfield stopped by frost.

Monday 9th December 1844.

Ice House completely filled with ice partly from our own ponds which were frozen again to a thickness of 1¼ to 1½ inches.

Tuesday 10th December 1844.

Men working on the new road to the back yard at Tyntesfield by the job at 5 pence per yard – Nicholls calculates that they will have dug it out in about twelve days. Dig.

Wednesday 11th December 1844.

The "Great Britain" got out of dock on the night tide having failed to do so in the morning.

Monday 27th January 1845.

The "Great Britain" arrived in the Downs….William and Blanche and little Dolly left Belmont.

Thursday 20th February 1845.

Sir John Naysmith (landscape gardener) came to Belmont in the evening.

Friday 21st February 1845.

Walked about Tyntesfield with Sir John Naysmith. William came in the evening.

Saturday 22nd February 1845.

The whole day with Sir John Naysmith and William at Tyntesfield. Sir John Naysmith left Belmont.

Monday 7th April 7th 1845.

William and Blanche came early in the morning.

Tuesday 8th April 1845.

Harriett, Ellen, Blanche, Susan, Lucy and Charles Crawley went with William to Bath on his way to London. Completed covering the ten acres with guano.

Thursday 10th April 1845.

Mr Foster came to Belmont and Tyntesfield.

Friday 11th April 1845.

Went to Watercress and met Chesterman there.

Wednesday 4th June 1845.

A good deal at Tyntesfield. Crops of grass looking very fair. Tyntesfield very beautiful.

Thursday 5th June 1845.

A great deal at Tyntesfield. Foster came over. Everything was shown to him. Ice in Ice House very much shrunk.

Friday 6th June 1845.

Walked with Bright to Tyntesfield. Harriett and Anne with William, Blanche and little Robert came in the morning from London.

Saturday 7th June 1845.

At Tyntesfield.

Monday 9th June 1845.

Sir John Naysmith left for Castle Hill and William and Blanche for London.

Friday 13th June 1845.

Had a washing tub of ice from Tyntesfield…Began the hay harvest in the Hither Let – a very good crop particularly the guanoed part.

Friday 25th July 1845.

Mr Glendenning came to Tyntesfield about conservatory.

Saturday 26th July 1845.

Haymaking finished at Tyntesfield.

Thursday 28th August 1845.

Joseph's child christened. Pleasant party on the West Hill. Foster came to Tyntesfield.

Friday 29th August 1845.

William and Blanche went to London and return tomorrow.

Saturday 13th September 1845.

With William and Blanche at Mr Ame's at Cotham about the Ice House and afterwards at King's Weston Hill. Went to Clifton and called at Mr Lane's to see his Great House heated by Hazard's stove.

Figure 3. Robert Bright, George Gibbs' partner.

Dined at Tyntesfield.
Wednesday 8th October 1845.
Went to Mamhead a most beautiful house built with a very fine terrace,
known for an extremely beautiful flower garden and Conservatory, but
principally for camellias. The grounds beautiful and we saw Mr Thomas
Newman. He makes great use of guano. He reaped several fields of
capital turnips.

Monday 7th September 1846

Found William very unwell with bilious complaint approaching jaundice.

Tuesday 8th September 1846

Some time at Tyntesfield. Dined at Tyntesfield.

Wednesday 9th September 1846

At Tyntesfield. Met Chesterman there. Rode with Nicholls about the grounds. Swedes and turnips looking very well.

Thursday 10th September 1846

Chesterman finished his job at the pond and came to Belmont about our pond.

Friday 11th September 1846

Bright came to Belmont. I went with him to Tyntesfield and took a very long walk with him.

Sunday 31st January 1847

I hear about daily correspondence with William Gibbs about guano matters, the price of which has advanced to £10. Most dreadful accounts of the famine in Ireland.

Sunday 10th February 1850

William with Harry (*Henry Hucks*), Charles, William, John and Francis came to Belmont. Mary arrived in the night. Caroline (their mother) certainly not worse. Dr Williams only came in the morning.

Saturday 11th May 1850

At the Exhibition we saw the pictures of William and his family by Ross. His is a great likeness.

Sunday 12th May 1850

At church. In the afternoon with Harriett in wheeled chair to Kensington Gardens. Dined at William's.

Monday 31st March 1851.

Blanche and the Clifton Hampden party left Belmont. Walked to Tyntesfield. Very much occupied with the Population Return.

Sunday 7th March 1852

At the sacrament and the afternoon service – Harriett I hope is somewhat more comfortable than usual – Anne much as yesterday after a better night. William and Blanche came out at five o'clock having left London; this in consequence of my letter of the 27th. Joseph in bed with a bad cough and attack on his chest.

Monday 8th March 1852

I took a drive with Anne, William and Blanche to the Castle and afterwards in the High Road. She was not comfortable all the way, but upon the whole she seemed the better for it and was very staunch the rest of the day. A good day with dear Harriett.

Saturday 11th June 1853

Heard from William with guano return. At Tyntesfield I heard from

Blackmore and also from Scott about Osman.

Wednesday 20th July 1853

After the rain was over we carried a load of hay from Home Field.
William and Blanche and their boys, Antony and George Abraham, came
to Belmont.

Wednesday 14th September 1853

William and Blanche came to Belmont.

Friday 23rd September 1853

Walked to William's Kitchen Garden.

Thursday 1st December 1853.

Letter from William. Heard from Harry - 20th November from Cadiz.

Friday 2nd December 1853

Heard from Scott about payment of his quarterage….Wrote to Scott.

Monday 2nd January 1854

Heard from Scott with particulars as to work at Tyntesfield and wrote to
William and sent him Mr Cosin's letter and also Scott's. Enclosed one
from Harriett to Blanche. Wrote to Scott and Joseph.

Monday 9th January 1854.

Heard from Mr Scott. Wrote to Mr Scott, Nicholls and his son George.

Wednesday 1st August 1855.

Flower Show at Tyntesfield which went off very well – Harriett came
late but enjoyed it very much and was not too much tired with it.

Wednesday 14th November 1855

William called on me about alteration of road and expressed himself
most kindly about his business and guano freights.

Monday 3rd December 1855.

William went to call on Dr Harris. I went with Harriett and Blanche in a
one horse Clarence first to the beach and afterwards in the town.

Tuesday 4th December 1855.

Took a drive with Harriett, William and Blanche to Mr Brunel's place –
only the foundations laid. The outlook very commanding but with too
much view of the town.

Wednesday 5th December 1855.

William and Blanche left for Plymouth by the 11 o'clock train.

The Diary of George Henry Gibbs.

GEORGE HENRY GIBBS [xi] was born in Exeter on 24th August 1785. He was trained in his father's business from the age of 15. He paid six visits of 6 to 10 months each to the Peninsula (Portugal and Spain) between 1801 and 1807. He was present in Cadiz at the Spanish revolt against the French in June 1808, after which he reopened his father's house of business there and remained till 1810. He was a partner with his father in Antony Gibbs & Sons, London, (and in the Cadiz branch) from the founding of the firm in September 1808. From 1815 until his death in 1842 he was head of Antony Gibbs & Sons, which, under him and his brother William, opened Branches in Gibraltar 1818, Lima 1822, Arequipa and Guayaquil 1823, and Valparaiso 1826. He was director of the London Assurance Corporation from 1822 to 1842, a member of the club *Nobody's Friends* (1832 to 1842), and of the *City of London Club* (1840 to 1842).

He was also a member of the London Committee which (1832-1835), with the Bristol Committee, promoted the Great Western Railway and an original Director of that Company (1835-1842). Between 1819 and 1840, he and his brother William voluntarily completed the payment of those of their father's and grandfather's debts which were still outstanding from their bankruptcy in 1789. A few months before he died in 1842, he succeeded to most of the properties which his cousins Anne Noyes (died December 1841) and Sarah Noyes (died April 1842) had inherited in 1814 from their uncle Robert Hucks of Aldenham, Hertfordshire, (his mother's second cousin). As heir at law to Sarah he received Aldenham House and other estates in Hertfordshire and Middlesex; and under Anne's will on Sarah's death, he received estates in Oxfordshire and Berkshire, and in Lambeth, Surrey. With these properties he became Lord of the Manors of North Moreton, Berkshire, (sold by his son Henry), Burston, Hertfordshire, (sold by his grandson, Alban), and Clifton Hampden, Oxfordshire; and patron and lay rector of the last named. His residence was at 2, Powis Place (1817-1821), and 11, Bedford Square (1821-1842), both in the Borough of Holborn.

He married Caroline, the sixth daughter of the Rev. Charles Crawley, the Rector of Stowe-the-Nine-Churches, in July 1817. They had eleven sons – Henry Hucks (1819-1907), Antony (July to November 1821), Antony of Merry Hill (1822-1856), Charles Crawley (August to November 1824), George (1827-1846), Charles (1829-1890), William Lloyd (1830-1860), John Lomax (1832-1914), Francis (1834-1857), Joseph (1837-1838) and Robert (1839-1856), and three daughters – Anne (1818-1820), Caroline (1828-1859) and Mary (1833-1906).

Figure 4. George Henry Gibbs by Sir William Charles Ross R.A., 1840.

The Diary

Friday 24th June 1837
George and William left us for Belmont.
Thursday 7th July 1837
Mr and Mrs Merivale and Reginald with us.
Tuesday 2nd and Wednesday 3rd August 1837
Set off in a carriage for Belmont with Caroline, Willey, Johnny, Mary
and Frances. Slept at Newbury and arrived at Belmont at 6 o'clock in the
morning. Harry and Antony had gone off by coach ten days before, and

Thomas followed on the 5th. Since we have been here we have had very hot weather with wind in the east, but we have enjoyed ourselves very much, particularly one day which we spent at Cheddar. William is with us, having determined not to return to London till tomorrow night.

Wednesday 21st December 1837

William left town with Capon for Bristol.

Monday 13th February 1838

Letters from Valparaiso (*Chile*) announcing the arrival and landing of the Chile expedition and their entry into Arequipa on 12th October.

Saturday 24th March 1838

William went on board the Great Western and I went to the depot, where, though there is still a great deal to be done, I do not see anything to retard our opening beyond the 21st May.

Saturday 31st March 1838

William and I went in the afternoon to Acton, and walked back along the (*Great Western Railway*) line. What I saw did not give me much confidence as to our opening in May. We had a very cold, uncomfortable walk with the wind in the North East and cloudy.

Monday 2nd April 1838

I was shocked to hear of Mr Brunel's serious accident on board the Great Western.

Thursday 12th April 1838

William went this evening to Salthill and Eton to stay a few days.

Good Friday 13th April 1838

Went to Paddington after Church with Charley and Trilly and was much pleased with the progress making there.

Monday 16th April 1838

William came back from Eton this morning.

Sunday 22nd April 1838

John Yonge of Eton is with us.

Sunday 29th April 1838

East wind with occasional snow. Walked today after Church to Paddington with Tom and William.

Thursday 3rd May 1838

South Easterly wind – warm and pleasant weather. I went in the evening with William to Miss Etalls' where we met Sir L. Glynn and Mrs Short.

Friday 11th May 1838

In the chair at the Railway office for two or three hours examining candidates for situations on the railway. Left them at 2 o'clock and set off with William, Antony and Wetherall for Maidenhead in William's carriage. Walked about the works for two hours at Maidenhead and returned to sleep at Salthill.

Thursday 17th May 1838

Letters have been received from Lima to the 13th January with the account of the house to the 31st October 1837 showing $35,000 profit in Lima for the half year, and a considerable reduction of the debts.

Saturday 2nd June 1838

Eton College applied to the Court of Chancery for an injunction to prevent our stopping at Slough. The application was dismissed with costs. Dined at Mt Justice Coleridge's with Caroline and William and met the William Yonges there.

Sunday 3rd June 1838

William went to Englefield where all the children and Antony are.

Monday 4th June 1838

Our railway opened to the public this morning and I went to Maidenhead with the first train and came back with the third which started from Maidenhead at a quarter past ten. I was disappointed with regard to speed as we were one hour and twenty minutes going down and one hour and five minutes coming up....We carried altogether 1479 people and took £226.

Tuesday 5th June 1838

I went yesterday evening with Caroline to Englefield in a fly, and found William, Anne and Joseph arrived there. Joseph had gone to Eton with William. The children were all very well and rejoiced to see us. Caroline and I slept at Egham. This morning they went to Eton, and I proceeded in my fly to Slough, and joined the 10 o'clock train and returned to Paddington in 45 minutes or 29 miles per hour.

Saturday 9th June 1838

Went after an early dinner with Harriett and Anne and William by the Railroad to meet George. Spent two hours there and got home comfortably to tea.

Saturday 30th June 1838

It appears likely that Eton will allow us to have a station at Slough and strange to say a train was promised on Thursday at the request of the Master to bring the Eton boys up to town.

Thursday 6th September 1838

Mrs Yonge and Charlotte came to us with her younger brothers and Mrs Sage dined with us.

Monday 24th September 1838

The Chapatyra arrived today from Valparaiso with letters to 1st July and bringing us $28,000.

Thursday 11th October 1838

The (*Great Western Railway*) Meeting separated in very good humour. Soirée of the Directors, and Saunders returned with me to Belmont to dinner and spent a very pleasant evening.

47

Saturday 27th October 1838

Heard from George from Dover where he had just arrived with William, Harriett and Anne.

Tuesday 6th November 1838

I dined late at the Wyndham with George, William, Mr Short, Lewis and George Crawley.

Wednesday 7th November 1838.

Dined at the Wyndham with George, William, George Crawley, Lewis and Mr Short – very busy connecting to Villamail, Marco and Negrete.

Saturday 17th November 1838

George left Gravesend today at half past two – little wind – He was in good spirits I was glad to hear and had enjoyed the previous evening very much with William and his brothers. John Yonge called having just arrived from Heidelberg.

Tuesday 20th November 1838

William went off to Liverpool by the mail train this evening to negotiate for a vessel to take out our Mexican cargo.

Sunday 24th November 1838

William arrived in the morning from Liverpool.

Wednesday 27th November 1838

John Yonge and Charles Daubeny dined here.

Friday 29th November 1838

Charlotte (*Yonge*) left this morning. Charles Daubeny, John Yonge and Anthony Crawley dined here.

Monday 15th December 1838

William sent off today in capital order and in very capital style all the instructions and letters necessary for the expedition of the Venus.

Sunday 23rd December 1838

The Venus sailed at half past twelve from Liverpool for Valparaiso and San Blas.

Monday 24th December 1838

William went off by the Mail to Belmont.

Wednesday 2nd January 1839

Went early to Paddington where we had a very useful meeting with Gooch (*railway engine production*). We went afterwards to Ealing to try a carriage. William came home this evening.

Tuesday 15th January 1839

In the evening I went with William and the boys to the play and was very much less ached up.

Thursday 17th January 1839

Harry (*Henry Hucks Gibbs*) was at the Merivales last night and is gone to the play tonight with William.

Tuesday 22nd January 1839

The Margaret is in from Lima. The many arrivals lately have given us a great deal to do. The railway calls for a great deal of my time.

Wednesday 30th January 1839

William and I dined together and afterwards talked over many interesting matters.

Tuesday 4th March 1839

The Pattersons, Corries, Susana and Blanche Crawley, the Turners and Merivales came in the evening.

Saturday 8th March 1839

William arrived. Mrs Crawley breakfasted here.

Sunday 31st March 1839

Harry (*Henry Hucks Gibbs*) is paying too much attention to his cousin Blanche which I must check as he is young and too poor to marry and I have not the means to make him do so. He spoke to me the other day of his wish to come into the business, and I shall tell him that he must first take a creditable degree, and then I will let him do as he pleases.

Monday 1st April 1839

I went in the evening to Paddington, where we agreed to accept tenders for about 30 engines. We had a pleasant dance in Bedford Square afterwards and kept it up till past 1.00 a.m.

Saturday 6th April 1839

Harriett and William with the Crawleys went to the Opera. George stayed at home and I was busy about the house accounts.

Saturday 13th April 1839

Harriett, Anne and William dined at Highgate.

Sunday 22nd April 1839

William made an offer on Friday morning to Blanche and then became very nervous that he had done wrong in endeavouring to gain the affections of one so much younger than himself. He carried his scruples in this respect too far and made us very uncomfortable for some days as he placed Blanche in a very trying and uncomfortable position. She returned his affection and apprised him that his fears of entailing unhappiness in her were entirely groundless. Her friends had made ready to give their consent and yet William hesitated. The fit however went off on Saturday and they have both been very happy ever since.

The Matilda arrived today from Lima.

Tuesday 23rd April 1839

Sir Thomas told me today that he'd given Blanche £7000 and I said plenty afterwards about settlements.

Wednesday 24th April 1839

North Easterly – a beautiful day, but cold. At 11 o'clock we left town

with Caroline, Sir Thomas and Susan (*Crawley Boevey*) by the B.
Railway for Stowe and arrived in four hours. The hedges beginning to
look green, and the grass growing, but no trees and Stowe looked very
pretty.
Friday 26th April 1839
Walked to the station at a quarter past three and reached Bedford
Square at half past seven much pleased with the travelling, the
ability and the appearance of everything on the line. Found William and
Blanche very happy.

Figure 5. Flaxley Abbey from the Church, Blanche Gibbs, 1840.

Thursday 2nd May 1839
Got to Oxford by half past twelve and found Joseph and Emily there.
William and Blanche and Susan came at 3 o'clock by the coach, and we
all dined with Harry (*Henry Hucks Gibbs*) and had a merry party....
William had completely lost his worries. Blanche and Susan went on
immediately after dinner to Gloucester, and we went to Clifton Hampden
from where William walked back to Oxford to get onto the Gloucester
mail to London.
Wednesday 15th May 1839
Sir Thomas Crawley and Mrs Crawley came over (to Belmont) from
Flaxley.
Saturday 18th May 1839
Sir Thomas and William left us this Morning (from Belmont).
Tuesday 28th May 1839
William left us this evening by the Mail for Flaxley.

Figure 6. Flaxley Abbey from the Gardens, Blanche Gibbs, 1840.

Friday 14th June 1839
William, Blanche and the rest went to the Nightingale Valley
(from Belmont).
Monday 17th June 1839
William left us this evening for London.
Wednesday 19th June 1839
Sir Thomas Crawley and his daughters left Belmont.
Saturday 6th July 1839
The Great Western sailed.
Thursday 25th July 1839
Left Belmont for Westbury (*on Severn*) at 2 o'clock and arrived at 8
o'clock.
Saturday 27th July 1839
Harry (*Henry Hucks Gibbs*) arrived at Flaxley from Belmont.
Sunday 28th July 1839
Went to Church at Westbury in the morning and at Flaxley in the
afternoon.
Monday 29th July 1839
Left Westbury for Flaxley.
Tuesday 30th and Wednesday 31st July 1839
George, Harriett, Anne and Charley arrived here from Belmont, and
William, Joseph and Emily from Clifton (*Hampden*).
Thursday 1st August 1839
We all assembled today at nine o'clock in the little church to witness the
marriage of my dear brother William with Blanche Crawley. It was a

lovely day and everything combined to make it a happy one. The bride and bridegroom left us about twelve for Malvern, and we went most of us to take a drive to call on Miss Bennett.

Figure 7. Flaxley Church, Blanche Gibbs, 1840.

Still lovely weather and we took advantage of it to go to Tintern by the Speech House (*Hotel*) and St Briavels which we enjoyed exceedingly. I never saw the forest or the Abbey to so much advantage. We did not get home till 12 at night.

Monday 5th August 1839, Flaxley.

South Westerly and beautiful summer weather. We went, 21 of us, on a picnic party through Newnham, Blakeney, Whitemead and Parkend to Staunton and the Buckstone, a most delightful drive. The views of Newland, the Winecliff, the Sugar Loaf and other Welsh mountains, Malvern and the Wye were very striking indeed.

Monday 12th August 1839

Left Flaxley today with all our children except Harry and Willy in William's little carriage – eleven in all and we left with regret all the kind friends with whom we had been living so pleasantly since William's marriage.

Saturday 24th August 1839

Fine weather. Simms and I received the Duke of Wellington at Paddington and showed him the Electro Magnetic Telegraph and the station. He was accompanied by Lord Bathurst, Lord Fitzroy Somerset, and three ladies and looked very well.

Monday 26th August 1839

Left London with Francis by the 12 o'clock train for Bristol, in William's carriage, and arrived there at half past ten.

Saturday 12th October 1839

Antony, Harry and I went to Reading to meet William and Blanche, and Albinia came up with them from Twyford. Harry left us this evening for Oxford.

Saturday 2nd November 1839

William returned from the Isle of Wight.

Tuesday 24th December 1839

The Eton people have at last conceded to our having a station at Slough.

Friday 10th January 1840

The Penny Post began.

Monday 20th January 1840

We had in the evening a dinner party. William, Blanche, Susan, George and Caroline, Mr Dallon, Mr King, Mr Venables, F. Daubeny and his sister and Miss Hall, and in the evening young Hawkins.

Tuesday 21st January 1840

Caroline and the boys went in the evening to the Merivales.

Wednesday 22nd January 1840

Harry left us for Oxford.

Sunday 1st March 1840

We (the Great Western Railway) shall probably open to Reading on 6th April, Steventon on 4th May, Farringdon on 29th June, between Bristol and Bath on 24th August, to Swindon in November and the whole line in August 1841.

Monday 9th March 1840

North Easterly wind – the same fine weather. The first of our new engines arrived today. William, Blanche and Susan drank tea with us.

Saturday 14th March 1840

Some of the directors went with an engine for the first time to Reading. I went over the Paddington Station in the evening, and I think it will be all finished in a fortnight.

Monday 30th March 1840.

Our railway opened today to Reading

Monday 13th April 1840

Traffic increasing famously.

Tuesday 14th April 1840

Shares continue to rise (10 to 10½) and the traffic also.

Wednesday 22nd April 1840

Our traffic continues to improve and shares are at 17.

Thursday 7th May 1840

Great Western Railway shares after rising after much excitement to 25

have fallen again and are now at 19.
Tuesday 30th June 1841
The Great Western Railway opened from Paddington to Bristol
Temple Meads.

Figure 1. Temple Meads Station, Bristol in 1850.

**Figure 2 The broad gauge steam train arrives at Bristol Temple Meads
Station.**

Diaries of Henry Hucks Gibbs,

The First Lord Aldenham

Figure 3. Henry Hucks Gibbs.

HENRY HUCKS GIBBS, THE FIRST BARON ALDENHAM

xii was born at 2, Powis Place, Bloomsbury, London on 31st August 1819. He was the eldest son of George Henry Gibbs and his wife Caroline, the daughter of the Rev. Charles Crawley, Rector of Stowe-the-Nine-Churches in Northamptonshire. He was educated at Redland near Bristol and at Rugby School before going to Exeter College, Oxford.

In 1843 he joined Antony Gibbs and Sons and after initial uncertainty settled down into the family firm. He virtually ran the company after his uncle, William Gibbs, retired in 1858 and on the death of his uncle, in 1875, became the Prior or Chairman of Antony Gibbs and

Sons. In 1853, he became a Director of the Bank of England, a position he held until 1901. Between 1875 and 1877 he was Governor of the Bank of England. He advocated 'bimetalism' that is using both silver and gold to back the currency of a country, and for international monetary affairs.

Under Henry Hucks Gibbs, the family firm closed its Peru branch in 1880 at the time of the War between Chile and Peru/Bolivia, and concentrated on Nitrate Production in Chile. The family firm took over Gibbs, Bright and Company in 1881 with branches in England and Australia and business in the West Indies. He was a Member of Lloyds from 1855, and a Director of the Mexican Railway (1864-1905), of the Indemnity Mutual Marine Insurance Company (1869-1906), and of several other companies.

He was involved with other members of his family in establishing a Conservative newspaper in 1880 – "The St James Gazette" – which the family owned until 1888. Although he was invited to stand for parliament for Bristol in 1862, he declined this and other offers and only agreed in April 1891 when he won a by-election in the City of London. He stood down at the General Election of July 1892.

Henry Hucks Gibbs was a Justice of the Peace in both Middlesex and Hertfordshire, and served as High Sheriff of Hertfordshire in 1884. He was appointed a trustee of the National Portrait Gallery by W.H. Smith in 1890, and he was President of Guys Hospital from 1880 to 1896. He was a great lover of books with a celebrated library. A High Churchman, Henry Hucks was from 1876 a trustee of the English Church Union. He restored the churches at Clifton Hampden and Aldenham. He was on the Council of Keble College, Oxford from 1873 to 1907, and a life member of the Corporation of Church House, Westminster, from 1888 to 1907. He was elected Fellow of the Royal Geographical Society in 1859, and Fellow of the Society of Antiquaries in 1885.

His services to the New English Dictionary, edited by Dr. James Murray, were noteworthy. He undertook the sub-editing of the letters C and K. He assisted Dr Murray considerably in settling the final form of the work for Oxford University Press. When the dictionary was menaced by financial stringency at Oxford University Press, he gave a generous donation to keep the dictionary project a going concern. Indeed he was the man who saved the dictionary.

He was created Baron Aldenham on 31st January 1896. He was a member of the Club "Nobody's Friends" and its President from 1895 to 1907, of the Roxburgh Club of which he was President from 1903 to 1907, of the Carlton Club and the Athenaeum Club.

He married Louisa Ann Adams in 1845 and they had six sons – Alban, Walter, Vicary, Herbert, Kenneth and Henry – and one daughter –

Edith. Louisa, Lady Aldenham, died in April 1897. Lord Aldenham died on 18th September 1907.

The Diary

Journey to Italy

During the spring and summer of 1846 Henry Hucks Gibbs journeyed through Italy. During March and April he visited Rome, Albano, Terracina and Naples. He spent the whole of May in Sicily visiting Palermo, Sciacca, Monte Alegro, Selinuntium, Syracuse, Catania, Etna and many other places. In June, Henry Hucks and his party visited Rome and Florence. He had instructions from Uncle William (William Gibbs) to purchase works of art.

Sunday 26th April 1846, Naples.
Mr Furze gave me a letter from *my brother* Antony in which he mentions that… poor little Antony has been very dangerously ill, but is better.
Thursday 4th June 1846, Salerno.
Letters from Uncle William and Uncle Joseph. Wrote to Uncle William about pictures and giving an account of our movements.
Wednesday 10th June 1846, Naples.
Went to the Museum this morning and walked through the sculpture rooms – to remind myself of the beauties of the collection. Bought some cork models of the temples of Paestum on Uncle William's account.
Monday 15th June 1846, Rome.
Went to Paggioli's and stayed there above an hour choosing different marbles for Uncle William's chessboard, which will form an oblong table with its sides of Nero Rosso Giallo and Bigio Antico. It is to cost $45. Went to Luchetti's at 11, where by appointment I met Mr Furze, and proceeded to look at his pictures. Those two which Antony recommended (by Le Moyne) I bought and also one by Nicolas Poussin. (I never saw one by him like it, though L. says the pendant, bought by a Mr Drury, was verified in London), one by Schnellinck – two by Ruysdael (according to L, the smallest is by Jacob R.), one by a scholar of Rembrandt and one by Carlo Maratta. The sum asked was $756. I gave $450. At Paggioli's I bought a little Flemish piece for $6. Went home to dinner and wrote half a long letter to Uncle William recounting my exploits. At half past two, Furze came again and went on with me to Capraneri's where I bought two pictures said to be Canalettos (and indeed something in his style) with figures by Zuccarelli – exceedingly pretty. $100 asked $80 paid – also made an offer of $150 for two real

Guardis very beautiful, both works of art and pleasing pictures.... On a second visit I found my offer had been taken. In this shop I saw a picture by Astades of a Chymist in his Laboratory – the most exquisitely finished picture of the kind I have ever seen – price $500. I must write to Uncle William to buy it. Furze much approves both purchases and taste. From hence we went to Barberi's who after some preliminary conversation about mosaics, and after a visit to the Marquis de Gorgorji's to see the Murillo (with which Furze was as delighted as I am, and not withstanding that the Marquis will not abate a jot from $3000, I do hope Uncle William will buy), he opened the question of the Francia and the Raffaelle. It appears that the Count entirely rejects the offer of £250 for the former, but is disposed to treat for the purchase of both, on the basis of my offer of £400. This however he says is far too little and desired Barberi not to go lower than £500, to which Barberi rejoined that if he, as he wished were to be arbiter, he must be left unshackled. The Count assented, and he therefore on consideration named the sum of £475 – I heard him all out and answered that it was not my affair, that I must follow my instructions, that as therefore his was a definite answer, I must much as I regretted it, leave the pictures in his possession. "When do I go to town? I could then induce Mrs Gibbs to increase her offer." I answered that I should be in town shortly, but I could answer for it that the offer would not be raised, but that she would be rather glad that it was not accepted. He promised to call in the evening, and I have not the least doubt the pictures are ours. I bought a beautiful mosaic table for Uncle William (£30) and two paper weights – one for Whitman and one for Uncle William if he chooses. Went to Trebbi's – Lunchettis and Capranesis (to ascertain the fate of the Guardis) – then to Flatz, who with his pupil Finck received me most heartily – not the less so when I seemed like a purchaser. I should have at once given an order for the Magdalena, only that I again saw the Saint Cecilia which so charmed me that I must try and induce Uncle William to have that instead. As to Furze's copy of the Sassoferrato I hope he will have that too. Sat some time with the Furzes and returned at half past nine to tea, journal and letters. As I expected, Barberi who had been sitting here for some time has come down to our price of £400 – so the pictures are ours.
One o'clock and I am only just going to bed after finishing Uncle William's letter.
Tuesday 16ᵗʰ June 1846, Viterbo, Rome.
I began the morning by going to Trebbi's seeing that he had got all the pictures and instructing him what to do with them. Then to Ploweden and Cholmeley's Bank, where I drew the money for Barberi, and also some for myself. Met Furze in the Piazza Colonna and made him take 5% on the purchases.

Friday 19th June 1846, Perugia.

Sent a message to Uncle William in John's letter to say that we would probably be at Milan Monday or Tuesday fortnight and begging him to write and tell me if I am to order any alabaster for him, seeing that I had already exceeded his commission by £10 or so.

Tuesday 23rd June 1846, Florence.

We went in a carriage to the Pitti Palace to see Hughes' copy of the Persigino. Very much pleased with it, though we suggested one little alteration. Saw also the Madonna del Gran Duca – much above any copy I ever saw. Went to Pifani's and bought some alabaster for ourselves and some for Uncle William – the latter conditionally.

Wednesday 24th June 1846, Florence.

Louisa wrote to Uncle William mentioning among other things the beautiful mosaic tables we had seen at Bianchinis near the Capella de Medici, and asking if he would like one of them for £20 or £25.

Tuesday 30th June 1846, Florence.

I fear from the receipt of a letter from Uncle William and Blanche directed Milan and dated 17th that the two intermediate ones are lost. They order the Sassoferrato, but I shall not execute the order till I hear again. I wrote to Uncle William to say so, and to correct an error in his statement of the sum owing by me to the house.

Sunday 19th July 1846, Lausanne, Hotel Gibbon.

A letter from Blanche ordering the Florentine Mosaic table which however I have hesitated about as it seemed doubtful whether they did not mean in lieu of Barberi's. Wrote to Uncle William (to go by Mrs Thompson) to ask – and the Alabaster. Wrote to Risani to tell him.

Tuesday 21st July 1846, Lausanne.

Louisa wrote to Blanche. I wrote another letter to Uncle William giving an account of the orders sent to Furze, to Flatz, to Capranesi and Bianchini to whom I send letters tomorrow.

Saturday 1st August 1846, Vevey.

A long letter from Uncle William chiefly about the expenses at Clifton Hampden Church and House, and about my debts to the house (Antony Gibbs and Sons). I can understand his mode of thinking on the subject, and without being prejudiced by my own interest must think my view of the case the right one until I talk to him more about it. Wrote to him but did not enter very deeply into the subject.

Monday 31st August 1846, Aldenham.

Baby was received very well and behaved most graciously to his Grandmother and Aunts. He has been very well since he has been here. He is to be called Henry, or more probably George after all. We thought it would please my mother, so we told her it should be so….Also I wrote to Uncle William….Antony had a letter from Uncle William in which he asks us to Tyntesfield if we can spare the time. We amuse ourselves with cricket in the park and have a pretty good ground. On Saturday we fetched our first parcel of things from Trebby which seem to please very much. Especially our pictures and mosaic paper weight and Blanche's commission.

Thursday 10th September 1846, Thorpe.
I had a note from Blanche.

Tyntesfield, Belmont and Aldenham.

Friday 11th September 1846, Tyntesfield.
A note from Blanche this morning to say we were to come today but that Uncle William had got the jaundice. Packed up and packed off by 11 and leaving Slough by the 12.38 train arriving at Bristol by 4.45 p.m. where we found Luke waiting for us. Left Louisa and Nurse at the station and went to the Post Office where I found Uncle William's letter mentioning my mother's intention of paying the whole of the surplus for Clifton Hampden house and church, and also increasing the endowment of the living by £100 a year in the hope that I would agree with her to present it (if the presentation should ever fall to me) to one of my brothers. I do not like the idea of making a positive agreement – it is looking forward too far. A promise that no temporal reason, such as preferment of a son of my own, should interfere with my doing so, does not appear to have any objection against it.

A letter from Flatz agreeing to do the two pictures for Uncle William. Arrived here at 6 and found Blanche very well and Uncle William, though much depressed, better than I expected – William Henry here – Uncle George and Aunt Harriett dined here, the former looking very well. The house beautiful and the formal terraced garden very good. I am glad and surprised to find Blanche's opinions of and feelings towards Thomson (*their baby's wet nurse*) exactly coinciding with ours.

Saturday 12th September 1846, Tyntesfield.
Walked about the grounds after breakfast with Uncle William and talked over business. After luncheon drove out in the pony chaise to the farm and round by Belmont. Dined there at 6 and spent a pleasant evening with them.

Sunday 13th September 1846, Tyntesfield.
William Henry told me he'll probably go to Genoa. Talked to him a great deal to make peace between him and his brother Charles. Uncle William talked to him on the same subject. He thinks Charles' conduct has been on the whole very creditable.....Uncle George has been very poorly today. Louisa and I walked up before tea. He is rather better tonight.

Monday 14th September 1846, Tyntesfield.

William Henry went to day….Called on the Edward Vaughans – dined at Belmont. Uncle George better.

Tuesday 15th September 1846, Tyntesfield.

Copied between us a letter of Uncle William to Mr Hayne.

Finished posting our expenses while on the continent. Mr and Mrs Vaughan dined here. A very long evening, scarcely enlivened by a vehement talk on politics towards the end.

Wednesday 16th September 1846, Tyntesfield.

Letters from Antony (*Henry Hucks' brother*) and from Methuen, the former saying that my Gun case hat box etc. had been booked on the G.W.R. so that they have certainly been stolen or miscarried. Wrote to him. Uncle William and Blanche went to Belmont after dinner. I stayed with Louisa who had a cold in her system.

Thursday 17th September 1846, Tyntesfield.

Letter from Antony saying my things are being enquired after. Also one from my mother. Wrote to both, to the latter about endowment of Clifton Hampden church and accepting her offer of paying the balance of the Clifton House and Church account. Dined at Belmont. Aunt Anne, Uncle Joseph, William and John came in the evening. Uncle Joseph sleeps here. The Charles Vaughans come to Clifton (*Hampden*) next Tuesday and stay for a fortnight – as they cannot receive us until the 7th or 8th. We shall probably therefore pay our Farndon and Stowe visits first going round by Birmingham and Gloucester and perhaps taking a peep at Flaxley on our way. It will probably delay us a little.

Friday 18th September 1846, Belmont.

George and Albinia came today. The Belmont party dined at Tyntesfield, and we have come back with them. I find my mother has determined not to have the Billiard table in the hall but in the bachelors' room – so there will be about 2½ feet between it and the wall – it will be of course impossible to use it. I wish she had consulted me first. I might have saved her ordering a lamp for that room – and I fear a table for the hall. If the Billiard table has to be returned I shall have been made a pretty fool of – ordering it in the name of A. Gof. Wrote to Aldenham…so as to be sure to catch my mother and give her a chance of repairing any evil that may have been done.

Uncle William told me the other day of his having engaged Mr Davy and Mr Hayne to be partners in the house from January 1848, and that he hoped that I should be able to be a partner at the same time. I must work hard to enable myself.

Saturday 19th September 1846, Belmont.

Sent letters to my mother. Went out shooting with Uncle Joseph but had but two shots, with the first of which I killed one hare. At last my gun and other things are come from town having been eight days on the road; and after all Antony (*Henry Hucks' brother*) has not sent my journal. Tyntesfield party dined here and I played whist with my three uncles – Uncle William and I winning four points.

Wednesday 23rd September 1846, Belmont.

Aunt Emily, Uncle Joe, and John and Francis dined at Tyntesfield. Mother, Louisa, William and I played whist.

Thursday 24th September 1846, Belmont.

The Tyntesfield party dined here.

Friday 25th September 1846, Belmont.

At Tyntesfield I found two letters. Antony says Mr Cracken sent off Uncle William's pictures yesterday. Uncle William, who dined here today, sent for them but they were not to be found.

Saturday 26th September 1846, Belmont.

A most rainy day, but fine between the showers – the Tyntesfield party dined here to help us eat an excellent haunch of venison sent by Mr Robert Bright. The pictures are at last come and are safe in their boxes at Tyntesfield.

Sunday 27th September 1846, Belmont.

Walked with William to church by way of Tyntesfield and back with Uncle William and my mother.

Monday 28th September 1846, Belmont.

Aunt Harriett sent for the pictures up here, and after breakfast I opened them all and was no less pleased than when I bought them. Uncle William and Blanche came up after luncheon, but were I fear rather disappointed. Had they given me more liberty both as to subject and price, I would have pleased them better. My mother is very much pleased with the Raffaelle and Fra Francis. The Tyntesfield party dined here. Everybody else seems to admire the pictures and Barberi's table very much. My mother wishes to have the Guardis because one represents the view from our window in the Europa at Venice.

Tuesday 29th September 1846, Belmont.

Took the pictures to Tyntesfield in the market cart, and spent the morning arranging them. They have determined to put them all in the Gallery where they have an excellent light; they look very well there and I think find more favour in their master's eyes than they did yesterday. Uncle William lets my mother have the Guardis – excellent pictures they are.

Wednesday 30th September 1846, Broughton.

Drove after breakfast to Tyntesfield in the gig to wish them good' bye – brought up Blanche to see Louisa. Forgot to mention that Uncle William gave us the picture of the man drinking which I bought at Luchetti's.

Thursday 3rd December 1846, Aldenham.

Still at home (with a sore throat). Mother planted an oak in the park opposite our windows. I wrote to Uncle Charles. Uncle William and Blanche came.

Friday 4th December 1846, Aldenham.

Drove Uncle William, three in a gig with Ruth to Bushey; he came back in a fly. Eliza Hughes left baby alone to cry. Louisa gave her a proper scolding saying she must go if ever it happened again.

Saturday 5th December 1846, Aldenham.

Fly with Uncle William to Harrow.

Sunday 6th December 1846, Aldenham.

Elstree morning and evening. Uncle William to Aldenham.

Monday 7th December 1846, Aldenham.

A letter from Susan to Blanche gives a very bad account of her father. She thinks he cannot last much longer. Blanche goes down there tomorrow.

Wednesday 9th December 1846, Aldenham.

Blanche went yesterday and today there was another letter from Susan urging her to come if she wished to see her father alive.

Thursday 10th December 1846, Aldenham.

Letter from Hughes. Sir Thomas much the same, but I think frailer. A most miserable drive home – hail and snow in our eyes all the way.

Friday 30th April 1847, Bedford Square.

Yesterday I took the Pages and Susan to the Thames Tunnel, where I had never been – it is a wonderful place, but a neighbour also to the Bank, of which the same may be predicated, but it is most interesting, especially the weighing machines, and the telltale.

Friday 7th May 1847, Bedford Square.

Uncle William came to Bedford Square to talk with my mother, at her request, about Antony's health and prospects in the business. We began to be much persuaded that London and a sedentary life are not consistent with his health, besides that his temperament rather unfits him for the business. My mother has therefore determined to make him the offer of even now sending him to college, with a view to his taking holy orders. She has spoken to him about it, and he as is natural and right says it requires a great deal of thought to decide on the subject – he is loath to change and in that I think he is right, but I do at the same time think it is what he is more fitted for by nature.

Saturday 29th April 1848, Forest Hill.

We went on Thursday to Hyde Park Gardens to celebrate the baptism of little George Abraham, the 7th Abraham in 7 successive generations of our family.

Figure 11. Aldenham House, Hertfordshire.

Figure 12. The Church at Clifton Hampden.

Tuesday 15th August 1848, Hyde Park Street.

I arrived at half past ten last night and found Uncle William, here. I have managed to get a very bad sore throat. I have got on pretty well with my packet work, but throat or not I must go in tomorrow.

Saturday 19th August 1848, Hyde Park Street.

Uncle William came home at three and dined at 4 o'clock, he starting for Tyntesfield by the Express. He takes with him Flatz's picture of the Magdalene. It is beautifully finished and he is on the whole well pleased. Only the depth of thought in the eye gives the face too masculine a look – and it is quite right for the penitent pale Magdalene.

Wednesday 3rd January 1849, Hyde Park Street.

A long time has elapsed since I last wrote anything in this book…I will now take it up as well as I can from where I left off….The fatigues of nursing me in my illness make it very necessary that Louisa (as well as myself) should have quiet and a change of air; we are accordingly going to take possession of the empty house at Belmont for a month or so knowing that Uncle George and Aunt Harriett in their kindness would be glad we should do so, if they were here. We are to stay about a month till the William Gibbs's leave Tyntesfield when we shall probably take a little run into Devonshire.

Hughes has quite finished my father's picture, and besides making a good painting has certainly made a better likeness than either of Gill's – Uncle William was so pleased with the copy that he bought it at once for Tyntesfield and Hughes is to make another for the Counting House, and then probably another for Aldenham. Uncle William will probably sit for his own likeness to Hughes, to be put in the Counting House.

Friday 5th January 1849, Hyde Park Street.

Uncle William called in the morning – The Morning Chronicle is full of an arrangement which Osma has made with the Peruvian Bond Holders, and which appears highly favourable to them – and to offer a probability of their dividends being really paid. It is based upon a contract which he appears to have made with us, and which has occupied Uncle William and Hayne all this week and is likely to occupy them some days more. I know nothing of particulars yet, but I am to hear them at Tyntesfield. Moreover Uncle William has carried off my Paper of today which leaves me still more in the dark.

Friday 12th January 1849, Belmont.

Left town by the 9.50 Express and reached Bristol without much fatigue by 12.30 where we found Blanche's carriage with a hot water tire inside which was a great comfort to my frozen feet – We got here by about 1.10 and found dear Blanche here to meet us. Alban looking very well and having been very good by all accounts….Uncle William is good enough to say that we are his guests here. He must have thought it very encroaching of us to talk of bringing Frank but he told us by all means to persist – so here he is. I hope he will be able to make himself useful. I love every tree and stone of this place. And it really seems much more like going home than even going to Aldenham. This is what I remember from childhood but that is not even yet formed.

Saturday 13th January 1849, Belmont.

I don't think I mentioned that in the hurry and confusion of Tuesday morning that our dear little girl was baptised "Edith Caroline". George Daubeny (*married to Matilda Blanche Gibbs' sister, Albinia*) and Susan came to see us today, and Uncle William has just arrived from town.

Sunday 14th January 1849, Belmont.

We have had a miserable rainy day but in the afternoon the sun came out and we ventured to take a walk – my first walk since my illness – down to the farm. We enjoyed it exceedingly. Looked at many odd numbers of the Town and Country Magazine and the European Magazine. We had letters from Eliza, Barbara, Robinson our dentist and Megan, the latter enclosing a short one from Uncle George. We have written tonight a very long one to him and Aunt Harriett.

Monday 15th January 1849, Belmont.

Blanche called to see us before dinner and finding myself none the worse but rather the better for my walk yesterday, I walked with her and Louisa to Tyntesfield and that without being tired. Blanche kindly sent us back in the carriage…The children (Blanche's) are greatly improved especially Dolly (*Dorothea*). I like the pictures very much and their frames become them. I must say I do agree with the general opinion about Flatz's Head of the Magdalene. It is not a happy idea. They have hung the picture too high.

Began today to write the History of our Family and finished the introduction thereto.

Tuesday 16th January 1849, Belmont.

A few letters from tradesmen and an old letter from my mother. I sent off my letter to Uncle George. Miserable weather, but Uncle William and Susan have come up here – we managed to get a walk up the West Hill to Ellen's and back again.

Wednesday 17th January 1849, Belmont.

Pouring weather but in the evening it cleared up so that, with Antony (who had come from Aldenham looking very well) and Louisa, I walked about for some time and then to Tyntesfield and back without fatigue. Uncle William was up here and advised me to give £20 a year to Clifton (*Hampden*) School instead of £10, and I shall certainly do it. Our children are improving and Mr Davis says he is quite satisfied with both of them. Alban got a good walk today. Antony (*Henry Hucks' brother*) is not going up this time; and William (*Henry Hucks' brother*) is beginning to funk matriculation. He has been foolish enough not to work this vacation. I have written to say that he must go up, and that if he is turned back he has only himself to thank for it.

Tuesday 23rd January 1849, Belmont.

I have left off my journal since the 17th by reason of illness on Friday last which kept me in bed until now..... Owing to the remedies applied by ourselves and I have been going on sufficiently well to have been allowed to sit up today to dinner and eat some excellent roast chicken and blancmange. The evening before last I had four leeches put on the affected part.

Wednesday 24th January 1849, Belmont.

Both Blanche and Susan, and Uncle William paid us nice long visits today. They have all been very kind in sitting with us. I wrote my mother a long letter about her boys – (*Antony, William and Charles*). A very kind note from Eliza today.

Monday 29th January 1849, Belmont.

We are reading Lord Harvey's "Memoirs". Wrote part of a letter to Aunt Harriett.

Tuesday 30th January 1849, Belmont.

Went on with the letter. We had a long letter from my mother. The two boys (*Antony and William*) go up to Oxford today, I believe to be examined tomorrow. Walked as far as the farm and round by the road – beautiful camellias in the greenhouse. Muggy weather with a soft rain.

Wednesday 31st January 1849, Belmont.

A beautiful day, but with occasional mist – The Glass rising – We walked to Tyntesfield. All the children there have colds.

Thursday 1st February 1849, Belmont.

Glass steadily rising, but the day has been miserably misty and even rainy. Robert Bright called and sat some time. Louisa and I are improving I think. We walked to Tyntesfield.

Friday 2nd February 1849, Belmont.

The same odd weather here – The glass is Fair, and the land covered with mist amounting to rain. Walked before dinner to the iron gates calling on the way on Betsy Heaven. After dinner to Tyntesfield. Colds bad there.

Saturday 3rd February 1849, Belmont.

A beautiful day at last. We went to Tyntesfield before dinner, and afterwards Uncle William came up here for me, and walked with me down to his farm, round Tyntesfield and so home here. The Farm looks very nice. The baby at Tyntesfield had a slight attack of inflammation in the chest, but is better this evening.

Sunday 4th February 1849, Belmont.

The poor little boy (*William Gibbs aged two*) is very ill this morning and has been so all day. However I hear he is better tonight. He was prayed for in church this evening. Mr Davis is to stay there tonight. Louisa went to church this evening. She is better. She is to use Belladonna ointment. Our little girl (*Edith*) was vaccinated this morning.

Monday 5th February 1849, Belmont.

I took a longish walk with Uncle William today.

Wednesday 7th February 1849, Belmont.

Uncle William went yesterday to his new house. I think my walk the day before was rather too long for I was a good deal tired today with walking only to Tyntesfield.

Thursday 8th February 1849, Belmont.

Still uncomfortable and walked no further than the Iron Gates.

Friday 9th February 1849, Belmont.

A letter from my mother enclosing one from Robert (*Henry Hucks' young brother*) in which he said he was not happy at Radley. Louisa and I think of going there to see him. I wrote to him. After dinner we walked to Tyntesfield. Mr Kington called, also Blanche and George.

Saturday 10th February 1849, Belmont.

Uncle William returned this evening. I have a mumpy kind of swelling in my throat, arising from cold, but it is not much. I see from the paper that young Charles Blackstone (I suppose the son of my tutor) has shot himself through the heart with a pistol…It appears that it was an accident, the pistol being kept under the sofa pillow, and the young man being at the time asleep on the sofa. He was a scholar of Corpus.

Sunday 11th February 1849, Belmont.

Most lovely cold weather. A letter from mother which I answered. Louisa went to church this evening. Poor little Edith has to be vaccinated again. We walked over to Tyntesfield after breakfast and found them still at their breakfast. Uncle William had returned. A letter from Harrison.

Monday 12th February 1849, Belmont.

Still the same delightful weather. We walked twice to Tyntesfield. Finished the first volume of Lord Harvey's Memoirs.

Tuesday 13th February 1849, Belmont.

Uncle William, Blanche and the children actually went this morning. A lovely day.

Wednesday 14th February 1849, Belmont.

Cold and fog this morning, but fine in the afternoon. A letter from Robert saying the masters are very kind, but the boys not so. William and John came this evening looking pretty well.

Thursday 15th February 1849, Belmont.

Walked to Tyntesfield in the morning and drove to call on the Vaughans in the afternoon. Lovely weather.

Friday 16th February 1849, Belmont.

Still fine weather and not quite so cold. We drove to see Backwell

Church and returned in time to see the boys off to join the 4.50 train from Nailsea.

Saturday 17th February 1849, Belmont.

Most beautiful weather, only the evening was spoilt by a thick mist which filled the whole valley. Little baby is looking very nice. Wrote to George E Adams, Blanche and my mother....We went to Barrow Court – a fine old place. The church grievously bepewed, but capable of improvement, and the house and situation glorious.

Sunday 18th February 1849, Belmont.

A letter this morning from Uncle William being dated the 16th ought to have arrived yesterday. It brings me a copy of one from Aunt Harriett telling him of the illness of dear Uncle George. Some letters however appear to have miscarried as he refers to a former letter of the 4th, and this brings an account of his being better and going on favourably – so by this time please God he is convalescent. We do not know what has been the matter but he is now suffering from fever. This evening he was prayed for in church.

Monday 19th February 1849, Belmont.

A windy drizzly day. We took a drive to Ashton and a walk to Tyntesfield. No letters.

Tuesday 20th February 1849, Belmont.

Uncle William has sent me two letters from Aunt Harriett and Aunt Anne written before the one I read on Sunday, and telling of Uncle George's illness with a gastric fever, but though he has been very ill, it does not seem so alarming as her letter of the 7th taken without these as context. We went in the fly to Clevedon to have Alban's hair cut, but the man was out and called here. It rained all day.

Wednesday 21st February 1849, Belmont.

Today has brought us an excellent account from Aunt Harriett saying that dear Uncle George was much better and had lost but little strength considering his illness and his age. Ash Wednesday – better weather.

Thursday 22nd February 1849, Belmont.

No news today. I went alone and called on the Kingtons (*at Charlton House*). They have a handsome house, with a fine hearth and carved chimney piece.

Saturday 24th February 1849, Belmont.

We were to have gone to Glenfrome today but that the weather has been very rainy, and besides I was taken ill last night in consequence of indigestion owing to my eating some mackerel and rhubarb – both which things gave me more violent pain in the stomach than ever I had in my life. The day had been lovely and we had been to Cadbury Camp, and feeling remarkably well and hearty, when just approaching Tyntesfield the pain came suddenly on and by the time I came here at about a quarter past five I could not stand upright. Louisa said I looked like a woman in labour! The pain lasted till about ten o'clock when it yielded to 30 grams of Rhubarb and 30 of soda administered by Mr Davis.

Sunday 25th February 1849, Belmont.

Uncle William sent yesterday an excellent account of dear Uncle George. The fever has wholly left him. Sent it to Lucy Hendy. April weather.

Monday 26th February 1849, Belmont.

A very fine day. I hope we may have the like tomorrow. Finished a copy of the Daubeny Pedigree for George. Worked hard yesterday and today at a Scripture Genealogy. Mr Bright was so good as to call and left us the second volume of Lord Harvey's Memoirs which we began. Louisa wrote to my mother and hers. Little Edith is getting more and more intelligent every day. Alban too is pretty well in health and very quick. He has an excellent memory and really seems to enjoy his lessons. He has a bad ear though for sounds. He is a dear good little boy – most obedient and good tempered.

Tuesday 27th February 1849, Belmont.

We were to have gone to Glenfrome but Lucy being poorly they were obliged to put us off. The accounts of Uncle George continue to improve and I trust he is now quite out of danger. He has been prayed for here in church.

Monday 19th March 1849, Belmont.

I have been most idle about my journal; but will try to make amends. We paid a very pleasant visit to Glenfrome on Tuesday 6th March – having a lovely day. The Hendys all kindness as usual. Jane Hendy was there. I was a good deal tired with my jaunt. The next day Christopher Harrison came and stayed till Friday.

In India Mooltan has fallen but we have had a defeat on the plains of Chillianwallah with dreadful slaughter – 95 officers and 2500 men killed and wounded. It is called a victory so no doubt the Sikhs lost as many or more. In Parliament Disraeli's resolution for the "Relief of burdens on agriculture" was lost 289 to 190 – a large minority. We finished Lord Harvey's Memoirs on Friday last – a most entertaining book – but showing how utterly corrupt the Court and Kingdom were at the time. Of the Royal Family, disgustingly bad as he was, the King was the best. Lord Harvey spares no one – not even himself and one rises from the perusal of his book with a thorough disgust for his character as pictured by himself.

Tomorrow we leave Belmont I am sorry to say, and that as it is just coming out into its beauty. I have not made as much progress as I had hoped – nor poor Louey either. She still suffers from this grievous irritation. Davis says we ought to go to Hastings for a month or two, and so I think we shall – though I am really exceedingly sorry to be away so long from my business. The last two Sundays I have been to church, but the Sunday before I was detained by another attack of indigestion. We have had an excellent account from Uncle George himself, giving the best possible report of his own recovery.

Sunday 10th February 1850, Belmont.

Uncle William came this morning before church with the sad news that my dear mother is dangerously ill. He had had a letter from Uncle George who, by Dr Symonds' desire, had sent an express for us. We went to town in his carriage for service at the small new church, and here with him and Francis (whom we found in Sussex Square) took the 2 o'clock train *to Bristol* meeting at Swindon Antony, William, John and Charles (who had walked the preceding day from Heyford) and who had joined the train at Didcot. Thank God she is better but still in great danger.

Monday 11th February 1850, Belmont.

She has been no worse today though the fever is somewhat more tonight, but that, Dr Symonds said, was to be expected. It must have its course and we have only to hope that she may have the strength left to meet it. I went to see our dear mother today. She is dreadfully altered and grown very like her father; so weak I could hardly hear her voice which has been much altered since I saw her, about five months ago, by the loss of two front teeth.....Uncle William and Aunt Charlotte came yesterday. The day has been wretched.

Tuesday 12th February 1850, Belmont.

Tonight I am grieved to say she is not so well, the fever having increased as we expected, but the debility has increased out of all proportion. I fear Mr Davis thinks very badly of the case. Dr Symonds opinion this morning was much the same as yesterday. May God spare us so great an affliction as her loss would be. I have begged Mr Davis to let me know very early tomorrow morning how she is that if necessary I may send for Uncle William and Robert. Mary came the same night as we did by the mail.

I had two comfortable notes from my dear wife (*at Frognal*) and Eliza giving a very good account of her and the children. Uncle William will have been there tonight. When I saw mother today she seemed to suffer greater pain in her limbs and to feel more the want of sleep. She had seen Rev. Edward Vaughan for a short time, who had read prayers for the sick. She told me she knew she was in great danger. Dr Symonds comes tomorrow at nine.

Ash Wednesday 13th February 1850, Belmont.

Jane Glover came to my bedside at 5 o'clock to say that mother has passed a better night, having slept more and taken more nourishment, that she was asleep then so Mr Davis had not seen her. Therefore I have not sent and I hope it will not be necessary.

Alas my hope has been overthrown, for Hines has just come in (8 a.m.) to say from Mr Davis that she had grown decidedly weaker during the night. I shall send certainly if Dr Symonds confirms this report. 9.30 a.m. He has just been and I am sorry to say he seems to think even worse of her than Mr Davis – and has ordered her champagne or, if she cannot retain that, brandy. I have sent Hines to go by the 11 o'clock with notes to the Warden of Radley, Uncle William and Louisa. He will bring back Robert and nurse by the mail. I hope they may not be too late, but greatly fear it myself.

At half past four today it pleased God to take my dear mother; none of the stimulants we gave her remained in her stomach 5 minutes, and being unable to take any nourishment, she sank rapidly and departed, I trust without much pain to a better and happier world to join my dearest father – May we in our time be found fit to form part of the same blessed company! At one o'clock I took Aunt Charlotte to see her, and she remained in her room. She, though with great difficulty, found breath to say a few kind words to some of her children. God comfort us under this heavy affliction. Robert does not come till 3 in the morning. Uncle William only came at half past eight. I wrote many letters and one to Eliza to prepare dear Louey for the sad event. I sat up talking with Uncle George and Uncle William about the necessary arrangements.

Thursday 14th February 1850, Frognal.

This morning I had the painful task of telling poor little Robert, who arrived in the night, but was not told of my mother's death. By the express train Uncle William and I left Bristol, he stopping at Didcot to go to Milton and Clifton Hampden where he has kindly offered to make all the necessary arrangements about the funeral. I made the best of my way here and arrived about the same time as my letter (12 o'clock), which I therefore sent to Louisa by Eliza, not going up myself until 2 o'clock. I found poor Louisa most dreadfully agitated, much thrown back by the grief and fear which our sad reports had caused…. Talked a long while with her and I think she is more composed. Wrote several letters. Eliza has been the greatest possible comfort to her.

Friday 15th February 1850, Frognal.

At 12 o'clock Uncle William's carriage and the Aldenham carriage came here, the latter to take him and me to Aldenham. Uncle William took the carriage as far as Edgware to bring us back. We went to see my mother's Will there or any memorandum relating to the disposal of her property, but looked in vain partly through not having all the keys, and partly because Gibson has, I have no doubt, got the Will itself. Returned to dinner. Dear Louey I think a little better, though she did not sleep at all last night. I have a headache.

Saturday 16th February 1850, Frognal.

Went to town by the 10 o'clock train to meet Gibson.

Tuesday 29th May 1850, Frognal.

Just a month has passed since I last wrote in my journal, and that for no other reason but that we have had a house full and I have been too lazy to set to work at night. George Daubeny (*whose mother Elizabeth was William Gibbs' first cousin*) and Uncle William are going to build a new church at Flaxley as a memorial to dear Albinia. Harrison is to be the architect. Blanche still keeps up though she has been expecting her confinement any time these three weeks. Uncle William has had two smart attacks of lumbago – one succeeding the other. Aunt Harriett is still very poorly though at times cheerful enough. Uncle George and Aunt Anne are pretty well…On Saturday last I went with Uncle George to see the House of Lords, and was very much pleased.

Thursday 26th December 1850, Belmont

This has been rather a harassing day what with trouble at home and festivities abroad. The latter have consisted of a fine game of blind man's buff and a dance at Tyntesfield, in which (blind man's buff) Mr Bright, Antony and Charles played very amusing parts. We had also dissolving views – a little galvanized battery and a Christmas tree – Alban was very much delighted with the Christmas tree and behaved very well indeed. He is staying there tonight. This morning as well as yesterday, John and I breakfasted at Tyntesfield, but my particular errand there this morning was caused by Louisa having heard from Mary, a confirmation of our own suspicions, that John was very much attached to Milly and she to him, and that they have spoken to one another on the subject. I therefore went to Uncle William to ask his opinion, and on our walk back I spoke to John about it, when he most candidly told me the whole affair, and that knowing the evils of such an intimacy, he had already determined to go away – that in all he had said to Milly, he had carefully kept in mind, and repeated to her, the wishes of her parents on the subject – Poor fellow, he was and is very sad about it and is to go tomorrow. The absurd part of it all is that William and Charles are in the same boat, in different degrees. William reserved and quiet and Charles more so, philosophical, funny and fervent by terms. His is a mere smite, William's something rather more serious, but neither of them are much to be pitied for Milly has always decidedly preferred John, and they have known it; as they have been moths round a candle, and Charles especially is a most absurd moth. Milly does not yet know anything of their going. Neither John nor William were at Tyntesfield – nor Mary.

Friday 27th December 1850, Belmont.

They went away today by about four o'clock – poor dear John very sad indeed – Charles alternately in high spirits and for a few moments sad. I wish in his lightness of heart he would show more consideration for the feelings of others. Both Uncle Joseph and I have spoken to Milly who behaved very well indeed, and certainly none could have conducted themselves better under such circumstances. They are both quite satisfied that all has been done well. Charles went with John. In the morning we had good sport at coursing and killed five hares. All the house was present except Uncle George and Uncle Joseph who have both got colds, this evening we have dined at Tyntesfield (Mr. Roos being there) and played a game at whist.

Saturday 28th December 1850, Belmont.

Uncle George's cold bad – Aunt Harriett going on much the same. She had a letter from Charles. The Tyntesfield party came to tea and Antony, William, Mr Roos and I had a game at whist. William, Mary and Robert still bark a good deal, and Mary has been poorly all the while we have been here under Mr Davis's care. We were to have gone today as John will be alone tomorrow at Frognal, but Louey (*Louisa*) was suffering too much from a sore throat, and the others also were poorly. I wrote to John to say we would be there tomorrow.

Sunday 29th December 1850, Belmont.

So miserable a day that what with colds and rain we did not go to church at all. I had gone yesterday to see Wraxall Church with Mr Roos and Uncle William. They have made a sad mess of the pewing of the Chancel and also of the Chancel roof (which cuts the East Window). They have also left the wretched East Window as it is!

Monday 30th December 1850, Belmont.

I wrote to John yesterday to say we could not come today for the same reason as before. I have been out shooting with Antony and Reginald Bright, but only killed one rabbit and brushed a hare – a wretched drizzly day. Uncle Joseph in bed all day with bronchitis. He is better tonight. Mr Roos, Antony, Joseph and I have been playing Whist.

Tuesday 31st December 1850, Frognal.

Went in the market cart this morning to Tyntesfield to talk over poor Cady's affairs with Uncle William. He has written to Uncle George Crawley to present a deed for her signature. At twenty past one we went in his carriage to the station, and arrived here by the express train in time for dinner.

Thursday 1st May 1851, Frognal.

The Day of the Opening of the Great Exhibition – A most lovely day – Queen's weather! I am sure no one of the 25,000 persons who were in the building had ever seen or will ever see such a magnificent spectacle as this. We left here at half past six and got to Hyde Park Gardens to breakfast about 7 o'clock. Found Aunt Anne, Uncle Joseph and Aunt Emily there; started at a quarter to eight and reached the line about midway between the Marble Arch and Apsley House, about 9.30 entered the building. John, Mary, the three above mentioned, Blanche, Miss Snow, Louisa, and Martin were our party, and we all, I am sure as everyone else, enjoyed the day thoroughly. All seemed in a good humour and happy. Her Majesty left the Crystal Palace about one o'clock and we got home to Hyde Park Gardens at about three. After a little rest, I took a walk with Martin and we left at five fifteen, John staying to dinner. We dined at the Lovejoys – in very good spirits and full of the Exhibition.

Friday 2nd May 1851, Frognal.

Uncle William stayed away from the Exhibition and was one of only three occupiers of the Counting House yesterday. He went today. Hayne, Davy and I made an arrangement to have if we liked two holidays a week each to see it.

Saturday 3rd May 1851, Frognal.

Left at half past twelve and had luncheon in Hyde Park Gardens. Took Aunt Emily with Louisa and Mary who met me there in a fly to the Great Exhibition to join Uncle William and the rest who were there, and without going in drove through heavy rain to Chiswick. The weather cleared up just as we arrived at the Gardens and we enjoyed our walk through them very much. The azaleas, heathers and roses very lovely. Martin Crawley came back with us to dinner, Uncle William and Miss Snow going to the Opera.

Monday 5th May 1851, Frognal.

Dined at Hyde Park Gardens and went with Louisa, Mary, Martin and Withy to the Princess's Theatre to see Charles Kean in Hamlet. He acts very well. I don't however like the funeral scene on the stage. It seems a profanation. My new Brougham sent home.

Tuesday 6th May 1851, Frognal.

Our Wedding Day – Mary and I and Martin went to the Exhibition and walked about getting a general idea of the place. Uncle William, Blanche, Martin, Aunt Anne, Mr and Mrs Davy, Escandon, Millam, Bourdeux, Curtis, Barandiaran and Achaval dined here.

Thursday 8th May 1851, Frognal.

Louisa and Mary with the Hyde Park Garden party went yesterday to see the Exhibition and the Lucens carriage and stud.

Saturday 10th May 1851, Frognal.

My holiday – went with Mary to the Exhibition by 12 o'clock – new boots – hot weather – very tired indeed – so much so that by 3 o'clock when I left I had a very bad headache which has been increasing ever since, so that I have done my part in entertaining my guests very badly.

Thursday 26th June 1851, Frognal.

Took Louisa this morning to see Lord Ward's Collection with which she was very much pleased. She left me near the Exhibition where I stayed for an hour and a half and went to luncheon at Hyde Park Gardens. Afterwards I took Joseph and Antony to the Exhibition and got home by a quarter to six. Slept for 20 minutes, then Uncle William came back. Rosales, Riviero, the Baring Youngs, Mrs John Sewell, Mrs Henry Sewell, Ugarte, Achaval, V. Marco, Mrs Walsh, Mr Wilson and his daughter dined there – a pleasing party. Mrs Henry Sewell playing very nicely – a clever woman.

Tuesday 8th July 1851, Frognal.

Went to Hyde Park Gardens with Antony and John after breakfast, and after some shopping with them to the Exhibition. Luncheon at Hyde Park Gardens and then with Antony to the City.

Thursday 10th July 1851, Frognal,

Yesterday Uncle William besought me to go to the Ball at the Guildhall instead of him as he hates a crush, so I sent up to Hampstead for my bay, and dined at Hyde Park Gardens at five o'clock and proceeded with Blanche to the Guildhall where we both enjoyed ourselves very much. We got excellent places, and were among the very first to walk before the throne and bow to and be bowed to by the Queen and Prince Albert, before there was any crush at all. We saw the Duchess of Kent, the Duke of Cambridge, the Prince of Saxe-Weimar, the Marchioness of Douro, Miss Burdett Coutts, Lady Aylesbury, Lord Normandy and many other great folks among whom was the Duke of Wellington, who walked all round the Hall, the people making a lane for him. We got home by three and found Uncle William still up. Blanche lost an emerald drop of her brooch. Very tired today as might be supposed. We should have been home sooner but that George the footman was foolish enough to stay by the carriage instead of being in the yard of the Hall. Today though a holiday, I went to the City with Uncle William but came back to Hyde Park Gardens by three o'clock and went to the Royal Academy Exhibition with Blanche. Found George E. Adams here and he dined with us. Suggested to him to buy the Grove at Kingsbury.

Saturday 11th October 1851, Tyntesfield.

I went to the Exhibition and then found Louisa. An immense crowd! Bought myself a cigar case – embossed, plated with oxidized silver – also got a ticket for Monday and the two following days as *there will be an Exhibition on behalf of the Peruvian Government*. My head ached a little and by the time I reached Swindon by express it ached badly, and for my sins I there ate some soup thinking it might be tire and exhaustion that made me ill, but it became worse and worse, and I could hardly speak all the way, and shortly after I arrived at Belmont, I was very sick twice, which a little bettered me, but I was exceedingly glad when the carriage came to bring me here and I was no sooner in bed than asleep and awoke this morning refreshed and well, only rather weak. I walked about the grounds with Uncle William, and then went up to Belmont, Louisa having gone before me. Aunt Harriett very comfortable for her – that is quite cheerful though suffering – Aunt Anne and Uncle George very well. I took a walk with him to the farm. Frances and Lucy Hendy well but grown old. Honour Davy and Mrs Branscombe very well, but both very stout. I really should not have known Honour if I had not met her elsewhere but it is ten years since. I last saw her here when she was 20 and I was 14 or so….Uncle Joseph and Aunt Emily are at Belmont and pretty well. Caddy much as usual poor girl – she was 23 in July. Mary is a poor rheumatic creature, which is absurd. We have a most comfortable room and dressing room here looking West and North. Uncle William and Blanch went on a sad errand today – to Shirehampton to send off G. Daubeny's children. The Brights (Robert and Sam) were at Belmont and had luncheon there.

Sunday 12th October 1851, Tyntesfield.

Uncle Joseph went to take Mr Woolley's duty at Portishead, he having gone to Clifton Hampden. Frances and Dolly and Joe went to Portishead. I walked twice to Church and back with Uncle William. The church looks very nice, but they have square pews in the Chancel, and doors to the seats! The painted window is very poor. The altar flimsy. The reredos handsome. The old Gorges Monument is restored and painted beautifully. It has been put into the wall of the Chancel in the position of a founder's tomb – which is incorrect but much more convenient than its former place out in the Chancel – Chancel rails bad.

Went to the farms and chose a young pig – Boar Berkshire: sow half Naples half Berkshire, also two young China cocks….The Hendys are obliged to leave Glenfrome! Mrs Branscombe says she is 82! She is neither deaf nor blind nor lame in the least. Honour says her little Harriett is the plainest of the children. What beauties they must be! Mrs Branscombe says she was always told she should like Louisa and she does very much. We dined as usual at Belmont and I also lunched there. Frances and Lucy Hendy look oldish, for according to Uncle William's account Lucy is 66 and Frances 60 or thereabouts. They look 58 and 50 respectively.

Monday 13th October 1851, Tyntesfield.

Uncle William went to London by the afternoon express in order to be in time for poor Mrs Mallet's funeral. I went out shooting all day with Isaac, the keeper. We saw or rather heard a great many pheasants, but could not get many shots. I bagged a leash and knocked over one more but lost him in the underwood. Little Joe went with me after luncheon at Belmont. Dined there and have said good bye to the dear friends there. Aunt Harriett seems in good spirits enough.. Mrs Branscombe and Honour go to Clifton on Thursday. Uncle Joseph goes with the foreign party tomorrow by the afternoon express. Aunt Emily is going to Marlborough to see George. They sleep at Reading tomorrow and go on to Folkestone on Wednesday, and cross to Boulogne on Thursday.

Tuesday 14th October 1851, Frognal.

Left Tyntesfield this morning with my spoil – also Blanche and Louisa at 7 o'clock and came into town by express. Found a letter from George Crawley of Sydney in the city which I did not reach at once having gone with Blanche and Louisa to the Exhibition. The building of course very empty and therefore very pleasant. Uncle William there also but I did not see him. William called and told me John had been home since Sunday. Asked William to dinner. Uncle William and Blanche sleep here….

Letters from George Adams, Mary Crawley and Miss Poole. I wrote to George Adams and Mary – the latter about her indolence and lack of regular employment pointing out to her how injurious it was to her health both mental and bodily.

Wednesday 15th October 1851, Frognal.

Went with Uncle William into the city rather early and sent the carriage back for Blanche who came for Uncle William at one, and went with him, John and William to Folkestone to see the Belmont party off. Meanwhile Arthur and I went to the Exhibition to see the Closing, which however was a tame affair compared with the opening; though the numbers were very great – I could not hear a word of what was said by Lord Canning, Prince Albert or the Bishop of London, only it seemed to me that both speeches and prayers were too long. Special prayers always are nowadays. Got back to the Counting House by a quarter to two.

Thursday 16th October 1851, Frognal.

Rode into town and had a busy day….At 6.20 p.m. Uncle William and Blanche, John, William and Francis came to Bishopsgate Street on their way back from Folkestone where they had seen the Belmont party off in pretty good heart. All came up here to dinner in the carriage and we got our dinner by 8 o'clock and played a rubber afterwards.

Sunday 22nd February 1852, Frognal.

Mary and William went to St Barnabas, going in a cab part way – then to luncheon at Hyde Park Gardens. Aunt George and Blanche were very angry with her for going in a cab and gadding from her parish church, but especially the former which my mother and father would never have done. Now I have a distinct recollection of going once to Kensington Gardens and once to the Zoological Gardens of which my father was a fellow, on two Sunday evenings with him and my mother in Hackney coaches, and that my mother went with us one Sunday evening to Forest Hill. But I had (nor have) not the smallest idea of any wrong in going in a public carriage on a Sunday, and would have without scruple asked *a friend* to come with me. It is different hiring a fly or using one's own

Figure 13. Aunt Anne, William Gibbs' sister who lived at Belmont, miniature by Sir William Charles Ross R.A.

carriage though with Aunt George's brother and niece, and many others of her kin and acquaintances, and with the knowledge and full approval of the Archbishop of Canterbury I went with two carriages last year to St. Thomas Charterhouse. But most absurd of all Uncle William and Anne gadded up here today. This day fortnight he and Mary and Uncle George gadded to Lambeth in the morning and to St Andrew's in the evening; and last Sunday Blanche herself, Aunt George's daughter Caroline, and the two Hartperry girls with Uncle William not only gadded to Westminster Abbey, but came back in a cab! I think we may fairly have the last laugh against them. But Aunt G. should not scold Mary who is under Louisa's care, for the fault if any is Louisa's, and to upbraid Mary is to teach her that she is not to trust Louisa.

Monday 23rd February 1852, Frognal.

This evening I dined at Nobody's (*The London club "Nobody's Friends"*) Uncle George not there because of Mrs Powell's death. Lord Nelson proposed Judge Patterson's health. We had a poor account of dear Aunt Anne today though there is no decided disease reported. Uncle George wishes Uncle Joseph to come out to them.

Tuesday 24th February 1852, Frognal.

Louisa and I slept at Hyde Park Gardens tonight and met at dinner Pedro Escandon, Martinez del Rio, Henry Lewin, Frank Wilson and Mr and Mrs Davy.

Wednesday 25th February 1852, Frognal.

Louisa went back this morning, but hearing that Uncle Joseph and Aunt Emily were coming on their way to Nice, I have stayed thinking I might be of use. Uncle Joseph looks very well. Uncle William is in bed with a cold.

On October 6th 1852, Anne, William Gibbs' sister, died at Belmont.

Monday 11th October 1852, Frognal.

Today Louisa had letters from Blanche and Georgiana and I from Uncle William. Antony….will have heard of poor Aunt Anne's death and have gone to Belmont. I wrote to Uncle William. My foot rather bad with rheumatism.

Tuesday 12th October 1852, Belmont.

It was still worse this morning, and is now so bad that I can hardly hobble. Antony and Francis went down with me, but Mary who had intended to be here was not well enough.

Uncle William and Blanche, Uncle Joseph, Aunt Emily, Milly, Dolly and George were here, but Blanche and Uncle William have gone back for the night. Uncle George, Caddy and Aunt Harriett all look particularly well and so does William, but he seems as is but natural to have been particularly affected by the loss of dear Aunt Anne.

Wednesday 13th October 1852, Belmont.

My brothers sat up some time talking with me last night, and Aunt Emily came in and sat with us talking about Aunt Anne's last hours. Certainly a more blessed death none ever died. Uncle William too told me today many things she said which showed her lovely frame of mind. Her last words, as she composed herself to the sleep from which she never woke, on seeing him come into the room – "Ah there is my dearest brother William!" Then to herself softly, "In my Father's house are many mansions." When she died, lying on her side, they did not know but that she was still asleep. Uncle Joseph said that in all his ministerial experience he had never seen such a death. While feeling ill in the morning she called on all the servants and wished them each good bye.

Our sad task of her burial was finished today, and was done well – much better than most. I mean with less undertaker frippery. When I die I hope that all people by that time will have yet less. What a blank there is in this house without her – and how Uncle George and Aunt Harriett will feel it. They do feel it now most deeply, but scarcely as they will when her room is open again, and her familiar face is no longer there. May she rest in Peace! But we need hardly say so, for the spirit of one so good must be among those who cry, "Lord, how long?"

Last night I put Hayne's remedy on my foot, an alum flannel bag, and I had a good night and was really almost well all day, but tonight, though the middle of my foot is no longer painful, I feel a little gout like pain in the large joint of my great toe. Mr Davis who saw me this morning said the pain was Rheumatic Gout. I wrote to Hayne, Dr Saunders, Louisa and John.

Sunday 17th October 1852, Frognal.

The pain in my toe got no less when I got to bed by 12; and at a quarter past two I woke with a regular fit of the gout, which of course allowed me no sleep.....I could not walk at all and my toe ached horribly all day. They were all very good to me and pitied me as much as I suppose one can with the gout; but everyone seems rather amused with another's having the gout....Uncle William and Uncle George seemed to have none of that feeling; and it almost made me laugh, though I was so much obliged to them, to see those two old gentlemen coming one on each side of me to help me out of the room. I would not let Uncle George, but took Dolly's shoulder to help me to get into Blanche's carriage which took her and Aunt Emily to Bristol. I suppose I ought not to have gone for the journey was a very painful one, but I preferred being ill at home, and besides had no wish to frighten Louisa by my non-appearance. I was kept 20 minutes on that miserable, cold Express Station at Bristol waiting for the train without however catching cold most fortunately.

Saturday 18th December 1852, Tyntesfield.

I went to see Exeter Cathedral Registers and then went down to the train at 12.35 with the Oxenhams and Mary, where we found Louisa and the children. I joined them and we arrived here at 4 o'clock. All pretty well here but Edith had a very bad cough, Louisa says within the last two days. I hope it is not whooping cough.

Sunday 19th December 1852, Tyntesfield.

Miserable day. Edward Vaughan preached us this morning a worse sermon than ever I heard from him. He enunciated as clearly as possible the true doctrine of the Catholic Church on Baptismal Rejuvenation and declared his full belief in it; but told us most inconsistently that we could not have perfect confidence in it, as the regeneration of the child must depend on the faith of the God parents!......He gave us a thoroughly good practical sermon this evening. I had a long talk with Uncle William about John going abroad, and I think he modified his objections.

Monday 20th December 1852, Tyntesfield.

Rainy day. I walked to Belmont and Charles and I drove over to Abbots Leigh to call on the Brights. Sir William Ross has kindly made a very nice pencil sketch of Louisa...Charles dined here. Antony went back to Torquay.

Tuesday 21st December 1852, Tyntesfield.

Mr and Mrs Brown and Mr Joseph Brown and the Edward Vaughans dined here, and the two Böhls. Mr Sandford and little Antony came at 9 o'clock in the evening,

Wednesday 22nd December 1852, Tyntesfield.

Out shooting in the morning and walking in the afternoon. Dined at Leigh with Emily and Dolly, Charles and Mary. Mary and Robert came yesterday evening.

Thursday 23rd December 1852, Tyntesfield.

Bad cold and rainy weather prevented me from going out all day. I had a sitting for Sir William Ross.

Christmas Eve 1852, Tyntesfield.

Rainy morning but fine afternoon. Went coursing with little sport. Dined at 1 o'clock. Miss Courtenay Boyle, in a crop like our grandfather's and wearing a hat like a Quaker dined here.

In the evening came all the Brights, the Vaughans and Mrs Burrows, and the children had a very Merry Evening with the Christmas tree etc. etc.

Christmas Day 1852, Tyntesfield.

All but Louisa went to church this morning and stayed to the sacrament – a very good sermon from E. Vaughan. I did not go in the afternoon because of my cold and Louisa and I spent the time at Belmont. I had a letter from Anna.

Sunday 26th December 1852, Tyntesfield.

Mr Vaughan ignored St Stephen today except in the second lesson where he could not help himself, and I am sorry to say he ignored St James too for in his sermon on "Faith is the substance of things unseen" was very different in teaching from what I was taught…..The difference is that the faithful Christian, as St James says, shews his faith by his works and life. I find nothing in the Bible or Prayer Book to say that Faith is "Trust in God"….. In the afternoon I went and sat with Aunt Harriett and some time also with Mrs Prosser. Louisa and I dined at Belmont and they sent the carriage for us from hence.

Monday 27th December 1852, Frognal.

A fine day for our journey. We with the Böhls started by the 2.35 but did not arrive here till about half past six – the Böhls going to Sydenham. Uncle William told me he should like to buy the estate at Clyst St

82

Figure 14. Pytte, Clyst St George.

George, as it was by his father's misfortune that it was alienated from the
family. I told him that it rather appertained to me as the representative of
my father, his father's eldest son, for if his father had ever had it, he
would never have inherited it; but my father and I. I hope he won't stand
between me and it; but if he does I trust my son, if he has an opportunity,
may at some time have a chance of buying it back into the elder branch
of the family.

Monday 4th April 1853, Frognal.
Head uncomfortable all day but not very bad. I went in to Chancery Lane
by 11.35 and met Uncle William there by appointment to make an
affidavit to get back some money on the account of my mother's estate. I
had a letter…from Mary Gibbs, enclosing a note from a friend to say that
Pytte at Clyst St George is really to be sold shortly. I talked to Uncle
William about it, and he did not seem to care much to get it for himself,
but thought I ought not to spend more money on land – I would not do so
for any other purpose, but I should like to do it for this. But I suggested
to him that I believed I might exchange the Lambeth property away
placing Clyst St George under the same entail. I wrote to Gibson about it.

Friday 20th May 1853, Frognal.
I called at Hyde Park Gardens after breakfast. Uncle William was going
to meet Tom who had written to him and begged him to do so. (*Tom was
the Rev. Thomas William Crawley, who succeeded his father, the Rev.
Charles Lloyd Crawley, as Rector of Heyford, Northamptonshire in*

1851) His wife's mother had died suddenly, and he had thought well to prevent her from going to see her father, but Uncle William pointed out to him the impropriety of such a course, and I was glad to hear that he had had a kind letter from Henry to the same effect. Dr Carr of Northampton had been attending her in the hospital or infirmary, and when Tom went and asked him what he thought of her health, he said, "Ah you ask after that young woman – a most interesting person!", and this seems to have confirmed Tom in his intention. He means to do his best to educate her, but Uncle William shewed him that a school would be very bad for her, and that it would be hardly possible to get a governess, or at least a good one worth having, to undertake the charge. Besides it would be bad for Tom to have a lady in his house as a contrast to this uneducated girl. He should on all accounts find a curate for Heyford, and himself get a curacy in town where he could have masters for her. Her name is Hannah Carter. Uncle William is to see her tomorrow. I dined at Hyde Park Gardens today, and rode home by 9.10.
Saturday 21st May 1853, Frognal.
Uncle William saw Tom and his wife this morning and spoke to them very fully and frankly on the subject. He was pleased with her appearance, and says she is an interesting looking, pretty, modest girl – very timid, bashful, and taking in very good part all he said. He has now advised Tom not to think of a curacy for himself but to devote himself entirely to her education. I doubt he is not well fitted for that as he is irritable and therefore teasing by nature. Masters will hardly be sufficient for her as she will require a lady to teach her to behave entirely as a lady. She might get a daily governess in London I should think. Uncle William has written to Aunt Lloyd to advise her and Henry to see Tom, and telling her what had passed between them this morning. He suggested Sheppard as a curate, and kindly said moreover that if Tom could not get on comfortably otherwise, he would pay the curate.
(*Tom had just married Hannah Elizabeth Carter in 1853. They went on to have six children – all boys*)
Friday 18th September 1853, Frognal.
Went to the Registrar to enter little Vicary's name and had to pay seven shillings and six pence for being too late – i.e. more than six weeks after the birth.
Thursday 29th September 1853, Folkestone.
This morning we were up by a quarter to seven, got through our breakfast early, finished our packing, and were ready to start. I rode to Hyde Park Gardens and on to the city, leaving Louisa to go by the 11.30 train with the children and they all accomplished their journey safely as we found when we, William, George, Edward and I, arrived by the 1.30 at half past five. I rushed about completing my shopping all the morning

84

till half past eleven when I went to the Bank (*of England*). Louisa and the children are all I am happy to say pretty well.

Journey through France and Spain

Thursday 30th September 1853, Paris, Hôtel Bedford.
Here we are after a fatiguing journey and very ill lodged. Louisa with the children while the nurses are supping so that I, having nothing to do, can write my journal. Marco had taken rooms for us on the first floor, but the land lady has actually put us on the fourth giving as an excuse that the lady below was ill, but was going tomorrow. If she was well enough to go tomorrow, she was well enough to take these upper rooms – a letter from Marco who I found expressed great indignation at her conduct, (which I also did in words as well as I could) and told me that after much search he had got us good rooms at the Hôtel Smit at 56 Rue Faubourg St. Honoré, which we might occupy at once. As however it was a quarter past eleven and we were all at the top of the house very tired, we determined to stay for this night vowing to go tomorrow. The boat from Folkestone did not start till nine (when George left us), and we proceeded on our way – *my brother* William and I and Alban going after a while to the fore part of the vessel close to the bowsprit so as to enjoy the pitching of the vessel, for I thought that if I was to be sick it was better to have it over. The passage was very rough but I was pretty comfortable for the first hour and a half really enjoying the breeze, but the last half hour altered the face of affairs, and although never feeling very ill, I was sick two or three times. Alban only began to feel uncomfortable at the same time – William had a head ache – all the rest were very sick and ill, but are alright now. The boat being half an hour late, and we requiring rest, we unfortunately got to the station too late for the 12.30 train and had to wait for the 5.15. The inn we went to, the Hôtel Maurice, is a very respectable one, but not so good as the Hôtel du Nord, to which we hope to go any other time we chance to visit Boulogne.
Saturday 1st October 1853, Paris, Hôtel Smit.
This morning before breakfasted I descended from my high estate, and called on Marco who sent Ventura with me to this Hôtel, which seems very respectable. The landlady, Mme Rouget tells me it has been in their family for 102 years. I went back to the inn, breakfasted and sent Louisa and the rest off here; she chose one of the two suites at 40 francs, and in the course of the day I took the others (50 francs) for Uncle William engaging them for tomorrow and telegraphing to Antony Gibbs and Sons to tell him. I however had an answer from them saying he had started, and I had a letter from Blanche saying they were starting, and enclosing

one for Miss Maclean. I went to Meuniés to enquire for them and to tell Cailly that he need not trouble himself about rooms for them as I had taken these. Those knaves at the Bedford charged us for three nights, which of course I repudiated, being supported therein by Marco, and a hint of the Juge de la Paix soon brought them to their senses. It is a nasty rainy day which William and I employed in running about Paris. Louisa and I called on the Marcos. Lunched at the Café de Paris.

Sunday 2nd October 1853, Paris, Hôtel Smit.

Breakfasted at home, and after church in the Rue d'Agnesseau . The Lathams who had seen us there called on us. Mr Barnes and Reginald were there too. William and I went for a walk with them, and ordered ourselves dinner at the Café Philippe where Monsieur Pascal gave us a good sensible dinner, which we have just now been discussing. It was excellent, not over loaded, costing us 90 francs – that is 15 francs a head for the six…..I found letters from Freshfield, John, Charles, Antony and Uncle William, the latter telling me they had crossed and would be here tomorrow evening by the 5 o'clock train.

Monday 3rd October 1853, Paris, Hôtel Smit.

They did not arrive till about seven but are now comfortably settled in. We have been dining at the Marcos and playing bagatelle afterwards with Ventura Marco. William, Marco and I went with the Barnes this morning to the Marché St Honoré and ate some fruit. Then Louisa, William, Marco and I breakfasted at the Café Durant near the Madeleine. Reginald Barnes, William and I had been yesterday up to the top of the Panthéon St Geneviève, and through the Exposition of Industry. Today we all went to the Madeleine and then to the beautiful Sainte Chapelle, a most glorious specimen of Early Gothic and of painted glass, and of modern decoration. Thence to the Gardens of the Luxembourg where the party separated, Louisa and I going to Meuniés to enquire for Miss Maclean and the children, who we found were coming today, and who are here accordingly, then home and then to the Louvre which we found shut. Walked about the Palais Royal, lunched at the Trois Frères on our return from a visit to Père la Chaise.

Tuesday 4th October 1853, Tours, Hôtel de l'Univers.

I am not very well tonight having something of a colic and diarrhoea. Louisa and *my sister* Mary have both of them bad colds, so we have determined to send for Dr Croisin. We started by the 9.20 train and got here at about 2.30. I walked about with William, and went into the cathedral where the painted glass was most beautiful – We yielded to the earnest solicitations of an old woman that we should go up to the top of the tower, availing ourselves of the beauty of the day, for she averred that it would not be fine tomorrow. We were well rewarded for our trouble for the view was most lovely. We all dined at the table d'hôte.

Figure 15. Palais du Luxembourg, Paris.

Figure 16. La Madeleine, Paris.

Wednesday 5th October 1853, Tours, Hôtel de l'Univers.
The old woman was right in both respects, for it has rained nearly all day, and I have been in bed most of the time. Dr Croisin gave me some medicine which has done me good, but I am not yet well, and my head

aches from the opium. The children are better though not well. Wrote to John and to Santa Coloma. The William Gibbses come here tomorrow. Thursday 6th October 1853, Angoulême.

Deceived by Goldschmidt who in his turn was deceived by the landlady at Tours, we went to the Hôtel de la Croix d'Or, which Murray calls "good but dear". We found it a clean pot house sort of a place, apparently cheap enough. William and I had gone on to see, leaving Louisa and the others to follow with the luggage in the omnibus, but they unfortunately only sent the servants and the luggage up, being afraid lest the omnibus break down....We went to the station. There we found them sitting much discontented with the place, and at last Louey and I walked up through the town to the Hôtel des Postes, a most excellent inn, the rooms clean and comfortable, the dinner the best we have had since that of Monsieur Pascal.....Goldschmidt is at the Hôtel de la Croix d'Or with the luggage. The weather has been abominable and has prevented us from enjoying as we should the beautiful view from this terrace and the picturesque character of the town, which is one of the most foreign looking we have been in. Really Goldschmidt is of no use! A travelling servant at a third of his wages would have been infinitely more use. When we had completely settled all that was to be done, he came in with "Now Sir I'll tell you what we had better do" to which I replied – "Don't trouble yourself! We have done it!" Whereat he looked crestfallen and foolish. For a wonder he was on time this morning and had our tickets ready when we came to the station, and forthwith in his pompous manner began to praise us for our punctuality! An old owl!

The William Gibbses have written here for rooms for tomorrow. We are all much better today. Louisa's cold is still heavy but much better. We were all up by six. I bought the Journal des Débuts which says that the Sultan has declared war.

Friday 7th October 1853, Bordeaux, Hôtel de Paris.

I was up at about a quarter to six and went up to the cathedral, a curious church covered with carvings at the West End, which they are restoring, and very plain within, with stone galleries. Also I went a great way round the walls enjoying the most lovely view over the river and valley. By seven we were in the omnibus and got to the station long before the time the train really went, which was not till eight o'clock. We arrived here before eleven and found Monsieur Santa Coloma waiting for us with his carriage, in which he conveyed us to the rooms he had taken for us where we were agreeably surprised to find John (*my brother John Lomax Gibbs*) looking very well, and as tall as I am. He arrived this morning to meet us. He talks very well. At 3 o'clock Madame and Mademoiselle Santa Coloma, Monsieur Sloane, and Monsieur Santa Coloma came here. We were invited to dine with the Santa Colomas tomorrow.

Saturday 8th October 1853, Bordeaux.

It rained all day and William, John and I went to play billiards after we had seen the William Gibbses safely lodged here in their rooms, and we lunched at the Café de Paris. The Heros' called and the Santa Colomas, and we have just come from a most excellent dinner at the Santa Colomas' house, where I have eaten, drank and smoked, and danced better than ever. We talked more French than ever I did before. They are a most amiable and pleasant family.

Sunday 9th October 1853, Bordeaux.

I am glad to say that neither Louisa not Blanche seem any the worse for the party, but she has done quite right not to go to the Heros today for what with packing and cold and cough she will be too tired as it is. Except for church, all this day has been taken up with receiving and paying visits – Sloane and his wife, O'Ryan and his wife and daughter, a pretty girl, and Mr and Mrs. Heros were here, and John, Uncle William and I went to the Santa Colomas'....Blanche and Uncle William are here at tea with us. Sloane has sent us a present – 10 pints of sherry and muscatel, and Heros two pints of another wine.

Monday 10th October 1853, Mont de Marsan, Hotel des Ambassadeurs.

Notwithstanding that it has rained more or less all day and that we started at half past eight and did not arrive until five to eight this evening. We are not nearly so much tired as we should have been with half as long a railway journey. We like our carriages very well – the one *in which* we, Louisa and I, Alban and Edith came is the one which was used by the Emperor when he made his presidential visit to Bordeaux. It is very comfortable. I hired it and the other which was Heros's, a comfortable handsome Landau from one Burgeon, a coach maker near the hotel, agreeing by Santa Coloma's help to pay 1000 francs for 4 months. Santa Coloma came to see us off and brought me the £100 I had asked for. The road is very singular through great sandy wastes covered with heather and pines, and though seldom beautiful is even picturesque. I am glad I have seen it. It is a pity the William Gibbses are going to sleep at Roquefort (2 stages back) so as to avoid coming here as being a trifle out of their way to Pau for that seems a poor sort of place. And this is really the best inn we have been in. The rooms excellent and the dinner nearly as good as Philippe's, and the attendance perfect. All the party are pretty well.

Tuesday 11th October 1853, Bayonne, Hôtel St Etienne.

We started at a quarter past eight and should have arrived here by four but that at Dax, where we had found soup and some Sauterne for luncheon, and admired the hot springs in the middle of the town, we had to wait an hour and a half to have a band put on the near hind wheel of our carriage which was broken – and also that at Cantour, the next stage to this, we had to scold the postmistress because there were but four horses; so that we had to leave the servants behind to wait two hours till others should come in, while we came on straight. Monsieur Bourdeux met us at the gate and was very profuse in his civility, and has since called and sat half an hour. He speaks very well of Biarritz. We shall try and see tomorrow. The inn is not very good, or at least our rooms are not; and the small and horrid Mr Soulé, the Yankee Ambassador to Spain is here, which causes a considerable commotion in the inn; but he goes at six tomorrow and we shall have his rooms.

The road today was through beautiful forest scenery, bounded during the latter part of it by the Pyrenees. There is quite a forest of oak trees looking lovely in the sun.

Wednesday 12th October 1853, Biarritz – Hôtel des Ambassadeurs.

This morning I had a letter from Uncle William enclosing a letter from John sent back from London, and he on his part found at the post two letters from me, and I, to make it even, have found one from him at the post office by where we are at Biarritz – Hôtel des Ambassadeurs a very comfortable inn, with as many fireplaces as we can desire, not withstanding what folks told us. The place is lovely and looks under the sun of this glorious day as pretty a watering place as ever we saw. I think Louisa will be able to stay six weeks here. We shall however I dare say all go to St Sebastian for a week when we pay here 25 francs a night for good rooms – but that would I think be too much except for this one week. Monsieur Bourdeux called and saw us off in hired carriages. We took only nurse and the children, leaving the servants behind, and after luncheon, William, John and I returned, and saw things put up and brought them, all but Goldschmidt, in Heros' carriage for which we had to have post horses and to pay twelve kilometres for eight! Monsieur Bourdeux called and sat a long time with us in the Hôtel St Etienne. He is a kind, good old man I think – plenty of newspapers here but no letters except that from John. I wrote to Uncle William and began a letter to George, and Louisa to Aunt George (*Georgiana*).

Thursday 13th October 1853, Biarritz – Hôtel des Ambassadeurs.

We are at home in a manner now and our days are more humdrum.... Poor Louisa has had the colic all day, but is a little better tonight. I had to get up and give her physic in the night and woke with a headache myself which has now gone off. I had a good scramble about the rocks with William, John and Mary, and another in the afternoon with them and Alban, the latter enjoying it immensely. I had too a most delightful bathe in the sea and afterwards practised with a pistol and a carbine at a mark and pretty successfully. William hit the bull's eye precisely in the centre. Mary fired two shots and Alban Two, to his great delight. No letters.

Friday 14th October 1853, Biarritz – Hôtel des Ambassadeurs.

Sent my letter to Aunt Harriett and John's to Aunt Raine in the morning. Bathed – shot – Mary hit the white twice out of seven or eight times! John not well so we called in a gentlemanlike doctor who has given him some physic and ordered him a bran bath. Said doctor says that all last winter he had no fire in his house here except in the kitchen. Louisa had a letter from her mother dated the 10th. The George Adams (*Louisa's parents*) are at Broadstairs in the Paragon House.

Saturday 15th October 1853, Biarritz.

No letter except one from Uncle William announcing his arrival at Pau. He hadn't received my letter of the 12th, and so rather expected me to be coming to Pau one of these days. I wrote to him. We took a long walk with Alban which he enjoyed most exceedingly. We had some shooting too and Mary acquitted herself very well. I too hit the white twice out of seven times. Louisa and I took a nice walk in the morning which I am sure did her a great deal of good as anything must which she enjoyed as she did the lovely air of this morning.

Sunday 16th October 1853, Biarritz.

At 11 o'clock this morning we read the church service with the servants and children, and read also the sermon of Butler's of Wantage on Whitsunday. After luncheon, William, John and I walked to Bidart over the sandy dunes along the coast, and then struck across country through the beautiful lanes and heaths to Arbonne, and so through the same sort of land home. We were out about four hours and a half. Bidart is nothing in itself; but the church is very curious, at least to my unaccustomed eyes. There is a large reredos occupying almost the whole of the East End, with niches, statues and figures, and giving somehow an oriental effect, but the most singular thing is that the three other sides of the church are clothed with galleries of wood with railings like the outside of a Swiss cottage – three tiers of them one directly above another. The women all wear mantillas and the men their jackets and red fajas and blue flat caps. The whole village was playing at Pelotas (Bobot I think my informant also called it in Basque I suppose). At the end of the Square the wall was built up with square flat stones (having a date of 1823) against which the ball was thrown, one man standing apparently as the defender of that side of the square, and having one or two others as his allies, all of whom seemed to endeavour to strike the ball away from that side. On the other side there was a tripod of wood placed like some ancient altar, on which the man who might be called the bowler "dapped" the ball (as in trap-ball) and then struck it across with his hand. They all had the most curious bats, shaped like canoes and hollowed out and having a leather glove fastened on the back in which they placed their hands. I could not quite understand the game. At Arbonne they were playing a game of fives in a similar court. They all spoke Basque and could speak but little French – some a little Spanish. We talked to an old man at Arbonne who had been a prisoner in England…..

Monday 17th October 1853, Biarritz.

I had a letter from Aunt Harriett….and also a letter from Uncle William, and I wrote to him. After luncheon William, John and I walked to Bayonne stopping on our way to see the church at Anglet which also has galleries like those we saw yesterday. At Bayonne we went again into the cathedral which is really a very beautiful Gothic building internally, with some fine glass in the Clerestory. The triforium is very handsome. There is also a fine cloister which they are restoring as they are also some parts of the church. Monsieur Bourdeux caught us just as we came out of it and remained with us all the time. I had a walk with Louisa this morning on the rocks, and afterwards some shooting with Mary and the others in which we all proved ourselves better shots than before.

Tuesday 18th October 1853, Biarritz.

There was a terrible storm last night so much so as to keep me awake…. We all took a drive to Bayonne on a shopping expedition, and happily owing to the rain escaped Monsieur Bourdeux, who although very civil and kind is somewhat oppressive in his attentions and delays….I went this morning into the little chapel here. They certainly seem enamoured of galleries, for they have a horrid west end gallery, for all the world like the old one which used to be in Clifton Hampden Church…. It is raining very hard tonight, so I dare say we shall have just such a storm as last night…..

Wednesday 19th October 1853, Biarritz.

Bathed this morning in a very rough sea. A letter from Uncle William this morning which I answered. After shooting very badly, William, John and I went up to the lighthouse to see it and to shoot there. We were more successful at a greater distance. Coughs still bad probably owing to the nurse letting the boys get their feet wet.

Thursday 20th October 1853, Biarritz.

The sea exceedingly rough, so much so as to dash over one of the bathing houses and carry away the steps. John and I bathed however very pleasantly. After breakfast John, William and I walked up to the church where I observed a quantity of inscribed stones let into the floor marking the seats appropriated to different persons or families. One was "La siège d'Elisade 1730"….One of the gravestones in the churchyard had on it, "Ici gisent les Décèdés de la noble famille de Silhouette". Next to it another says "Ici repose de Lampunde 1696". On a scroll on one of the pillars was a date 1541…..After going to the church we took a long walk over furzy and heathy hill and dale. I should like to be here longer to find my way about the country which is very beautiful and very intricate. I had a letter from Uncle William which I answered before luncheon. After luncheon, Louisa and I took a walk and a very pleasant one, though the weather was bad.

Friday 21st October 1853, Biarritz.

The post did not arrive till this afternoon by reason of an accident on the railway between Orléans and Blois, and then brought no letters from Paris. I wrote to Uncle William…and the Master of the Fonda Nueva at San Sebastian.

Saturday 22nd October 1853, Biarritz.

Two letters from Uncle William today, one of the 20th and one of the 21st, which I answered having taken meanwhile for us all the places in the Correo to Burgos, with the option of proceeding to Madrid. John called on Ellis, who gave us £40, and put our names down at the "Cercle" where we played billiards. Then we called on Bourdeux and got from him an introduction to enable us to pass our carriages at Irun. We had luncheon at the "Panier Fleury".

Sunday 23rd October 1853, Biarritz.

This has been a most lovely day, warmer I think than the hottest day in July in England, and giving us a most charming variety of colours on the foliage and heather. We had our bathe as usual, in a very rough sea – and after reading prayers and a very good sermon of Butlers on "Dearly beloved I beseech you as strangers and pilgrims", we went out and took a long walk. Louisa and I had been up to the church for the morning service, and now William, John, Mary and I went up there for the afternoon service, but we were too soon so went back with Mary, and went back ourselves for our walk through the Communes of Bassart and Angelet and came in at half past six not a little tired. We had a letter this morning from Uncle William and I had a letter from Mary Crawley and one from George, a very amusing one. Monsieur Bourdeux called here on Louisa while we were away.

Monday 24th October 1853, San Sebastian, Fonda Nueva.

Con que estamos en Espana, after a most lovely journey through beautiful scenery, and under a summer sky. Indeed the only drawback to our comfort was the exceeding heat. Louisa has enjoyed both the country and the fine soft air very much – only she has got a headache this evening which took off from our pleasure, but she is gone to bed and will I hope soon get over it. The posting (*coach driving*) here has been just as good as in France - better indeed in some respects for one does not need to pay the postilion to drive well; one has rather to beseech them not to go too fast. The beginning of the first stage from Irun was passed so rapidly that I began to fear for the safety of our carriages, and I think the exceeding swinging helped to give poor Louisa her headache. It was a pleasure to get from the straight French roads to the sinuous ones of this mountainous country. The peaks of l'Arrhune, Tres Coronas and Fuentarrabia looked most lovely. We started this morning at ten past ten, lunched at Irun where I had a letter of introduction to Garcia and where the partner met us at the post house, and was very civil and got us the permit for our carriages for forty days. We tasted Chacoli wine, which from its strong tarry flavour brought me back to the wines of Greece – accordingly I alone was able to drink it. I think William however was not "proud" as they say at Oxford. We started from Irun at two and arrived here at four and find it a comfortable inn with W.Cs. of the best. I only fear whether the diet will agree with the young ones. It is very curious to observe the complete change of language on the two banks of the Bidassoa.

We had our accustomed bathe this morning and that a very pleasant one; and since we have been here we have all except Mary had warm baths.

Tuesday 25th October 1853, San Sebastian.

This has been a very sad day, for, added to poor Louisa's having a very bad headache, she has been most grievously depressed and miserably out of sorts about my going. It has been a great pain to me to see her, and I do now feel very sorry the plan was ever thought of. It cannot now be given up; but I would not willingly have given the dear affectionate creature so much pain. I trust she will not find herself so lonely and that William and Mary will be tender of her. I believe they will and that she will find the pain greater with anticipation than in the reality. I think she is a little better tonight but I look forward with dread to tomorrow. We called today on the Vice Consul, Lieutenant Marsh, who was civil and kind to us – gave us some English tea, lent us a book, recommended us a Doctor, whose services I trust we shall not want. The day has been very hot and sultry, and yet the wind is now blowing a hurricane. We had a nice bathe today on the beach. I had a note from Uncle William. Mary, William, John and I went up to the top of the fort, and enjoyed a most lovely view from it. A ship stranded in our sight, but all the people were saved. The town looks exceedingly picturesque, and very singular like a doll's town, the Playa Mayor very conspicuous and pretty. The town looks equally pretty from the other side of the bay. (*Fig. 22, page 120*)

Friday 28th October 1853, Madrid – Fonda de las Peninsulares, Calle de Alcala.

After a very bad night on Tuesday poor Louisa became more comfortable and happy, and was I hope really better in health. She even for a few minutes thought of coming with me, and I said she should be quite well if that was possible – but we were soon convinced that the children could not properly go, and that she would not wish to leave them, so it remained that if she found it practicable she might come with all the rest to meet me on my return, or if not at least as far as Vitoria always supposing that she found it comfortable to remain in Spain, and she was to get a Spanish mistress to get her on in the language, and Mary and William were to study hard in the same work, but how much will be done I cannot foresee. I feel quite satisfied that if as is probable she is in the family way the journey from here to Vitoria would be a most hazardous one, both for the badness of the road and the insufficiency of the accommodation, though to John, Uncle William and me it presented no difficulties. Meanwhile I did at last quite repent of having wished to go, but she did not now wish me to give it up, as she had had all the pain, and besides she thought it would not be fair upon Uncle William so I determined to go and accordingly here I am, having arrived about 11 this morning. I must never think however of leaving her again unless there is necessity. I was very sorry too to come away without seeing the dear children, but they were out when I left the house. William and Mary walked out with me to the Casa de Postes outside the town area where we bathed, and about a quarter past one up came the Correo with Uncle William therein, and a gentlemanlike young Spaniard named Masardo who had taken the Conductor's place as far as Vitoria. John and I went with Uncle William in the coupé and James in the interior and we came along a beautiful road *through* lovely country till night overtook us and we reached Vitoria at about 11 o'clock, and had a cup of chocolate, and composed ourselves for the night, preparing ourselves for a good sleep by a long walk up the Cuesta de Salinas. Uncle William and Masardo had many common friends – amongst others he knew Pedro Escandon whom he was rather like. The sleep was rather better than I expected though of course it was off and on, and in the morning about a quarter to eleven we arrived at Burgos, where we breakfasted very well on eggs, mutton, chops and coffee at the Parador de las Diligencias…..It was the same inn where Uncle William put up many years ago. I forgot to mention Villafranca where it was market day and a very curious scene it was. The first I had seen of Spanish costume and Spanish people actively engaged…..We were at Briviesca about sunrise, and the scene there was curious enough. The wretched people standing round the carriage, and the ragged goatherds coming in with their slouched hat and ancient tawny brown cloak ragged and torn, but thrown over their shoulder in true Spanish style. Hard rain all Thursday and at 8 o'clock we reached Aranda, where we took our chocolate and then slept more or less until six in the morning, and at a quarter past eleven we arrived at our destination, and after no little trouble succeeded in getting rooms in this dirty inn….. Though however the Inn looks dirty, and the company diligence company, we have had a particularly good dinner. We have called on O'Shea, and Don Francisco has traced us and has sat with us for some time after dinner. We went to the Teatro Lope de Vega, where we have

seen at least two acts of a very good play called "El Oro y el Oropel", (*the gold and the glitter*) well acted, a Spanish ballet and a *comedy*. We are all not a little sleepy and hope to make up for the last two nights.
Saturday 29th October 1853, Madrid, Calle de las Carretas Antigua – Casa Filippinas.
The inn was not so bad after all, the beds were clean and we slept very well, but as we had agreed yesterday with the landlady here, we have taken these lodgings, which certainly look better, and if not more comfortable in themselves are fitter for the reception of any visitors. One thing we enjoyed not a little yesterday and that was a thorough wash and shave and dress, which took about two hours – not to mention a bath which we had just before dinner. I wrote to Louisa from Burgos and from the Hotel yesterday…I was disappointed not to hear from her today, but I trust that no news is good news….We came to breakfast at half past ten escorted by the Achavals and Don M. Hippolito Niesco, and after breakfast went to their house to see Doña Transitu, Don Nicola's wife – a very nice woman. Thereafter we went to the Royal Armoury – a most beautiful collection excellently arranged. What I most admired were two helmets of Charles V, one of his son, Don Juan of Austria, and a breastplate with the Battle of St. Quentin most elaborately chiselled thereon in silver belonging to Philip II.
We walked about with our friends till dinner which was a pretty good one. I talked to my neighbour Don Cipriano del Mayo – a civil sort of loose fish, an Andaluz from Seville. After dinner we went to the Teatro del Principe and saw "Adriana Lecouvreur" beautifully performed especially by Theodora Lamadrid and Manuel Arjona. We were not home till 12 o'clock.
Sunday 30th October 1853, Madrid.
At last we have our letters through…. Uncle William had one from Blanche saying they had been nearly upset (*carriage turned over*) on their way back to Pau, and I two delightful letters from my dear wife…..
She writes so considerately of my plan, and I never can be too thankful to her for her constant endeavours to please me in everything. Joaquin José Mora called on us today. James went to the Bull Fight, but I did not as Uncle William did not like to do so, nor should we under ordinary circumstances, but this was said to be the last of the season, and if I had been alone, I think I should have gone; it would be such a pity to leave Spain without seeing one at all. We had read our own service, there was no public service in which we could join. We have just come in from a very good dinner at O'Shea's where we met his two sons, the Duke of St Lucar, and a younger one just come from a College in England. We also met the Swedish ambassador, an Austrian Attaché, and the Russian Consul and his wife. Afterwards we went to the Café Suizo and talked

some time with John's friends there – including Cornellas, his master, and a Monsieur Buisson whom Uncle William knew something of. In the morning John and I had taken a run through the Museum just to take a glance at the pictures….It brought back my Florence recollections so vividly – I think that this is even a better collection than that.

Monday 31st October 1853, Madrid.

We have occupied all the day making enquiries about our journey south…I have considerable doubts of our being able to see Cordova for though the Diligence stops there for an hour or two, I am afraid we shall not arrive till sundown and we can't stop there because no other Diligence of the same company passes till two days after…We have settled therefore to go direct to Seville by the Diligence which starts on Thursday, by which we shall arrive early on Sunday morning – a toilsome journey. Uncle William called on a few friends today – Muchada, Escudero and a niece of Achavals.

Don Francisco and Don Domingo have been with John and me tonight to the Teatro del Circo, where we have heard a stupid Sarguela called "Le Estrella de Madrid". The acting was not very good neither was the music, and we were intolerably sleepy. If the Achavals had not been with us I should have come home after the first act. I wish our friends would not pay for our places – that is rather an oppressive civility. I saw young Goyeneche in the theatre, the son of Juan Mai de Goyeneche, our Arequipa friend. He is now Conde de Guaqui, a Grandee of the First Class. His father would not take the title so it passed to him. He seems a nice sort of young man; Achaval says he does not care about his title and does not call himself by it. I don't see why he should, for they have no political power or privilege….

John's friend Cornellas called this afternoon. I wrote to Mr Graham, the Consul at Bayonne, about a servant for Louisa, as Goldschmidt wishes to go back – also to Louisa and to Harrison from whom I had a letter on Saturday about the purchase of a little piece of land at Clifton Hampden.

Tuesday 1st November 1853, Madrid, All Saints.

Today after breakfast we went to the Achavals as we had promised and from thence we went to the Museum intending to meet them and Don Niesco there, but we were sorry to find the Gallery closed, a mortification which was only mitigated by our escaping from our kind friends whose assiduous attention, though springing from the kindest feelings, is too much like that of Monsieur Bourdeux, and somewhat destroys our liberty.The porter told us to go and see the Campo Santo, and thither accordingly we went.

I can't understand why people should go to pray over the graves of the departed today rather than tomorrow, which as All Souls Day would seem the more appropriate occasion.

We all called on Pepe Campana, a very amusing Cadiz friend of Uncle William's like Sam Bright and full of fun.

Uncle William and John called on Doña Angela, and I went home to write to Louisa. I have had no letters today, but Uncle William has one from Blanche and one from Uncle Joseph…..Several friends called here today – Escudero, Echerri, Gajo, who left their cards; and O'Shea whom we saw. We have just come from dining with him – a family dinner, but a very good one. The Duke of St Lucar not there but the younger son was – also Mr Middleton.

Wednesday 2nd November 1853, Madrid.

We have spent most of this day writing letters, paying bills, calling on O'Shea and the Achavals and packing up, but we have found time to visit the Museum, and to eat an immense dinner at the Achavals, and it was indeed no fault of theirs that we have come away sober, for I was never so plied with wine in England. I left a whole battery of five glasses in front of me untouched…

Sunday 6th November 1853, Fonda de la Europa, Seville.

We are very well lodged here, and are very little tired after our formidable diligence journey of no less than 75 hours. The first part of it was a very prosperous one for we had excellent weather, and the road was in very good condition so that we more than kept our time, but on Thursday it began to rain and has continued ever since so that the road was a perfect slough, and for many stages we had to go at foot pace all the way, and consequently arrived about 12 hours after our time. Still I like Diligence travelling on the whole better than Correo, because the many stoppages, which make it longer, give one also time to stretch one's legs, eat and rest. We did not do much in the eating way at the inns, for we had laid in a very good stock of provisions at Lhardy's and O'Shea had made us a most acceptable present of three bottles of excellent sherry, so we fared sumptuously in our coupé, or Berline as they call it here. At night John went into the Rotunda with James so that we all had a corner a piece, and all slept tolerably well. We started…….from the station at seven reaching Tembleque at ten….As far as Villa del Rio, about 6 leagues before Cordova, we had kept our time very well, but as it rained all yesterday and the day before, the result was that instead of being here last night we did not arrive until half past ten this morning. I have been quite unhappy all day at not having had any letter from my dear wife….I trust I shall have a letter tomorrow with good news….I don't know that I can say we enjoyed our journey for a more miserable, uninteresting country than Spain at this time of year I never saw. Fertile as it really is, it looks like a desert with a monotonous road running through it. What a great thing for Spain and for her visitors will a railroad be! It will hurry one through the uninteresting country to the

PEASANTS OF ANDALUSIA.

Figure 17. Peasants of Andalusia (mid nineteenth century).

Figure 18. The Alcazares, Seville.

towns which really are worth seeing. The Somosierra, which we passed over in the North, is wild and ugly as far as we could judge in the dark, and although the Sierra Morena is I have heard very grand and really worth seeing, we passed at about four in the morning and cannot say much about it. Indeed we have been unfortunate in this respect for we passed through Cordova at night and also Carmona. There is little to see in the latter, but the Mezquita at Cordova may make us take another journey or leave it unseen which would be a pity. Our halts were at Madridejos where we first saw the curious patios of the South of Spain. They are surrounded with galleries like the three sides of a Basque church – or like the Green Dragon, Bishopsgate Street, and many other old English inns, except that they are supported on columns. There is a huge church there with scarcely any windows which I should have liked to see, but as we were there between 12 and 2 o'clock, it was not open. We saw the people collecting their crop of saffron which cover the fields by the road side with a garment of purple crocus…The old women pick it and dry it. They are more elaborate in the ironwork of their doors than I have seen elsewhere. The doors of quite poor houses are studded with nails the head of which are often well and tastefully worked….At Tremblique the plaza mayor is very curious like a huge patio of a house surrounded as those are with balconies on pillars…..The only alleviation of the journey were the curious hills rising lazily out of the plain around the so called Pass of Puerto Lapiche. We stopped at about nine o'clock at night to sup at Val de Peñas, and had some very good wine there. In the interior of the Diligence there was an English family of the name of Murray – Mr and Mrs and a governess with a little boy of six and a half or so – a wonderfully fine child like Georgey Whatman only handsomer. Mr Murray is Consul at Tenerife; they are now in this hotel. They had two or three fellow travellers inside, and were consequently very uncomfortable – one a fat man and a sort of Gacioso amused us a good deal, though he was rather troublesome by continual repetition of complaining that Miss Hopton, the governess, had thrown his hat out of the window. He had of course gone to sleep and dropped it. We thought we would never hear the end of "La cachicuerna" as he called his cap. The little boy is a capital traveller born in Morocco.
A little while before we reached Carolina we began to see that we were in the south by the hedges of olives and cactus which lined the road. After Baylen we saw one picturesque view – viz the stony valley of the Rio Relimgar (*Rumblar*). We ought to have arrived at Ecija at about nine o'clock yesterday morning, but we were not there until about 1 p.m. As we had already dined we amused ourselves by walking about. The houses are very pretty with marble patios filled with plants. The house of the Marquis Peñaflor is a curious one, painted outside like those of

Genoa. A great many nobles live there – rich haciendas of the fertile corn and olive plains near it. The society, is good I suppose, and makes up for the great lack which there appears to be in Spain of country houses. I suppose they would not know what to do if they lived in the country, and I don't see how they are to begin. When we came to Alcala close to this place, the country began to be pretty, and the road though in some places horrible, was generally better after Alcala, however it was a sandy swamp. Don Francisco Buiga de Beas, nephew of Don Juan the son of Uncle William's old friend, Don José, met us at the Diligence and brought us here, and by the time we were dressed called again with his uncle, a very good natured fat man. I don't like their Andalusian tongue at all. We hoped to have arrived in time for the High Mass at half past nine, but contented ourselves with the Vespers in this glorious cathedral after reading our own service at home. We walked about a little before dinner, and took a bath, and shall now have great satisfaction in turning in to bed.

Monday 7th November 1853, Seville.

At last I have a letter from my dear wife….She is quite well thank God, and the children too except that Alban has fallen down and hurt his arm a little, but I hope that will soon pass. William and Mary are good and considerate to Louisa. I have just posted a letter to her. I called on Buiga de Beas to get the letters. Uncle William has one from Blanche, and John from Charles, and went again with Uncle William to call on them. We saw his daughter who was having a music lesson from Don San Clemente, one of the canons here in minor orders and organist of the cathedral. There was a piano we had sent out for them, a very good one, and he played to us most beautifully a composition of his own. He has promised to play something more than ordinary at Mass tomorrow for our gratification. There will be no extraordinary function till the 27th, St. Clement's Day, when we shall not be here. We called on the Viuda (*widow*) de Tide, also on Balmaseda, the Representative of Valvidario – he was not at home – nor was Urbina, to whom Achaval had given us a letter. Then we went to Williams the Consul and had a long talk with him and saw his pictures – some very good. A St Francis de Paula by Murillo, two by Orizzonte (Jan Frans van Bloemen from Antwerp), one very good Rembrandt-like landscape, a Monk by Murillo's master, a San Sebastian moderately good by Vargas, a fine Parmagiano Replica or original of that in the Bridgewater Gallery, and a fine figure by John Matsys, having a modern young lady's dress painted over it. The head was very good. Uncle William took a great fancy to the Murillo.

He and I then called on Doña Teresa Lerdo of Tereada, sister of Mrs Charles Vaughan of Bristol, a very nice woman. At dinner we met the Murrays as usual, and a very intelligent Yankee, a Mr Niven, a very gentlemanlike, unprejudiced man. I never knew such a traveller. He has been to Japan, China, and everywhere except Australia and South America. At nine in the morning we went to the Cathedral and went about it with one of the vergers. I should like to know if there is any Cathedral in England or elsewhere that can compare with this. I believe the height is greater here which gives a grand effect, and as richness I never saw anything to equal that of the Roof above the Choir and transept dome….To my eye it is the perfection of architecture. Here there have been no puritans to break the painted glass which fills every window. It seems to be mostly of the sixteenth century, but the colours are most rich and the general effect magnificent….There was a Tintoretto of the Last Judgement…and a St John the Baptist by Zurbaran. The other pictures were all of the School of Murillo. In another chapel further on is a beautiful little "Mater Dolorosa" of Murillo, and a large St Peter by Zurbaran….But the great glory of the Cathedral is the picture of San Antonio by Murillo. It is the best picture of Murillo I ever saw.

Tuesday 8th November 1853, Seville.

At Mass this morning we were much pleased with San Clemente's playing. He spoke to us after the service, looking very fine in his canon's vestments, and has promised to play something new for us every day of this week. It is very kind of him. Young Williams called while we were at breakfast and sat some time with us. He is a very intelligent young man, knowing a good deal both of art and music. He had brought us tickets for the casino and we went there today. Our chief sight seeing today has been the Hospital of the Caridad, where are some of Murillo's choicest pictures – very few but very good – Moses striking the rock, Our Lord feeding the Multitude, the Annunciation, San Juan de Dios burying the dead, and a lovely little brown picture of the child St John, and another opposite of the Infant Saviour…..Buiga es Beas and his nephew have been inflicting on us a two hour visit. We have had a good dinner at the "Madrid"…….

Wednesday 9th November 1853, Seville.

We have seen wonderful pictures in the Museum – Murillo's Immaculate Conception, Zurbaran's large altar piece representing St Thomas Aquinas and a multitude of saints, Murillo's St Augustine praying with the Holy Trinity represented. At the side is a good picture by Alonso Cano of the Souls in Purgatory, and on the opposite wall a curious one by Zurbaran of some Carthusian monks at their meal……Mr Murray has been painting a dancing girl in our passage, and is getting on very nicely. The mother of the girl has such a clever poodle with her.

We went as usual to Mass this morning and saw Dr San Clemente. After breakfast we went to the Giralda and enjoyed the beautiful view from the top. Went at one with the Murrays to see and hear Mr Sanz, a famous amateur guitar player. He certainly has a great command of his instrument....There was an Italian painter there naturalised as an American, who had some capital cosmorama pictures of Niagara, New York, Granada and other places.

Thursday 10th November 1853, Seville.

This morning before Mass we went and saw the handsome rooms in the Louja where all the documents connected with the Spanish Colonies are labelled and put away in perfect order. It is a very fine building. The music was beautiful today and after service Dr San Clemente sent a peon with us to get admittance into the Sacristia Mayor, and much fine plate – especially a tabernacle or ciborium (Custodia) weighing more than half a ton. Among the relics is a beautiful monstrana resplendent with pearls and diamonds an a cross of pure gold brought by Columbus, and the Keys of Seville presented to San Ferdinand – also a cross of wood curiously carved out of one piece by Orientals, representing on the cross itself the passion and its attendant circumstances. Of religious relics there don't seem to be many – two pieces of the true cross.....and the arm bone of St Bartholomew.....There are two Murillo's in the middle of the room, one on each side, of St Isidora and St Leander – fine pictures.......In the Chapter House is a fine "Consumption" by Murillo and several nice portraits by him and his school.

I was surprised and delighted to see the beauty of the Alcazares. I had no idea of there being such exquisite work in such perfect preservation. The Sala de los Embajadores is particularly beautiful....In a little chapel where Charles V was married the altar is of Raphael ware.

Uncle William called on Mr Richards, an old acquaintance whom he had not seen since 1802! The man had become quite a Spaniard and has really forgotten his native tongue. I forgot to mention that we called this morning on Mr Urbina, a nice intelligent old gentleman with a capital library.

Tonight we have been to a dancing academy to see some Spanish dances. The ballet girls and men and children having got up a dance for us. Some of the figures and attitudes were very pretty – especially of the little girls. The Murrays were there and Mr Bruen, the American, and his Irish friend Turner. I had a nice long letter from Louisa saying among other things that they mean to go to Bilbao.

Friday 11th November 1853, Seville.

I had another letter this morning saying Captain Graham had found a Courier for them – one Gabriel, and that they would probably leave San Sebastian today for Tolosa, Loyola and Bilbao. She enclosed a letter from *my brother* Charles telling me he is ordered to the Cape and will probably have to go before we return....

Before breakfast we had been to walk in the pretty gardens by the river, and had unsuccessfully endeavoured to get into those of the Infanta. Also we had been as usual in the morning to Mass at half past nine, and had seen Doctor San Clemente.

After breakfast we went to the Universidad and saw a fine Retablo chiefly by Roslas – the centre group in the large picture of the Holy Family is a very good one. The monk below on the right is as Ford says a sleek grimalkin Jesuit. I never saw a man so like a pious cat. There are two fine images of Francis de Borja and San Ignacio…and two fine marble tombs of the illustrious family of Ribera – husband and wife and in between them on the floor a grand brass of their son, Perafan – evidently a portrait……Afterwards we went with Uncle William to call on his friend Murphy, a gentlemanlike man, but very ill with diabetes. We met him walking slowly out before his door. He went back with us to show us as he said the finest Murillo in Spain; and though I can't think it to be that, yet it is a lovely picture….representing the nativity. The colouring is charming and the picture untouched……Don Julian Williams took us to the studio of one Bekker where we saw an original by Francisco Herrera el Viejo of St Peter and the cock crowing. Many pictures attributed to Velasquez are really by him. Bekker's own pictures were a good one of Seville from Triana and a tolerable one of the Giralda.

Went to the house of the Viuda de Olea, Calle Gugman El Bueno, to see the Moorish work which exists in it. Could not get in but saw through the window a room like the Sala de los Embajadores only of course not so rich and without colour. Also to another house where there were handsome ceilings of a later date, but the work of Morescoes.

Just before two we went into the gardens of the Alcazar, very pretty trim orange hedges. Jets d'eau all over the walks with which the gardener delighted to catch us. We called on Buija, but saw him not, and they have just returned the visit but not given us such a benefit as on the former occasion. I have written to Louisa to say that as Uncle William would not go by sea to Gibraltar and Malaga, we thought of leaving him to go to Valencia and going south ourselves and either joining him there or meeting him in Madrid, but I don't at all like breaking up this party, and doubt whether it will do.

In the church of San Isodoro we saw a very fine picture by Borlas representing the death of the Saint. The heads in the foreground especially those on the left are excellent….they are certainly portraits of the Florentine School.

Saturday 12th November 1853, Seville.

John and I are settled that we do not break up the party, so we have given up the south, and are only comforted by the thought that we could not see Gibraltar without undergoing a week's quarantine on our return which we would never do with our limited time…..We went at half past eight with James in a carriage to Cartuga, now the earthenware manufactory of Mr Pickman, who seemed to know all about us and received us most hospitably, taking us all over his very interesting works, and over his gardens and all the premises and giving us a nice luncheon. Moreover he sent…for a ticket for the Infanta's Gardens which we have made use of this afternoon. They are very pretty, tidy English gardens of considerable extent with the addition of palms and ferns and other tropical plants, but hardly pay for making us three quarters of an hour late for dinner as we were. The old church in the Cartuga is the principal hall of the factory. (They have less scruples here than in England in desecrating churches I think.) But the external church is still retained as a private chapel for Mr Pickman's family and the workmen. There are very beautiful carved stalls therein like those at the Museum, and a charming full size statue in white marble of the Virgin and Child by some Fleming. Mr Pickman is very anxious about the railway, and I dare say he would be glad if Antony Gibbs and Sons would take shares in it. But who, that knows Spain, has confidence enough in the Spanish Government to do anything of the kind?

Our American friend Mr Bruen is gone, and another has come, a good looking young fellow, but a great contrast to the former, whose gentlemanlike manners we all liked, for he is a rough, bearish, dogmatic sort of fellow……We called on young Williams by appointment and went with him to see Don Francisco Romero Balmaseda's pictures. There is another picture just like Hayne's St Joseph by a pupil of Murillo, a fine landscape, and several good things amongst more rubbish, but the collection contains one gem which almost surpasses anything I have yet seen of Murillo. I thought Murphy's excellent, but this as far as it goes is much superior…It is a half length of a Mater Dolorosa, and the expression of the countenance I think I have never seen surpassed…..

Afterwards we went to Don Frederigo Ludwig who had some nice little pictures – six by Montaliro and two by Jameson – scenes from the life of the Prodigal Son excellently painted.

After we left Pickman's we went to the Ruins of Italica – now called Sante Ponce – where there is an amphitheatre, well defined though not in very good preservation of course. I saw some cool looking frogs basking in the burning sun on the fig leaves of their own colour. We meant to have gone on to San Juan de Aznalfarache, but had not time to do this and keep our appointment with Manuel Williams.

Sunday 13th November 1853, Seville.

After reading the Service this morning we went to the Cathedral, but had no time to stay through the Mass; as the procession took up a long while, and we had more to do than we could crowd into a short day.

We have been disappointed in not being able to see the Museum which closed at three just before we got there; so we shall endeavour to take a day as we come back. We went to Herman, the Confectioners in this street, who has a most excellent collection of prints, and looked over most of them, and then called on Manuel Williams. He says he can't value Murphy's pictures because such things are so much matters of caprice, but he has seen worse Murillos sold for £3000. As to Balmaseda's, he will endeavour between now and our return to find out what the values of his other paintings are besides the Murillo. He asks £150 for his St Francis de Paula, an early Murillo, and £100 for St Antony with a book, an earlier one, which for my part I prefer…His two Orizzontes are worth what he asks £10 each, and there is a picture I know very well – a little boy's head by Raffaelle. This however portends to be an original and is indeed a good little picture. A sweet little Morales "Virgin and Child" at £40 – rarity not beauty.

I have been looking several times at the Luis de Varga I mentioned in San Sebastian, and admire it more and more each time, and have finished by buying it for £10…..Also I have bought for $90 a very fine head by Murillo of St Francis in his early style, a fair representation of it and a picture of much expression…..Also I have bought a pretty little sketch of the St Thomas of Villa Nueva in the Museum, a very good reminder thereof. It is by Barrera.

We have taken places by the "Diligence del Medio Dia" for the 24th and mean to go to Aranguez, Toledo and Madrid, and stay at Madrid till the 7th or 8th. I have written to Louisa and Charles and as it is now a quarter to twelve I must go to bed. It has been raining cats and dogs this afternoon and is doing so still.

Monday 14th November 1853, Port St Mary's Fonda de la Vista Alegre. Up at six this morning and off by the 8 o'clock boat down that very tortuous river the Guadalquivir seeing scarcely any scenery worth looking at after passing San Juan de Aznalfarache. All the rest marsh, marsh, marsh, and ducks, plovers and gulls. On the left side indeed the dullness is relieved by the mountains of Ronda in the distance which really looked pretty, not elegant as our Yankee acquaintance would say. The Murrays came with us of course and we took leave of them on arrival at Bonanza. Mrs Murray sends her pictures to the Royal Academy every year so I shall look after them. Any pictures we may order from Barrera this time are to be sent to her at Tenerife; because as he has to send some to her for transmission to England, she may as well send ours at the same time. He lives at 74, Calle de la Palmas.

We got a Coche de Colleras at Bonanza, and came here, a drive of some 2¾ hours, four leagues on a good road through St Lucar and a most uninteresting country to this place, paying for the drive $6. At St Lucar, the principal church has pillars before it like Seville Cathedral. We are pretty well lodged here, and have already done some of our calls. Osborne lives at his house out at Cerillo, about a mile off, but we called here and intend to breakfast with him tomorrow. We called on Don José O'Neale, and Don Tiburcio Ochoteco brother of Mrs Achaval, and they also called here and have been with us all the evening; the latter a great sportsman and a great talker. I kept awake with difficulty. We all went to the Casino and saw there Don Carlos Carrera, and Don Jorge Thuiller, the former a very gentlemanlike person. I hope we shall have letters tomorrow.

Tuesday 15th November 1853, El Puerto Santa Maria.

We walked this morning to Cerillo to Mr Osborne and breakfasted with him. Doña Aurora was there and one of their daughters married to a M. Rueda y Quintanilla of Carmona, who was also there. Also young Thomas Osborne, a very gentlemanlike young fellow of 17, a school fellow of young Henry O'Shea's who has since accompanied us to Xeres where we have seen Mr Gordon's immense bodegas (*wine cellars*) and Mr Pemartin's, and tasted some excellent wine at the former's. We went also into the church of San Miguel the interior of which is very handsomely ornamented both roof and columns. The latter clustered and foliaged between each shaft…The façade is a fine specimen of the Renaissance. Ate some prickly pears which were very fine indeed. This evening we have dined with the Osbornes and met Mr Souter their head clerk, a pleasant man. They sent us in their carriage into Port St Mary; hired a carriage for Xeres; paid for it and the turnpike. The higher the toll, the worse the road! I left my gold pen at Seville. Wrote to the landlord to take care of it.

Wednesday 16th November 1853, No 65, Calle Camino, Cadiz.

I don't think I ever saw such rain as has fallen most of this day unless it was in August 1839 after Uncle William was married. During the time we were at Chiclana it poured down like water out of a bucket, so that the streets ran in rivers – at the bottom of the Calle de la Vega where our inn was, there ran a wide and rapid stream, too wide for John and me to jump. We left Puerto in the same carriage we had yesterday taking our luggage in a Calesa (Osborne paying for all we find when we arrive here!) and arrived at Chiclana about eleven, and breakfasted there. Then we wandered out and paid a visit to Doña Francisca de la Peña, Uncle William's old love – a very nice woman – not so thin and elegant as she was; really something like both Aunt Harriett and Aunt Anne, very lively and with plenty to say. She did not know him at first, but when he spoke and said, "No me conoce señora?", she cried out, "Por la certeza, si! Gibbs!" – And they embraced most lovingly in Spanish fashion. She seemed a good deal agitated at seeing him for it was the first time for 30 years, and since their engagement was broken off. She has a beautiful Murillo there belonging to her landlord – a San Antonio embracing the infant Christ. She was making Garlands and making them beautifully for the Chapel of the Virgin…She almost made us promise to go there for one day at least before we go, and we shall try and do so on Sunday.

This is a very nice English house kept by Mrs Stanley, the widow Uncle William says of a bad sort of man of good birth who used to live here. She was in her time Kitty Costello, an Irish lady, and the handsomest girl in Cadiz.

Mr Boom is here now having called on us with his pocket full of letters and papers – two for me from my dear wife, who reports all well, and that they were going last Friday to Tolosa on their way to Bilbao. They talk also of going to Madrid but I do not think that will really come to pass. They like their servant Gabriel. John has a nice letter from Mary, and Uncle William his usual letter from Hayne – All going well in Bishopsgate Street (*Antony Gibbs and Sons office*).

Uncle William called at Chiclana on Doña Angela Böhl sister of Doña Aurora.

Thursday 17th November 1853, Cadiz.

This morning we took a walk about the town to learn it, and then came back, and I then finished my letter to Louisa, and wrote to Rodriguez of Granada, and Loring of Malaga telling them to forward to Madrid any letters that might come for us, while Uncle William wrote to O'Shea detailing our plans, and asking him to take our places for Toledo, and also wrote to Blanche, suggesting that she should meet him at San Sebastian, and John wrote to Robert, and to Robert Crawley. We then called on the Echecopars, on Luis Crosa, Mrs Lonegran and the Geislers….On our return we met Boom who brought us our Galignani (*a daily newspaper, the Galignani Messenger printed in English*) and me a letter from Louisa, and Uncle William one from Uncle George. Louisa was to start on Saturday last for Aspeytia and for Bilbao on Monday. We meant to go to the theatre tonight, but though we arrived rather late, the doors were still shut, so we suppose something has happened to prevent the function announced. We walked about till a quarter past nine in the Plaza de Mina under a lovely moon.

Señor Echecopar met Uncle William and gave him two bottles of sherry under the just belief that we should not have any of the best here.

Friday 18th November 1853, Cadiz.

Today has been chiefly occupied in hiring our coach to Chiclana, Port St Mary and San Lucar for which we are to pay $27 including turnpikes, buying books and various Malaga figures… We saw nice copies of Don Quixote and Solis, but the prices were $32 and $25 respectively so they remain to be thought about. I spent $21, John $6. Uncle William bought four figures of $8 – I three of $8 and three of $4, and John two of $8 and three of $4. We called on Don José Seron, a very amusing fat friend of Uncle William, and Doña Isadora Harmony (sister of Don Carlos Carrera) whom I remember to have met at dinner at Bedford Square. She is a very nice woman. We saw also her sister and some five nieces. One of her nieces, a daughter of Don Carlos, sister of one of those we saw today, is to be married at Port St Mary tomorrow. It is a great pity we shall not arrive in time to be at the Bodas (*wedding*). I wrote to Borlase (*Louisa's brother*), and to Uncle George. Uncle William had a letter from him with a good account of our dear baby.

Uncle William wrote to Osborne and to Doña Francisca…We have dined at Boom's and been to the casino since, watching the people play Tresillo. I have a book about it. It seems to be the game of Ombre, and the same more or less for three as quadrille is for four. Mrs Boom is no great things, but they have a sweet little girl called Ana, as pretty a child as one could see. I have got Mrs Stanley to get me three scarves (Velas Mantillas) which seem to be more wearable than real Mantillas. Uncle William has got the same.

Saturday 19th November 1853, Cadiz.

This morning we got some money from Boom, and then went to see some Malaga figures representing a Bull fight, very well executed, but consequently too horrid for a drawing room. Uncle William bought the only one, a contrabandista on horse back, which was not horrid. John and I bought some gloves, and found that Mr Younger, the Swedish Consul, who had this morning brought us tickets to see the ceremony of laying the first stone of the highway from Cadiz to Seville, had sent his son to fetch us and accordingly we went (that is John and I did, for Uncle William went making calls) to his house and accompanied Mr., Mrs. and Miss Younger to the Punta de la Vaca where half of Cadiz was met, and where much music and singing and processioning of folks in uniforms was gone through all having a pretty effect in this glorious weather; and afterwards a grand cold collation, when champagne flowed most abundantly so that we were not home till dinner time and had not the least appetite for our dinner. Mr and Mrs Younger are pleasant old people – He an old friend of Uncle William's. Miss Younger a pretty girl, lively and accomplished, the young man something of a rake. We all took a walk with them in the Plaza till half past eight to see the gay doings there. Illuminations and also music, singing and dancing on the platform in the middle. Then we went for tea with Mrs Lonergan where we met a Mr Loyo. She is such a nice pleasant old lady.

I had a cheerful long letter from dear Louey (*Louisa*) from Aspeytia – they have been delighted with the drive and were to start on Monday 14th for Bilbao. I don't think they will come to Madrid, and I should be sorry to induce them to do so. It would be very pleasant, but no risk might be run. I have written to her tonight to go tomorrow, and my letter to Uncle George will go by the same post as I forgot it today.

Sunday 20th November 1853, Port St Mary's. Fonda de la Vista Alegre. This morning we drove over to Chiclana starting at half past seven after reading the Service – and breakfasted with Doña Francisca, who received us very kindly, and gave us an excellent meal. We saw also her aunt Doña Juana Espelata, a nice old lady of about 78 – very thin but handsome, and having all her faculties about her. In her youth she used to go out shooting and do all sorts of things. Doña Francisca delighted us by her playing – her touch is beautiful, and if her music is good now on a cracked piano what must it have been in Uncle William's eyes 30 years ago? I don't wonder at his falling in love with her – so clever a woman, so full of imagination, and such an excellent musician. The only wonder is how he could have made up his mind to give her up so lively, good tempered and affectionate as she seems. If however the obstacle was, as I believe it was, that he was to have the children educated as Romanists, I am sure he was quite right. She received us very kindly – I wish we could have stayed longer. She says she will come to England some day, but I don't much expect it. While she was playing I said to myself – "Now Uncle William will buy her a new piano", and accordingly when he went out he told me the idea had passed through his mind at the same time. She said, talking of Pepe Campana – "Todos quiersa casarse con muchachas – siempre muchachas! ("All the men want to marry young girls – always young girls") A little shaft which missed Uncle William because he did not hear it! He asked me if I did not see a likeness to Blanche – finding or trying to find any excuse for his infidelity. Her landlord's name to whom the picture belongs is Espelosin – a friend of Achaval's. We took a walk to the Cuesta de Santa Ana, a sort of St Anne's Hill to which I think Uncle William had often walked before and there in the ruined church Uncle William and John sang many things. At two we took our leave and started for this place where we arrived before five and having called on O'Neale and Don Carlos Carrera and gone over the handsome, regularly built bodega (wine cellar) belonging to the latter and the Harmony family. We went up to dine with Osborne, having the interlude of an upset in our way up, our Mayoral having gone the wrong way, and endeavoured to rectify it by going up a bad road. Happily no one was in the least hurt. We walked on to the Cerillo, and met with a hearty welcome from our kind friends there. The Buedas were fine, and the other daughter Manuela with her husband Mr Morgan (a very pleasant fellow) were there. It is now nearly 12 and we are quite tired.

Monday 21st November 1853, Seville – Fonda de Europa. This morning we went to breakfast with the Osbornes, and at half past ten went on in our coach to San Lucar and Bonanza, which we reached at twenty minutes to one; and beguiled the time till the steamer came, which was half past one, and started by buying a handsome poodle named Lucero for Uncle William – very like Tanny which my grandfather had at Stowe, and which Uncle Charles bought for him in Cadiz. We paid our Mayoral the $25 agreed on for the journey from Cadiz (including pikes) and $2 for himself …and have arrived in the steamer sin novedad (*without any incident*); the only mistake being that we sent for a coach which caused us to wait nearly half an hour opposite the Infanta's Palace where we arrived.

Tuesday 22nd November 1853, Seville.

Uncle William had a letter from Blanche. Before breakfast we called on Barrera, the painter, and went to the Cathedral as usual; heard the Mass and saw San Clemente, and walked round to see the pictures. Looked again especially at that of Louis de Varga at the West End – a fine picture. One cannot see the Gamba de Adam. After breakfast we called on Buiza de Beas, and then went to the Museum, and rejoiced ourselves with the pictures in the Sala de Murillo – Barrera was there and I have ordered from him three more little pictures (at $5) namely the Nativity, the San Antonio and the St Francis – a larger copy of the Nativity for Mary. Uncle William ordered a still larger copy thereof, and one of the Santo Thomas. He is painting my little one of San Felix very well. Should have liked a copy of the lovely Madonna de la Servillete, but I doubt whether Barrera could do it satisfactorily. The pictures I like best are that and the St Thomas, St Felix, the Nativity, St Francis and St Antony. St Leander and St Bonaventura is a fine picture – both as to the heads and the general arrangement…

After leaving the Museum we called on the Marchioness of Castilleja, Osborne's daughter, a pretty agreeable little woman – exactly like both father and mother. The Marquis called afterwards and saw Uncle William, but we were out taking a walk with Lucero the dog, who follows us well and fetches and carries and goes into the water very well. After our call, we went to Williams' to talk about the Balmaseda's collection. Balmaseda values them at 210,000 reals, but Williams thinks he would take about 145,000 reals, and Williams himself valuing the Madonna at 40,000 reals or £400, considers them worth 114,000. It remains to be seen whether the Madonna is worth more. Tonight we have been to the casino where we found Williams, who gave us a nice cup of coffee – We met Balmaseda there and appointed to go and see his pictures tomorrow.

Wednesday 23rd November 1853, Seville.

And accordingly we have been and have gone through them, thoroughly taking a note of those Uncle William would like or would think worth

111

carrying to England, and making a calculation to see what they are worth. I put down about 40 pictures as being worth £684; the Dolorosa £400, and about 80 or 90 more – copies and third rate pictures and rubbish about £130; or some £1200 in all, and tonight at the Casino we have seen Balmaseda, and have tried him with $5000, thinking that we might get them for six which Don Julian Williams said was the lowest calculation he could make for them. Balmaseda however did not seem likely to accede, and I have been up till now – 12 o'clock – maturing a proposition of $4000 for the Dolorosa and some 30 pictures, Balmaseda however, after long consideration and much talk with Williams, has refused. I think them well worth $5000, and would even cast out some of the pictures reducing them to 24 or so, and proposed in response to Balmaseda's answer which offered us only 10 and the Dolorosa for £1000 ($5000), to offer $4500 or $5000 for the 31, but Uncle William has become shy and would not let me do more than repeat the offer, cutting out 5 pictures of small moment. We shall see if it will be of any use. I fear not; and hope Uncle William has not thrown away his chance. This morning after breakfast at half past eight we went to the Cathedral and saw the procession with the banner and sword of St Ferdinand – this being the day of St Clemente, the anniversary of the Conquest of Seville in 1248 – and heard the Mass – the music very grand representing a battle – some of it very beautiful.

We also saw the body of San Fernando in the Capilla Real. This is a real relic, and it requires an ingenious amount of incredulity to disbelieve it. He was King here and lived and died here, and if that is not his body, I don't see who else it could be; nor why they should have substituted another for it – a profitless lie for a profitable truth…….

We saw the San Antonio today in a really good light and were more than ever pleased with it. I think there is not better picture in the world, by whomsoever it may be.

After the service we went to Williams' and saw some nice old copies of heads by Murillo, and then went to Balmasedas as I have said. Nuedas saw us at the casino and has given us a letter to procure us a seat in the Congress one night. He is a very nice fellow. We had called after dinner on old Williams and had been with him to the Café Lombardo, an immense room 150 feet by 25. At the Casino Don Frederico Ludwig gave us some tea, which did not pay for his tiresome talk. I occupied the time while Balmaseda and Williams were talking, in writing to Louisa. We paid another visit to the Caridad, and impressed ourselves with the lovely pictures there. Notwithstanding a blue pill I took last night I have had a baddish headache today, but it is nearly well now.

What interested me most in the service today was a most eloquent sermon by Father Rafael Levin of the course of the conquest of Seville. It

112

was ex tempore and yet without any useless repetition, shewing a wonderful memory for dates, names and events. It was an excellent peroration very practical and gave a vivid picture of the sordid avarice and self seeking of the present day, as compared with the faith and good works of the days of old. Then he said there was faithful service of the heart – now nought but miserable money getting calculation of the head. I was particularly struck with the turn he gave to the falling off in the reign of Alonso the Wise from the Glories of San Fernando. Then it was hoped he said that the Victorious Spain would stretch forth her arms to the stronghold of the infidel, and pursuing her enemies into Africa would raise again the Church of St Cyprian and St Cyril – then might the Holy Sepulchre conquered and guarded by Spanish breasts, have opened a refuge for the pilgrims. But cares of state prevented this holy work. Yet weep not Seville. Dry your tears ancient and illustrious city – a Queen shall arise, and shall send forth her servants who shall give a new world to Spain. In Mexico and in all America a new nation shall embrace the Cross; amid a new people shall the sacred rites of Iberia be reproduced to the glory of God and of his Church.

Everyone attended most earnestly and ourselves among the rest; and except that our time was so short I was very sorry when the preacher said, "He dicho" (*I have spoken*) and came down from his pulpit.

Sunday 27th November 1853, Aranjuez, Fonda de las Cuatro Naciones.
On Thursday morning at nine o'clock we started our journey hither after having had a long visit at breakfast time from Don Manuel Williams wherein I was quite convinced that Uncle William had made a miscalculation in offering $4000 and sticking to that price….If he (*the seller*) asks £1000, it is that he values it at £500; and if you bid £400, it is because you know his real price is £500 or somewhat less, and mean by negotiation to bring your price up a little, and his down a great deal. What a man should do is first to consult a good judge such as Williams what the real market value is as far as it is determinable; then consult his purse whether he can give that value; then *ask* the seller for his price……
Uncle William was not convinced, and would not take my advice to revise his offer to $4500 so as to open a further negotiation, and so get them at worst for $5000 if not even for $4500. I believe however he has now discovered that he has made a mistake, supposing himself to have offered on Williams' evaluation, whereas his offer is some $980 short of it.

We arrived at Carmona 2 p.m. At Carmona, which is a place beautifully situated on the crest of a hill, we (having already dined in the carriage) left James to his dinner and walked on – strolling in the Alameda, and walking up the steep hills outside the town to the picturesque Roman and Oriental fortress. We enjoyed our walk very much, for it was a lovely day.

We slept very well after our chocolate at Ecija (12.30 a.m.) and woke to a fine day on Friday and to breakfast about 10 o'clock at Cordova. The Mayoral put us down close to the Mezquita so that we had time to see it thoroughly before we went to our breakfast. I should have been very sorry to have missed that sight.

It is a perfect forest of pillars, and the small holy of holies at the end a very beautiful specimen of Moorish work reminding me of the Mosaics at Monreale.

After breakfast we went on our way singing and cracking jokes and bottles till it was dark, and then slept a little till we were roused up by our arrival and supper i.e. Chocolate at Andujar (9.10 p.m.). At Baylen (2.20 a.m.) we were stopped an hour by meeting a Galera (*a heavy covered wagon*) in a narrow road, and had all to put our shoulders to the wheel to back the diligence out of the street – such swearing by all possible things in Heaven and Earth and elsewhere! But no attempt at action for the first quarter of an hour!!

Yesterday we breakfasted at La Catalina (7.15 a.m.) and were to have stopped at Puerto Lapiche for supper but had no time, lest we should be too late for the train at Tembleque; so we held straight on and have been employing ourselves today after breakfasting and reading the service in walking all about Aranjuez seeing the Casa del Labrador, and the two Royal Gardens, which even at this season of the year are worth seeing. The Casa del Labrador strikes me as very pretty, very costly and very silly; like in the latter respects to its builder Charles IV. There is one room fitted up with ornaments of gold and platinum which are exquisite. Another room has many pictures of the Escorial, some fine Sevres vases and a malachite table and chair…..The Epergne in the first room of gold and precious marbles is very handsome. With all this the rooms are too small for use, and the king never did anything but smoke a cigar there once or twice a year.

We arrived at Tembleque at 4.45 a.m. and after having had a good cup of chocolate, started by the half past five train, and arrived here at 6.55 a.m. and have got very comfortable quarters, (Fonda de las Cuatro Naciones at Aranjuez). The landlord here has excellently good Val da Penas, which we have been just rejoicing in. He is an Englishman – his wife French.

A letter from O'Shea with the ticket for the places in Villa Sequille, but with no letters for us enclosed. This evening brought us an express letter from Senora Ramona saying we should have rooms in her house in Madrid, I wrote to Louisa.

Monday 28th November 1853, Fonda del Lino, Toledo.

Started this morning after breakfast by the half past eight train for Villa

114

Figure 19. View of the city of Toldeo

PEASANTS OF TOLEDO, CASTILE.

Figure 20. Peasants of Toledo, Castile.

115

Sequilla which we reached in time to start by the diligence at half past nine, and came here over such a road as I never travelled on in my life.... and we nearly upset I think a dozen times – once within an ace of it. Murray says this is an indifferent inn and indeed one near the Plaza Mayor looks better. It was a most dangerous road but this is tolerable enough. We got a light luncheon, took a guide and went to the Cathedral. I had expected something more nearly approaching to Seville, but this cathedral falls far short of it. Still it is very beautiful especially in minor details.....but here the glass is glorious especially the ruby colours; and better even than the lovely windows at Seville. The woodwork of the choir representing the wars of the Catholic kings is far above anything I ever saw and should be studied for days. The carving of the screens and parcloses is very beautiful – but for general effect and grandeur of sentiment Seville is far superior.......The pictures in the Sagristia are not very great......The Christ bearing the Cross in a fair specimen of El Greco. The head of the Saviour is good, and the man stooping down in the right foreground and boring holes for the Cross is a striking figure. I begin to know El Greco (Domenico Theotocopuli) by his cold colour. His heads are generally very good and he paints armour well.......The Custodia is very beautiful of wrought silver and gold, and the silver statues of Saint Ferdinand and Saint Augustine are good.......The screen work of the Choir and High Altar is very beautiful, solid yet light, filled with excellent carving....

We went to the Synagogue, now the Church of El Transito, an oblong building rich in Moorish carving. I suppose the lower border of flowers in something of the same sort of work with Hebrew characters in stone and with the arms of Castille and Leon introduced is of a later date to the rest.

We saw also the other Synagogue, now the desecrated church of Santa Maria La Blanche, consisting of a nave and four aisles with Moorish columns and arches and beautiful honeycomb and arabesque work in their peculiar hard white plaster. There are also open-work windows ... and beautiful sort of network patterns in the spandrels of the arches. In both Synagogues the roofs are of Cedar of Lebanon.

From thence we went to the curious little Mezquite in the Calle Christo de la Luz – now a church. The Mosque part consists of little domes supported by a nave and two aisles. Ford says that this building belonged to the Templars.

("Hand-Book for Spain" – first edition 1845, an immense and deeply learned work by Richard Ford. Ford (1796-1858) was a wealthy British aristocrat who travelled throughout Spain from 1830 to 1833. In 1839 John Murray asked him to write a book about Spain for Murray's new

series of traveller's hand-books. Six years later it was published in two thick volumes of tiny print and sold out immediately.)

We had a few minutes of light left to go to the Museum which is over the beautiful cloisters of the convent of San Juan de los Reyes, where there are a number of pictures in very bad condition – Some I think of considerable merit of the Early German School.

We called on Don Onofre Rodriguez to whom O'Shea had directed us, and find that he has taken us places in the direct diligence for Madrid which starts at 7 on Wednesday.

Tuesday 29th November 1853, Toledo.

I did not sleep well somehow and woke with a headache; nevertheless at seven, after chocolate, Uncle William and I sallied forth leaving John to get up at his leisure. We went to the Cathedral, to the Capilla de los Reyes Nuevos where the chief thing to remark is the beauty of the grained roof, and the quasi chancel by which one enters the chapel (which lies parallel to the Cathedral). The statues too of the Kings and Queens are worth notice – and one more interesting for being the daughter of John of Gaunt....

Before breakfast we had been up the tower and seen the lovely panorama of the town. On the highest stage, to which there are stone steps, the wise Toledans dragged two pieces of cannon when they were attacked by the French, but it never occurred to them to fire them off! They might as well have saved themselves the trouble.

This afternoon we have taken a walk all round the outside of the town – a charming park giving us beautiful views of this queer rock-built nest, and as good an idea as possible of its position in a sort of loop which the river forms. There are but two land gates – the Puertas Visagra and del Cambro, and two river gates over the bridges of Alcantara and San Martin – the latter a very picturesque bridge. We have been on our legs perpetually and are not a little tired. The Zocodover or principal plaza and market place struck us as very picturesque – full of people in various costumes looking lively and active. The houses and galleries having their share of the picturesque appearance. The Calle Ancha (The Broad Street of Toledo) is not much wider than Lime Street in London, but…the streets here are all narrow and crooked, and all up hill and down hill. The town looks very ruined, dirty and dilapidated, but it takes a long time to recover from the burning and destruction of war. One of the streets out of the Zocodover leads down to the Hospital de la Santa Cruz – now a military college, where with some difficulty as it was late we got permission from the Commandant to see the handsome patio and staircase. The cadets were going through their drill at the time. We also got his permission to see the Alcazar which is just above – a huge square

117

pile, gutted and never repaired – Ionic without and Corinthian within. It is finely situated and seems to command the town…..In the Street of Torneria we saw a very good specimen of a Moorish private house. The rooms in the same style as the Sala de los Embajadores but small and without ornament. Ford calls it "El Taller del Moro".

Ford says the Church of the Convento de los Silos is a beautiful Ionic chapel – but I could not find anything to admire in it. The Assumption by El Greco was a characteristic picture.

We went to San Roman, but did not discover the Moorish work which Ford mentions…On our way to the Fabrica de Armas where there is a tolerable collection of specimens of arms, we went into the little church of the Cristo della Vega, the foundations of which were a small Roman basilica, but which has Moorish arches on the outside. The chief attraction was a very pretty little statue of Santa Leocadia by Berrujuste now over the door of this church, but heretofore in a niche in the Puerta del Cambron.

Wednesday 30th November 1853, Madrid, Casa de la Bizcayna –
Casa Cordero, Calle Mayor.

We started at seven in bitter cold and arrived here at about half past one, and found ourselves exceedingly comfortably lodged. I have no less than six letters from my dear wife from Bilbao. All going on well except that both Joseph and Jane have been disagreeing with the servants, and have, I am afraid, not been conducting themselves well. *(Joseph Hucks Gibbs, William's nephew and son of his brother Joseph.)* Louisa talks of sending Jane home by sea. There is also one thing rather unpleasant in the letters, and that is that Mr Clark the Consul, an American who lives in the same house and is very civil to them, has a pretty ladylike daughter with whom *my brother* William seems to be falling in love – and Louisa wants to know what she can do.

I have written to her to say she must either go back to San Sebastian or Pau, or else send William and Mary *(his youngest sister)* here, unless talking to William seems to suffice. The Clarks are poor as church mice, and besides the education must be bad, living as they do in Bilbao, and what should William do with a wife with £300 or £400 a year to keep her! Uncle William had a letter from Hayne and three from Blanche – all good news. Also one from Osborne, and one from Williams saying that Balmaseda was still stiff, and that he (Williams) thought of offering $6000 for his own account – in which case Uncle William should have his list for $4500.

O'Shea called in this evening, sat with us for a while – till dinner – and asked us to dine with him tomorrow. We dined very well here at half past five – the waiters very attentive. Altogether the house is much better than that in the Calle Carretas. One of the waiters has good cigars, of which we bought 25 for $1.

Thursday 1st December 1853, La Vizcayna, Madrid.

We have just come back from our several amusements. Uncle William from the French theatre where he has been with Mrs O'Shea, and John and I from O'Shea's where we have been playing whist, and losing two or three dollars a piece. We met there a Mr Ilavat, the Duke of Cauzano, and a Mr Hofer who with O'Shea, his partner Kennedy and ourselves constituted the whist players. We dined there and that well. The mantilla which Mrs O'Shea has bought for Uncle William is so beautiful that I think I must have one for Louisa notwithstanding what she says. I have ordered one for Mary not quite in the same style. This morning after breakfast we went to the Academy and spent much time in looking at the charming pictures there. The "Dream of the Roman Senator", the "Completion of the Dream", and the grand picture of Santa Isabel (Elizabeth of Hungary I suppose) nursing the sick – a fine companion to the San Tomas de Villanueva. The figure of the Senator in the dream is as perfect a representation of sleep as can be imagined…The "Procession to the Consecration of the Church" is excellent. These three are so good that they have put all the others out of my head.

Afterwards we went to the Museum and examined some of the wonderful pictures there. The more I look at the Conception by Murillo, the more I prefer it to any other of the same subject by him or anyone else. When I was here before I did not see the "Noli me tangere" by Correggio. I don't think the figure of the Saviour so striking, beautiful as it is, as that of St Mary Magdalene, but hers is all that can be desired, for the expression of her love for our Lord. Correggio has evidently desired to express that love as human affection as well as spiritual love and adoration, and her attitude and gaze most happily represent this…….We have called today on Dona Angela and the Achavals – also in the morning on O'Shea. There were two letters at the Correo for me – one from George Crawley and one from George Gibbs enclosing a letter of introduction from Mr George Robert Smith to Lord Howden. We found the latter there but some rogue had drawn the former!

Friday 2nd December 1853, Madrid.

John and I had a long talk at the Café yesterday and today also after going to the Theatre del Principe and seeing "Mr Capricho" and "Acerta per Carambola." At the Café I met a painter Don Francisco Carse and had a long talk about early Italian art, wherein he seems very intelligent. I am to go to his studio tomorrow. We went of course to the Museum as usual, and John and I went to the Quarto Reservado and saw the pictures of the Royal Family, three pictures by Titian, one of Danae and two of Venus – the latter just the same as at Florence, but the Danae really a very pretty picture though of a subject not to be hung in the drawing

Figure 21. Madrid 1850.

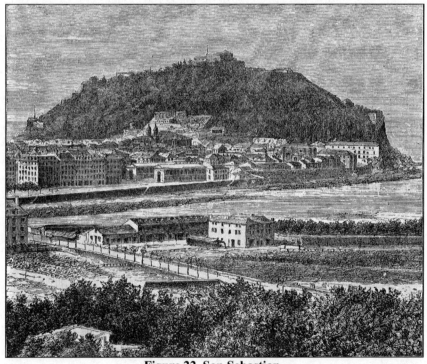

Figure 22. San Sebastian.

room. The face is beautiful and the upturned look. We called on the Achavals and saw Dona Transitu and Mr Riesco. Called on Lord Howden who was not in.

Saturday 3rd December 1853, Madrid.

This morning Uncle William and I called on Mr Aarom, husband of Doña Cecilia Böhl, Doña Aurora's sister. He is going to Sydney as Spanish Consul there. Also after a long discussion as to which would be the best road to go to Valencia we have at last decided to give up the Cuenca Road, and have taken our places for the other for Wednesday next. We had to go to the Consul's to exercise a power, which we received from Hayne in a letter sent back from Malaga yesterday and there we saw Mr Middleton, and when we told him about our movements I felt sure from his manner that Lord Howden had asked us to dine on Wednesday next, and accordingly at O'Shea's, where we have been this evening, we learn that that was the case, and that he had in fact been asked to meet us – while Middleton had suppressed our note. O'Shea asked us to dine on Monday, a family dinner he said, and now the matter has been complicated by our find of three notes from Lord Howden for the same day (very civil of him for he must have got up a party for us). Uncle William has just concocted a note to O'Shea to find out if there has been a mistake. I played Ecartè and lost two dollars.

We paid our accustomed visit to the Museum spending our time in the Flemish and Dutch Schools. Afterwards we went to the painter's and saw two or three good pictures which he had collected, and two most excellent copies – one of the Transfiguration (price $1000) another of the Little Madonna del Libro at Perugia.

Sunday 4th December 1853, Madrid.

I have had two letters from Louisa chiefly about William…and strongly urging me to send John and have William here, but I am writing to say that…it is too late as we shall be gone to Valencia. I do think the better way is to speak seriously to William who is now old enough to judge for himself, and is of course only amenable to persuasion. They have all been more or less ill with diarrhoea especially Nurse and Edith, but they are I hope better. Jane went home by the "Taunton Pilot" on the 2nd. O'Shea answered Uncle William's note to the effect that we ought to accept Lord Howden's invitation, which we accordingly did. After a half past nine breakfast we went for two or three hours to the Museum, and then Uncle William went to make some calls, and John and I seeing that there was a Corrida de Toros, and that it was the only chance I should probably ever have of seeing a bull fight, went accordingly, and I am very glad I have seen it. The first two bulls were "Novillos" brought up to try their mettle. They had large balls on their horns and could hurt no one nor could the Picadores hurt them much. They were not professionals, but jovenes aficionados. They made good sport and the bulls charged well. The conclusion of the entertainment too was very amusing, for six novellos were let out one after another into the plaza where a great number of young men and boys unarmed actually played blind man's buff (boeuf) with them – the bull acting the part of the blind man, and catching them when he could – they then teasing him with their cloaks. He tossed two or three but no one was at all hurt. One lad seemed bruised a little, but he got up smoking his cigarette as before. It was the funniest thing to see three oxen come in as each novella had had enough and was tired, and pitch him out! They seemed quite to know what they were about, and yet looked so stupid. The real part of the performance consisted in the death of four old bulls who were killed secundum artem (*according to the art*).

It very nearly made me sick for I could not bear to see the poor animals be stabbed and die nor the wounds they inflicted on the horses. It was quite shocking! They killed four horses. No men were hurt though the falls looked terrific. One bull was a poltroon and they had some fierce dogs to bait him. He killed one, but the others pulled him down. The whole scene was one I shall never forget. This evening after dinner we have been to the Achavals and found them playing Tresillo, which we sat and watched.

Monday 5th December 1853, Madrid.

Tonight we have been there again and I played a hand or two, and begin to understand it practically. We dined with Lord Howden and met Colonel Stopford, a Doctor Lovel, Mr Aspinall, young Owens, young O'Shea, a Frenchman name unknown, and a Lieutenant Burnaby. We had a very good light dinner and my Lord was very civil to us….We had no time to go to the Museum, so occupied were we in going to the Achavals and with Don Domingo to the shop of or studios of a famous armourer by name Zuloaga. Since the plate in the Pitti Palace and other work by Bevenuto Cellini, and some of the armour in the Armoury here, I have seen no chiselling so beautiful. He shewed us several small scent bottles enclosed in boxes – all of steel inlaid with silver, costing £30 or £40 each, and full of work. But the finest things were the Gun for the King, carved all over and inlaid with gold – a cover of a great folio book to enclose the titulos of some new noble. There were a sword, dagger and shield for the Queen to be placed in the Armoury – the pommels and sheaths covered with arabesque figures and battles carved in steel and the wax model of the shield (now finished) representing the various battles of Charles V and Francis the First, ending in the centre with the famous Battle of Pavia. The sword and the dagger were $6000. He shewed me a nice sword he had made for the King of Sardinia with the Battle of Goits on the Hilt (value £100) and another (value £50) which if I was a rich man I should like to have bought. But if "money was no object", I should say – Mr Zuloaga, make me a casket of steel inlaid with silver and gold with arabesque round it and subjects on the top and sides. Moreover if I wanted an Epergne or anything of that sort, I should not go to Hunt and Roskell, but to him. We are to go with him on our return to see the armoury.

Lord Howden gave us the best Val de Piñas I ever had and a curious bitter sweet wine – not too sweet – called Alba Flor (which he thinks comes from Palma) of which I should very much like to have some.

I sent Louisa the letter I wrote yesterday, and since post time I have had a long and pretty satisfactory letter from her. She had spoken to William who was of course very contradictory and inconsistent como suelen los amantes (*as is usual with lovers*), but I think in better train. Poor dear Louey was not quite well of her ailment......

Tuesday 6th December 1853, Madrid.

Achaval has this morning sent us a couple of bottles of wine, a miniature Don Quixote for John and an "Espiritu de Cervantes" for me, also two packs of naipes (*Spanish playing cards*) – They are very kind indeed to us......We employed our morning in taking our places, getting money from O'Shea's (and directing him to send letters to Valencia till Sunday inclusive) buying our provisions, and going thoroughly through the room above the sculptures, and the right hand room of the Spanish School, as one enters the Museum.

Then we called on Mr Escudero who was not in and came home to receive our letters, acknowledge them and dine. Colonel Stopford called and sat awhile before dinner. I had a comfortable letter from Louisa giving a better account of herself and Edith, and also of William's affair.....We called after dinner on the O'Sheas and sat till a quarter past nine when we went to the Opera to hear Lucretia Borgia. The House is a very pretty one – white and gold with no draperies – the boxes and stalls most comfortable. It is a very large theatre. We did not think much of the singing, but some was tolerable. I like the last act of that Opera very much.

I have forgotten to say that we called on Carderera, a painter to whom Williams gave us a letter. We saw there some good portraits, and one large and very beautiful picture by Zurbaran – the Annunciation. I think I like the figure of the Angel better than any I remember. He is on both knees, the grand flowing drapery falling soberly down, and the head bent in reverence before the Blessed Virgin. Over the drapery is a sort of close garment of wool with pearls and jewels. The figure of the Virgin is pleasing, and the drapery excellent. He asks 60,000 Reals for it....It has unfortunately been raining a little most of the day and is now raining hard. It is a great pity as the roads will be spoilt for our journey.

Friday 9th December 1853, Valencia, Fonda del Cid.

I don't know that that can be called spoilt which was never other than execrable; and that is the true description of a great part of the road between this city and Madrid; and now since the rain, what with torrents on the good road, and what with the bad being no road at all, it may be characterized as almost impassable. Still here we are, quite safe and having on the whole slept very well through all the bumps and jolts, and as far as scenery goes enjoyed our journey especially the latter part of it very much. The view of the mountains, some of them crested with snow was very pretty, and the view looking back on the little town of Chiva, charming. We left at eleven o'clock on Wednesday, made our dinner, procured as before at Lhardy's, in the Diligence and took chocolate at Tarancon where we arrived at eight, the road beginning to be bad some time before we reached that place, and continuing so more or less till just before we arrived at Motilla yesterday evening. Since then with some atrocious exceptions, such as when just after passing Chiva, about 11 o'clock today, a torrent had undermined a bridge and made it unsafe, so that the coach had to go round a quarter of a mile through ploughed fields while we walked on, it has been tolerably good, and in some places admirable. The Spaniards are good road makers, and all their stone work, bridges, curbs etc are beautiful and strong, but when made, for want of ordinary attention, they suffer them to go completely to decay. Here, therefore, some of the main road is in a dangerous state, and besides that the Government has been so negligent as to leave a great part unmade, so that one has between Olmedilla and Motilla, and also I think before we reached Taracon, to drive at hazard across a heath; and if we had not happily had an excellent Mayoral we could hardly have failed to be upset – as it was we rocked sometimes like a ship in a storm….After all we shall I believe try the Cuenca road on our way back.

We stopped at Olmedilla yesterday at half past twelve and ate an egg and drank some wine out of a decanter with a little curved spout the size of a quill through which we poured the liquor down our throats Catalan fashion, without touching our lips. This was meant for breakfast, but as it was so late we used it only as a whet for our dinner, which we began as soon as the coach started again and finished our grog, and the remaining bottle of Achaval's excellent sherry. We had discussed the "Viajado" on Wednesday, and now paid out attention to the Amontillado…….. At Minglanilla we stopped and had a tolerably good supper in company with our friends in the upper part of the banquette, one a lively little man in a white hat, a great admirer of dogs and especially of Lucero (whom by the bye James has washed and made to look lovely after his dipping), another a Basque with a red beret, a contractor for a part of the road now being made, and the other a Doctor Fernando Weiler, a resident at Palma,

Mallorca, where he is a physician to the military hospital, a very intelligent, pleasant man. He tells us the Albaflor wine belongs all to the Captain General, Cotoner, and is sold exclusively by the agent, a friend of the doctor's, Mr Ramon Bauza. It is made at Baña Albujar, and is a kind of Malvoisie. We shall order some through Trenor who is to desire his correspondent to communicate with Dr Weiler who will see that we have it of the best. He says also that the Muscatel grown on the same estate is very good. As we had the whole of the Diligence – nine places – we left Uncle William at night the whole of the coupé to sleep in, while John, James and I took three corners in the interior. We did not sleep very well at first – at least I did not, till I got John to take the opposite corner to me, and so leave me the whole of one side, whereon for the little that remained of that night and the whole of last night I slept most soundly. I hardly liked having half the interior to myself, but John was just as comfortable in one corner as the other, and I reflected that "when two men ride one horse, one must ride behind", so reconciled myself to taking the best place.

One curious part of our journey was when a torrent had swept down the middle of the road, and though not deep was rushing pretty rapidly across. The Mayoral (overseer, man in charge) told us to cross on foot, and then he steering the horses as well as he might, dashed through it and the crowd of galeras (wagons) waiting their turn to cross after us. Another time, on one of the heaths, while we were cruising across the country, we had to dash down into a deep road and up the other side – the Diligence taking the leap as it were at a run. The heaths were very beautiful and smelt at every footstep of rosemary and thyme. That of Olmedilla was covered with a little low dull holly with a leaf about an inch long not polished as ours are.....

We arrived at about two o'clock and have excellent rooms in this hotel, taken for us by Mr Trenor who has called on us this evening, and brought Uncle William letters from Blanche and Hayne... Mr Matthews, Trenor's nephew, called on us while we were at breakfast at about 3 o'clock. We may say breakfast for we had nothing but a little jicara (*cup*) of chocolate at Duñol, it was I think quite early in the morning. We dined at half past six, and everyone enjoyed our "Arroz à la Valenciana". The country wine is not good and the sherry is not sherry, and bad; the tea is tolerable. We have all enjoyed a tepid bath.

Saturday 10th December 1853, Valencia.

We have settled to go home by Cuenca and have taken our places accordingly. After breakfast and reading we went to Trenors and sat with them at breakfast – Mr and Mrs Trenor, Henry Trenor and Matthews. Mrs Trenor (Doña Brigada) is a very nice woman. Trenor took us to the Cathedral, and there we saw over one of the altars a most beautiful Head of the Saviour by Juanes, soft in expression and exquisite in painting. There is a fine Holy Family in the Sala Capitular, and two good paintings one of St Michael and the other of some monkish saint. Also a Last Supper in the style of Juanes if not by him. The Baptism of our Lord, over the font, also by Juanes, is very good....

In the Museo there are not many pictures which struck me much. There are two of the Saviour with the Sacramental Bread...both are good, and an Ecce Homo by the same painter (Juanes) which I don't admire so much. Between the two first is a fine picture by Ribalta of St John in the Wilderness.....There are some good pictures by Borras, a pupil of Juanes – especially one of the Holy Family. I should have enjoyed these pictures more with a catalogue and without a guide.

I forgot to say that we had been up the Cathedral Tower and greatly enjoyed the view of the town and of the Huerta thickly studded with villages and isolated houses. It is indeed a garden of fertility.

We went with Trenor (after calling on Xavier Paulino and Servet, correspondents of ours....) to the Ayuntamiento where we saw some beautiful roofs, carved and richly gilded – and the sword of the King, James the Conqueror. Thence to the Audience or Judgement Hall, where the principal thing to be seen was the old hall of the Valencian Cortes, covered with frescoes representing the several estates, with their titles written above them in Valencian dialect. The roof and the galleries here were beautiful. The Dado of Azulejo (*Spanish painted, tin-glazed, ceramic tile work*) is very beautiful. The rest of the day was spent in seeing the Azulejo manufactury, and the Presidia, which last was the most interesting of all. The prisoners (an evil looking set of rascals) were all either working at their own trade or learning one. They are obliged to work a certain time and have for themselves half at once and half when released of half the sum earned. The other half goes to the government for food etc. Some people object to this treatment as offering encouragement to vice, but I don't see how it can do so. It must be better to have them employed than idle and the small earnings are necessary as an encouragement to the best among them to amend and improve. They seem, to have little spiritual instruction. They have a chapel and must go to Mass and have a sermon on Sundays and holidays, but they have no daily service... The chaplain however goes in and out amongst them in their several workshops.

They are under excellent control and very respectful in their manner to their superiors. The best among them are promoted and have superintendence over the others... There were two or three decent looking boys and men, but on the whole I never saw such a desperate looking set of ruffians.

Tonight we have been to the theatre and have seen a very stupid play, not very well acted. We were in the Trenor's box with the young men. We went to see the casino which is very comfortable and snug. They only pay $1 a month.

I have had two nice, comfortable letters from my dear Louisa. She is going to leave Bilbao on the 16th for San Sebastian…I had also a letter from Antony (*his brother Antony Gibbs of Merry Hill*) giving a good account from *my youngest brother* Robert. *My brother* Charles is I am sorry to say to sail on Wednesday from Plymouth to the Cape. I am very sorry not to be home to see him off.

Sunday 11th December 1853, Valencia.

While we were at breakfast Mr Aparici, father of poor Ramon Aparici our clerk who has just died, and the director of the Fabrica de Tabaco here called on us and sat a long while – a man full of talk, a great egoist and very conceited – but his conversation was very amusing and much of it very much to the point and very clever. Then came Trenor with his youngest son, Ricardito, and in an excellent Tartana with windows all round, four wheels and three horses like a Coburg… We went to Lake Albufera, the only one in Spain, and round about there some time – spending our time very pleasantly in the nice weather we have had. The rice lands are so overflowed in consequence of the continual rains that it is impossible to say when the lake begins and the land ends. There is plenty of waterfowl, and good fishing and shooting. The view of the mountains in the background is charming. When we came back we went round to the Gras, the port of Valencia, where they are making a new harbour, and walked about there for an hour enjoying the view of the Mediterranean. Then back by railway – an eight minute journey – in time for a walk on the Alameda where Matthews joined us. We went to dine with Trenor. At Trenor's we met a Colonel Pratt, his father in law, Captain Biedman, John's friend, a very nice fellow, Mr Duke, Colonel Lafuente and another engineer officer. They played Tresillo in the evening and we watched them, and no doubt got some knowledge of the game. Home here by 10.45.

Monday 12th December 1853, Valencia.

In the morning we went with Don Guillermo Matthews to see the Lonja de Seda , a most beautiful Gothic Hall with twisted pillars reaching the ceiling; and then the Church opposite of the Santos Juanes; where in the chapel there is a very good picture by Juanes of the Coronation of the Blessed Virgin Mary – the face beautiful. The priest was administering the Communion to the laity as we came in. No words were said to each other than Corpus Domini, and Uncle William remarked on the irreverence of the mode of administration. It certainly seemed so and always I find the same when I see Edward Vaughan at Wraxall, doing precisely the same thing. Yet that never displeases Uncle William but rather he approves of it. In that prejudice has no little weight I think. Afterwards we went to Trenors and chose divers mantuas, I buying one for Forbes and one for Uncle Joseph and two for myself – Uncle William one for himself, one for someone else and one for James; and John one for Barnes and one for Aunt Harriett. They are to follow us and also some Turran we have bought. Then we visited the Fabrica de Tabaco where Mr Aparici shewed us all that was to be seen, and afterwards overwhelmed us with cigars which we don't know what to do with. After calling on Mrs Aparici, and Mrs Ferras, a friend of Uncle William's, we went out to Villanesa Trenor's fabrica where I was much interested in the process of winding the silk; and also a most capital dinner of pollo con arroz and many other things which he gave us. On our return we found a letter from Louisa and one from Mary Crawley. I have written to Louisa to go tomorrow.

We have had tea at the Trenor's and I have played a hand at Tresillo, Biedman kindly instructing me. I won at Ochavos 6 Reals.

We went for an hour or so to the theatre, and saw "Los Zelos de un Corazon noble", a most atrocious play, and as stupid as it was immoral. We had been today to the British Vice Consul's and had signed a power before him for the sale of the South Sea Stock standing in Davy's and my name, so I wrote a line to Hayne sending it.

Thursday 15th December 1853, Madrid, Fonda de la Bizcayna.

Here we are again in our old quarters after a long and bad journey, not a little tired and ready to go to bed after our tea. Therefore I shall write no more tonight except to say that we have arrived at ten minutes to eleven p.m. instead of at 6 a.m.

Friday 16th December 1853, Madrid.

It rained most part of Monday and all Tuesday, the day we started, so that the roads were in the worst possible state which was the cause of our being so late. We left Valencia at half past six by the Diligence of the "Generales" and arrived at….Cuenca at 10.50 p.m. the following day, where I wish we had thought of asking the Mayoral to stay the night, for he would have done so if we had wished and spoken about it in time. However we started at 12.55 a.m. and reached Madrid at 10.50 p.m. and got ourselves to bed by half past twelve and have had a comfortable night's sleep. This was a longer journey than our former one and perhaps a worse one; but that was probably only on account of the rains, for I suppose now the stage between Olmedilla and Motilla would be almost impassable…..The Diligences on this road by Cuenca have never yet been upset. They are stronger and broader than the others; otherwise I think we must have been overturned in some parts.

At Requena (1.30 to 2.45 p.m.) we stopped for a while and made some tea in a tea pot we had bought, and with some excellent milk Mrs Trenor had given us, which we enjoyed very much. Two gentlemen who came into the inn apparently for shelter told us how bad we should find the road, but congratulated us on being on this rather than the other road. At Minglanilla (9.05 p.m. to 12.20 a.m.) to which we got without any difficulty, the road being tolerable, we had otro tanto (*a further amount*) of tea, and as the coach stopped about three hours so as to go on with the same horses, John and I laid down on the only beds there were of the host and hostess, and had a comfortable sleep for an hour, Uncle William doing the same but preferring a chair. However the beds were very clean. Then we started and our troubles began. The roads were execrable, and when we had reached as far as Puebla (3.30 a.m. to 7.15 a.m.), two leagues off we were awakened out of our uneasy sleep by finding the carriage irrecoverably stuck in the mud! We had therefore to walk about 200 yards to the village and take refuge in a cottage and sit in the chimney thereof till daylight, when the people dug and tugged the carriage out and we got on as far as Campillo (9.30 a.m. to 10.20 a.m.), where we breakfasted sumptuously on a dozen eggs and some tea, sitting in the chimney of another little venta (*country inn*); and went on warned that after Almodovar (2.00 p.m.) we should have the worst part of the road on the mountain called El Pinar, which as the name betokens is a pine forest, and although on the way there we thought nothing could surpass the badness of the road, which was…almost impassable mud, we found our mistake when we arrived, for although there had been a track, there was really no road, and by night we could not possibly have ventured. As it was light there was no danger, though it seemed that the only thing that could account for us not upsetting was that the coach couldn't do it. After we got out of this we came on to the Camino Real and beyond a few bumps and thumps…when the road was nearly as bad as the Pinar….we arrived at our journey's end safely. We had most lovely weather on Wednesday night at Cuenca (10.50 p.m. to 12.55 a.m.), where we had our tea. We walked out to the astonishment of the natives (who thought us mad) to see the city by moonlight, but fearful of detaining the Mayoral, we did not go quite up the hill nor see the Cathedral which I much regret. We did see the Puente de San Pablo which connects the cliff on which the town is built with the one on the other side of the river. It is a lovely bridge of about seven immensely lofty stone arches and is altogether the most picturesque I ever saw. The town is beautifully situated, perched on a high pointed rock surrounded by the river – much as Toledo is – only more compact, more on a peak and so more striking at the first view.

We were to have supped at Tarancon, if we had arrived there as we ought on Wednesday night, but as we did not arrive till Thursday at one o'clock, we proposed taking our breakfast – again on eggs and chocolate and under a cottage chimney at 10.25 a.m. at Alcazar. Notwithstanding the poverty and dirt of the place, we got very good fare, and particularly some excellent light biscuits, which the women called bizcochos de Canela…..We dined well in the carriage, and then finished our journey by the light of a lovely moon.

This morning we went to O'Shea's and sat in his room to read over our letters. I had 5 from my dear wife, giving a very good account of everyone but not a little perplexing our plans by proposing that I should leave the Correo on Tuesday morning and go to Bilbao to fetch them. I should like to have gone there and especially to have accompanied her on her journey, which I do feel somewhat anxious about considering her state, but if I did go now we could not possibly go to Pau by Xmas, and I have been a pagan here long enough to be very sorry if I should miss going to church on Christmas Day. The only plan would be to stay at Bilbao for Christmas, and that would be bad for William in respect of Isabel Clark, whom by the bye Louisa describes as a sweet pretty innocent girl. What a pity William can't have her! But it would be madness – poor as they would be. (*William never married and died at Belmont, in 1860, at the age of 30.*)….Uncle William had a letter from Blanche, one from Hayne and a delightful one from Aunt Harriett with a good account of our dear little boy (*Vicary*) . Thank God for that! …. We have had little time for anything today beyond answering our letters, but we have called on the Osmas, O'Sheas and Achavals. The Osmas have just arrived posting (by Mail Coach) from Paris which they accomplished perfectly. Tonight we have been to the O'Sheas and played at Whist, and to the Achavals and played at Tresillo. Mary's and Louisa's mantillas are most beautiful. Soulé, the Yankee Ambassador, whom we had met with at Bayonne, and who had made himself notorious by an audacious speech about Cuba just before he was sent home – so audacious that it is astonishing that this government received him – has now again been making himself notorious, and moreover a fool here. Don Modesto told us tonight that he, originally a Frenchman and a violent republican, was a barber in the "Havannah", and was afterwards naturalised in the U.S.A. When we were in Madrid before, we heard the story. It seems that he and his wife and son came to the French Minister to an evening party, Mrs Soulé being very strangely dressed. The Duke of Alba remarked to a friend in Spanish, "How oddly that woman is dressed. What a Guy!" Young Soulé turned round and said, "Sir, what do you mean by that? Do you know that lady is my mother?" "I did not know it, Sir, but you must be aware that Mrs Soulé is strangely dressed. At any rate I had no intention of offending you." "Yes you had – Wait a minute." He then went to his father and said, "You must fight him", and accordingly young Soulé insulted the Duke provoking a challenge, and saying, "I am very glad that I a republican have this opportunity of giving a lesson to a Spanish Grandee."

What a thoroughly vulgar speech – a saying of a parvenu of low and brutal mind. The Duke the next morning still expressed his readiness to have the affair settled peaceably and his regret at having unintentionally wounded Soulé's feelings. Soulé declared that sufficed – he had got all he wanted, and should now publish the story and the correspondence in every paper in the U.S.A. This he has done, and in so offensive a way that when it came to the Duke's ears there seemed no remedy but a challenge. Accordingly they fought the other day with swords for three quarters of an hour, and no one being wounded, they separated – not however before Soulé had promised to return all the Duke's letters and to publish a contradiction in the papers. He had talked very valiantly about their fighting till one should fall; yet on the ground he asked three times to be allowed to rest to which the Duke very good naturedly consented. Now Soulé, the father, had written to Turgot, the French Ambassador, before the duel to say that he should hold him responsible for any evil consequences which might result from the duel, because forsooth it took its origin in his house! And accordingly he has challenged him! Turgot referred him to Lord Howden, saying he was an old man and a man of peace, but still, if pressed, he would do what was right. I hear tonight that they are to fight, but that Soulé has begged to delay till Sunday that he may practise a little with his pistol!! It seems quite a farce, but no man ever deserved chastisement better than Soulé. He and his son appear to be pests of society, and I hope they will be punished with their own tools. His hostility to Turgot has something political in it. There is another quarrel on foot. Perry, one of the American attachés, a nice sort of young man, had to take one of Soulé's letters to Turgot, and a friend of the latter, a Frenchman, had some words with him, and finally put him out of the room by the shoulders. There's a pretty enredo (shady affair, mess) – and altogether a nice piece of gossip to sit up till one o'clock to write. We slept more comfortably on our late journey; for as the wind was from the North West, we had it just in our teeth in the coupé and suffered greatly from the cold – so that we transferred ourselves to the interior, and having six places for three and putting our legs up and enveloping them in our cloaks, rugs and mantas (blankets), we managed to make ourselves very comfortable.

Saturday 17th December 1853, Madrid.

We find it difficult to go on with our sightseeing as we have many preparations to make for our journey, however we managed to be at the Museum for two of three hours and looked thoroughly over the remainder of the Spanish School, and the Flemish and Dutch Schools…We called on Lord Howden – not in – also on Middleton

131

whom we saw and sat a while with. Also on the Achavals, and saw Doña Transitu and Don Domingo. They were to ask the price of the Murillo belonging to Mr Espelosin (*Doña Francisca's landlord*) but they found the poor man had just died! We amused ourselves – Uncle William buying sweetmeats, and I books at Cuestas. He is to pack up all those I don't want and send them to Cadiz.

In the Gallery we met Bland (Myer's partner) and his wife and sister in law – nice pleasant women who understood and enjoyed the pictures…After dinner we went to O'Shea's and played "Twenty One", John winning 11 Reals and I losing one!

Soulé has shot Turgot in the knee! The practice will be his punishment from someone sooner or later. I am sorry to say there is now a quarrel between Lord Howden and Count Esterhazy, the Austrian Ambassador, who were the French ambassador's seconds, and it is said they are to fight. Lord Howden too is a married man…..

Sunday 18th December 1853, Madrid.

Had prayers before breakfast, and went afterwards to call on the Ashavals. Don Nicolas gave me a book called Figaro, and Don M. Riesco promised to enquire about Espelosin's picture. Then to O'Shea's to call on Owens. Yesterday's mail brought…a letter for Uncle William from Blanche and one from Uncle George, and today's mail has brought one of the 16th *from Louisa* still speaking of my going to Bilbao….

Don Modesto Cortaza called. We have dined with O'Shea, and met Mrs Xifra y Casas, whose husband Uncle William knew years ago. They live apart. She is like Mrs Herman Merivale. The others of the party were the Austrian Secretary of Legation and Baron d'Anethe , the Belgian – both very nice fellows especially the latter – and O'Shea's two sons.

There is no truth in the story about Lord Howden. John and I spent an hour in the Museum today and mean to go tomorrow if possible. We also had a warm bath.

Monday 19th December 1853, Madrid.

We are now just getting ready for our start at six by the Correo, and are going to take our farewell dinner of Garbanzos (chick peas). This morning we made our farewell visit to O'Shea, and sat with him and Don Tomas Owens a long while, finally arranging our accounts with them, Then we went to the Achavals to bid them good bye, which took up most of the morning. However we had time for a Farewell walk round the Museum, and to call on Mrs Osma in their old house, and afterwards on Osma in his new one in the Palacio Villahermosa. The French post has not come in yet and I don't suppose it will in time for us to get it.

Wednesday 21st December 1853, Bilbao, Fonda de Bilbao.

Here I am after all, where I had no intention of finding myself, but at Vitoria I had notice from the man who came for our passports that the carriage with all the family was at the inn. All the family however proved to be only *my brother* William who had come for me with Heros's carriage and after a little consideration John determined to come with me – not liking to be away from us at Xmas, and considering that it is now impossible that we should spend the winter at Pau.

We were very sorry to let Uncle William go on by himself, but there was no remedy. I find my dear wife looking pretty well, but very thin. I hope she will now with better spirits get better health. *My sister* Mary is very well and William too – the latter tells me he cannot deny being "smitten" for the lady is really he says quite worthy of it, but that there is nothing more but a smite for in his circumstances it would be quite absurd that there should be. He does not seem in very low spirits, but Louisa says he is sometimes. The children are well, so that I may consider my journey to have been successful and happy throughout. Thank God for it! However till we are out of Spain we can't call it ended. We are to go pasada mañana (*at last tomorrow*). Gabriel, the courrier, seems a decent enough sort of man – much more active than Goldschmidt. We have not yet heard of Jane's arrival out (*in England*). Joseph has been behaving quite well since she went.

We left Madrid at 6.00 p.m. and reached Burgos at 7.40 p.m. the following day. We arrived at Vitoria at 10.10 a.m. today, and here John and I branched off – starting after our breakfast, at 12 o'clock, and Uncle William at 10.55 a.m. He should have reached San Sebastian at 9.40 p.m. We passed through a most lovely country especially the descent of the pass called Puerto, the beauty perhaps heightened by the contrast with the ugliness we had passed in our travels through Spain, but it seemed as beautiful as any scenery I had ever seen. We dined in the carriage at the top of the hill and stopped for our first halt at half past five. There were some ill looking or rather wild looking fellows rather drunk at the Venta, and some of them miqueletes or rural policemen. I was glad to get out of their company and proceed on our way, when in about three hours, darkness and a nap brought us safe here by about a quarter to ten. The rooms seem very comfortable, but I being very sleepy can say no more about them.

Thursday 22nd December 1853, Bilbao.

The children all look pretty well, and I thought dear Louisa well in the morning, but tonight her head aches violently and I am quite shocked to see how pale and thin she looks. After looking at the mantillas, which have pleased Louisa and Mary much, we walked out to pay visits. I liked Mrs Barry, the ladylike young wife of the Vice Consul, and her aunt Miss Heron, Mrs Ansell also, and her two daughters are nice people, but not of the first class. The girls understand English but speak only Spanish. Carolina is going to see a married sister in Hampstead – Mrs

133

Lancaster. Then we went to the Clarks, who live above our rooms. Mr Clark is vulgar in speech but pleasing in manner and hearty – I should say a gentleman in conduct and feeling – Mrs Clark disagreeable in manner and vulgar; clipping the Queen's English too much to be ladylike. We have been out for a walk with the girls this afternoon and have had them down here tonight to play "Vingt et Un" with us. Mary Anne good natured and not unpleasing – Isabel exceedingly pretty – a beautiful companion and most agreeable. Both girls have apparently had very little education, and what they have had, not of the best, and I should think a Bilbao life none of the best for a young girl. But they are clever especially Isabel, who is but 17, and are capable of education, and it surprises me not to see the little harm that Bilbao life and education and somewhat vulgar parents have done her. She and her sister too appear very innocent and artless ladylike girls, and if they neglect the "h" sometimes it is as Spaniards. In short I am not surprised at William falling in love with her. I should have done the same thing were I in the same place except that Mrs Clark might have acted as an antidote – a remedium amoris. He has behaved very well indeed – paying her no more attentions than he ought – but he is grievously dull tonight after the leave taking. We go tomorrow.

I have had our bill (it is too large to pay) and it does not surprise me – no less than 17,288 Reals! For five weeks and five days. I remonstrated with the landlady, but she said everything was so very dear that she had to charge so much to make her fair profit. So may it be.

Friday 23rd December 1853, Vergara, Parada de las Postes.

This morning I sent up to Mr Clark who was so good as to come down to see us off, and also to promise to pay the Bill for us, drawing on Antony Gibbs and Sons for the amount. We started at 9 o'clock, amid an admiring crowd, and with handkerchiefs waved at us from the upper windows, which did not tend to make William a very lively companion to me on the dicky (seat) for the first twenty minutes; but on talking to him I found him disposed to be partly philosophical and what was of more consequence to set to work at something, and if he could not find employment in England to seek it in America….. If it really persuades him to endeavour to employ himself, this will have been a fortunate encounter for him. Moreover she really is a very nice girl, and if he could keep a wife would be a good one for him.

Our journey, though the day has been miserable, has been most beautiful. It is a land of mountains and bridges – most picturesque bridges they are too – generally only wide enough for two foot passengers, yet of massive construction. We stopped to dine at Elorio, a curious town with apparently a small inner town entered by gates. Over one was, I think, the Coat of Arms of the Emperor Charles V. We went into the Church, an ill shaped building with a huge handsome gilt retable over the high altar….We had brought food with us, and got there, in the very decent venta (*country inn*), from the civil mistress thereof, excellent Rioja wine, cherry jelly or sweetmeat, and some maize bread called borona which was like a good batter pudding. Also we got in a shop some excellent sponge cake – such as we should not have expected to find in so poor a place. There is a good deal of architectural and heraldic ornament about the town. We arrived at Vergara at about half past five and have comfortable rooms in one of the best inns in Spain (which is not saying much) and have had a very good supper.

Saturday 24th December 1853, Fonda Nueva, San Sebastian.

This morning we meant to have started at a quarter past eight notwithstanding the rain which came down in torrents, but poor dear Louisa is so very poorly that I feared we could not go at all. Still the want of a doctor there and the knowledge that we should find a tolerable one here made us press on, and as she felt herself somewhat better we started at 9.45 and arrived here at about seven or rather before. Thank God without any evil consequences, either from the journey or from the illness. I am very glad I was with them for I am quite sure that they would neither have got away so well from Bilbao without me nor have gone through this journey without my help…We enjoyed the journey very much after she began to get more comfortable. The scenery was quite Tyrolean, the hills studded everywhere with cottages; and a village or town in every dip of the mountains. What a contrast to Castille! The snow lay thick on the ground on the steep pass between Vergara and Villareal. We reached Villareal at 11.20 a.m., Villafranca at 1.00 p.m. and Tolosa at 2.40 p.m. At Tolosa we dined tolerably well at the Parador de las Diligencias, and waited there for about an hour. Here we had tea and an omelette – the people were very glad to see us.

Nurse is I am sorry to say very poorly with diarrhoea…We have called in Doctor Passements, a very nice looking old gentleman who speaks French, Spanish and English, and he says she must be carefully tended tomorrow and even then will hardly be able to move on Monday. Uncle William left Blanche's Mantilla and three letters for Louisa from me, and one for me from her sent by O'Shea – and a basket of Manteca de Prevalè (a variety of butter or lard).

Sunday 25th December 1853, Christmas Day, Fonda Nueva, San Sebastian.

Nurse still very poorly and her doctor who has been twice today says we must not go tomorrow, and perhaps not the next day. William, John and I went after our service to the Military Mass, which is very grand. I then after luncheon took a nice walk up the citadel hill with Louisa, and then a long hard walk up the opposite hill with the watch-tower on it. It took us

35 minutes from the foot to the top, hard walking, and about 5 minutes coming straight down, instead of by the circuitous paths. They gave us a tolerable good dinner

Monday 26th December 1853, San Sebastian.

Nothing new today. Nurse is better and wished us to go on but the doctor advised our staying till tomorrow....John and I wrote to Uncle William. We all took a nice walk over the bridge and on the beach, and have played a game at whist with Spanish cards making tens out of the eights of another pack.

Thursday 27th December 1853, Hôtel des Ambassadeurs, Biarritz.

After paying our bill and breakfasting comfortably, nurse being better, we started at 10 and came with four horses to each carriage, paying therefore $40 in full, through the lovely country lying between this town and San Sebastian in 6 hours and a little more – having very fine weather till the end of our journey, when it began to hail. It is now blowing great guns as it does here I believe all through the winter. We were stopped about 26 minutes at Irun not only having to present permission for our carriages – Mr Aguinaja facilitating the matter for us – but also to get a permiso for the horses, which took an additional 20 minutes...We also stayed another 20 minutes at Behobié to have our luggage examined. The officers found nothing to tax except John's prints, and my Manta which they ignorantly said was new though I had worn it or rather used it 20 times. However one wiser than the rest found out their mistake. We arrived here at half past three, finding nothing prepared; though Gabriel said he had written a letter which the people of the house denied having received.... However they soon got our old rooms ready and gave us an excellent dinner. Louisa has a cold. I posted my letter to Mary Crawley.

Wednesday 28th December 1853, Biarritz.

A beautiful day, but an evening full of snow and hail. We spent the day in going to Bayonne, and calling on Captain Grahame, Ignacio Garcia, and Bourdeux, and doing some little shopping. Did my accounts and played at whist. John and William rather poorly. Drew on Antony Gibbs and Sons in favour of Ellis and Co, and wrote to advise them thereof.

Thursday 29th December 1853, Hôtel de l'Europe, Pau.

One would think we were at the North Pole instead of in the South of France. Never have I felt it colder in England certainly than it has been today and never I think so cold in the house as I am at this moment opposite a large wood fire. This inn is not of the best though we have three large fine rooms – they are full of cold and smoke, and there is no egress from the centre room except through the others. Mary is in it – the children in our outer one and we in the others. We have no sitting room as our bedroom should be the salon so we have dined in a miserably cold salle à manger off a dinner not too good. John and William have another small room. When we awoke this morning the ground was covered with snow, and as it has been snowing more or less all day our journey has been exceedingly slow and not very comfortable. Our carriage has met with no mishap, but the horses of the other fell down several times. We left Biarritz at about a quarter past nine and reached Bayonne at about ten. We stayed there until 10.45 a.m. and bought some gloves and took leave of Bourdeux who met us at the post. At Peyrehorade we stayed at the Post House and ate our lunch, the woman giving us two bottles of wine for which she would take no payment. We reached this house in Pau at 8.40 p.m. making a nearly eleven hour journey of what should have been not more than seven.

Friday 30th December 1853, Pau.

We have made ourselves more comfortable in our rooms today, though they are very cold and the wind is howling dismally outside. Our room has become the sitting room and we have taken Mary's putting her in William's, and William and John in a nice room upstairs. We were not up till eleven when we breakfasted downstairs – two uncivil French gentlemen, as the custom of this once polite nation is, blocking up every inch of the fire from the ladies. Uncle William, Blanche, Miss M. and three of the young ones called, and we three men have dined in their very comfortable house – the Château Montfleury, about 2½ miles out. I have had nice letters from Aunt Charlotte and Mr Barnes; and John from Reginald Barnes and Antony – Louisa from Mrs Vaughan with a good account of Baby, and from Aunt George and Robert.

Saturday 31st December 1853, Pau.

Today has been a continual thaw and it is consequently much warmer tonight, though still very cold especially in our room. The papers today report Lord Palmerston's return to office, of which I am rather glad. We all dined at Montfleury at thee o'clock and came back at a quarter to five. Nurse was downstairs and seems better.

After all Uncle William will have his pictures and for less than I thought. He will have to pay $4200 and William's commission. He has got them very cheap and made an excellent negocio, and I am glad therefore he did not implicitly follow my advice. So ends eighteen hundred and fifty three. I trust next year may be a happy and satisfactory year and may be well spent by all of us.

Sunday 1st January 1854, Hôtel de l'Europe, Pau.

We went to church this morning at half past ten and were very glad to join again in the English service. It was pretty well done, and reverently. The only thing I did not like being the delivery of the bread and wine not to each separately, but to the whole "rail". This even was better done than generally in such cases e.g. at Wraxall. The excuse is want of time, and indeed as there is a second morning service at half past twelve, they

Figure 23. Panorama of the Pyrenees from the Château of Pau.

Figure 24. A diligence arriving in Pau.

did need to save as much time as they could. There were between seventy and eighty communicants. The time saved is very little, as so much time is lost while one party goes away and another comes to the altar. There is a complete thaw today, and it has been raining most of the time. I wrote a few lines in Uncle William's letter to Hayne.

Monday 2nd January 1854, Pau.

A fine day and very wet under foot. We all took a walk together after luncheon by the river. Uncle William, Blanche and Antony called just before Louisa had a letter from her mother giving a bad account of George Adams…..I wrote two French exercises.

Tuesday 3rd January 1854, Pau.

We called on the Bells and I took a walk with Louisa about the Castle Grounds which are very beautiful. Blanche called. Louisa wrote to her Spanish mistress, a lady who is the daughter of Don Martin de Bartolomé, now married to a Pole – Smolenski – and in great distress, her husband being gravely ill. She came today and gave her a lesson. She speaks French and English well and is a very nice person.

Wednesday 4th January 1854, Pau.

Louisa and I took a little walk in the gardens, but our time was chiefly occupied in a wool shop and a lace shop – more amusing to the ladies than to me. Mary called on the Miss Bells. William, John and I dined at Montfleury, and we walked back thorough the mud. We were to have come back with the William Gibbs in their carriage as they were going to a ball, but while we were at dinner a note came from the entertainer putting off the ball because of the death of poor Mr Tornis who was thrown from his horse yesterday and injured his spine. He died today leaving a widow here. What a sad death –"In the midst of life"! ….Mary had a note from Charles written just as his ship was about to sail. John and Mary had letters from Francis. Our baby had cut four teeth and was very well. The Chronicle and the Times both make now no doubt of immediate war with Russia!

Thursday 5th January 1854, Pau.

I woke this morning with a colicky sort of diarrhoea which though better now under the influence of Gregory's powder, lying in bed till two, and semi-starvation, is by no means well. The day has been lovely, and Louisa enjoyed her walk with William and Mary. William and John have been working hard at their French. Uncle William and Blanche came to call. James is better.

Friday 6th January 1854, Pau.

Better this morning, but I did not get up early. Uncle William and Lowe called, and Mary and I went up in the carriage to luncheon at Montfleury, and I walked back with William and John who walked up there. Uncle William has written to Williams and so have I. He is buying the pictures and I am offering $100 for the Complutensian Bible. (*The Bible is called Complutensian as the town where it was printed, Alcalà de Henares, is known as Complutum in Latin*). I see on looking back that I have not told him the truth exactly for I give its value at from £24 to £30 when well bound and in good condition; but not very far wrong. I don't expect to get it for $100. The letter is to go tomorrow.

Louisa and I did not go to church as I was not quite well. The others did. Tonight we had a game of cross questions and crooked answers which delighted Alban.

Saturday 7th January 1854, Pau.

This morning a note came from Uncle William enclosing Hayne's usual despatch in which he said he was suffering very much from his usual winter cough and found great difficulty in getting to his work every day so that he should be glad when I was once again at home, for that the work was too heavy to be all on Davy's shoulders; begging me however not to hurry. It was very evident however that it was my duty not to stay here any longer than was necessary to get our army in motion. I went up to and talked to Uncle William and we agreed that I should go to Eaux Bonnes leaving Louisa to get the things packed up, and that we should go on Thursday, and I wrote to Hayne to say so – adding however that owing to Louisa's health I could not be home for some time as our journey must needs be slow. On further consideration I have written to him again to night to say that we shall start on Wednesday, as a Thursday start would oblige us to stay two days in Bordeaux. I have also written to Coloma to take me rooms in the Hôtel de Paris for the 11th, and to Marco to take rooms in the Bristol for the 18th. Also I have written to George saying that Thursday's and Friday's letters could reach us at the Hôtel de l'Univers, Tours, and till the Saturday following at Marco's at Paris. I have also asked Hayne to discontinue our papers except the Guardian which might come to Tours and Paris; and Galignani to send his Wednesday paper to Bordeaux, Thursday to Angoulême and Friday and Saturday to Tours.

We are much disappointed at having to go for we like this place very much, and dear Louisa was I am sure gaining strength day by day.

Sunday 8th January 1854, Pau.

After sleeping upon it we have determined to give up Eaux Bonnes and go on Tuesday so I have altered the instructions to Santa Coloma, Hayne, George and Marco as above – only the latter two letters don't go till tomorrow. Uncle William had a letter from Doña Angela, whom (though I had quite forgotten) he had by my desires begged to make enquiries about Espelosin's San Antonio. The family ask 4500 Reals which is a great deal more than I would give. I have written to her today thanking her for making enquiries, and saying it was beyond my ideas. It is well that I should have thus got an idea of their pretensions, but it is a pity that with her and Riesco, I should have two enquirers in the field, who may hinder one another. I have written today to Don Nicolas de Achaval, telling him all about it, and begging him to let Don Manuel (*Williams*) know that he might go further than the 1000 Reals he spoke of – even as far if he needs as 2500. Uncle William, Blanche and Lowe came to luncheon after church, and Blanche stayed here till after Evening Church – she, Louisa, Mary and Uncle William having had a walk on the slopes while I was writing my letters. I had a headache and went for a walk with John – he by reason of his bad toe, wearing my gouty shoe.

The poor man who was killed the other day by a fall from his horse was Richard Torin, son of Dr Adams' old friend.

Monday 9th January 1854, Pau.

Most of this day has been occupied in packing and preparing for packing. They sent the carriage for us, and we went to Montfleury, to luncheon. Blanche came back in the carriage and Uncle William walked back with us. He had a letter from Hayne saying he was still poorly. Lowe had one from Uncle Joseph, saying the Bishop had told him he had heard from a member of the Government that war was considered inevitable. We might gather that from the papers…. I wrote to Mr Clifford at Madrid about some photographs of the pictures there. Mary and John called on the Bells. Miss Georgina Bell called here.

Tuesday 10th January 1854, Roquefort, Hôtel des Princes.

We started at 9.20 this morning from Pau and arrived at Roquefort at 5.15 p.m. We stopped at Aire for half an hour to eat our provisions, and poor Louisa got frightened by some horses which made her very uncomfortable for the rest of the day. The countryside is less ugly than between Bayonne and Bordeaux, having some redeeming hills and dales and winding roads.

John had a nice letter from Aunt Harriett with a good account of Baby. The day has been drizzly and rainy, but the afternoon tolerably fine. This is pretty comfortable for a village inn.

Wednesday 11th January 1854, Bordeaux, Hôtel de Paris.

We meant to start this morning at seven but could not get off till 7.20, and we arrived at this inn, *the Hôtel de Paris*, at 4.15 p.m. thus doing the whole 109 kilometres in 8 hours and 50 minutes which was pretty good going… Santa Coloma had taken us our old rooms, which have been altered and made very comfortable. I went at once to call on him and meet his wife and divers daughters, Mrs Sourget among the rest, who all went to call on Louisa, while I went and sat with old Mr Santa Coloma who gave me a good cigar, and has moreover brought me kindly a whole bundle of excellent ones. Heros called while I was there and has since been here and sat an hour, talking very agreeably. Mrs Heros is ill. Santa Coloma called here and did otro tanto (likewise), and with him, his son and Sourget. We played our usual game at Whist.

Thursday 12th January 1854, Angoulême, Hôtel des Postes.

I wrote a line to Uncle William before breakfast, and afterwards walked with Don Eugenio and his son and Heros. The latter sent his carriage for the ladies, and we left by the "train" at 11.04 and got here by 2.45 p.m., and to this hotel where we have bespoken rooms by 3.30 p.m. We were delayed by the trouble of getting our luggage and sending some part to Paris straight. Monsieur Dauriac gave us an excellent dinner, and we are going to bed in pretty good time....Before dinner William, John, Mary, Alban and I walked *along* the *town* walls and enjoyed the lovely view. We went also into the Cathedral, the restoration of the front of which is going very well; and into the new church which certainly is very pretty. It is a Gothic church with Romanesque ornament, especially about the porch. It looks within and without like an English church chiefly because as one walks up the nave only one altar is visible.

Friday 13th January 1853, Poitiers, Hôtel de France.

Before breakfast this morning William, John and I walked right round the walls, a sharp 35 minutes walk, very beautiful. We left the hotel at 10.00 to leave by the 10.10 train, but we were sorry to find that an electric telegraphic message had just been received to the effect that there would for some unexplained reason be two hours delay, and accordingly we did not get off until 12.15 p.m. nor arrive here until 3.20 p.m. Louisa was very tired with waiting, and with the bustle of getting into and out of a carriage which was too small for our own party, and she was so poorly in the train that I was quite alarmed, but she is now quite well again. Thank God. I am very glad we did not go on to Tours as the journey would have been certainly much too long.

William and I walked about the town after our arrival – saw the Promenade which is like the "Buen Retiro" in Madrid and very pretty, a church with a handsome Romanesque gate near the Place, the Court Yard of the Hôtel de Ville… and the Salle des Pas Perdus, a handsome kind of Westminster Hall used for the same purposes. I am quite surprised to see what a good town this is. There seem quite excellent shops in it. It is far better than I expected to see. Our inn here is very comfortable, the people civil, the fires plentiful and the fare good. At the station at Angoulême was a capital refreshment room where the children had a good dinner and we a good luncheon.

Saturday 14th January 1853, Tours, Hôtel de l'Univers.

After breakfast William, John and I went out to the market – lively and full of mob-caps – to see the beautiful Romanesque Church of Notre Dame de Poitiers, and visited it again afterwards with Louisa, Mary and Alban. The West Front is most picturesque – two little turrets flanking each corner something like a ball gable – only much richer. The general effect is like that of the churches in the north of Italy – covered with grotesque sculpture. The interior is painted all over – but coarsely… One regrets that they did not leave the shafts of the pillars their natural colour.

The aisles are very narrow but none the worse for that. We all went to the Salle des Pas Perdus which is certainly a fine handsome hall.... Before the ladies joined us we went to see the Cathedral, a very handsome church... Then we went to the very curious church of St Radegunda at the East end of the cathedral – very picturesque. We saw the tomb of the saint and bought a medal a piece..... We took the children in the omnibus to the station and gave them dinner there, but Alban would not eat. We started at 1.32 p.m. and just as we got to the station before this, Alban was violently ill with diarrhoea and vomiting and sent us all but Louisa and nurse out of the carriage. However he is pretty well again now. We arrived about 3.50 p.m. here, a little before our time, and, with John and William, I took a walk to the bridges and to the Cathedral.

Sunday 15th January 1854, Tours, Hôtel de l'Univers.

This morning Mary and John and I went to see the Chancellerie, Tristan l'Hermite's House and the other old houses mentioned by Murray, and this afternoon Louisa went the same round after attending vespers in the Cathedral. The service at the English Chapel was partly well performed, but we heard as silly a sermon from an Irishman as ever could have been preached..... Yesterday I had a letter from Hayne saying he was better, and one from Marco telling us that the rooms were taken at the Hotel Bristol. I have written today to the former and am writing to Uncle Joseph. Louisa has written to Blanche.

Monday 16th January 1854, Hôtel de l'Angleterre, Blois.

This morning William, John and I took a walk after breakfast, and went up the North Tower of the Cathedral, having been up the South Tower when we were here before. One ascends much higher on this as there is a small spiral staircase.... rising from the platform to which one ascends alone on the other *tower*. The day was very fine. Letters arrived from Uncle William, Mrs Adams, Antony and Aunt Harriett. We started at 11.42 and got here at four minutes past one, and set out almost immediately in a good carriage which we had bespoken from the hotel for the Château of Chambord – only stopping to buy some luncheon and to dispute with the superintendent about our tickets.... taken through for Paris...... which here they would not allow to serve for tomorrow's journey. Our drive by the Loire was very pretty. On the right bank of the river after passing Menans, is a village called Cour sur Loire, the church of which has a steeple exactly like that at Clifton Hampden. I did not like the first view of the Château as much as I expected. It is rather more curious than handsome – but it is nevertheless a grand building – and the façade opposite the little river is very handsome. It would have been better I think if the four conical domes finished in a point as a cone should do, instead of breaking off into skinny little bell turrets. The staircases are quite worth seeing – especially the double spiral one. I

143

think it is that mentioned in De Vigny's novel of "Cinq Mars". There were some interesting historical portraits – one of King Henry III – an evil looking wretch; one of Queen Christina of Sweden – as bad; and one of Marie Leczynska wife of Louis XV. She was I think the heroine of the "Cinq Mars", a pretty woman well painted; a little bronze statue of Henry V; a miniature Park of Artillery given by his grandfather Charles X. Altogether it was well worth seeing…. We got back here to dinner at seven and found Louisa not at all tired with a walk with Alban to the Cathedral. The inn is very comfortable, and our sitting room and bedroom quite handsome and in good taste.

Tuesday 17th January 1854, Hotel d'Orléans, Orléans.

All our morning was occupied in seeing the Château at Blois, which surpasses in interest any I ever saw except Windsor. One part of the building is said to date from the sixth century and the old Counts of Blois. Another something like Eton College or a very superior St James's Palace of the time of Louis XII, another wing and that the most beautiful is that of Francis I and his son Henry II, and Catherine de Medici. The fourth side was built by that ass Gaston d'Orléans, who destroyed the old wing, and much that was good about the others. The chimney pieces in Francis the First's part are very handsome, and as well the frescoed and painted and arabesqued walls are being beautifully restored in excellent taste. I think those I like best are the Oratory and bedroom of Catherine de Medici. There she died ten days after the murder of Henry of Guise, the victim no doubt as well of her astute and plotting brain, as of the fears of her son, Henry III. It is – or was then – an evil thing to be a king…. We saw the spot where he (*Henry of Guise*) fell – stabbed by the "forty five" to whom the King had given the dagger. We saw the prison where the Cardinal *de Lorraine*, his brother, was placed, and the spot where he too was killed the next morning, (*23rd and 24th December 1588*).

Gaston's wing had nothing worth seeing except some good carved ornament where a circular staircase should have been. In the other wing are two staircases something like the single one at Chambord. The man who took us over the principal part spoke most excellent French. No doubt this is the place to come and learn the language.

Louisa was delighted with the visit, and I am glad to say is not at all tired even with it and the journey and the walk here (*Orléans*) over the Cathedral which is externally handsome especially the great gabled porch with its three tall arched entrances. There is scarcely any painted glass – neither is there in the Cathedral at Blois where we went this morning. Alban was disproportionably pleased with the Château of Blois which has so excited him that I fear he is still awake thinking of it. After seeing it we went to the church of St Nicholas, a very handsome Gothic interior but horribly whitewashed and frightfully cold. The arches of the Aisle are very curious – each one differing from the other so as to produce a very curious effect.....We left Blois at 1.15 p.m. and arrived here at 2.35 p.m., and have very tolerable rooms, and have eaten a good lunch and had some tolerable tea. We went into the churches of St Paul and the Recouvrance… In the pillars of the first are inserted stamped leather Reliefs of the Passion – very well done.

Wednesday 18th January 1854, Paris, Hôtel Bristol.

We went out to see the Museum, wherein there were many pictures not worth much, and a good number of carvings in wood, stone and ivory which were rather interesting. The Hôtel de Ville wherein they are is a fine old building. We also saw the houses of Diana of Poitiers in the Rue Neuve, of Agnes Sorel, and of Joan of Arc in the Rue Tabourg and of the Duchesse d'Etampes in the Rue de la Recouvrance. Joan of Arc's was not hers but Jacques Bouchier's where she lodged, and the existing rooms are in fact only buildings of the 16th century or so with handsome carved ceilings, on the same site as those occupied by her. We saw the Church of St Paterne and St Peter, and went in search of that of St Aignan, but instead came on that of St Euverte with a pretty Rose Window, and tracery in the West Door. It seems now unused.

We left *Orléans* at 2.45 and arrived here through a dense fog at about a quarter to six, and got to the hotel at half past. Our suite of rooms (at 50 francs) is most comfortable. I find letters from Hayne saying he is much better, George and Georgiana giving a sad account of her husband's state. Mary has a bad sore throat.

Thursday 19th January 1854, Paris, Hôtel Bristol.

This morning brought letters from the Poste Restante, from Aunt George, Francis and Mrs Williams – the latter giving a good account of baby, whose four teeth are quite through with four others showing signs of coming. John wrote to Francis and I to Hayne saying we should perhaps delay a little. We were most of the morning among bootmakers and tailors. John, William and I lunched at the Trois Frères – called on Marco and got the address of a good livery stable at Borrel, 37 Rue Neuve des Mathurins, and of the best Bronze Shop, Raingo, 102 Rue Vieille du Temple. The Marcos called here in the afternoon. We all went to the Louvre and walked through the Gallery. The Conception by Murillo is a charming picture, but I certainly don't like it so well as that at Madrid. We only took a general view, but hope to go more particularly through all the rooms. Mary's throat is still bad and she has stayed in today. We three men went to the opera and were delighted with the Italiana in Algeria (*Rossini*) – Marietta Alboni (*contralto*) and Giorgio Ronconi (*baritone*) sang, and a tenor whom I had never heard, but whose singing I liked very much – Bartolini.

Figure 25. The Trois Frères Restaurant, Paris.

Figure 26. The Art Gallery in the Louvre.

Friday 20th January 1854, Paris, Hôtel Bristol.
I went out before breakfast and hired a very good carriage for 20 francs a day. We have been all through the galleries of Antiquaries at the Louvre, and again into the picture galleries. We took the servants and Alban – the

latter was much pleased with the sculptures. Afterwards we went to the bronzes and bought a few for presents, also to the Palais Royal and got some little things there, and also to Jean Marie Farina's and bought Eau de Cologne. Mary's throat is better though she suffers just now from a tiresome long visit of a most fatiguing doctor, and particularly from his having causticked her throat. Lowe and little Antony (*William and Blanche's son, aged 12, probably on his way back to school*) arrived looking very well.

Saturday 21st January 1854, Paris, Hôtel Bristol.

This morning Louisa and Mary, who is better, went out shopping, and I stayed at home and wrote to Uncle William, Leathwaite, Antony and Francis. We went to the Louvre and visited the China Room and the pictures again and after luncheon to the Luxembourg where the Gallery is not worth seeing – though there are two or three good pictures – one of the last days of the Reign of Terror struck me a good deal.

This evening, all but Louisa have dined at the Marcos, and have been to the funniest play (or spectacle) that I ever saw. I have laughed more I think than I did at my first pantomime. I had a letter from Hayne confirming the good account of his health and saying it could be no inconvenience whatever my staying a week or a fortnight....The Riveros have called here and have asked us to dinner on Wednesday. I have accepted.

Sunday 22nd January 1854, Paris, Hôtel Bristol.

After church at half past eleven this morning Louisa and John and I went to call on the Riveros and were very kindly received by them. He has given us a host of permissions for various things. We came home for luncheon and then I went with John to call on Rosales, Generals Blanco and Santa Cruz, and Costas, of whom we found only the latter at home. Then Mary, Louisa, Alban and I went for a drive in the Bois de Boulogne and saw the Empress *Eugénie*. Lowe and Antony dined with us, and we had a vol-au-vent of frogs. They are like delicate, tender chicken with scarcely any taste. Louisa has written to Aunt Harriett, George, Aunt George Crawley, and I to Charles – all to go to England by Lowe tomorrow. Alban has fallen down against the table and given himself a terrible black eye. We at last have a tolerably fine day.

Monday 23rd January 1854, Paris, Hôtel Bristol.

Today the fog has been thicker than ever – really as yellow as in London in November. I wrote to Uncle William. We made an expedition, as when we were last here, to the Louvre, only to be turned back with the information that it was always closed on Mondays, so we went instead to Sèvres and enjoyed the sight of the China Works very much. We bought a few things – some for presents and a vase for ourselves. We were obliged to leave Alban as his cold was too bad for him to leave the house. This evening William, John and I have been to the Opéra Comique and have heard the "Nouveau Seigneur", and the first act of "Marco Spada". Louisa is not at all tired with her exertions. She has given Alban some of Dr William's medicine.

Tuesday 24th January 1854, Paris, Hôtel Bristol.

He is better today, but still the cough is bad, so that he has not been allowed to go out. I wish Louisa had not either for she woke with a slight sore throat, and has I am afraid increased it by going out after luncheon. We went to the Louvre twice and saw the Naval Museum there and walked hastily through the drawings and prints. What a pity that the grand collection of prints which is in the British Museum should not be open to the public, and that beautifully arranged as these are! I hope when they build the National Gallery they will provide for this… At the Théatre Français I met Hankey, who was in the stall just in front of us. We saw "The Caprice" very well acted, and four acts of "La Pierre de Touche".

Louisa had a short note from Antony saying that Baby was cutting his sixth tooth. John had a letter from Francis saying, amongst other things that it was reported that Mr Pott, the Bishop's chaplain and an excellent man – Rector of Cuddesden – was very much at Clifton Hampden, and that people did say very much with Milly. Love gone to Pot!

I think John has got over his love, but it makes him nevertheless rather dull, poor fellow. He and William went buying tortoiseshell snuff boxes, and I to keep them company bought a niello one. Moreover I bought a Rhinoceros horn staff. It is certainly not a stick nor a cane. I must call it a baton. I have managed to catch cold also. The weather has not been foggy but it has rained hard tonight. Mrs Marco called.

Wednesday 25th January 1854, Paris, Hôtel Bristol.

General Blanco called here and saw Louisa. Louisa's throat still rather sore, but as the day has been remarkably fine she went with us to the Gobelin where we were much entertained in the ateliers of the tapestry; and also to the Hôtel de Cluny, a beautiful old house, used as a Mediaeval Museum where there is a great deal worth seeing. Louisa has stayed at home, while we have spent a pleasant evening with the Riveros. We met the Marcos, Mr and Mrs Baleazar (she the daughter of General San Martin, *the Liberator of Argentina, Chile and Peru*) and their two daughters, all speaking English excellently, and a Spaniard, Mr Olivares. Dinner very well served. Little Natividad Rivero is grown a fine tall girl of a very pleasing expression.

Thursday 26th January 1854, Paris, Hôtel Bristol.

We occupied this morning shopping, we getting a little more china, and Mary a ball dress. In the afternoon we went to the tomb of Napoleon in the Church of Les Invalides under the Dome – a very handsome sarcophagus of porphyry, surrounded by statues of white marble. Then we took a drive in the Champs Elysés and saw the Emperor well (*Napoleon III*), and leaving Louisa to go home went up the Arc d'Etoile, and enjoyed the view therefrom. Then a walk to the Palais Royal where George bought a stick for Uncle George. Tonight we have been dining with Marco and going to the Opéra Comique, where we have been beautifully pleased with "Les Papillottes de Monsieur Benoit", and "Les Noces de Jeannot".

Friday 27th January 1854, Paris, Hôtel Bristol.

This morning brought a letter for me from Uncle William and one for John from Uncle Joseph, the latter announcing Milly's engagement to Mr Pott, the Vicar (not the Rector) of Cuddesden. We went to the Louvre in the morning, and Louisa, John and I again to Sèvres in the afternoon to buy two little vases for Aunt Harriett and Uncle George, as we had transferred those we bought yesterday to Milly. We have dined at home today and played Whist. I wrote to Uncle William.

Saturday 28th January 1854, Paris, Hôtel Bristol.

Went to bed last night and woke this morning with a bad cold, which I have industriously made worse today, in the first place by going to Notre Dame, and in the second by going to the Grand Ball at the Hôtel de Ville. Went to the Bibliothèque but found the only days were Tuesday and Friday. William and John went for a walk and I to the Louvre.

After lunch we went to Notre Dame (observing the Hôtel de Ville on our road, which is a grand building). Admired the West Front of Notre Dame very much. The inside "no vale gran cose" (*is not worth much*), but there are some good monuments – especially one of the Duke of Harcourt by Pygale, representing a dream of the Duchess. The anatomy of the dying man is very good.

I never saw such magnificent rooms as in the Hôtel de Ville, and the Ball (to which we went with the Riveros, and where we met and accompanied the Marcos) was very handsome and well worth going to. There was an English beauty there like one of Beato Angelico's angels. Mary was very nicely dressed – as well as anyone. As we went under Rivero's wing we did not have to have la Cola (the queue), which was very agreeable and we were not ten minutes going there instead of two or three hours as some were. Louisa has still a bad cold and poor Alban's cough is by no means well. He did not go to sleep till a quarter to twelve tonight.

Saturday 29th January 1854, Paris, Hôtel Bristol.

I have passed most of the day in bed suffering from my bad cold and from colic.

Sunday 30th January 1854, Boulogne, Hôtel des Bains.

We left Paris by the 9 o'clock train and arrived here without accident at half past two, my cold being better generally….John and William stay in

Paris, intending to leave Wednesday night. I am afraid we shall not be in England much before them, for the wind is blowing great guns and it would not be right for Louisa to attempt to cross except in a moderately calm sea.

Tuesday 31st January 1854, Dover, Lord Warden Hotel.
Here we are at last on English ground – quite safe though rather sick even now with the remains of our dreadful passage. The wind had lulled in the morning, and the good report of everyone made us not fear to start, but besides the swell from yesterday's storm the breeze freshened almost immediately, and we had a regular storm and were all as ill as could be…

Thursday 2nd February 1854, Frognal.
Here we are safe again in our own house – thanks to God for his merciful care of us throughout our long journey… William and John came this morning at 5 o'clock having had a 2½ hours passage, and a very rough one, and came with us in the 8 o'clock train.

Belmont, Frognal and Tyntesfield

Friday 18th May 1855, Belmont.
I spent most of the day walking about with Uncle William and talking with him and Uncle George. The Tyntesfield folk dined here.

Sunday 20th May 1855, Belmont.
Uncle William and Blanche dined here yesterday.

Tuesday 22nd May 1855, Belmont.
William and I walked with Uncle William to and over Charlton – a very pretty place and park. The house old with a good hall. It will be a capital dower house, or a place for a dower house, or for Antony (William Gibbs' son) when he marries some ten years hence. Then after lunch Louisa and William and I walked about Tyntesfield. Devéria's pictures of Uncle William and Blanche are very good.

Wednesday 23rd May 1855, Frognal.
After going to Tyntesfield and having a long talk with Blanche, and after luncheon, Louisa, William, Miss Vaughan, Milly and I started by the afternoon Express, Milly and her Aunt stopping at Bath.

Saturday 11th August 1855, Belmont.
Francis, Louisa and I left London this morning by the morning Express Train and came here by about two, leaving Francis at Tyntesfield on our way. Antony (Henry Hucks' brother) seems a lot better and took a walk with me up the West Hill.

Sunday 12th August 1855, Belmont.
After church and dinner I went down to Tyntesfield and took a long walk with Blanche round the grounds and afterwards with Louisa and Kate walked back to Tyntesfield.

Monday 13th August 1855, Frognal.

James took a photograph of me, John and Francis together and another of me, John and Blanche, but Blanche's and John's in each picture were failures. We came back by the Express and found the children well except Alban who has a stye. Uncle William dined here. Letter from Uncle Joseph.

Tuesday 14th August 1855, Tyntesfield.

Went back to Tyntesfield today. I wrote to Uncle Joseph and Francis.

Wednesday 15th August 1855, Tyntesfield.

Mary went to Belmont. I had a letter from Francis.

Thursday 16th August 1855, Tyntesfield.

William dined here yesterday. I had a letter from Francis. Louisa called today on Dr Williams…. Louisa took Edith with her and I am very sorry to say thinks her delicate in the chest, the chicken pox having left some mischief behind it. Wrote to Uncle William.

Friday 17th August 1855, Belmont.

Wrote to Gibson, Uncle William and Francis. George and William dined here. The latter has bought à Court's mare for £40 – a very nice animal.

Sunday 27th January 1856, Frognal.

Uncle William and John called before morning church. Young George Gibbs and Smith dined here.

Monday 28th January 1856, Frognal.

Uncle William and Blanche dined here.

Wednesday 26th November 1856, Cheltenham.

Uncle William and Blanche came tonight.

Friday 28th November 1856, Tyntesfield.

Antony (Henry Hucks' brother) certainly is better, and the blister has risen a little though not enough. Both the doctors saw him at 11 o'clock and have some hopes they may remove the pressure on the brain. Uncle William Crawley and Aunt Charlotte and the two girls came today, and Uncle William and I came here; the Belmont party and William also going back. William Crawley is going to be married to a Miss Clara Maddock, a nice girl I hear with £20,000. Poor Isabella (Antony's wife) bears up very well and her mother and Anne Maria are very kind. They are quite willing the marriage should go on.

Saturday 29th November 1856, Tyntesfield.

I had letters from Mary and Louisa with as good accounts of Antony and Francis as we could hope for. Blanche went on Friday to Monks Kirby for her girls, stopping at Rugby to see Georgiana, with whom also she sat for an hour on her way back today. She arrived with Uncle Joseph, Dolly and Harriett; and her own daughters about 7.00. Uncle Joseph left Antony a little more himself – conscious but unable to show his consciousness, Letters from G.B. Crawley and George Gibbs – Wrote to them, George Abraham, Mary and Louisa.

Sunday 30th November 1856, Tyntesfield.

Letters from John reporting no change in Antony; from Louisa to say they had moved Francis to Eversfield Place and from George Adams. Read an excellent letter from the Bishop of Exeter to his clergy about the Bath Judgement. Wrote to Ellis, Louisa and Lady Pilkington (Henry Hucks cousin and Sir Vicary Gibbs daughter and heiress), the latter too late.

Our dear Kenneth is a nice flourishing little boy thank God. He is a handsome looking child with bright curly hair. Very like his uncle Henry.

Monday Ist December 1856, Belmont.

A sad and melancholy night this is to me, for I have just had a telegraphic despatch from Mrs Gordon to tell me that we have lost poor dear Antony (*Henry Hucks' brother*) – The message said all is just over and was received in London at 10 past 6 – I have told Blanche, and we have agreed that it is impossible to stop the marriage, and that far the kindest thing will be to let it go on now that it is so near. Evered knows; Luke and Miss Watts for they saw the message brought; but they will keep silence, and I must put the best face on it I can, and act my part; though it will be difficult enough, God knows. John, Mary and Aunt Emily left Cheltenham at 12 today, and brought word that there was no change, for though he was still unconscious, the doctor said that he was not materially worse. I can hardly believe it – we were beginning to have some hopes that it might please God to spare him from this attack – Tomorrow immediately after George and Mary are gone, I also shall go to poor Isabella. I have telegraphed to her. Borlase, Henry and George Adams, George Crawley and George Gibbs came today, also Robert and Larry Crawley and the two girls from Broughton. Blanche was very kind and helpful to me. Louisa came with her brother 5 minutes after I heard, but I have not told her anything.

Antony Gibbs *of Merry Hill (1822 to 1856). He was the third son of George Henry Gibbs and his wife Caroline. He worked in Antony Gibbs and Sons, London, from 1839 to 1841 and from 1844 to 1847. In the interval, he spent a year with Feldman Bohl and Co., merchants in Hamburg. After taking his Oxford degree, he was in 1852 a student at Wells Theological College. Merry Hill was bought by him from his mother's executors. On December 7th 1854, he married Isabel Margaret Gordon at Great Malvern. At his death his brother Henry Hucks Gibbs bought Merry Hill and in 1878 sold it out of the family.*

Tuesday 2nd December 1856, Cheltenham.

The day has been beautiful and all went off perfectly well at the wedding, Mary seeming quite happy, and Aunt Harriett very well for her; and all the party enjoying themselves very much throughout the morning and at the breakfast. To me the position was dreadful and I felt it all the worse for having slept very little all night. The bride and bridegroom went off to join the 2.45 train, George looking very well after all his anxiety – and immediately they were gone I told Uncle George and Uncle William that I had had bad news and had promised to go, but did not tell them how bad and begged them to let no one know more than that I had gone in consequence of a promise. I told my dear wife and she insisted on coming also.

Sunday 28th December 1856, Belmont.

Walked twice to church – very cold and frosty – Antony at Tyntesfield does not look very well. Alice gets more beautiful every day I think. Our dear little boys, both at one house and the other, are very flourishing.

Tuesday 30th December 1856, Belmont.

Miserable, rainy, misty day. Uncle William went into Bristol, Blanche and I walked round the road in the rain, and Louisa and Aunt Harriett went out for a drive. I had a letter from George Gibbs of Chichester who had sent me a hamper of woodcocks and clotted cream, which helped out our dinner the evening we were at St Dunstan's very well.

Wednesday 31st December 1856, Belmont.

Uncle William and I took a walk in the afternoon. Thus I bring to a close this sorrowful year.

Thursday 22nd January 1857, St Dunstan's,

Uncle William came with all the party yesterday, but he has not made his appearance today. (*St Dunstan's, Regent's Park, rebuilt as Winfield House in the late 1930s and now the residence of the US ambassador to the UK.*)

Friday 23rd January 1857, St Dunstan's.

Uncle William came today to the City. I was much disappointed to find that he had been applying through Uncle George to Knapp and Dovetons of Exeter for the Clyst St George Estate. I should certainly feel a great injustice done to me if he were to stand in my way for no doubt had my dear father been alive, he would have bought it and it would have of course have come to me – Uncle William imagines my father might have appreciated his motives however, but I think he might fully accomplish his end by seeing the estate restored to the family, even if not by his means, but I have proposed to him that he should buy it, keep it for life thus restoring to the family possession of the estate he remembers in the hands of his grandfather, and which was lost, as he says, by the misfortunes and in some degree the misconduct of his father, and then

153

that he should leave it to me, or if I am gone to the head of the family whichever it is, at the same cost. He does not seem to like it however, and it may be that he will press his claim, when of course I shall not oppose him, and although I cannot but be much disappointed – very much – for it has been my cherished wish all my life, I can at least find some satisfaction in knowing that Uncle William has gratified a strong wish of his, and in seeing him enjoy it. He has been too good to me all my life for me to have any unworthy feeling towards him. However he has written asking Uncle George's opinion and I also have written to him. I do hope however that if he does take it, yet some time or another it will come into the right line – for his children can at all events care very little for it in comparison with me, and, I daresay, will sell it to my son if I am not alive to buy it. I would just as well see Uncle William in possession as myself, but I should think it hard that his family should supplant my father in the inheritance of their ancestors.

I have talked to Hayne about it who I believe quite agrees with my view, and certainly quite approves of my letter to Uncle George which was of course a very temperate one.

Monday 26th January 1857, St Dunstan's.

A note from Uncle George saying he would answer in a few days. He has evidently made up his mind against me which surprises me very much. I wrote to him again giving my reasons more concisely, and also to Mr Barnes begging him to withdraw my proposal for the present. I had a letter from him saying that very likely it would not be sold just yet. It would be curious if we had had all this discussion for nothing.

Tuesday 27th January 1857, St Dunstan's.

Louisa and I went to Hyde Park Gardens. Milly looks very well, and she and Pott seemed much amused with mine and Uncle William's war. I should not have discussed it before them but I was speaking of it to Blanche and as she spoke out there was no help for it. Of course she wishes Uncle William to have his will, but she says that what justice there is in the matter is on my side. They none of them can agree to Uncle William's idea of what my father would have done. Nevertheless, as I told her, I would not oppose Uncle William. I will convince him, if I can, but if I can't there's an end of it. I can't buy it and keep it while he thinks he ought to have it. He certainly still thinks so as sincerely as ever.

Wednesday 28th January 1857, St Dunstan's.

No letter from Uncle George, but he said in a letter to Uncle William yesterday as much as that I was in the wrong.

Friday 30th January 1857, St Dunstan's.

Heard from Uncle George today. He decides against me as being he says consonant to what my father would have wished. I don't think he makes out his reasons well.

Plate 1. Vicary Gibbs as a young lawyer   Plate 2. George Abraham Gibbs as a boy.
by Mrs Hoare.

Plate 4. Eleanor Hucks, Mrs Townley Ward by George Romney.

Plate 3. Antony Gibbs by Edmund Patry R.B.A.

Plate 6. Dorothea Barnetta Hucks,
Mrs Antony Gibbs.

Plate 5. Salvina Hendy, George Gibbs'
first wife by James Leakey, 1802.

157

Plate 8. George Gibbs. Miniature by
Sir William Charles Ross, 1840.

Plate 7. George Gibbs as a young man.
Miniature by James Leakey, 1802.

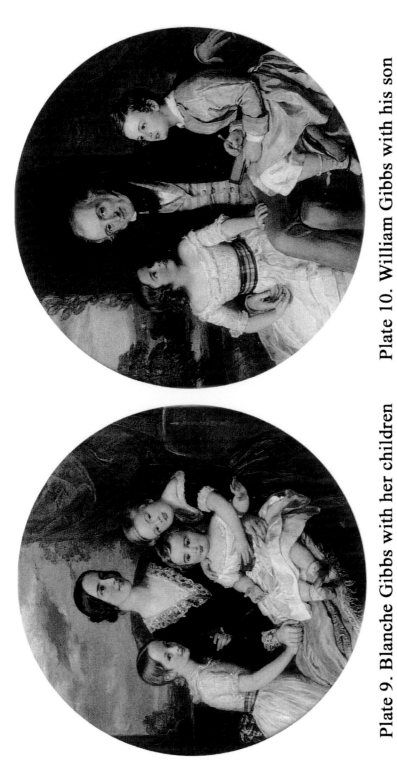

Plate 9. Blanche Gibbs with her children by Sir William Charles Ross R.A. 1850.

Plate 10. William Gibbs with his son Antony and daughter Dorothea, by Sir William Charles Ross R.A. 1850.

Plate 11. A Water Colour of Tyntesfield, which shows later extensions to the original house. Matilda Blanche Gibbs.

Plate 12. Tyntesfield from the Park. Henry Hewitt, 1855.

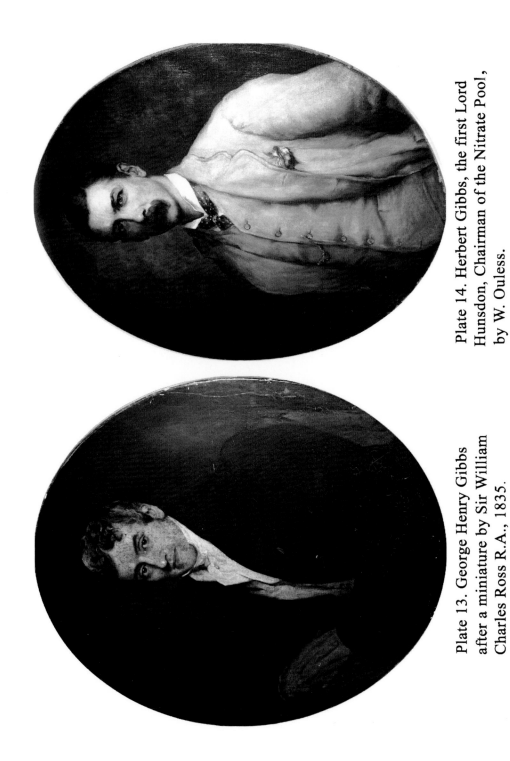

Plate 14. Herbert Gibbs, the first Lord Hunsdon, Chairman of the Nitrate Pool, by W. Ouless.

Plate 13. George Henry Gibbs after a miniature by Sir William Charles Ross R.A., 1835.

Plate 15. George Henry Gibbs
by Edmund W. Gill, 1840.

Plate 16. Caroline Gibbs (née Crawley)
by N.C. Hughes, 1849.

Plate 18. Matilda Blanche Gibbs by
Eugène François Joseph Devéria, 1854.

Plate 17. William Gibbs by Eugène
François Marie Joseph Devéria, 1854.

163

Plate 19. Hyde Park Gardens from Victoria Gate.

**Plate 20. Seville from the Rio Guadalquivir
by Manuel Baron y Carillo, 1846.**

Plate 22. Edith Gibbs by F.G. Cotman, 1876.

Plate 21. Vicary Gibbs by T.R. Wirgman, 1890.

165

Plate 24. Alban Gibbs, the Second
Lord Aldenham by Sir H. Herkomer.

Plate 23. Henry Hucks Gibbs, the First
Lord Aldenham by G.F. Watts, R.A., 1876.

166

Thursday 24th December 1857, Belmont.

Louisa, Alban and Herbert went down by the Mail, and I by the Evening Express, and found all things much as usual here. George and Mary seem pretty happy and comfortable.

Christmas Day 1857, Belmont.

We wanted some more young folks to have a jolly Xmas but still we did pretty well. I had letters from Uncle Joseph and Charles – the latter enclosed in one from his friend Steele. The service here is as little of a festive service as can be imagined. They sang the Christmas hymn as if it were a dirge.

Saturday 26th December 1857, Belmont.

George and I walked over to Barrow Court today. Tyndall Bright and Mr Sage called.

Sunday 27th December 1857, Belmont.

After luncheon, George, Alban and I walked over Backwell Hill, down the Combe and by the church. I wrote to Uncle Joseph and Steele.

Monday 28th December 1857, Belmont.

George and I walked over to Leigh to luncheon. Mr Bright looking very much better. Met two Hills there, pleasant fellows, and one in Daniell's house here. Tyndall and his wife and two nice children, Catty, Isabel, Constance and George's son Robert made our luncheon party.

Tuesday 29th December 1857, St Dunstan's.

Left Bristol by the 8.05 train this morning and went straight into the City.

Friday 13th August 1858, St Dunstan's.

Uncle William and Isabella dined here and so did Henry Adams. George Gibbs came up from Eastbourne in the evening to stay with us. He is much better.

Saturday 14th August 1858, St Dunstan's.

Uncle William went to Tyntesfield and Isabella to Cuddesdon. Henry Cokayne came to stay. Our boxes came from Florence. The Mercury is set up in the saloon and looks very well.

Wednesday 18th August 1858, St Dunstan's.

Letter from Uncle saying he is ill with an attack of strangury and wished me to consult Evans, who had before attended him for the same. But we find that he never did and I have telegraphed to Uncle William to say so and to advise him to send to Bristol for a prostate surgeon.

Thursday 19th August 1858, St Dunstan's.

Letter from Blanche saying Uncle William was better, but still very poorly. I wrote to him.

Friday 20th August 1858, St Dunstan's.

He wrote today, saying he was much better, but the complaint he has is disease of the prostate gland and is a very troublesome one. Heard from John. Wrote to him and Uncle William.

Saturday 21st August 1858, St Dunstan's.
Heard from Uncle William with a much better account of himself.
Monday 23rd August 1858, St Dunstan's.
Uncle William not quite as well yesterday.
Tuesday 24th August 1858, St Dunstan's.
Letter from Blanche with but a poor account of him. I wrote to him today.
Wednesday 25th August 1858, St Dunstan's.
Antony came from Tyntesfield saying his father is no better. He sleeps here tonight. Wrote also to Blanche.
Thursday 26th August 1858, St Dunstan's.
Heard from Uncle William and Blanche, the latter saying about the same things to Louisa as I suggested to her in my yesterday's letter, which crossed hers.
Friday 27th August 1858, St Dunstan's.
Letter from Blanche this morning requesting me to call on Dr Suto, the Head of the German Hospital. This I did and he urgently recommended Uncle William to go to Koeznach, the waters of which place were a specific for glandular disease, especially for the one from which he is suffering. He does not say it will cure him which I fear is impossible, but it is the best hope of doing so, and will most likely alleviate the evil. I telegraphed and wrote to Blanche to that effect.
Saturday 28th August 1858, St Dunstan's.
Blanche's letter this morning says that Mr Harrison quite forbids Uncle William to travel because though the baths would probably be good for him, the inflammation that the journey would increase might even prove fatal. This makes me think worse of the case than I did. I mean that I understand from it that there is more present danger. I have written today I shall go down and see him on Friday.
Monday 30th August 1858, St Dunstan's.
I had a note from Uncle William saying however nothing about his health. George Gibbs returned from Eastbourne where he went on Saturday and brings but a bad account of poor Aunt Harriett. They have all come up today and are going back to Belmont on Wednesday.
Wednesday 1st September 1858, St Dunstan's.
Letters from Uncle William and Blanche and Mr Adams, the surgeon, giving a much better account of him and making us quite easy as far as present danger goes, but I fear he will be all his life debarred from his active habits. Wrote to him today.
Saturday 4th September 1858, Tyntesfield.
Alban and I came down here by the Express, and I left my great coat in the carriage. Mrs Wood (formerly Mary Jones of Hay Hill) met me at the station and went with us in the Tyntesfield carriage. She makes me

feel very old, seeing that I remember her quite a young pretty woman. She has grown quite stout, though she is still pretty and the same kind pleasing woman she always was. I found Uncle William so very much better than I expected that it has been a great relief to me. He is quite cheerful and lively and has been getting steadily better since Monday. He took a slow walk with me all around Belmont and Tyntesfield. Uncle Joseph is here and Mr Wade, the Tutor, a very agreeable and clever young man, son of the Rector of St Anne's Soho, and Miss Stignant, a nice, clever, ladylike girl as Governess. Wade sings very beautifully – a tenor voice – quite self taught

Sunday 5th September 1858, Tyntesfield.

Uncle William had not so good a night but is not much worse for it today. I have had a very long talk with him about his will and the mode in which he will leave his money in the business.

Monday 6th September 1858, St Dunstan's.

Alban enjoyed his visit very much and his rides with Georgey. We returned by the Afternoon Express. Frampton, a great friend of the James Powells was in the carriage with us. Uncle William was not very well last night and seemed depressed, but I don't think but what he is on the right way to get well. I called in at the Great Western Railway Station to see Uncle George and Aunt Harriett.

The Richest Commoner in England

Tuesday 7th September 1858, St Dunstan's.

The Belmont party went home. I wrote to Uncle William. This morning I called in at the G.W.R. and talked with Uncle George about Uncle William's will and, as Uncle William said he should talk to him, I thought it well that he should know my feeling on the subject.

Saturday 11th September 1858, St Dunstan's.

John went down to Tyntesfield, and I wrote to Uncle William. I had also written to him yesterday by Penny whom I sent down to see the garden and to take him a young boar as a present.

Wednesday 15th September 1858, St Dunstan's.

Letter from Uncle William and Blanche. He is not quite so well again. George Gibbs dined here – we stood outside on the Balcony to see the comet.

Thursday 16th September 1858, St Dunstan's.

A very fine day but somewhat cooler. Wrote to Uncle William with a copy of our letter to the minister about not raising the price of guano.

Friday 24th September 1858, St Dunstan's.

Despatched a long letter I had written to Uncle William about his will, and about his leaving the money in the business.

William Gibbs' Capital in Antony Gibbs and Sons[xiii]

The point you have in view being the preservation of the business both for the benefit of those who are now working in it, and for an employment and means of wealth of such of your children as may choose to follow their father's profession, your natural course will be to consider first what amount of capital shall remain for any length of time in the business and next what rate of interest thereon will give your estate sufficient additional income to compensate for the inferior security of such an investment as compared with others of which you would be likely to direct your Executors to avail them a living, and at the same time will not be so dangerously onerous for whoever will have to employ the capital as to make them anxious to pay it off as soon as possible.

If you are satisfied with the security it is for the advantage of your Estate that you should fix a rate sufficiently high to give you a profit above ordinary good securities but also sufficiently low as to be an inducement to your successor to keep it for the longest possible time.

Now so long as the guano business remains with us and on its present footing, no doubt the capital might safely be left large; and the interest payable might be fairly high, and yet the burden might not be very great; but it would be highly unsafe for us to count upon that business either on the present or any future footing; and it would need all the disparity between a moderate interest and the presumed profits contingent to the capital you would leave to compensate for the difficulty of making even a small interest on so large a capital, unless with the aid of so exceptional and extraordinary a branch as the Guano.

No doubt, in case of the guano business falling off, I could pay off whatever capital was superfluous; but it would be some years before I could call it in, in order to do so, and in the meanwhile the interest on £1,200,000 would easily devour not only the current profits, but much of those of preceding years South American profits not to mention your share of the profits already earned in the third concern, your capital must at least amount to that; but we are now talking of the arrangements for your will, and there is no knowing what sum it may be not much before they come into operation.

It will be, then, for the good of all parties that the capital should be limited, and that the interest on it should be so fixed, that the process of payment off should be delayed as long as possible.

I think that you should order your capital to be reduced as soon as you conveniently can to a million, and you might even express your wish (as a guide to your Executors) that when that result was attained, a further reduction should gradually take place, so as to place about half your fortune in other investments.

I say this because I think that especially as the interest cannot be high, you ought not to allow the whole of the fortune of your family to be exposed to the risks of trade, small as those risks may be (comparatively) with such a House as ours; and for the same reason I think it would be well for you, when the present position is over, to begin by slow degrees to reduce your capital employed in the business, and at any rate to prevent its further accumulation by investing at least your annual savings in funds or in land or at all events in some other security than this. By this time twelve months we shall probably have plenty of money disposable, and I do not see any probability of the business ever requiring so large an outlay again.

I dare say if you withdraw none, we may still find profitable employment for the money even if it was remaining at its present amount for some few years longer; but I am speaking of what would be the best course for your own interest.

Henry Hucks Gibbs   September 24th 1858.

Saturday 25th September 1858, Tyntesfield.
Came down here by the morning express, and found Uncle William looking all the worse for a slight attack of lumbago. Otherwise his complaint is decidedly better just now. De Gaja and his daughter Geraldine are here (*see Biographical Note page 322*); and Mr Cosens from Dawlish, a nice old gentleman, came by the afternoon Express from Exeter. I went up to see Uncle George and Aunt Harriett and had a long talk with the former about the object of my visit here, and about my prospects in the business. *Young* William is not looking quite so well though Dr Symonds who has seen him today, says the disease has made no progress in his lungs. Dr Blake says he has committed some imprudence in his dinner which has disordered his stomach.
Sunday 26th September 1858, Tyntesfield.
A foggy day. I walked back from church in the morning with Mr Cosens. A Mr. Norman of Portishead preached a good sermon but oddly delivered. I did not go to afternoon church but took a walk with Blanche talking de omnibus rebus. Uncle William does not look, I think, well today; but he does not say so. He had a long letter from Ellacombe about various improvements to Clyst St George.
Monday 27th September 1858, Tyntesfield.
I breakfasted at Belmont with Uncle George, and had a long talk with him about future arrangements in the business, and the share which I ought to have in it. He shewed the old books of "Munckley, Gibbs and Richards" beginning years ago. Mr Munckley was much in Uncle William's position as regards to the business receiving half, and the other

171

two equal shares. Uncle George himself joined his father (on equal terms) in 1802, and they established their Liverpool House, then Gibbs, Thomson and Co., in 1804.

After breakfast I had a long talk with Uncle William about divers matters, and principally about his will. I only alluded to the shares, which he said he would have settled before, but for my absence, and our press of business at the end of last year. He is to talk with Uncle George on both matters tomorrow. Meanwhile he knows (more or less) through Blanche my view of the matter. He has been much more comfortable today. General de Gaja has been singing very nicely tonight – and his daughter also. She and Blanche also played very well on Piano – "Hark – Here in cool grot" and "The heavens are telling".

Tuesday 28th September 1858, Tyntesfield.

Occupied nearly all day about Uncle William's will arrangements, on which I am to confer with Upton when I go up to town. Meanwhile it is all nicely settled and I have drawn out a codicil for Uncle William to sign ad interim. I went and had a conversation with Uncle George after breakfast and he came here and discussed the matter with Uncle William giving him I am sure very valuable advice, in all of which Uncle William agreed and I also as I was concerned. I had a letter from Louisa in which she said that poor Alban was feverish and had a sore throat; but was better. He seemed she said very happy at school.

Wednesday 29th September 1858, St Dunstan's.

This morning talked with Uncle William again and talked with him about the will, and finished drawing up the codicil which he signed – Mr Adams and Mr Cousens witnessing – also about the shares which we are quite agreed about. He considers that he ought to retain half, but if I find as I suppose that Hayne and Davy would feel uncomfortable at being left at their present shares, he will content himself with two fifths during the time Hayne remains in, and after he leaves two quarters, Davy and I dividing the other half; giving however to Hayne the option of being in but 6 months of the year and taking the 1/12 shares which would reduce Davy's and mine to 5/24 each much to our satisfaction if he will consent. Blanche took me in with Dr Blake to see Dr Symonds who examined me, and gave a very satisfactory account of my heart symptoms. I came up to town by the 2.50 Express.

Thursday 30th September 1858, St Dunstan's.

Talked to Hayne and Davy about the shares, and think from their tone that they will be dissatisfied with their sixths and that Uncle William will have to concede the fifths – an arrangement which Uncle George seemed to consider a very proper arrangement though a liberal one on Uncle William's part. Although I had hard work at Tyntesfield, I had a very pleasant visit there – everyone was so kind.

Monday 10th January 1859, Addington.

This morning we all came up (*to St Dunstan's*), and found plenty of letters, two or three from Uncle William sending me up poor William Henry's will (*He was an independent trader in Genoa*), and desiring me to consult Orme about it. It was made in 1838, and has three codicils made as his circumstances improved, and distributing his £5000 or £6000 of property very properly making Uncle William his Executor and empowering him to do whatever he thought proper, altering and amending the bequests as might seem good to him. He had left the will in Genoa, and in February last instead of making a new will or Codicil he wrote a paper of directions for Uncle William Gibbs, entirely altering the previous distribution of his property. If he had not only signed this, as he did, and dated it, but had it witnessed, it would have been a good will and Uncle William would have had no trouble or responsibility, but as it is he will no doubt act on this memorandum, in the exercise of his own discretion, according to the power in the 3rd codicil.

Thursday 10th February 1859, St Dunstan's.

Uncle William and General De Gaja called in the evening

Saturday 12th February 1859, St Dunstan's.

Blanche and I went to Brighton this morning – she to see Alice and Henry Martin, and I to see Alban.

Saturday 12th March 1859, St Dunstan's.

I called at Hyde Park Gardens this morning and found Uncle William very busy with the project of a new church at Paddington which he hopes will be free seated.

Sunday 13th March 1859, St Dunstan's.

Uncle William called here, and John and I went with him to St Andrew's in the afternoon and afterwards to Hyde Park Gardens.

Saturday 18th June 1859, St Dunstan's.

We have a large party here tonight. The John Coleridges, Stephen Caves, Hankeys, Hubbards, Maurice Drummonds, Blanche, William Latham, the Baring Youngs and William Lloyd. We have a Miss Fraser to sing. Uncles William and Joseph are gone to the ordination.

Saturday 30th July 1859, Whitby.

Louisa has had a letter from Blanche and I from Uncle William who has bought sundry pictures at Lord Northwick's sale.

Monday 21st November 1859, St Dunstan's.

Letter from Uncle William mentioning some objections to our plan of giving *Augustus* Sillem (*partner in Antony Gibbs and Sons, 1865 – 1896*) the procuration, which I answered in a letter to go tomorrow.

Monday 24th September 1860, Collina, Torquay (*John Lomax Gibbs' home*).

Uncle William called after breakfast and walked with me to the Warrens again and then to Bollam where we met the Miss Barnes and then to Palace Gate – where after walking about a little while in the garden, Uncle William delighting in the old familiar place and half inclined to roll down the slopes as he used to do as a boy – Mr Barnes came in to us. Then we called on old Dr Oliver; and after calling myself on Turner (who was out) I got to the Oxenhams again to luncheon at 1.15 where Blanche and her daughters were – Louisa and I came here by the 2.30 train. The place is beautiful and in this weather better than any other I know.

March/April 1861

My illness began on 26th March. I had been out for a delightful ride – though by myself – to Kingsbury – the Saturday before, and the wind having changed to the N.E. in the course of it I caught a chill which took away my voice. On Tuesday my cough was too bad to go out. For several days or rather nights I barked continuously, getting (and allowing Louisa) scarcely any sleep, and on Monday 1st, I moved down into the drawing room – a most delightful bedroom. Uncle William was here all that day helping me to write a long letter to Eggert. He has been most kind to me all the while, missing no single day in coming to see me.

Thursday 25th April 1861, St Dunstan's.

Went to the British Museum to look through Gould's Birds of Australasia, before writing to Charles Bright.

Friday 26th April 1861, St Dunstan's.

Went to luncheon in Hyde Park Gardens.

Sunday 19th May 1861, St Dunstan's.

A lovely day – but cold. N.E. wind. Uncle William and Blanche called. They had had but a poor account of dear Isabel (*John Lomax Gibbs' wife*), who seems very weak and poorly.

Monday 20th May 1861, St Dunstan's.

Blanche and Louisa have both heard from John, the latter by this evening's post, giving a much clearer account of his dear wife. It has been fever and has now happily departed.

Wednesday 22nd May 1861, St Dunstan's.

This is Uncle William's 71st birthday. It is a great pleasure to see him looking so well and robust as he is.

Friday 24th May 1861, St Dunstan's

Both today and yesterday I have been dining in Hyde Park Gardens. Today meeting Dr and Mrs Goulburn, the Eltons, who are staying in the house, and Mr and Mrs Brookfield, the latter a sister of Sir Arthur Elton. Mr Brookfield is a very amusing talker, the more amusing to me before I knew he was a clergyman. Yesterday Lord Denbigh and three daughters (who sang beautifully), Algamora, George Adams, Mr Prescott and the Eltons, Hardie and Antony came in the evening, the latter from

174

passing his exams at Exeter for Matriculation.

Saturday 25th May 1861, St Dunstan's.

Mrs O'Shea and her two sons, and George and Mary dined here.

Sunday 26th May 1861, St Dunstan's.

They came also to luncheon today, and went to the Zoological Gardens.

Saturday 25th October 1862, Tyntesfield – Letter from William Gibbs

My Dear Henry,

I wrote to you yesterday and I am glad to see from a few lines of that date that a couple of hundred thousand pounds is of no consequence to the House of which my dear Father was the Founder. How little did that good man foresee such a result when he was travelling through France and Spain with your dear Father and myself on our way to Cadiz just 60 years since!! But I verily believe we owe our success under God's good Providence to the principles of honour and integrity which he instilled into us by precept and example. However I did not certainly imbibe at that time any aristocratic tastes nor have I acquired them since and therefore I don't feel at all inclined to buy the Estate of which you sent me the advertisement, but I am glad that we are so full of cash as I may wish to employ some of it in quite another way …………. (*Rebuilding Tyntesfield*).

Blanche has received Louisa's letter and in consequence of the kind wish she expresses that I should go to St Dunstan's on Tuesday night, however late, I will do so with great pleasure and think it very likely I may be able to dine there but as it is very uncertain how long I may be detained elsewhere or whether I may not find it save time to dine with Hawkins at the Athenaeum, do beg her not to wait for me a minute after seven, which I believe is your hour.

Your affectionate Uncle,

William Gibbs

Tuesday 3rd February 1863, Torquay.

Dear Alban does seem a little better I am happy to think but his cold is still heavy. Louisa, he, Edith, Vicary and I left St Dunstan's on Friday last, I stopping at Tyntesfield so as to see dear Uncle George again, and as I fully expected, for the last time. Aunt Harriett looked thoroughly worn out with her anxiety and her own ailments. Uncle William was too much depressed, but was cheered by my coming.

Mr Hogg had kindly taken No 10 for us with leave to come into this house if we did not like the other, and as that turned out to be the case, the work was a great deal too much for Louisa, and I wish I had been with her instead of at Tyntesfield. However all is pretty comfortable now. Mr and Mrs Hogg and Dr and Mrs Goulburn were at Tyntesfield when Alban and I were there, and I was very glad to make their better acquaintance. This time the only guests beside myself and the aforementioned in the house were Blanche and Douglas Page.

The Hoggs have called - a reconnaissance in force. Also I met Wade.

Monday 23rd March 1863, Torquay.

Uncle William, Blanche and Alice came down the day after I wrote last; but the next morning I had to run up to town. I returned here on Monday 5th, having taken in Tyntesfield on my way from town on Saturday evening. Alice was staying here, having before been with the Hoggs and Miss Parsons and stayed till Friday. She had had her horse down here and enjoyed her rides very much. Willy has been very poorly at Tyntesfield with the old abscess, but is now better.

Thursday 26th March 1863, Tyntesfield.

They sent us this morning to Clyst St George (The church is a perfect jewel, and the school very good indeed. I saw Pytte, and Mr Courtenay, the tenant thereof, and Ellacombe, of course) and took, in the afternoon, to Veitek's where I saw many beautiful flowers; and amongst others a Phalaenopsis Lobbi – a most lovely flower – between Rosea and Amabilis – perhaps a hybrid. It is the only one in England. By the 3 o'clock train we came down here arriving in time for dinner. I have been with Uncle William and Blanche to Belmont, and have seen poor dear Uncle George. He lies utterly unconscious and has done so almost continuously since Saturday. They do not think he can live through the night. Aunt Harriett is very composed, and for her, even active in doing what she can to help him; but he is past her help – or indeed any help, and the most merciful thing would seem to be that he should now be taken. He suffers no pain; but in all but breathing he seems to be really dead.

Friday 27th March 1863, Tyntesfield.

This morning, and up to now (midnight) he remains in nearly the same state; but his pulse is almost gone, and he may, since Uncle William and Blanche came in (for they have spent the evening there) have ceased to breathe.

It has been a lovely day and we have been on a long ride to and from Dundry going as much through fields and over hedges as we could – but Tredegar has lost courage since his falls, and is quite shy of jumping so also is Charles' chestnut mare, but she is not well. Georgia behaves admirably; but I regret to see she 'speedy cuts' on the road. Alban and I, Alice and Harriett were of the party; Albinia and Miss Digby coming part way. Dundry Church has been restored; and the interior is very pretty – especially the pulpit. I had a letter from home from Louisa. They had all arrived well.

Saturday 28th March 1863, Tyntesfield.

Dear Uncle George breathed his last this morning at half past one. Shortly after Uncle William and Blanche left. He died almost without his last moment being perceptible. His long state of unconsciousness had broken the shock to poor Aunt Harriett, who is very calm and as much comforted as possible under the circumstances of so heavy a loss. A heavy loss he is to all of us and all who knew him. Uncle William is the Executor, and read the will today. He leaves both him and me £1000 (after Aunt Harriett's death) which we won't want at all for the money's sake; but it is I am sure to both of us a great pleasure that he has so thought of us. There are other very liberal legacies, and the residue and the land to Aunt Harriett, Uncle Joseph and Aunt Emily successively for life, the land then I think to George L.M. Gibbs and the personalty in certain shares between him and his brothers, but the disposition of the residue of the personalty to be alterable at Aunt Harriett's pleasure.....I wrote to Louisa.....I saw dear Aunt Harriett today, and she talked just as one would wish her to talk.

On Thursday (the 2nd April) I went back again to the funeral which took place on Saturday (the 4th April), the body being carried all the way and attended by all who were there in the two houses. Several of the Brights and their friends, and a considerable concourse of neighbours. Aunt Harriett also came to the church and bore the trial it must have been to her very well.

I stayed at Tyntesfield till the Monday week (the 13th April) helping Uncle William as much as I was able about the Worship, and also discussing with Mr Norton and a Committee of the whole house the alterations they are about to make in it and about it. They have some hopes of taking Mamhead for a year during the alterations. Alban is still at Tyntesfield enjoying this lovely weather and I have had plenty to do since I have been away with packet work (*shipping*) and other business.

Saturday 18th April 1863, St Dunstan's.

I hope to go to Tyntesfield to discuss with Uncle William a Greenland business which has been proposed to us by a Mr Taylor – it is a charter from the Danish Crown to the Hudson's Bay Company.

Wednesday 22nd April 1863, Tyntesfield.

Left home by the two o'clock train…A pleasant old gentleman named Fitzgerald, an old Walcheren and Waterloo man was my companion on the train. All well here, especially Alban – George has gone back to school.

Thursday 23rd April 1863, Tyntesfield.

Dear Alban's 17th birthday. He and I and Harriett and Alice, Miss Digby and Albinia rode over Cadbury and through Sir Arthur Elton's grounds

Figure 27. Mamhead Park near Dawlish, rented by William and Blanche Gibbs (1863 to 1865).

Figure 28. William Gibbs and family on holiday in the Alps in 1867. Seated from left – Dorothea, Blanche, Albinia, William, Alice and Alfred Gurney. Standing behind from left – John Lomax Gibbs, Antony, an unknown lady, the Rev. John Hardie, Colonel Charles Gibbs, and William Gibbs Junior.

178

to Walton Castle and home through Clevedon and up a very pretty lane before one comes to Tickenham. Heard from George Louis and wrote to Louisa.

Friday 24th April 1863, Tyntesfield.

Heard from and wrote to Louisa – also from Dr Rae about Taylor and Greenland. Talked about it with Uncle William and found him not disinclined to enter into the business - being fearful only that it may involve some political responsibility.

Walked with Blanche and Alice through the wood behind the Cottage to Abraham's Corner. Wrote to George Louis.

Monday 27th April 1863, Oxford.

Blanche drove in with me and Alban in the morning and I called in on Davy who seems much as he was. Then we came on here by the 2.55 train, Joe accompanying us, and Harriett also as far as Didcot. Alban dined with Antony, and I with Sheppard and afterwards they came up to his rooms and we played a rubber (*of bridge*) – Douglas Page and Evans of Pembroke being his guests.

Tuesday 28th April 1863, Oxford.

Antony's rooms are very comfortable and himself going on very quietly and gentlemanly as far as I could judge… I enjoyed my little visit to Oxford. We had luncheon at the Mitre, and came home by the 1.55 train.

Thursday 30th April 1863, St Dunstan's.

Wrote to Blanche. Had a long talk with Goschen about the railway to connect the Riga and Donauberg with Vitepsk; and about a Moscow and Sebastapol line. Dr Rae called and talked about Greenland.

Friday 1st May 1863, St Dunstan's.

Wrote to Uncle William about Dobrer's and Mr Mallet's plan for a financial association of the leading merchants. I don't myself incline to it.

Saturday 2nd May 1863, St Dunstan's

Heard from Blanche and wrote to Uncle William.

Monday 16th November 1863, London – Letter from Henry Hucks Gibbs.

Dear Uncle William

I wrote a line from Nailsea with part of the packet letters and I now send you the rest…………

Louisa will have told you that we found Georgey (George Abraham) looking really in excellent health, grown both tall and straight. His ailment had been very little indeed, and although he had some relics of a cold, there was no cough, and indeed nothing to complain of. He had hardly the face to ask for leave for him, but we did and Yonge said it would be quite in vain to ask the headmaster (*of Eton College*). I was

179

much pleased with Yonge's manner and with the interest he showed in those of his pupils about whom we asked, and in whom we ourselves having but slight interest, he had no need to affect any. Altogether our impression was that Blanche may make herself more easy than she had done about John Eyre Yonge's (*Charlotte Yonge's brother*) management.

You and I know boys well enough, having been classed ourselves in that department of Zoology, to know that we must not make too much account of their complaints in either sense of the word. A whole school day has very often great weight in determining the character of a slight cold. Mammas however don't always see things in the same light. Blanche might at any rate take comfort from the fact that Louisa and I should be most happy if we could always see our children in such good health as Georgey is.

Thank Blanche for her letter to me. I have found Alice's photograph. It was in my bag. As to the House – liberavi animam meam – you asked me to report, and I have. If you think it's better as it is, there is no more to be said – Only Blanche says you have considered the Drawing Room question in all its bearings – I say not <u>all</u>; for you have not <u>seen</u> it, and eyesight may lend you a new light as it has me. 'If you had pulled the house down it might have been different'. As far as this is concerned you <u>have</u> pulled the house down.

I don't think heightening the rooms above at all a necessary part of the changes, and I don't think widening the Drawing Room will at all increase the appearance of lowness. Quite the reverse – It now looks like a low <u>corridor,</u> and it will look like a low <u>room</u> if you widen it. Ask Robert Bright what he thinks. As to the earth before the school room wing, the more you move the better, not completely opening the road. You must have the earth away from the end, and it is already nearly wide enough for carriages. You will find the spot that the said wing will completely mask the old road; and as to the land, here you will be obliged to depress the old road whether you will or no. Depend on it, when you see it yourself, you will treat it as I suggest, and the chief advantage of doing it now is that you can make use of the earth you take away. You won't want a wider opening; but the slope should not be abrupt.

In both cases – Drawing Room and Bank – all I want is that you should <u>see for yourselves</u> without loss of a day – It would be a great pity that you should allow an irreparable mistake to be made for want of a visit from the chief persons interested. If you see it, and don't agree with me, I can only say I am wrong. But no plans can shew you the present effect. As to the Oratory – corriente – as to the Drawing Room – much is to be said on both sides – this amongst others, that if you don't like it shut you can always open it.

I remain with kind love to all.

Your affectionate nephew,

Henry Hucks Gibbs.

December 17th 1864, Mamhead Park – Letter from Blanche Gibbs.

My Dearest Henry

I have nearly finished putting things in a little comfortable order to sit down to thank you with all true affection and love for your welcome letter and birthday greetings, but you surely forget my advanced age which is I believe my 47th birthday – not 42 as you suppose, much has indeed passed since the young days to which you allude. Years full of blessings and though not without a very full share of anxious care have passed over my head, and I am rapidly nearing the ultimate age that any of the young branch of my family have been allowed to reach, but the future is in God's hands and in this thought in ones thoughts is comfort. I cannot help looking for you dearest Henry at your old place at the writing table and expecting dearest Louisa to come in every moment to talk over your health and probably best plans for you. How nice it would have been if one could have persuaded oneself that Mamhead had been the best place for you, but as it is I care too much for you to wish you here again until you can come in received health and strength. We are keeping a degree of warm air, but still the house is bitterly cold, and three of the young ones are all in bed – Harriett, Alice and Henry – not a bright Christmas prospect. Your letter is full of interesting detail about Tyntesfield. If you really think the old mantle piece with which I had determined to be content for my room will not do, do by all means tell Wall so he can beg Mr Norton to send down another of the pattern I chose for the Green Room, which had in it a little colour, and the old white mantle piece can be put into one of the boys rooms. I quite agree with you about the avenue and I do not think that William has any strong affection for it but the fact is we are born down by public opinion and afraid to act which is perhaps cowardly, yet I do feel always afraid of being too independent in matters of taste for years past. I should like to have destroyed the appearance of avenue and have kept a few of the finest of the trees in irregular positions for I do think that old branches even though ill-shapen are the making of a place and in old homes are very valuable for the shade. William will probably digest your remarks and come to some conclusion in time but he will determine, waiting I think until the sheds are down and the coast is clear. I am glad indeed to hear your more cheering conclusion with regard to the hall. It will be a most pleasant surprise if after all, it is light enough. I am sure you may be right with regard to the door in the porch and this point can quite well stand over for the present. I cannot realize your idea of a tower, if you mean quite a low one like Jason's porch in Rome, we suggested this again and again, but Mr Norton could not or would not carry it out. Everyone must feel that a great mistake has been made about the entrance altogether, and that it is evidently no original design, all owing to Mr Norton's having so obstinately persisted in a high church tower. Will you tell Mr Hardie that James is very anxious about the reservoir and feels sure we shall have no water next year unless it is commenced immediately, and James hopes that Mr Hardie will speak about this at once. I am so sorry to hear that Louisa has not been well. I must now say good bye dear Henry with love to you both.

Believe me your ever affectionate

Blanche Gibbs

Friday 23rd December 1864, Belmont.

Page 173. Not withstanding the wise reflections at the beginning of my journal for last year, I did not long keep it up, and now 19 months instead of nine have passed over me since I last wrote in it, and now, alas, I am never to write in it again in the old familiar hand on the opposite page. It makes me sad to look at it like the picture of a lost friend – but, as in all other things, one must make the best of one's lot whatever it is, and I have only to be very thankful that I have a left hand with which I can still write with tolerable ease, and especially that through the sacrifice of my right hand, my life has been spared. (*Henry Hucks Gibbs lost his right hand in a hunting accident in September 1864 at Mamhead Park, rented by his Uncle William.*) [xiv]

Page 176. We have built at Clifton Hampden, with Scott's help a sort of Organ-chamber and Vestry in one, as an extension of the north aisle, but wider than it and gabled like the chancel. We fill the two windows therein with stained glass by Clayton and Bell (one of them being after two of Ainmiller's cartoons for the East Window of Uncle William's beautiful church of St Michael's Paddington), we improve the organ and re-arrange the woodwork of the chancel, substituting a low screen for the high one, and a small wooden pulpit for the large stone one; and with whatever money is left we shall do more there.

The old stalls and pulpit we have offered to Uncle William for the new church which Rhode Hawkins is building for him in the parish of St. David's, Exeter, in memory of his father and grandfather.

After talking about it for a long time, I have at last built a bridge over the river in place of the ferry, and I am told it is very handsome. Scott gave me the design after Homfray had done the engineering part. It has cost £3617.15.10 of which no less than £628.12.6 has been for parliamentary expenses.

Figure 29. The bridge over the Thames at Clifton Hampden.

Christmas Day 1864, Belmont.

It is very pleasant being here with all our children about us after being so long separated from all but Alban, and for a short time Edith.

Charles too is here having come up last night from Plymouth, and excepting Miss Watts, of course, and Aunt Harriett we have the house to ourselves. Our only trouble is poor Aunt Harriett's state (which is certainly no better though no worse in the last few days) and my own loss for which there is no remedy but patience (*of his right hand*). I have been to church today for the first time since my illness here. The said illness was a congestion of the liver, accompanied by the passage of gall-stones through the duct. I was taken ill on the night of the 13th, the day after we came here from Torquay; and frightful pain I suffered, as bad I am told as severe labour.

Then came on a threatened attack of inflammation of the bowels, which was happily subdued before it became very bad; but with a slight interval I was full 3 weeks in bed and remain an invalid (for a few months only, I hope) with an enlarged liver. I am much better however, thank God, already. Harrison, the Bristol surgeon, has been out to see me every week, and Mr Adams has been in constant attendance; they are both very kind and skilful and Harrison is the more useful to me and takes the more interest in the case, because he is a fellow sufferer having lost an arm. I have been in hospital ever since the first of September last. Louisa had some undefined presentiment of evil and urged me not to go that day; but I wished to go to Mamhead where Stubbs (*Charles Edward Stubbs, Partner in Antony Gibbs and Sons 1865 – 1876*) was that I might "presenciar" (*attend to – Spanish*) Uncle William.

Page 178. Our party on the first of September were myself, Edward Crawley Boevey, Charles and Captain Drake, a friend of his, and George Abraham. I shot unusually well for me, having missed but one shot, when after lunch we came to a high bank, too high to climb with gun in hand. The men had gone over first with Edward and Drake, and Charles and George behind me. The bank was broad and flat at the top, and had a stake sticking up at the left hand side of the opening which was bare of hedge. I thought the safest way was to lay my gun at the top, and so I did laying it across the bank at right angles ; and I then sprung on to a ledge of stone projecting from the bank about 18 inches from the ground and caught the stake in my left hand to aid me in clambering up. I suppose the stake being firmly fixed in stirred the earth of the bank when my weight rested on it, but from that or some other cause down fell the gun slipping backwards, the muzzle trending towards me as it fell; and the hammer struck the ledge of stone, the blow breaking off a bit of the hammer, and bending the tumbler like a hook, so that the hammer being free, fell and discharged the gun, the whole charge passing into my right hand, shattering almost the whole of the palm, and a great portion of it passing through into my right cheek and lower jaw. If it had not been for the interposition of my hand, I must infallibly have been killed, and very thankful I am to have saved my life though at so great a sacrifice. I felt no wound at the moment, but I saw my bleeding hand and cried out, and jumped onto a lower bank which struck the other at right angles, and so down into the field where the others were.

Page 179. They at once made haste to tie up my wrist, to send for a cart, and for the Doctor, and to Mamhead to beg Uncle William to telegraph to dear Louisa, who arrived (with Edith and Clark) at 5 the next morning, dreadfully shocked and suffering mentally as much as I did bodily.

Thank God who has given me one so loving and so devoted to care for me and watch over me.

Uncle William was like a true father to me, to both of us, and Blanche like a most affectionate sister, and all the rest especially good and kind in their several ways.

We had sent for Mr Knighton from Dawlish, and Mr James, a surgeon

from Exeter. It was not until 9 o'clock that Mr Knighton and his nephew having come, and all things having been got ready they proceeded to take off my hand below the wrist, which was quite successfully done, and thanks to chloroform, without my being in the least conscious of any pain. The whole affair took I think 22 minutes. Alban and dear Blanche stayed outside the door all the while. It was almost worse for them.
Tuesday 27th December 1864, Belmont.
On Xmas Day I had very pleasant letters from Blanche, Alice, Harriett, Hardie and Harrison. I wrote to Blanche the same day and to Harriett today. Mr Pollard the surgeon had to open up *the wound* five or six times during our short stay in *Torquay*. I do believe it is now healed, for a few days ago came away a piece of exfoliated bone about 1/8 of an inch long which has no doubt been the cause of the mischief, and since then the small wound has been growing smaller and smaller, and these last three days it has been quite closed over.
I feared very much at first that the loss of my hand would make it impossible for me to continue my Dictionary Work, (*with the New Oxford English Dictionary)* but I soon began to write again and, indeed, on the 6th day after my wound I was able to write a letter to Mrs Adams, and passed few days after that without writing a little.
Thursday 29th December 1864, Belmont.
Letter from Blanche saying she, Uncle William and Willie would be here today by the 5.35.
Friday 30th December 1864, Belmont.
The William Gibbs's visit was a great pleasure to us, but I don't like Willie's looks, nor the sound of his cough. I went all over Tyntesfield with them and we condemned trees on the south side of the 'Avenue' and one on the north. They have now been two winters at work on the alterations during which time they have occupied Sir Lydston Newman's place at Mamhead (*Mamhead Park near Exeter*) and they will have a most beautiful and comfortable house. It is my daily walk at least once. The chief faults I see at present are that the carriage road leads not to the door but to the dining room window which is the only ugly part of the house. The road therefore will have to be altered sooner or later, and the hedge row branchless elms which have long simulated an avenue will have to go. The other fault is the entrance which lacking as it does an upper storey and pointed roof looks mean. I have an idea about it and though I don't know that I shall have my way, I have leave to write to Mr Norton about it. There is a beautiful room with a turret on the N.E. wing, which while the plans were making I pitched upon as 'my room' and they laugh at me saying I have chosen the best room in the house! A proof of my good judgement! Wrote to Joe at Mamhead…. He is now in the employ of George Crawley who appears at last to be embarked on a

very prosperous career. He has sundry Contractors for his clients and with them at his back has become a promoter of their plans, managing the financial part of their business for them…Joe has carried through, or nearly through the great Vera Cruz and Mexico Railway project….

Antonio Escandon, one of our correspondents in Mexico, was the Concessee of the Railway and also the Contractor General for it, and he offered it to us some three years ago, promising great gains, but it was not the sort of business we understood, and we declined. But now under the new regime things looked much more favourable and consequently much more tempting. But when he again pressed it, we still refused, but agreed to lend him money up to £30,000, to enable him to go on with the works.

It (the Mexican Railway Scheme) came out as successfully as one could expect, considering the high value of money in the latter days of August; and but for some trouble in Mexico it would now stand very well. The trouble is that although the new Emperor had given his warm adhesion while in Paris, he had not thought it too late to object to some of the provisions in the Concession (granted by his predecessors), nevertheless we have set all engines in work to shake him, including his patron, the French Emperor, and other magnates in France. The William Gibbs's went at two, to town, to see Willie off with Hardie for a cruise on the Mediterranean.

Saturday 31st December 1864, Belmont.

I wrote today to Mr Norton.

Wednesday 11th January 1865, Belmont.

Finished my borrador (*rough draft in Spanish*) for Eggert, and sent it to Stubbs and also a copy to Uncle William. Joe came from Mamhead and Medley went to Bath. They have been acting "Done on both sides" which we acted twice at Tyntesfield in January 1863. The cast then was Whiffles – Joe, Phibbs (Piggy) – Henry, Mrs Whiffles – Harriett, Brownjohn – myself (Henry Hucks), Lydia – Willie. This year the same cast, but with Alice for Lydia, and Antony for Brownjohn, and they did very well "Box and Cox", which we had in 1863, and "A Thumping Legacy". I had letters from Uncle William and H. Crawley.

Thursday 12th January 1865, Belmont.

We were startled tonight by the arrival of Harrison of Clifton Hampden bringing I grieve to say a sad account of a sharp illness of dear Uncle William. A bilious attack which was very threatening all this day.

Saturday 14th January 1865, Belmont.

The gale last night blew down one of the trees in the Tyntesfield Avenue. Unfortunately not one of those we wished down. The scaffolding is now all out of the hall.

Sunday 15th January 1865, Belmont.

Letters from George and Blanche greatly increase my fears about dear Uncle William and Dr Adams who has read them thinks the same. Louisa wrote to her, and I to George.

Monday 16th January 1865, Belmont.

We are in somewhat better spirits today for I had a letter from Alice saying that Uncle William had had but one fit of shivering on Saturday night, and that a short one. Harrison had been sent for by telegraph, and was to return today; so Edith and I drove in to see him, and his account was a little more hopeful. He can find no additional local mischief beyond what he knew of before, and inclines to think it may be ague; and they are accordingly treating it with quinine. We saw the Cathedral (beautiful Norman chapter house and Early English North Chapel) and the Mayor's chapel.

Tuesday 17th January 1865, Belmont.

A much more hopeful letter from George though they don't consider dear Uncle William out of danger. Wrote to Alice and G. J. Harrison and sent the packet letters to George….Mr Bright came and walked over Tyntesfield with me. He quite agrees with me about the tower.

Wednesday 18th January 1865, Belmont.

A most happy account from Mamhead. Uncle William was certainly much better yesterday and Blanche, as we learn by letters from herself, John and Aunt Emily, thinks him out of danger. I fear however he may have some return of the rigor.

Thursday 19th January 1865, Belmont.

The morning account was not quite so comfortable, but in the afternoon came Henry Martin on his way to school bringing a letter from Aunt Emily saying he had had a very good night and was quite comfortable.

Friday 20th January 1865, Belmont.

Edith, Herbert and Henry Martin went to school by the 10.20 train. I had a letter at midday from Mr Harrison with a good account of Uncle William (based on Knighton's) I wrote to Uncle William….Lady Elton and Mrs Robins called..

Saturday 21st January 1865, Belmont.

A letter from Blanche with a comfortable account. I keep to the house with a baddish cold.

Sunday 22nd January 1865, Belmont.

We heard from George Louis, Mrs Yonge, John and Mr Norton, to which four I wrote.

Monday 23rd January 1865, Belmont.

Had a delightful letter from Uncle William written manu propria in pencil – also one from George Crawley.

Tuesday 24th January 1865, Belmont.

My cold and the weather still equally bad so that I can't go out. George and Beatrice and Major Robins came to luncheon, the two latter going back to Clevedon and George going to town by the 9.45, taking Mr Norton, who was elsewhere, as far as Bristol.

Wednesday 25th January 1865, Belmont.

Louisa heard from and wrote to Blanche and I wrote to Uncle William.

Friday 27th January 1865, Belmont.

Cold still great and the snow some 9 inches deep. Nevertheless as the weather was very fine, Dr Adams permitting, I took a little walk, ploughing my way hastily through the snow to Tyntesfield. Began a long letter to Blanche reporting progress and strongly recommending the tower. Louisa heard from Aunt Emily. Wrote to George Louis.

George Louis Monck Gibbs was the second son of the Rev. Joseph Gibbs of Clifton Hampden, Oxfordshire, and his wife Emily, daughter of the Rev. Charles Vaughan, descended from the Vaughans of Tretower in Breconshire. He was William Gibbs of Tyntesfield's nephew. He was born on 28th April 1838 and in 1847 went to Marlborough College. He continued his education from 1852 to 1855 with the Rev. Daniel Nihill, Rector of Fitz in Shropshire. He entered Antony Gibbs and Sons in 1855. He worked in London from 1855 to 1859 and Peru and Chile from 1859 to 1862. On 5th January 1864, he married Laura Beatrice Elton, the daughter of Sir Arthur Hallam Elton of Clevedon Court. He became a partner in the family firm from 1865 to 1881. In 1865 he inherited Belmont from his father who was left the house by George Gibbs. He sold Belmont to William Gibbs in 1870.

Saturday 28th January 1865, Belmont.

A sharp frost added to the snow. Finishing my letter to Blanche detailing my conversation with George Louis (to whom I wrote) about Belmont. By the 3.45 train came Alice, George Abraham and Willie Cobham bringing me a letter from Uncle William. I can't say I feel easier about him from Alice's report; partly because Knighton seems as much in the dark as ever as to what was the nature of the malady, and because as soon as ever Uncle William is a little better, he falls to at his occupations, and works too hard which is most dangerous for him.

Sunday 29th January 1865, Belmont.

Snow and a partial thaw with much wind. Letters from Norton… and George Louis, and Louisa one from Mrs Merivale, and she wrote to the latter and I to George L. and Blanche sending her the plans. To Norton also and *Frederick James* Furnivall (*Pioneer of the New Oxford English Dictionary and Philological Society Secretary*) for tomorrow's post.

188

Figure 30. George Louis Monck Gibbs, 1838-1881.

Sunday 29th January 1865, Mamhead Park – Letter from William Gibbs

My Dearest Henry,
Although it is Sunday, I cannot help writing now a few lines to say what a great pleasure I have derived from reading your long letter to Blanche which she received this morning – with regard to Tyntesfield. Really if the place were your own you could not show more interest than you now

so kindly and affectionately do in everything relating to it. With regard to the Tower, we have held a Council of War and overpowered by the furiousness of the assault, we have unanimously determined that we must surrender at discretion hoping only that you will now be merciful and not shed more of our blood/money than may be necessary to meet the ends of justice. As you have now kindly taken the matter in hand, my dear Henry, I will leave its execution entirely to your taste, so pray arrange it forthwith with Norton taking especial care to keep within proper bounds his extravagant loves of ornament and of producing an outside "feature". Bind Cubitt down to finishing the work within a certain time and to its not in any way retarding the remainder of the work now in hand, and cut down the price to the lowest point consistent with it being done well, for Norton is reckless of expense, and in the instance of the Drawing Room Mantelpiece we obtained one from Crace at less than a third of what he wanted to spend on another which in taste Blanche thought very inferior. I will only add that the sooner the matter is arranged and the work begun the better. I am pleased to think that this miserable weather will, or ought not to have retarded the indoor work which we were glad to hear is getting on so nicely. I suppose the carvers in the Hall will soon have finished – so much for Tyntesfield…….Blanche is anxious that we should leave for Belmont at the end of this week….God bless you my dear Henry and believe me

Your most affectionate Uncle,

William Gibbs.

Monday 30th January 1865, Belmont.
Letters from Isabella and Ellacombe and also from Uncle William who in the most pleasing manner desires me to settle the tower question as I like and leaves the management entirely to me so I have added accordingly to my letter to Norton. I wrote also a separate note to Blanche.
Tuesday 31st January 1865, Belmont.
Letter from Blanche.
Wednesday 1st February 1865, Belmont.
Georgey (*George Abraham, William and Blanche's son*) went to Eton. They began to cut one of the big trees nearest the house
Thursday 2nd February 1865, Belmont.
Aunt Harriett downstairs again for the first time after her illness. I had letters from George Louis, from Harrison and Turnivall. Wrote to all three, and Gibson, and Blanche. Very satisfactory letters from Mexico about the railway. Tree down.

Sunday 12th February 1865, Belmont.

Uncle William and Blanche, Albinia and Miss Barton came on Monday, he looking wonderfully well.

Thursday 7th September 1865, Flaxley.

I had luncheon with Aunt Charlotte, and then went out in a fly stopping at Highnam to see the Church which is indeed magnificent – too much so for a country parish, but not at all, as I thought it might be, tawdry but solidly gorgeous. Gambier Parry's own paintings of the door (above the Chancel Arch) of the Fall and the Annunciation on either side of it, and the Angels on the East wall are particularly beautiful. His second son came in and played the organ admirably.

I finished tonight my task of looking through the *Flaxley* Library – about 1500 volumes – in the back study, and it is now midnight.

Friday 8th September 1865, Flaxley to St Dunstan's.

Up at 6 and left Flaxley at 7 and reached Belmont about ten to 11. Milly and Dolly there and many children. Aunt Harriett much as usual. I walked over to Tyntesfield with Harriett and went all over the house. It is beautiful and quite outpasses my expectations. I wrote to Blanche, dating from thence, and writing as if I had never left the place, but was giving one of my usual reports. I left by the 2.55 train from Bristol.

Thursday 19th October 1865, Tyntesfield.

Went to the Bank in the morning and came down to Tyntesfield by the two o'clock train with George R. as my servant. George Adams came with us and sleeps here. We stayed a few minutes at Belmont on our way, and saw Aunt Emily, Harriett, Alice, Albinia, Miss Barton, Miss Watts and Dolly, and Dolly Heberden. Also we saw dear Aunt Harriett (deceased) today, her own sweet face freed from pain, and having returned to her old beauty. Only Uncle William and Blanche, Willie and Hardie are here.

Friday 20th October 1865, Tyntesfield.

It rained excessively yesterday until we got to Swindon so I feared the rain might have come thus far today, but the weather has been beautiful and our sad day's work well done. Dear Uncle William has been very low in spirits for though he cannot help knowing with all of us that a long and latterly painful life has been well ended, he cannot help also looking back to his former happy days with her and Uncle Joseph, Aunt Anne and my dear father; and looking upon her death as the breaking of the last cord. George came from Clevedon, Joe from Barnstaple, Antony, Henry and Willie (now a Cantab) from Oxford, Charles from Cork, Heberden from Ranmore, John and Isabel from Leigh, A. Pott also and S. Harrison from Oxfordshire and H. Crawley from Bath. We met the hearse, as hideous as plumes could make it, at the schoolhouse and the men carried it thence to the church.

Besides the will in which she left £1500 each to Mary, John and Charles, and a small legacy or two, she left a memorandum disposing of the residue which was nominally left to Aunt Emily. Under this, I take £200 and my children (all but Henry) £50 each, Charles, John, Isabella and Mary £100 each, Dolly (of Tyntesfield) £100 and the other Tyntesfield children £50 each, Dolly Heberden £1000 and Milly the same, £100 to each of their brothers and the same to Anne Pott and £50 to Mary Pott, and £100 each to Caroline Adams, William, Frank and Joanna Crawley, Susanna and Margaret Hendy, £50 to Margaret Crawley and to each of Charlotte Sayers' 5 children, £150 to Miss Watts and £2360 between Honour Davy's children – Mary, William and Samuel Taylor, Sibella Nichols, E. Vaughan's five children (£100 each), Pugh's seven children (£100 each), Davis and Adams, 3 old servants and Mrs Bedford (each £100), and £350 to house and £245 to outdoor servants, and £200 to Waymouth and £120 to 4 foreign friends. £100 each to the S.P.G. and S.P.C.K., Arthop Hospital Torquay, the Consumptive Hospital, and the poor of Wraxall.

There will not be enough I think of Aunt Harriett's own personalty to pay all these gifts; but it will not run very far short. The analysis gives £2750 to the Joseph Gibbs family, £950 to my father's (of which £450 to mine), £400 to Uncle William's, £500 to Aunt Charlotte's, £100 to Frank, £2370 (less £400 for those already deceased) to friends or their children, £1655 (less £50 for those already deceased) to servants and dependents or their children, and £500 to charities. Two of the servants are, I find, dead so that lessens that amount.

Sunday 22nd October 1865, Tyntesfield.

A miserable wet day. We went to church in the omnibus, and when we got there the handle had fallen off, and we had to send to the blacksmith for tools to force the door. In the afternoon we had prayers at home. Letters from Louisa.

Monday 23rd October 1865, Tyntesfield.

Very fine again. Uncle William spent most of the day at Belmont with Aunt Emily and Robert Bright. Aunt Emily is rather hurt, I am sorry to say, about the division of dear Aunt Harriett's personal effects; but it is all in the most amiable temper, and her feeling is I think formed on a mistaken idea both of what is done and what should have been done. I have not yet been able to speak to her about it, but Uncle William and Blanche have, and both Uncle William and I are quite determined to give up anything or everything that is left to us, rather than there should remain the least unpleasant feeling. I said as much to George. He and we all dined at Belmont. I went out for an hour with Isaac, and had four shots at pheasants and one at a rabbit. Knocked over two pheasants, but lost both of them. Wrote to Louisa.

Tuesday 24th October 1865, Tyntesfield.

Letters from Louisa and Baring. After breakfast I went up and had a long talk with Aunt Emily, leaving matters very comfortably settled. She and Harriett went away to Clevedon. Charles, Dorothea and Alice came here so Belmont is deserted. Edith had come home with a bad cold but hoped to go back to school today.

Wednesday 25th October 1865, Tyntesfield.

George came over from Clevedon and we had a pleasant walk and talk together. I was out shooting in the evening, and he with me for a short time. I had 14 or 15 shots and killed 2 brace of pheasants and a hare. I had a letter from Louisa and one from Baring.

I have been sitting up till midnight talking over various matters with Blanche and Uncle William, and the moral of all is that no-one should leave a legacy in any other way than definitely and expressly to the legatee, never by means of a residuary legatee with discretionary power – said residual is always aggrieved. Secondly any list of one's personal effects should be made and appropriated by oneself, manna propria, while one is yet completely compos mentis. Uncle William found a cancelled will of Uncle George dated 1855 in which although he left Belmont absolutely to Uncle Joseph after Aunt Harriett, yet provided that if Uncle Joseph should die before him, the estate should be sold after Caroline's death, and as he had always given Uncle William to understand, be offered to Uncle William or whoever might be owner of Tyntesfield, and it was not till 1859, 4 years before his death, and when his mind, though quite sane, was certainly somewhat impaired in memory and otherwise, that he changed this intention.

Thursday 26th October 1865, Tyntesfield.

A miserable blowing rainy day, which we spent from noon onwards at Belmont looking over the things with Aunt Emily. She is quite comfortable now and disposed to see all that has been done quite in its right lights. George also came over to see me. Heard from Louisa.

Friday 27th October 1865, Tyntesfield.

Letters from Louisa and Plumer. Passed most of the day arranging the plate and other things, and locking up all that appertained to our family in the white room, preparatory to having them packed. Elizabeth… came looking very much better than when I was at Flaxley. She is in the Red Room and I have migrated into my room, the Turret Room.

Saturday 28th October 1865, Tyntesfield.

Letters from Louisa, and Stubbs, and Mr Norton. I wrote to Aunt Emily. Charles and Alice, Ella, Albinia and I had a pleasant ride through Charlton and Wraxall.

Sunday 29th October 1865, Tyntesfield.

A miserable windy rainy day; till the evening when it became pretty fine.

We had our evening service in the Oratory. I heard from Louisa and wrote to her and to Mr Norton….

Monday 30th October 1865, Tyntesfield.

Letter from Aunt Emily; who also came here with Harriett, George, Beatrice and Agnes. She and George wish us to keep the things we had offered her; and I am more than glad to do so because when I told Evered that I was in doubt about the silver waiter as I wished Aunt Emily to have it, he said, "When I mentioned to the other servants that that was for you, Luke said he always knew that waiter was to go to Mr Henry"……..

My conversation with Aunt Emily was pretty satisfactory.

Tuesday 31st October 1865, Tyntesfield.

Went into Bristol with Blanche and Elizabeth and took them to call on Fry. They were much pleased with his bibles and china, and with his daughter's beautiful illuminations.

Uncle William read to Blanche and me an excellent letter he had written to Aunt Emily setting her right on various points in the history of Aunt Harriett's will.

Wednesday 1st November 1865, Tyntesfield.

Took a long walk with Alice in the morning, and had a beautiful ride with the 3 girls this afternoon towards Clevedon by the road and home by Cadbury Camp – the light and shades most lovely. I rode Queen Bertha again – a very pleasant mare. Aunt Emily and Harriett came.

Thursday 2nd November 1865, Tyntesfield.

Rode with Harriett, Alice and Ella to Cadbury and back.

Friday 3rd November 1865, Tyntesfield.

Went out shooting again and shot very ill, killing but one pheasant. John came over for lunch and he and I, Harriett and Alice rode over to Leigh. Letter from Louisa in which she says she is coming tomorrow…..

Saturday 4th November 1865, Tyntesfield.

Went in to Bristol after luncheon to meet Louisa at 2.50 but found she had after all come by the 11.45 and arrived at Bristol at 2.25 and was in trouble with contending cabmen.

Sunday 5th November 1865, Tyntesfield.

We have had a cold rainy Sunday as usual the last three Sundays.

Monday 6th November 1865, Tyntesfield.

John came over to breakfast, and Isabel to dine and sleep. John shooting with me all day. He killed a woodcock, 9 pheasants, two hares and a rabbit, and I my first woodcock, 6 pheasants and 4 rabbits (10 head with 25 cartridges), but I lost two pheasants for want of a retriever, and John lost some beside those above mentioned. He had very much the most luck at getting shots at pheasants, but I in the course of the day began to know my gun, and get my hand in. Alice and Martina came up to the Summer House with our luncheon and had theirs. Made Martina load my gun and shoot at a mark, and they came with us till I shot a pheasant, which Alice liked not though she is to have his breast for her hat.

Thursday 9th November 1865, St Dunstan's.

I wrote to Blanche.

Friday 10th November 1865, St Dunstan's.

Letters from the Bishop of Oxford, Mr Ridgway of Culham, and Uncle William, the latter enclosing a most satisfactory letter from Aunt Emily and his answer thereto. I wrote to Uncle William, the Bishop and Mr. Ridgway.

Saturday 11th November 1865, St Dunstan's.

Letters from Blanche, Alice, Alban, Hardie and John....

Wednesday 3rd January 1866, Tyntesfield.

Alban and I came down here by the 11.45 train and found all very well, and they are going to a ball at Clevedon Court, from which however Alban and I abstain, as do John and Isabel. It begins to look very well here and comparatively tidy. Henry Martin grown and looking well, and the others all well.

I wrote to Louisa from hence, and to Furnivall this morning. Sat up very late with the boys.

Thursday 4th January 1866, Tyntesfield.

Letters from Rowbotham, H à Court and Loveday. Answered the two last and wrote to Louisa and Birch. A wretched rainy day. Went however to Belmont and round the hill with Harriett

A Servants Ball tonight at which we all danced the first three dances – Country Dance, Sir Roger, and the Triumph, the latter capital. First lady down the middle with the second gentleman, his partner follows and brings her back in triumph (hand over head). She and he down the middle and back, pousette. She then with the 1st, 4th and 5th successively. We used to dance it in Bedford Square ten years ago.

Friday 5th January 1866, Tyntesfield.

Letter from Louisa and wrote to her. Occupied all the morning talking to Uncle William and walking with him while the boys were coursing in the fields. In the afternoon, George and I went through the papers relating them to the question between G.N.C and Uncle George's executors. I am sorry that we find that we must give our opinion mostly against the latter. Went in the evening to Belmont. Much singing and dancing merriment there with Milly and Harry, also Constance Bright who returned with Catty in the evening.

Saturday 6th January 1866, Tyntesfield.

Rode out with Alice, Albinia and John to Backwell Common. The Roan mare ran away with me, and pulled off my false arm but did no more damage. Walked with John and Alice, and then with Uncle William. Wrote to Hubbard, Stubbs etc.....All the Belmont party dined here and we had some merriment. Alban shot his first woodcock: he has got a little cold I am sorry to say. I wrote also to Rivero.

Sunday 7th January 1866, Tyntesfield.

Thunder and lightning this morning but the weather changed 10 degrees for the colder before twelve. I heard from Louisa, Furnivall, and Elizabeth, and wrote to them. Wraxall in the morning and the Union in the evening. Dinner at half past nine after service.

Monday 8th January 1866, Tyntesfield.

John and Isabel went away to Clifton Hampden. Blanche and I walked to Bourton to call on the Burrowes and were caught in the rain. Colonel Maunsell drove us home. Letter from Harrison. Wrote to Maurice Drummond and Cokayne Maunsell.

Tuesday 9th January 1866, Tyntesfield.

Letters from Stubbs and Furnivall. Wrote to Louise. After dinner, Alice, Willy, Bob, Henry Hetherington and I, George, Beatrice, Harriett and Stanley went to a dance at the Elton's. Home by two.

Wednesday 10th January 1866, Tyntesfield.

Letters from Louisa, Charles, Furnivall and Ridgeway. Alban wrote to Charles and Ridgeway, and I to Louisa. Shooting all day. We had not good fortune though we brought home a couple of woodcocks, but the pheasants though plentiful got up out of our way. I killed 8 and 2 rabbits – 27 cartridges. Charles Lambert came also the Rev. Henry Courtenay (*the incumbent at Mamhead*) and Lady Anne Maria (*his wife*), their boy Hugh and Miss Buchanan. Mr Wayte and his wife at Belmont.

Thursday 11th January 1866, Tyntesfield.

Busy all day rehearsing. After dinner went to Belmont where were the Eltons and some neighbours, and danced ourselves thoroughly mad. In bed by half past two. Poor Alban in bed all day with his cold.

Friday 12th January 1866, Tyntesfield.

Great excitement this afternoon because of our dresses not coming. However they appeared just in time, and we actors dined together in the Housekeeper's Room, and then acted our "Slasher and Crasher" to the satisfaction of the audience and ourselves. Only Mrs Mordaunt and her daughter were there of strangers. Heard from Louisa and Alban and wrote to her and Charles.

Saturday 13th January 1866, Tyntesfield.

Letters from Louisa, Elizabeth and Charles. Wrote to the two latter and to Inez. A miserable, windy, foggy, rainy day, but Lambert and I, George, Heberden and Stanley went out shooting in the afternoon nevertheless and killed a few pheasants. I three with eight cartridges. Whist with Lady Anna Maria. Egerton Hubbard could not come. He amused us a great deal by writing his letter of excuses to Alice instead of Blanche; I suppose thinking she had been the writer of the note of invitation. His answer came yesterday and was a very pretty one.

Sunday 14th January 1866, Tyntesfield.

Letter from H. Lewin asking me to second him at the club. Wrote to Louise.

Monday 15th January 1866, St Dunstan's.

Alban's cold seems nearly well, and we came up by the 12.20 train. All well here. Kate came with us as far as Bath.

Tuesday 16th January 1866, St Dunstan's.

An Extraordinary General Meeting of the Mexican Railway went off well. Poor Frank Crawley has met with an accident in Valparaiso, having been thrown from his horse in the street. He was insensible for 12 hours.

Thursday 10th May 1866, St Dunstan's.

Immediately I got into the city I was taken with severe spasms in the stomach. Crosbie, Sewell's partner, came to me and his medicine relieved me. I had another attack however at dinner time, not so severe, though it lasted long. I am a little better now. Uncle William and Blanche, Tom and Fanny have been dining here. H. Barnett called in the city to tell me that Overend and Gurney had stopped payment.

Friday 11th May 1866, St Dunstan's.

Better this morning: but Crosbie kept me in bed until half past four. Uncle William with his accustomed kindness sitting with me for several hours….It has been a day of wild panic in the City, a run on the bankers, ours among the number but I have no doubt they are perfectly safe. We had to help H. Edwards; whose Bills were to have been discounted by O. and G. the day of their failure, and the Consolidated Bank would not or could not do it for him though as his own bankers they certainly ought. There is a rumour that the Government has suspended the Act of 1844, and that the City is quieter from the news; but George says it is not true. There is however less panic perhaps because today again there are reports of the sale of Venetia to Italy by Austria.

Saturday 12th May 1866, St Dunstan's.

The Government did suspend the Act later in the evening; and the panic seemed over.

Friday 29th June 1866, St Dunstan's.

Uncle William in the City a long while about his Will.

Monday 2nd July 1866, St Dunstan's.

Took Uncle William to Upton's and had a long talk about his Will and Alice's marriage settlement. Rode with Albinia, Antony and Gurney. The two latter, Uncle William, Blanche and Alice dined here.

Wednesday 15th August 1866, Tyntesfield.

Started for the moor (Garrigill) at 9 o'clock yesterday. 26½ brace – we three and Liddle – and came by the 5.25 Alston to Carlisle, where we dined, and left by the Limited Mail Branch going on to London, and we changing at Stafford and Birmingham and coming here by about 7 o'clock. The four Miss Gurneys – Emily, Ellen, Rosa and Mary, their brothers Edmund, John and Harry, and Frederic (the eldest) with his pretty wife (a Miss Deffell), Mrs and Miss Deffell, Tracy Majendie, and Monro came in the course of the day. Alfred is at Belmont with all the party. The Goulburns here, and the Hoggs there. We had 30 to dinner. Dear Alice looks very thin and worn, but except for the dread of leaving home she seems very happy with Alfred. Louisa and Edith came.

Thursday 16th August 1866, Tyntesfield,

The wedding has gone off very well indeed, and very happily. Alice and Blanche both remaining quite composed till the actual moment of starting. There were 60 at the breakfast. The speeches were good, short and not lachrymose. Dr Goulburn proposing the health of Alice, and Alfred Gurney answering of course and very well. Frederick Gurney proposing Uncle William and Blanche's health to which Uncle William replied beautifully – the first speech he ever made! Antony proposed Dr Goulburn's health and Charles proposed E. Vaughan's. I proposed the health of the bridesmaids to which Emily Gurney answered. Others may say if my speech was good, but it was at any rate well received and young Gurney's was excellent.

The bride and bridegroom went away at four, and are gone to Exeter on their way to Lynton. All the Belmont folk dined here.

16th August 1866, report from the Bristol Mercury.

"The village of Wraxall witnessed the marriage of Miss Alice Blanche Gibbs, William Gibbs of Tyntesfield's second daughter, to Mr Alfred Gurney, second son of the late Rev. H. Gurney, Rector of St Mary's Marylebone. Lines of flags flaunted gaily amidst the trees of Tyntesfield, festoons of evergreens and flowers met the eye at every turn in the road, triumphal arches with mottos and devices spanned the road at short intervals, flags and banners floated from the tower of Wraxall Church and fluttered in the breeze from the glittering spires which grace the roof of the noble mansion of Tyntesfield; more humble but not less gay colours and floral devices and inscriptions added much to the picturesque appearance of the cots and homesteads which crop out here and there amidst the charming scenery and romantic woods of the neighbourhood. Everything that could demonstrate the hearty wishes of all for the happiness of the bride and bridegroom was done most spontaneously by the whole of the residents of the district.

Group after group of villagers, in a state of joyous excitement, greeted the happy couple with many a heart felt wish for their health and future happiness as they passed through their midst and ringing out right joyously the happy sound of the wedding bells floated over the hill and lea. Down the long carriageway leading to Tyntesfield were a number of floral arches with suitable mottoes erected by Mr James Nicholls, the steward.

At the entrance to Wraxall church Mrs Joseph Gibbs had caused to be erected a grand archway of flowers and evergreens of the most elaborate and artistic workmanship. On either side were numerous texts, mottoes and inscriptions. The walk leading from this archway to the church was converted into a corridor composed of a series of arches covered with an awning adorned with choice flowers, and looking like fairyland itself as the bride and her companions glided over the carpeted floor over the flowers which had been scattered there. The neighbourhood of the church was crowded at an early hour and great was the anxiety to obtain advantageous seats from which to witness the interesting ceremony.

The bridegroom arrived at the church at about 11 o'clock accompanied by his brother, Mr Edmund Gurney, as his best man. The bride who entered the church leaning on the arm of her father was richly attired in a white satin dress; an exquisitely arranged coiffure of orange blossoms and myrtle adorned her forehead, and from the wreath descended, in graceful folds, an elaborately wrought Brussels lace veil of a most rich and costly description. Her ornaments were pearls and diamonds, and the effect of the whole was as chaste as it was elegant. The bride was attended by nine bridesmaids – Miss Dorothea Harriett Gibbs, Miss Albinia Gibbs, her sisters; Miss Ellen Gurney, Miss Emily Gurney, Miss Rosamond Gurney and Miss Mary Gurney, sisters of the bridegroom; Miss Edith Gibbs and Miss Martina Crawley Boevey, cousins of the bride; and Miss Margaret Hogg of Torquay. These ladies were attired in dresses of white grenadine with small blue stripes, small gipsy bonnets of the latest fashion edged with corn flowers, and from these drooped long veils. The bridesmaids also wore broad blue sashes trimmed with white lace, and a more charming group we have seldom seen. Joy reflected in every eye as the fair bride and her charming attendants knelt at the altar side. Mrs Gibbs, mother of the bride, wore a brocaded silk dress of elegant light brown tint, a pink areophane bonnet and a point lace shawl.

The ceremony was performed by the Rev. Dr. Goulburn, incumbent of St John's, Paddington, assisted by the Rev. Frederick Gurney of Torquay, brother of the bridegroom, and the Rev. E. P. Vaughan. At the conclusion of the service, as the happy couple left the church, a number of the school children dressed in white, strewed flowers on the pathway. The numerous party returned in a long string of carriages to Tyntesfield, where a sumptuous breakfast was provided. Between sixty and seventy guests sat down for the wedding breakfast

The bride's presents were exceedingly rich and beautiful. Among them were a pearl necklace, a diamond cross and ear rings from her father, an elegant silver mounted dressing case from her mother, a richly wrought dessert service from the Misses Gurney, a handsome breakfast service in silver from Mr and Mrs G. L. Gurney, a marble bust of the fair bride herself from Mrs Russell Gurney, and two miniature clocks from Lady Pilkington, Sir Vicary Gibbs daughter.

The whole of the workmen, farm labourers and others on the estate headed by the Ashton Band (which had played on the lawn during the breakfast) walked in procession to the hall door on the reappearance of the bridal party, and here they were received by Mr William Gibbs and the bride and bridegroom. They formed a semi-circle and the happy couple passed round in front of the assembled work people and exchanged greetings with them all. Having given three times three hearty cheers for the newly married couple and Mr and Mrs Gibbs and family, the workmen were conducted to a large tent erected in the grounds, where a capital dinner was provided for them. In another tent the Wraxall school children to the number of 130 partook of tea.

In the afternoon the workmen, villagers and others assembled on the lawn in front of the house, and gave the couple a round of hearty cheers as they left the mansion amidst a shower of slippers thrown after the carriage. The bride's travelling dress was of violet silk tastefully trimmed with chalk beads, black silk cloak and white crinoline bonnet trimmed with pink roses and leaves.

In the evening the band continued to enliven the proceedings with some popular airs, and a large party of villagers assembled on the grounds with the workmen, and thoroughly enjoyed the festivities of the occasion.

The happy couple will spend their honeymoon in the south of England."

Saturday 18th August 1866, Tyntesfield.
After luncheon we almost all of us went to Clevedon in three carriages. Some walked up to Walton and enjoyed the lovely view from thence. We looked in at Clevedon Court as we passed. After dinner we went to Belmont – singing, supper and whist. Russell Gurney came yesterday. Wrote to Alice.
Sunday 19th August 1866, Tyntesfield.
Most of us walked to Wraxall in the morning where Goulburn preached us an excellent sermon. Some of us went to the Union in the evening and home to a half past seven dinner.

Monday 20th August 1866, Tyntesfield.

Drove over the bridge to Durdham Down with the Goulburns and Russell Gurneys, Blanche and Uncle William and Mrs F. Gurney. The Miss Gurneys and John and Harry Gurney went away.

Tuesday 21st August 1866, Tyntesfield.

Went to a dance, yesterday night, at Clevedon Court, being Edith's first dance. She enjoyed it very much and we enjoyed her enjoyment. We were not at home until 5 this morning and got up at 11 o'clock. An idle day – billiards and croquet all the while. The Russell Gurneys and Goulburns went away.

Wednesday 22nd August 1866, Tyntesfield.

Louisa and Edith went away, and later on Mr and Mrs Deffell, and Mr and Mrs Frederick Gurney. The Belmont folk came down after dinner. Heard from and wrote to Birch.

Thursday 23rd August 1866, Tyntesfield.

Letters from Louisa, Mrs Drummond, Shank and Malcolm. The boys went to play rackets, and I had a little rabbiting with Willy and George Heberden. Wrote to Louisa and Furnivall. Dined at Belmont.

Friday 24th August 1866, Tyntesfield.

Headache today, but not bad. It is well tonight. Finished my report to the Court of the Lead Company to my great satisfaction. Wrote to Birch and Louisa and Bateman. Walked with Blanche. George and Dolly dined here. Mrs Mordaunt and Milly called.

Saturday 25th August 1866, Tyntesfield.

Letters from Louisa, Alice and Birch and George Louis. The latter came here today and is gone to Clevedon. Wrote to Louisa, Alice and Stubbs. Mr and Mrs William Miles called, she a very pleasant, pretty woman. Also Mrs George Bright and her two sisters. Alban and I played croquet with the two young ladies.

Sunday 26th August 1866, Tyntesfield.

Wraxall in the morning and Union in the evening. Letter from Sillem. Wrote for Blanche a Brief Note of the causes and course of the Austrian and Prussian War.

Monday 27th August 1866, St Dunstan's.

Left Tyntesfield with Alban by the first express and was in the city by 12 o'clock.

Friday 28th September 1866, St Dunstan's.

Long and disagreeable letters from Mexico, the worst being that Barron is not able to go to New York to meet George Crawley. Wrote to both of them

Saturday 29th September 1866, Clifton Hampden.

Not much better this morning, but I came down here nevertheless with Alban and am all the better for the change. We came down in time for

201

the repast service when the new aisle was opened. Uncle William and Blanche were there….The choir had their new surplices, and had practised well and sang excellently. The Clergy and Choir walked in procession both before Matins and Evensong, the Bishop wearing his Beretta, Evans bearing the Pastoral Staff before him and looking grand. The church was very full both morning and evening, and looks most beautiful. The Bishop arrived in time for the Evening Service at 5. His 59 minute sermon did not seem long at all, so interesting was it; but the great sermon was King's, this morning; one of the best I have ever heard.
Monday 8th October 1866, Tyntesfield.
Called on the Gurneys and then left Torquay by the 11.40 train. At Bristol we found Paine and Hilda (*horses*). Paine a little fidgety, but not bad on the road. Mrs Hogg, Etta and Salmon here. We have dined at Belmont where was Mrs Henry Vaughan.
Tuesday 9th October 1866, Tyntesfield.
Letters from Louisa, George Crawley and *Thomas Collett* Sandars (*Chairman of the Mexican Railway Company*), the two latter sad enough. Wrote to Louisa and the Bishop of Oxford. Went out shooting with Joe and Alban and we shot 40 pheasants, rabbits, a hare and a partridge. Salmon went away.
Wednesday 10th October 1866, Tyntesfield.
Letters from Louisa and George Louis. Wrote to them and to Hubbard. Rode with Albinia and Willy. Mr Hogg came and Mary Parsons but she did not dine downstairs.
Thursday 11th October 1866, Tyntesfield.
Letters from Louisa and John. Wrote to them, Hubbard and George Louis. Went out rabbiting with Alban and the two Williams, but did not signalize ourselves much. The Belmont folk dined here. Finished Freytag's novel, "Die verlorene Handschrift".
Friday 12th October 1866, Tyntesfield.
Mary had a little boy born yesterday morning. Wrote to George to congratulate; also to Louisa in answer to her letter.
Alban and I rode Punic and Hilda with the Beagles, Willy running as huntsman. We met at Farmer Light's beyond Barrow and had a good run. Hilda behaving very well and Punic very ill. He leaps very little indeed when he does leap, but Alban could not get him to face his fences without great trouble.
Miss Snow came.
Saturday 13th October 1866, Tyntesfield.
Antony and George came, the latter having matriculated from Christ Church. Alban went to Oxford. I spent nearly all day auditing the Bristol Branch.
Letter from Louisa, and wrote to her by Parcel also to George Crawley.

Letters from Barron and Escandon of rather a more comfortable complexion.

Sunday 14th October 1866, Tyntesfield.

Misty, rainy day. Service at home in the morning: at Wraxall in the afternoon. Letters from Louisa, Roscoe and Redfern, Sillem and George Crawley. Wrote to Sillem and Louisa. Mary has been very poorly and Louisa can't come till Thursday, so I shall go home and return with her; perhaps going by Clifton Hampden.

Monday 15th October 1866, Tyntesfield.

It was so dull a day yesterday that as I heard from Louisa that she could not come till Thursday, I settled to come up today; and I am glad I did for I find dear little Harry far from well, and Herbert with a badly injured hand, utterly neglected by the matron at the school – so that Louisa could not have come on Thursday.....I found a letter from Alice saying they hope to be at home on Thursday.

Saturday 20th October 1866, Tyntesfield.

Came down by the 3.50 from Didcot, after shooting for 2½ hours with John and Harrison. 13½ brace of birds and 4 hares. Aunt Daubeny, Aunt Susan, Uncle Charles and Aunt Eliza, Miss Snow, Miss Parsons and Elizabeth Crawley Boevey are the guests besides me. Alfred and Alice came back yesterday. She is very much knocked up with her journey, but looks better that she did before her marriage.

Sunday 21st October 1866, Tyntesfield.

Heard from Louisa, George Adams, Mr Thornton, Ambassador at Rio de Janiero, and George Louis, the latter enclosing very satisfactory letters from Joe from Paris. He is going thoroughly into his subject and I think will be useful to us. Wrote to Louisa, George Louis and Alban.

Monday 22nd October 1866, Tyntesfield.

Wrote to Louisa. After luncheon Antony, Alfred and I rode to Clevedon with Emily Doyne and Albinia and back over Cadbury Camp.

Tuesday 23rd October 1866, Tyntesfield.

Letters from Louisa and George, and from the Imperial Library thanking me for "Sir Generides". Wrote to the first two, to Etta Hogg and Russell Smith.

Rode out with John Daubeny, Antony and Alfred running with the Beagles. We found hares and killed one but had no good run.

Wednesday 24th October 1866, Tyntesfield.

Heard from Louisa, Sandars, Bateman and Hubbard. Wrote to Louisa, Sandars and Hubbard also to George and to Davy, to the latter about changes in our articles of partnership.

Thursday 25th October 1866, Tyntesfield.

Letters from Louisa, John and Plumer, and wrote to them.

Had a good days shooting with Alfred and Antony.

Friday 26th October 1866, St Dunstan's.
Left by the early train and reached town at noon.
Saturday 22nd December 1866, Tyntesfield.
Louisa, Vicary and I came here by the 9.15 train. Alban still has a little cough. Alice not very well. Uncle William a touch of sciatica – all the rest in their usual health. Antony on Hilda and George Abraham had a good day's hunting with the Duke (*of Beaufort*). George Louis called.
Sunday 23rd December 1866, Tyntesfield.
Letters from Darkwood and Blake. Wrote to them and to Hubbard. Alice very poorly again tonight.
Monday 24th December 1866, Tyntesfield.
All the Belmont party dined with us so we were 22 at dinner. Much glee – singing in the evening. Shot at Charlton. I killed 4 pheasants, 6 rabbits and a woodcock.
Christmas Day 1866, Tyntesfield.
The Belmont party came again this evening. Louisa and Edith sat awhile with us in the smoking room.
Wednesday 26th December 1866, Tyntesfield.
Mr and Mrs Vaughan, Harriett, Emma and Anna Maria and Henry Vaughan came in the evening, also Aunt Emily, Harriett, Beatrice and Stanley.
We had a good day with the beagles, I riding Manchester, Alban Victor, and Vicary Cox. Martin rode Box and Antony his black mare Bitton, Alfred Hilda and Stanley old Tredegar; George Louis the Belmont pony. Willy, George Abraham and Harrison running. I called on the Woolleys.
Friday 28th December 1866, Tyntesfield.
A long day's shooting yesterday, in which we killed 106 pheasants, 32 rabbits and four hares. In the evening we went to Clevedon Court where they had the play of "Still waters run deep" George Louis – Hawksley, and Gordon Young – John Mildmay, Gertrude Young – Mrs Sternhold, and Agnes – Mrs Mildmay. Potter acted well by a Mr Grey. All did very well. Dance afterwards and home by 3.45.
Today we have had a most splendid days hunting with the Duke (*of Beaufort*). The meet was at Cross Hands. We were not unfortunately quite in time, but we came up just as the hounds were gone away and followed at the tail of the hunt with the last of the field, but not with the hounds. We ran the fox to earth after a short run at Syston, dug him out, soon lost him, and instantly found another, whom we ran to earth after a very quick long run through both country hedge and stone wall, at half past three; we five Tyntesfielders being well up all the day. I rode Manchester who behaved very well; Alban Victor who to our surprise turned out a very good hunter, though not being prepared for he was so tired half the way home that we lost our train, and had to cook ourselves

bacon and eggs at Yate Station. Antony rode his black mare Bilton, George old Tredegar, and Alfred Queen Bertha. Home at half past eight.

Saturday 29th December 1866, Tyntesfield.

Willy seemed so much more poorly yesterday that they sent for Adams who I grieve to say said his state is much worse than it was a week ago and he evidently thinks him in a dangerous state his weakness having much increased.

It is unfortunate that Aunt Charlotte, Joanna and Margaret have come to stay for a week.

We all went to dine at Belmont but for Uncle William, Blanche and Hardie who stayed at home with Willy. They have put off a ball which was to be held on the second, and our acting which was to have been on the fourth of January.

Sunday 30th December 1866, Tyntesfield.

Willy had a good night and was better this morning, and till after dinner but then he went to bed much exhausted.

Monday 31st December 1866, Tyntesfield.

Mr Adams gives a better account of Willy today I am glad to say; and he himself seems more comfortable. We shot at Charlton. The Belmont folks came here this evening.

Tuesday 1st January 1867, Tyntesfield.

We sat out the old year last night, but it was a painful ceremony, wishing each other a Happy New Year, when dear Willy seemed in such danger. He is however better today.

The boys went with the beagles to Charlton. I rode with Hardie.

Wednesday 2nd January 1867, Tyntesfield.

Had a long days shooting in the Great Woods, the snow being about three inches deep.

Thursday 3rd January 1867, Tyntesfield.

Willy still a little better. George Louis went to town about Devon and Somerset matters. Heard from Aunt Elisa, through Aunt Charlotte, that Charles has engaged himself to his governess, Miss Harrap! She is I believe a very good sort of person, but it is highly wrong of him, to think of marrying when he has not a shilling in the world, but heavy debts which he can't pay.

Weather very cold and snow deep.

Friday 4th January 1867, Tyntesfield.

Letter from George Adams.

Saturday 5th January 1867, Tyntesfield.

Aunt Charlotte, Joanna and Margaret went away. Letters from George Louis and Rati saying I am wanted in town about Moscow Gas. I wrote to G.E.A. (*George Adams*), Norris and Dashwood. We are to go on Monday, which is a day before I wished.

14 degrees of frost last night. It is now blowing a hurricane, and I think raining.

Sunday 6th January 1867, Tyntesfield.

A complete thaw. George Louis came back last night. The Moscow Gas works are lighted up with their own gas, and on Tuesday next there's to be a grand function, the Prince Mayor lighting the first public lamp with a silver torch.

Monday 7th January 1867, St Dunstan's.

We all (except Alban) came up by the 12.20 train.

Thursday 10th January 1867, Tyntesfield.

Sandars and I came here by the 11.45.

Friday 11th January 1867, Tyntesfield.

Pott, Milly and their four eldest children came here. Sandars went to Taunton and I came back to dinner. We had a good days shooting in the woods. Hard frost destroying hopes of tomorrow's hunting.

Saturday 12th January 1867, Tyntesfield.

Joe came this evening. Alban and I rode to lunch at Leigh.

Sunday 13th January 1867, Tyntesfield.

Letters from Louisa, Stubbs, Blake and Hubbard. Hard frost still. Dick and Emma Bright called.

Monday 14th January 1867, St Dunstan's.

Alban, George, Joe and I came up by the early train.

Monday 21st January 1867, St Dunstan's.

Uncle William's illness has been a very serious one, an attack of bronchitis, but we hear from Blanche that he is happily better. She wrote to tell of his illness on Friday, but her letter seems to have been a little too late for the post. Wrote to her….

Friday 25th January 1867, Tyntesfield.

Edith and I came down yesterday by the 9.15 and went to the Fancy Ball in the evening at the Merchants Hall in Bristol. It was a most complete success, the rooms beautiful and the dresses capital.

Some 350 people were there and only 3 or 4 in plain clothes. We eight danced the Lancers together – Gurney as Knight Templar, Alice as Hypatica, George Louis as Henry Esmair, Beatrice and Harriett as ladies of the same date, with powder. Antony as Earl of Leicester, Edith as Margaret of Anjou and I in my Deputy Lieutenant's uniform. We got to bed at 6.00.

Uncle William is better but still very poorly. He came down into his room today for the first time. I do think Moscow Gas is at last practically settled – the lawyers had their meeting yesterday and smoothed over all difficulties, and now it is only a question of time.

There is an alarm that the little Potts, George Louis's children, and Johnny have the measles, so we sent Edith off to sleep at Belmont.

26th January 1867, Norman Court.

I took Edith to Bristol to go to town by the 10.15. Annie and Charles Pott with the Governess went with her as far as Didcot. The measles were I think a false alarm. The whole house however has got colds and John was in bed with it. Uncle William had a bad night. I came here by the 1.25 train by way of Salisbury arriving about 5 o'clock.

Monday 4th February 1867, St Dunstan's.

Letters from Uncle William, Alban, John and Richard Bright. Wrote to all but John. Had a long talk with Upton about Uncle William's testamentary arrangements about his capital. Telegram from Egerton Hubbard and Co. that the gas coal at St Petersburg has begun to heat.

Wednesday 6th February 1867, St Dunstan's.

Wrote a long letter to Uncle William about his Will.

Friday 1st March 1867, St Dunstan's.

Spent four hours with Upton about Uncle William's will. No letters from Mexico City, the mail having been robbed. Went to a Ball at Lady Mildred Hope's with Louisa and Edith.

Saturday 2nd March 1867, Tyntesfield.

I came down here by the 11.45 and found Uncle William tolerably well. Had a long talk with him about his Will, to be resumed on Monday when we get Upton's amended clauses. Spent a long time sketching some amended ones of my own.

Sunday 3rd March 1867, Tyntesfield.

Letters from Alban and Upton. Wrote to Catten and Louisa.

Monday 4th March 1867, Tyntesfield.

Settled with Uncle William all his Will arrangements and shall send his new codicils to Upton tomorrow. Wrote to Alban and Louisa.

Tuesday 5th March 1867, Tyntesfield.

Wrote to Upton, Louisa, Robert Bennett (Sherborne, Dorset)…Aunt Emily, Harriett and Miss West.

Wednesday 6th March 1867, St Dunstan's.

Went to church at Wraxall and came to town by the 2.55 train.

Thursday 5th September 1867, Tyntesfield.

Came here by the 11.45 express joining it at Swindon. Blanche, Willy and Hardie in Ireland. Alice and Alfred Gurney are here and Ellen and Mary, his sisters, also Mr Field, Antony, Georgey, Dolly, Henry Martin and young Manuel Martinez. Uncle William very well and Alice much better. Wrote to Louisa.

Friday 6th September 1867, Tyntesfield.

Wrote to Louisa from whom I heard, also to Gibson and Mary Gibbs. I am very glad to hear that Eliza is today sometime with Louisa while we are away. Had luncheon at Belmont. Mr and Mrs Hancock are there. She a pretty and lively sister of Joe's wife.

Walked with Harriett round the hill.

Saturday 7th September 1867, St Dunstan's.

Alfred and his two sisters went to Torquay. He intends to return with the other two on Monday. I came away by the 2.30 train and found all well here.

Uncle William had a long talk with me this morning about his church in Exeter, which was to be consecrated at the end of the month. He fears the "Ritualism" of the Rector and has got into a correspondence with him, in which both parties are misunderstanding one another. Mr Joye is not altogether wrong in his argument, but I don't at all like his tone in writing to Uncle William, who after all that he has done for him and for the church, deserved to be treated with more consideration.

Thursday 12th September 1867, St Dunstan's.

Heard from Uncle William about his controversy with Joye, shewed the correspondence to Hubbard, and wrote to Uncle William with his opinion.

Saturday 14th September 1867, St Dunstan's.

George came up from Clevedon and sleeps here. Heard from Uncle William.

Wednesday 8th January 1868, St Dunstan's.

Heard from and wrote to Uncle William. George Louis went to Belmont.

Thursday 9th January 1868, St Dunstan's.

Letter from Alban at Tyntesfield, who says his cold and cough are not yet well.

Friday 10th January 1868, St Dunstan's.

Heard from and wrote to Uncle William.

Saturday 11th January 1868, Tyntesfield.

I am very sorry to hear a poor account of George Reynolds this morning. I came down here by the 9.15 to find Alban not looking particularly well, having still a bad cold, but they tell me he is much better than he was. Uncle William very well but more lame. Egerton Hubbard is here, Hector Monro and Rhode Hawkins (the latter came by night), Lady Anna Maria Courtenay and Miss Buchanan. At Belmont are Charles Lambert, Sidney Harrison (*the Estate Agent at Clifton Hampden*) and all the boys. They all seem to have enjoyed the Ball immensely. I have just written a letter to William Barron for the French Mail, after playing two games of pool, one of which I divided with Antony.

Sunday 12th January 1868, Tyntesfield.

Rain has melted all the snow away. I had taken the Blue Pill and have stayed in all day......Wrote to Louisa and John.

Monday 13th January 1868, Tyntesfield.

We had a pretty good day's shooting, not withstanding that it was blowing a gale all the while. This evening the servants had a ball, and we

208

all danced 3 long country dances, I dancing with Mrs Davis, Jones and Mary, the Cook. It was very good fun. Rhode Hawkins and Egerton Hubbard went away from here, and Harrison, the Lamberts, Kathleen Stubbs, George Louis and Stanley* from Belmont.

(* *Stanley Vaughan Gibbs, son of William Gibbs' brother the Rev Joseph Gibbs and his wife Emily Vaughan.*)

Tuesday 14th January 1868, Tyntesfield.

I heard from Louisa, with no account of poor George Reynolds; but her letter to Blanche written later in the day gives me the sad news that he died yesterday. He was indeed a faithful friend and servant, and I shall never have one like him. I feel very much for his poor wife. Reeks told me this morning with tears of his hopeless state. He had heard it from Mrs King. Lady Anna Maria and Kitty Buchanan went away today. Wrote to Louisa.

Wednesday 15th January 1868, Tyntesfield.

Antony went to shoot at the Miles of Leigh Court. I took a pleasant walk with Blanche before dinner. Heard from Louisa, Stubbs and George Adams and wrote to all three.

Thursday 16th January 1868, Tyntesfield.

Heard from Louisa that poor George was to be buried today. Wrote to her. Antony and Alfred went out hunting. Kate and Mary, Martin, George Heberden, Antony, Dolly the younger and Miss Von Pohl went to the Clifton Madrigals.

Friday 17th January 1868, Tyntesfield.

Monro went to Belmont. I dined there to meet Mrs Elton and Minna, Agnes and Edmund. Saw Beatrice and her three charming little children. Walked back in heavy rain with Sheppard, Edmund, Harriett and Minna. Heard from Louisa and Aunt Charlotte and wrote to them.

Saturday 18th January 1868, Tyntesfield.

John Pode came this evening. We were to have shot – but the weather was all too stormy – nevertheless Blanche, George and I were able to walk round the hill before dinner. Had a long talk with Uncle William, about Antony's allowance, about his going on the Bench, and (when he should find a wife) getting married and settled at Charlton. Letters from Louisa and yesterday from George Adams.

Sunday 19th January 1868, Tyntesfield.

A finer day, but the gale still heavy. I had a long talk with Alban about Oxford and consented to his going up in Law and History instead of in Classics. I must say I am much disappointed at it, because I consider the latter the best training; but as he has not left time enough for it, there is no remedy. He assures me he shall like his work and will apply himself heartily to it. Ojala! Letters from Louisa, Baring….and wrote to them.

Monday 20th January 1868, Clifton Hampden.

Came here by the 10.40 train.

Thursday 23rd January 1868, St Dunstan's.

Wrote to Fry, Alban, Uncle William.

Monday 27th January 1868, St Dunstan's.

Satisfactory accounts from Mexico and a remittance on Railway Account, though small (£1300).

Tuesday 28th January 1868, St Dunstan's.

Letter from Uncle William and I wrote to him.

Wednesday 29th January 1868, St Dunstan's.

Louis Mallet and Plumer called at the Counting House…Busy all day with the Mexican Railway Report.

Thursday 30th January 1868, St Dunstan's.

Tonight we have dined with the Coleridges.

Saturday 1st February 1868, St Dunstan's.

Busy all day about Mexican Railway and Moscow Gas.

Wednesday 12th February 1868, St Dunstan's.

Wrote to Uncle William.

Thursday 13th February 1868, St Dunstan's.

Joe goes with Antony to Paris. I wrote to Uncle William…and also to Suarez with introductions for Antony.

Friday 14th February 1868, St Dunstan's.

Antony goes to Paris with Joe tomorrow.

Wednesday 19th February 1868, St Dunstan's.

Heard from and wrote to Uncle William.

Thursday 27th February 1868, St Dunstan's.

Letter from Uncle William. Stuart discharged our writ so Ross will go free for the present.

Friday 28th February 1868, St Dunstan's.

Stuart gave a very unjust judgement yesterday. Sandars dined here and played whist. I wrote to Uncle William.

Sunday 1st March 1868, St Dunstan's.

Uncle William and Blanche came up yesterday to sit with Alice. I saw them this afternoon and Uncle William was not so much vexed as I feared he would be at Stuart's rash remarks. He and Blanche both said, "If we are right, it does not much signify." This morning we had an admirable sermon from McKonochie at St John's. I don't know that ever I heard one that so spoke to one. It was on "God my Saviour".

Monday 2nd March 1868, St Dunstan's.

Letters from Mexico tell us that we are not quite out of the wood as to the Concession, as the Congress are making an awful howling about it, but our lawyers think the Government will keep firm to their point.

Tuesday 3rd March 1868, St Dunstan's.
Uncle William and Blanche dined here, but I dined at half past nine at
the City Club.
Thursday 5th March 1868, St Dunstan's.
I came home to luncheon to which Uncle William came. Blanche also,
and Alice came in the afternoon after he was gone.
Saturday 4th July 1868, St Dunstan's.
We have had a great fright today in a letter from Blanche saying dear
Uncle William had a return of his Mamhead illness, with complications
of that which he had before at Tyntesfield. He was very ill yesterday, and
as he is four years older, even this lighter attack naturally made us all
very apprehensive. I was very thankful therefore to receive another letter
(by the hand of Morris who was there) tonight to say he was decidedly
better.
Sunday 5th July 1868, St Dunstan's.
At home all day with a bad cold. George Louis came back from Moscow,
looking very well.
Monday 6th July 1868, St Dunstan's.
He (George Louis) has gone today to Clevedon. A good account of
Uncle William, I am happy to say.
Tuesday 7th July 1868, St Dunstan's.
Went into the City today, and have done my cold no good.
Letter from George Louis and one from Blanche.
Thursday 9th July 1868, St Dunstan's.
Letters from Blanche and George Louis. Dear Uncle William is not so
well.
Friday 10th July 1868, St Dunstan's.
Letter from Mexico, saying that as we had foreseen, the Congress had
separated without settling our affair.
Saturday 11th July 1868, St Dunstan's.
The accounts from Tyntesfield not so good, in so far as dear Uncle
William, though no worse, gets no better. Wrote to Alban and Antony at
Hamburg, George having written to Antony at Copenhagen and Blanche
to the same at Berlin.
Sunday 12th July 1868, Tyntesfield.
I came down by the 10 o'clock train arriving at Bristol at half past three,
and find dear Uncle William better. I think he has even improved in these
few hours since I came. I hope he may really have turned the corner.
Willy too looks much better than he did. Alfred and Alice are here.
Monday 13th July 1868, Tyntesfield.
He has been decidedly better today and has sat up several hours and feels
much more cheerful. Harrison and Adams both told me that they thought
the danger was probably over for this time. Blanche is uneasy about

211

Alice who indeed looks dreadfully thin. I wrote to Louisa yesterday and today.

Tuesday 14th July 1868, Tyntesfield.

Uncle William did too much yesterday, and was consequently very low and exhausted all the morning. But he is better this evening and Harrison does not think very much of this little fluctuation. Still so long as they must keep the catheter continually in its place, the danger cannot be over. Wrote to Louisa from whom I heard and to Antony at Berlin.

Wednesday 15th July 1868, St Dunstan's.

Returned by the 10 o'clock train, leaving Uncle William a little more comfortable, after a good night.

Saturday 1st August 1868, St Dunstan's.

Letter from Blanche with a very good account of Uncle William.

Tuesday 4th August 1868, St Dunstan's.

Letter from Uncle William, who is going on well.

Wednesday 2nd September 1868, St Dunstan's.

Two scoundrels of Germans, one of them called Ritter, came to propose that we should abandon our concession of the Mexican Railway, and leave the field open to them, they paying us on a valuation of the works in shares in their companies. Blanche, Alfred and Alice (Gurney) dined here. Dear Alice looks very ill. Edith went to Flaxley.

Thursday 3rd September 1868, St Dunstan's.

Today Risley and Martina Crawley are married, and also George Henry Gibbs and Mildred Mordaunt. Blanche went home and Alfred and Alice start tomorrow.

Friday 4th September 1868, St Dunstan's.

We had a lively letter from Edith about the wedding. The Gurneys did go and cross tonight.

Saturday 5th September 1868, Tyntesfield.

Came down here by the early express and find Uncle William really very well, lameness excepted. John came in the afternoon.

Sunday 6th September 1868, Tyntesfield.

Blanche has a comfortable letter from Alfred.

Monday 7th September 1868, Tyntesfield.

Antony went to Flaxley. Mr and Mrs Bullock came to stay. Mr. Bright, Catty and Constance to dinner.

Tuesday 8th September 1868, Tyntesfield.

Willie went to Flaxley.

Wednesday 9th September 1868, Clifton Hampden.

Uncle William has kindly given Mary, John and Charles £2000 a piece to make up for some of the unproductive investments into which they have got. John, Georgie and I came here by the 10.40 train from Bristol.

Friday 23rd October 1868. Tyntesfield.

I came down here from town with Stubbs, and John and Arthur Birch, the latter joining us at Didcot, and J.B. at Bristol wither he had come from Salisbury – a wretched Captain Barnes from the Artillery has stolen my portmanteau, leaving his upon the platform so I am almost clothesless. This morning John drove me into Oxford, stopping to call at Littlemore. We had luncheon at Alban's rooms, and then called on Coxe at the Bodleian. I met him and had a chat at the Bodleian on my way to the station. Aunt Emily, Harriett and Willy are here. The Heberdens are at Belmont where their little Sissy is now really getting up her strength again.

Saturday 24th October 1868, Tyntesfield.

A miserable day with a hurricane of wind and rain – the latter ceased at three and we went out for a couple of hours, but got scarcely any shooting owing to the wet and wind. I got all the particulars I wanted about the "Chevelere Assigne" Ivory Basket, and copied the letters. Letter from Louisa.

Sunday 25th October 1868, Tyntesfield.

A wretched day of fog and rain. Morning service at Wraxall and evening here – George Heberden officiating. Heard from and wrote to Edith and Aunt Eliza. Also to Mr Bright and Uncle William.

Monday 26th October 1868, Tyntesfield.

We had a lovely day, half in Charlton where we had luncheon in the very nicely repaired house, and half in the woods here. We killed 99 pheasants and a great many rabbits. Aunt Emily, Harriett and Willy went to Clifton Hampden to stay.

Tuesday 27th October 1868, Tyntesfield.

We all came up by train from Bristol. We had a Mexican Meeting to discuss whether we should accept the miserable little subscriptions to the loan. Wrote to Uncle William.

Tuesday 3rd November 1868, St Dunstan's.

We have been present at a magnificent dinner given by the Lord Mayor at the Mansion House. George and Beatrice were there.

Thursday 12th November 1868, St Dunstan's.

I have been so busy with the Mexican Railway and other matters that I have always omitted to write my journal. We have returned the small contributions to the Mexican Railway loan, and have been anxiously considering what was now to be done for the company. Whatever we do we must do in conjunction with Barron, and his letter received today is not encouraging. I am going out tomorrow evening to consult Uncle William, stopping in Paris to see Escandon and George Crawley.

Saturday 14th November 1868, Grand Hôtel, Paris.

Wrote a long letter to Barron about prospective arrangements of the

Mexican Railway Company; and in the evening George and I and Edith came here by the Calais Mail, Sir Antony Rothschild crossing with us, and getting us a carriage to ourselves. Our first greeting was in the shape of two telegrams from Stubbs – one saying there was an important letter coming by post, which I hear in answer to a telegram I have sent, is from Uncle William and the others communicating a telegram from Barron, saying the concession has been satisfactorily settled.

We have been hard at work all day writing out the conditions of our proposed plan of operation, Edith acting as our copying clerk. Dined at the Café de la Paix.

Sunday 15th November 1868, Grand Hôtel, Paris.

Letter from Uncle William, in which he so thoroughly accords with our plan of action that I feel it quite unnecessary to go on and I shall return tomorrow. Escandon has gone today to Mexico.

George and George Crawley have just started for England.

Saturday 29th March 1869, St Dunstan's.

Wrote to Uncle William.

Tuesday 30th March 1869, St Dunstan's.

Letter from Uncle William.

Saturday 3rd April 1869, St Dunstan's.

Letter from Uncle William announcing their arrival in Paris.

Tuesday 6th April 1869, St Dunstan's.

Called this morning at Hyde Park Gardens and saw Alfred (Gurney) and Alice, who with Charles had returned last night. She looking very much better than when she went abroad; so we must give some credit to St Moritz. This afternoon I had the great pleasure of seeing Uncle William and all the rest of the party safe in their own home again. We have been to tea with them this evening. My Uncle is very feeble in his legs, but otherwise very well to all appearances. I got Sir Henry Thompson to see him, and he promises him some relief for his ailment in the bladder.

Thursday 15th April 1869, St Dunstan's.

Alban went back to Oxford. Louisa and Edith and I dined at John Lewis Merivale's where we met the Trollopes. (*John Lewis Merivale and Antony Trollope were at school together at Sunbury and Harrow, and his uncle, Harry Drury, was Trollope's tutor. They first met when Trollope was ten years old. For more than fifty years they were close friends.*) [xv]

Saturday 22nd May 1869, St Dunstan's.

We dined in Hyde Park Gardens to congratulate Uncle William on his 79th birthday. George and Beatrice and Kate dined there too, and Stanley and Harriett came in the evening.

Friday 28th May 1869, St Dunstan's.

Dined at Hyde Park Gardens. Matilda and Geraldine Fitzgerald and Douglas Greyley there.

Sunday 30th May 1869, St Dunstan's.

Went to luncheon at the Lamberts…Kenneth walked with me, and we went also to see the William Gibbses and Aunt Emily.

Wednesday 2nd June 1869, St Dunstan's.

Uncle William and Blanche, Antony and Alfred, Kenneth and I went to see the school, and Mr and Mrs Rhode Hawkins and their two nieces were also there.

Saturday 5th June 1869, St Dunstan's.

George and I with Hope (*Alexander Berseford Hope*) and his brother in law Grahame went down to Lodge Farm, taking Penny with us. We dined with Hope at Parsloes, a beautiful old house belonging to one of the Fanshawes – that is today; the interior is beautifully panelled in old Elizabethan wood – Hall, dining room and drawing room, and there is a fine and well stocked library something like the Abbot's Room at Flaxley. The Red brick outside is not so good, being uglily battlemented. In the evening we went to Hyde Park Gardens where George and Beatrice are staying, (now that Aunt Emily is there too), and I came home with Louisa who had dined there.

Tuesday 8th June 1869, St Dunstan's.

I am sorry to say that the William Gibbses have all hurried down to Tyntesfield, on the receipt of a very bad account of dear Willy. I don't know the particulars, but I shall no doubt hear tomorrow.

Wednesday 9th June 1869, St Dunstan's.

I hear that poor Willy has rallied a little, but is still in great danger. He had a burst haemorrhage, which as he was lying down remained in his lungs and nearly suffocated him. I am afraid the consequent exhaustion must be too great to allow for any hope of his recovery. It is most sad. I greatly fear the effect on Uncle William. I did hope poor dear Willy would have outlived his father! It was very unfortunate that Alice was there alone with him! In her weak state of health it must be so bad for her.

Thursday 10th June 1869, St Dunstan's.

No change in Willy's state. Alban and Edith came back from Oxford. Charlotte Yonge and Kate, Lord and Lady Houghton and their daughter, Mrs Twisteton, Sir C., Lady and Miss Isham, Cardwell, Hubbard, Cecil, Alice H, and Monsieur Michel and his son dined here.

Friday 11th June 1869, St Dunstan's.

A letter from Georgey to Harriett prepared us this morning for dear Willy's speedy release and they have a telegram this afternoon from Hyde Park Gardens saying that he died at one o'clock this afternoon. Though his life has been a suffering one it was always a happy one, as it could not fail to be for such a good and affectionate fellow surrounded by such a loving family. They will feel it most deeply, and to us also his loss will leave a sad blank.

We have put off a dinner party at the Greens, and have had to bring here to dinner George, G.B.Crawley and Sandars that we may have a long consultation afterwards on the course to be taken by the Mexican Board about William Barron's proposals.

Sunday 13th June 1869, St Dunstan's.

After Service I went to Hyde Park Gardens to see Aunt Emily who is still very poorly; but she was not yet downstairs. I had yesterday a most pleasing letter from dear Uncle William. I wrote to him.

Monday 14th June 1869, St Dunstan's.

Another letter from Uncle William which I had no time to answer so busy was I all day with William Barron's affair. Wrote to him and Escandon and Joe.

Tuesday 15th June 1869, St Dunstan's.

Letters from Harrison and John. Answered the latter and wrote to Uncle William.

Wednesday 16th June 1869, Tyntesfield.

Alban and I, George, Stanley, Clifford Pott and John have come down here to the funeral. I find Uncle William and Blanche also as well as I would hope to find them, but she is much worn out. Alice is better than I would have expected after the shock she has had.

Thursday 17th June 1869, St Dunstan's.

Alban and I came up by the 2.45 train, and Henry Martin with us. The William Gibbses come on Monday. I called in Hyde Park Gardens on my way and saw Milly. She gives a very bad account of her dear mother's state. The other Milly, George Henry's wife, is at Belmont and doing well after the birth of her little girl.

Friday 18th June 1869, St Dunstan's.

George came up this afternoon, and I found him at Hyde Park Gardens when I went to enquire after Aunt Emily. Sir Arthur and Lady Elton were there too, and Mary. Aunt Emily is no better.

Louisa, Edith and I went to the Duke of Newcastle's to see the House and the things to be sold. There was not much to see except a Ball Room with a beautiful chimney piece and door.

Monday 21st June 1869, St Dunstan's.

Uncle William and Blanche came up this evening to Hyde Park Gardens.

Tuesday 22nd June 1869, St Dunstan's.

They came here this afternoon to see us. I wrote to Alfred (Gurney) proposing that he and Alice should take Elm Lodge at Elstree. I saw the agent today and got the (first) refusal of it for them.

Wednesday 23rd June 1869, St Dunstan's.

Uncle William and Blanche came here to stay, and Alfred came up from Clifton Hampden.

216

Sunday 18th July 1869, St Dunstan's.

I went to church at St Mary Magdalene, Paddington and then went to luncheon at Hyde Park Gardens and afterwards called on the Coleridges.

Tuesday 20th July 1869, Tyntesfield.

I came down here by the two o'clock train and find Uncle William and Blanche both very well, and as cheerful as I could hope. The people down here are Dolly and Miss Townley (a pleasing person, but a plain likeness of Catty Bright), Albinia, Antony, George and Hardie.

Wednesday 21st July 1869, Tyntesfield.

Went into Bristol with Blanche, and occupied myself during our shopping with going to Fullers, and looking at his Dogcarts and Wagonettes. The former (with Break) £45, the latter convertible into Stanhope phaetons (or T. Carts as the present phrase is) £55. A second hand uglyish one £25. Wrote to Louisa.

Thursday 22nd July 1869, Tyntesfield.

Antony and George went to town this morning. Blanche and I called at Abbots Leigh on our way back yesterday, on Jane, Catty, Isabel and Constance. Catty particularly blooming and well, and dear Isabel much better than I have seen her for a long while. Mr Robert Bright is a little better today, but they were much alarmed about him on Tuesday. Today I walked with Blanche to Charlton, and took a good walk with Hardie after 6 o'clock. Heard from Louisa and Kate, and wrote to them and to George Louis.

Saturday 24th July 1869, Tyntesfield.

Antony returned from town yesterday, and went today to Weston to stand Godfather tomorrow to George Henry's baby. Kate and Charles Pode came this evening. Uncle William, Hardie and I went to Clifton to call on Ward to see about some of the late Sir W. Abdy's land which Uncle William may probably buy. Letter from Louisa of the 22nd posted too late – one of yesterday – poor Alban's lameness turns out to be a slight touch of gout! Early for him to begin; but I suppose some lameness which I remember to have had at Rugby was the same; so he need not fear to have it worse than I had.

Sunday 25th July 1869, Tyntesfield.

Rode over to church at Leigh and spent a pleasant day coming back by half past nine. Richard and Reginald Bright were there, Catty, Constance and Isabel. The latter looking well. She and John go tomorrow to Weymouth, where their children are. Mr Bright is a little better.

Monday 26th July 1869, Tyntesfield.

Spent the day at Weston, with Kenny and Mildred. Antony, George and Harriett were there for the christening yesterday. Antony, George and Harriett returned in time to dine here. Wrote to Louisa from Weston.

Tuesday 27th July 1869, Tyntesfield.

Heard from and wrote to Louisa. Letter from Stubbs and wrote to George.

Wednesday 28th July 1869, Tyntesfield.

Wrote to Louisa. Charles Pode went away. Charles came in for a few hours on his way back to Chatham. He had been staying at Glastonbury with his old friend Colonel Atty.

Thursday 29th July 1869, Tyntesfield.

Harriett came over here and Georgey went back with her to Weston.

Friday 30th July 1869, Tyntesfield.

Heard from and wrote to Louisa. Georgey's friend Drake came. Antony dined at the Mordaunts.

Saturday 31st July 1869, Tyntesfield.

Heard from George (with the Mexican letters), from S. Hawtrey, from Count Strzelecki, (*Sir Paul Edmund de Strzelecki, 1797-1873, explorer and scientist*), and from Harrison, Louisa and Alban. Wrote to the three first. Barron's letters are conciliatory, but not generous, and I begin to have some fears that they won't get the line finished in time to be open by September 19th. The line is finished but the rails are not up from Paso del Macho. Richard and Antony Crawley-Boevey came – nice lads they are. Dick plays the organ beautifully. Miss Graumann came.

Sunday 1st August 1869, Tyntesfield.

Letter from Louisa and wrote to her. Took a walk with Blanche after luncheon, and got caught in the rain.

Monday 2nd August 1869, Aldenham.

Came up by the 11.45 train, met Louisa and Herbert at St Dunstan's and came down here to a very late dinner. We are still in considerable confusion, but it is very pleasant to find ourselves here after so many years. We are sleeping in the Red Room, my dear mother's room.

Friday 6th August 1869, Aldenham.

Our new Wagonette came from Fuller's at Bristol. It cost £55.

Monday 20th September 1869, St Dunstan's.

Letters from George and Uncle William.

Tuesday 21st September 1869, Tyntesfield.

I came down here in consequence of Uncle William and George wishing me to intervene in the valuation of Belmont, so far at least as to settle the principle on which it is to be made.

There is a large party here, all the Belmont party and Doctor Daubeny and his wife – she is a most charming person; I have not seen him for he is and has been in bed for a fortnight with a severe rheumatic attack. He is the nephew of Uncle Daubeny and was he says at school with me at Rugby. John is here and Isabel. She is better now, but has been much upset by her good father's lingering illness and death. He died on

218

Sunday.

On my way here I called at Charles Ward in Bristol to see the draft of Uncle George's will, and consult him on some points connected with the sale of Belmont.

Wednesday 22nd September 1869, Tyntesfield.

A long letter from Blake, which I answered, writing also to Hubbard and Louisa from whom I had heard. I forgot to say that Lonergam and his wife came down here yesterday.

We all went out with the Beagles and had luncheon in the Summer House. I went up to see Dr. Daubeny. He is a small likeness of James, his and my cousin.

Thursday 23rd September 1869, Tyntesfield.

The Lonergams went away, and Henry and Mildred came. Wrote to George Louis a letter to serve as instructions to the valuer, Mr Thomas Ward. I thought it better to put it in writing though George is here. Uncle William won't say a word to me about the matter, nor allow Blanche to do so, so that no-one can possibly say that he has influenced his nephew. Meanwhile he expressed his anxiety to me that George should have full value of the Estate, and leaves it to me to settle. I call in Ward, and if the valuation he puts on it is very widely different from my idea, I call in another. Wrote to Louisa and to Stubbs.

Friday 24th September 1869, Tyntesfield.

All we men, and Blanche, went to Mr Bright's funeral. Ward called and had a conference with me about the valuation. Heard from and wrote to Louisa. Henry and Mildred went away.

Saturday 25th September 1869, Tyntesfield.

George and Dolly went home this morning, and in the afternoon George and Beatrice went to Wells (Milton House), Stanley, Harriett and Willy to Weston and Milly to Abingdon. George, Stanley and I had a pleasant ride across country with the Beagles, Willy running – but it was a blank day. I rode the brown mare which was Georgey's. Answered a letter from Louisa.

Sunday 26th September 1869, Tyntesfield.

Heard from and wrote to Louisa.

Monday 27th September 1869, Aldenham.

Came home by the 11.45 train. I wrote to Blanche.

Wednesday 29th September 1869, Aldenham.

George and Stanley came to town yesterday and to the City today, as I did….Wrote to Uncle William and found a letter from him this evening when I came home.

Tuesday 5th October 1869, Tyntesfield.

George, Stanley, and I came to Bristol by the morning express and I called on Mr Thomas Ward about the valuation. All well here except for poor Dr. Daubeny, who is much as he was. Sir Thomas Wallace is here, his two daughters, and Edmund and John Gurney.

Wednesday 6th October 1869, Tyntesfield.

We had a beautiful day's hunting at Broadfield Down. We chased two hares but killed none. George, Stanley, Georgey and I rode, the rest ran. Mr Edwards (the squire) and his son and two young Cartwrights ran also. Georgey's friend Jeffreys has come to stay. I wrote to Alban and Sir P. Duncombe.

Thursday 7th October 1869, Tyntesfield.

We shot at Charlton, and had very good sport. Yesterday I had a letter from Alban saying that Blackwell had at last consented to exchange his 12 acres between Grubbs Lane and our garden. I wrote to Louisa and to Tom Baring.

Friday 8th October 1869, Tyntesfield.

We have had a capital day's hunting in Portbury. We killed one hare before luncheon, and were running pretty nearly all day. I got a fall about 5 o'clock in one of the "keens" as they call the marsh drains, but was not hurt at all. On the other hand I won thereby a half crown apiece sweepstake amongst us 'for the first mucker'. Stanley's horse had indeed come down before, but he had ignominiously thrown himself off, and was adjudged not to have won. We had a great deal of leaping and some of it rather stiff.

A long letter from Alban about the exchange of Blackwell's land and one also from Louisa, and one from Harrison. Ward also sent me the valuation of the Belmont Estate It is about £43,000 – some £5000 more than I expected, but then the timber is worth just that sum more than I had thought.

Saturday 9th October 1869, Tyntesfield.

Sandars came last night and we had a long talk with him about Mexican affairs. The Wallers went away; also John and Isabel and their children to Weston, also the Lamberts. I went to see old Wade to talk over with him the long promised sale of his cottage and land; and I think I made some progress. Wrote to Louisa and Alban.

Settled the Belmont exchange. Both George and Uncle William are exceedingly well satisfied with the valuation of £43,707; and Uncle William makes it up to £45,000 as a gift.

Sunday 10th October 1869, Tyntesfield.

After morning church and luncheon, Sandars, George and I took a walk through Charlton.

Monday 11th October 1869, Tyntesfield.

Sandars went away; Alfred also, on a visit to Cowley, where there is a retreat, and Alicia and her baby and Harriett to stay with Henry and Mildred at Weston. Had a long chat with Wade again, and advanced I think another step in the negotiation. Called on Mr Way, Sir Grevill Smyth's Uncle and agent, to see if they would make some arrangement about the forthcoming sale of the Abdy property, by which they will exchange some of their outlying pieces in Wraxall for some of the Tickenham property which Uncle William may buy. He was very civil, but I am not sanguine of success. Emmy Doyne went away, and her sister Katy and cousin Miss McKonkie came.

Tuesday 12th October 1869, Tyntesfield.

Wade and his son were to have come to see me this morning, but the old man was nervous and ill, and took to his bed, and the younger one came up, and I had a long talk. He is to see his father and see him again tonight. We have had a capital day's shooting, and I think I never shot so well.

Wade had just been here and after much talk he has taken away an agreement for his father to sign. He is to sell his property for £235, Uncle William keeping the money and allowing him 5% during his life. He is to have a cottage at Charlton rent free for life, and my uncle is to take on William Wade as an under rector.

Wednesday 13th October 1869, St Dunstan's.

George and I came up by the early express and I came in time for dinner. Wade brought me his father's signature this morning.

Saturday 29th January 1870, Tyntesfield.

Alban and I went to town by the 10 o'clock train, I to the City for an hour, and then home, and so down here by the 2 o'clock train. My cold has I think made me blind as well as somewhat deaf and dumb; for I kissed Mrs Doyne thinking it was her daughter Emmy much to both our amusements. We heard this morning of poor Sam Bright's sudden death. He has followed Robert very soon.

Sunday 30th January 1870, Tyntesfield.

My cold very bad so I stayed in all day. Wrote to Louisa..

Monday 31st January 1870, Tyntesfield.

Much the same. Wrote to Louisa, Lord Shrewsbury. Henry Martin went away.

Tuesday 1st February 1870, Tyntesfield.

Heard from and wrote to Louisa.

Wednesday 2nd February 1870, Tyntesfield.

Mexico and Lima letters. Nothing disagreeable in them I am glad to say. Heard from Louisa, Gibson and Mrs Rendle. Wrote to them and to George Louis.

Thursday 3rd February 1870, Tyntesfield.

Blanche and Hardie went up to St Dunstan's by the early train. My cough is still very bad, but as the day was fine I went out for a walk with Antony; not much to my good I fear.

Friday 4th February 1870, Tyntesfield.
Blanche and Hardie came back again this evening, bringing me a letter from Louisa, and I also had one this morning. My cough is a little better.
Saturday 5th February 1870, Tyntesfield.
I took a walk with Blanche and the others went hunting with a wretched lot of staghounds kept by Mr Abbot of Knowle. Letter from George with a good account of the Mexican Railway Receipts.
Sunday 6th February 1870, Tyntesfield.
Letters from Louisa, George, Randall, and Sandars. Our cross examination comes on Wednesday; so I must go to town tomorrow. Wrote to Louisa.
Monday 7th February 1870, St Dunstan's.
Came up by the 11.45 train and found all pretty well here.
Wednesday 9th February 1870, St Dunstan's.
A letter from Uncle William tells us the comfortable news that dear Alice is safely in bed with her second boy, born at 6 yesterday morning. Geraldine de Gaja is going to be married to Mr Atkinson, Vicar of East Hendred, Alfred Pott's old living….I wrote to Uncle William.
Thursday 10th March 1870, St Dunstan's.
At last we have comfortable letters from Barron – and all things are going on well there (*in Mexico*), except the relations between Joe* and him; but I hope the visit of George and Stanley who have ridden across from Acapulco, may be useful to bring them at one again. They were to arrive about the 22nd or 24th of last month; and I believe our letters about the quarrel would be received a few days later. (**Joseph Gibbs, third son of the Rev. Joseph Gibbs and William Gibbs' nephew.*)
Friday 11th March 1870, St Dunstan's.
Letter from Charlotte Yonge. Beatrice went away.
Saturday 12th March 1870, St Dunstan's.
The Mexican Mail is in and with no bad news for a wonder. This evening however we sent to George and Beatrice to ask them to come up tomorrow to consult on something Mrs Lonergam has told Louisa, and which seems to give us a clue to the reason of their being no social intercourse between the Barrons and Joe. I wrote to Uncle William.
Tuesday 15th March 1870, St Dunstan's.
Wrote to Uncle William.
Wednesday 16th March 1870, St Dunstan's.
Wrote to Uncle William
Thursday 17th March 1870, Tyntesfield.
Most dreadful news was brought us by the mail this day. Poor dear Georgie and Stanley (*Stanley Vaughan Gibbs, sixth son of the Rev. Joseph Gibbs and William Gibbs' nephew*) were taken ill on the 20th February, the day after they left St Thomas's and Georgie died at

Jamaica on the 23rd of yellow fever. Stanley was still alive on the 25th when the mail left in the morning; but there were no hopes of his recovery! Louisa and I have come down here to tell Georgie's poor broken hearted father and mother; and George Louis has gone to tell his own brothers and sisters what a calamity has fallen upon them also. Uncle William bears up bravely though he also is dreadfully affected, but poor Blanche is completely crushed by the blow. Albinia and Martin are away. Antony came in to Bristol to meet us in consequence of a telegram which we sent saying we had bad news to tell.

Friday 18th March 1870, St Dunstan's.

We came up by the 11.45 bringing with us Edward Crawley Boevey who was staying in the House and who will now stay a few days with us. He went to tell Elizabeth. Wrote to Lady Essex – also to John, Charles and Hardie.

Monday 21st March 1870, St Dunstan's.

George Louis came back from having been to see his brothers and sisters, and also to Tyntesfield. He brings a pretty good account of Uncle William and Blanche. I had very nice letters from Charles and John, and from Sidney Harrison. Wrote to the latter. Heard from Aunt George.

Tuesday 22nd March 1870, St Dunstan's.

Heard by telegraph from someone in Liverpool who had come by the 'Australian' from the West Indies that poor Stanley only lived a short time after Georgey. I had indeed no hope, but it seems more sad now that we know he is gone! Wrote to Aunt George and wrote to and heard from Lady Essex.

Wednesday 23rd March 1870, St Dunstan's.

George had a very pleasing letter from Mr Milne, a Presbyterian Minister residing in Jamaica, and just arrived at Liverpool, telling him all he knew from his friends the Campbells of dear Georgey's and Stanley's end. Dr Campbell was one of the doctors who attended them, and Mr Campbell, his brother, was the Rector of the Parish from whom we had heard and who was most kind in his attendance on them.

Friday 22nd April 1870, St Dunstan's.

Called on Messrs Cooksons about Sir William Abdy's property which ought to have been offered to Uncle William but has not been.

Wednesday 27th April 1870, St Dunstan's.

Uncle William and Blanche went away to Hyde Park Gardens tonight. I have been very busy the last day or two in making arrangements for him with Upton as to altering his Will in some particulars. I have been dining with Stubbs to meet Mr Sandison, whom the Mexican Railway Board think of sending to supply Joe's place when he comes back. Sandars there and George.

223

Sunday 1st May 1870, St Dunstan's.

Alban and I called on Hyde Park Gardens.

Monday 2nd May 1870, St Dunstan's.

On Friday last Louisa, Alban and I went to the private view of the Royal Academy and were much pleased on the whole, though there is no very grand picture. I had written to Way about the Abdy Estate which he has bought over Uncle William's head, Sturge the agent having behaved very badly in the matter and I have now an answer from him, from which I hope he may surrender the particular lands we want. Had a long conversation about Uncle William's gifts to his children, and the alteration he proposes in consequence to make in his Will.

Thursday 5th May 1870, St Dunstan's.

We went to tea at Hyde Park gardens and found Antony and Martin just returned from Normandy. Hardie, Alice, Alfred and Albinia had arrived yesterday. Poor dear Alice looks deplorably ill.

Saturday 7th May 1870, St Dunstan's.

Louisa, Edith and I and the two little boys went down to Aldenham for the day. When we came back we found a telegram from Escandon saying that Joseph and William Barron had made up their quarrel, and beg us not to replace the former till we should hear by post. I am very curious to know what has brought about this conversion on the part of William Barron. Any way the news is good. (*Joseph Gibbs and Barron probably felt remorse at the deaths of George Abraham and Stanley Gibbs.*)

Sunday 8th May 1870, St Dunstan's.

Alban and I went to church at St Michael's, and called afterwards in Hyde Park Gardens. I took a long walk with Blanche in Kensington Gardens.

Tuesday 10th May 1870, St Dunstan's.

A kind letter from Barron about poor George's and Stanley's death – also an interesting letter to Joseph from a Captain Walker who accompanied them on their ride through Mexico.

Dr Weber gives a very bad account of dear Alice. I fear they have fresh troubles in store for them.

Wednesday 11th May 1870, St Dunstan's.

Called as usual in Hyde Park Gardens and found a somewhat better account of Alice.

Thursday 12th May 1870, St Dunstan's.

The packet brought a heart rending letter from Charles Lambert, reproaching himself for having let the boys go, and bewailing their death, of which as yet he had only heard rumours. It is a comfort to think that about this time he has received a very kind and consolatory letter from Uncle William. There was a kind letter also from Mr Marescaux of Jamaica, in view of which I think and hope the thought of bringing the bodies here will be given up. It cannot in any case be done till after the lapse of six months.

Friday 13th May 1870, St Dunstan's.

Uncle William signed all the letters to Antony Gibbs and Sons disposing of sixty thousand shares in favour of Blanche, Antony, Alice and Albinia, providing in anticipation for Blanche's annuity and giving the others part of their legacies in his life time. Louisa and I dined there, and Alban and Edith went to Madame Tussauds.

Saturday 14th May 1870, St Dunstan's.

Antony and I went to Aldenham.

Sunday 15th May 1870, St Dunstan's.

Called in Hyde Park Gardens and on Mrs Lambert. The Richard Brights called and I went with them to the Zoological Gardens.

Monday 16th May 1870, St Dunstan's.

Poor Alice is not so well today.

Tuesday 17th May 1870, St Dunstan's.

We dined at the William Gibbses today. Alice no better.

Sunday 22nd May 1870, St Dunstan's.

Uncle William's 80th birthday. We all went to dine at Hyde Park Gardens, where we found George Louis, who had come back to sleep here. Charles also was there.

Tuesday 24th May 1870, St Dunstan's.

Called on Eddis to ask him to go to Hyde Park Gardens one of these days to make a drawing of Alice, and this he has kindly consented to do.

Sunday 29th May 1870, St Dunstan's.

Went to St Michael's and then to luncheon in Hyde Park Gardens, intending to go to St Paul's with Blanche and Alfred to hear Liddon, but Alice was feeling so uncomfortable that neither of them liked to leave her. Later in the afternoon Alfred walked home with me. Borlase and Antony dined here.

Monday 30th May 1870, St Dunstan's.

Louisa and I dined at Hyde Park Gardens to meet Captain Walker, the companion of poor Georgey and Stanley.

Tuesday 31st May 1870, St Dunstan's.

Pretty comfortable letters from Mexico. I dined at Nobody's (*London Club "Nobody's Friends"*) and had a very pleasant dinner.

Sunday 19th June 1870, St Dunstan's.

Alban and I dined at Hyde Park Gardens to meet Dean Goulburn.

Monday 20th June 1870, St Dunstan's.

Alice seems better today under Jenner's prescription of a diet of asses' milk.

Thursday 23rd June 1870, St Dunstan's.

A bad headache all day. Uncle William sent out his letters to those who were to have been his legatees, and Stubbs and Sillem showed me their very pleasing answers to those addressed to them with a gift of £1000 each.

Saturday 25th June 1870, St Dunstan's.

Called at Hyde Park Gardens and found Alice a little better.

Saturday 16th July 1870, St Dunstan's.

Today I breakfasted at Strawberry Hill; but Chichester Fortescue had to leave for a Cabinet Council. He said it was the first of the horrors of war that he had to leave his friends. This morning has brought from Paris the horrible news that France has declared war against Prussia.

Thursday 21st July 1870, St Dunstan's.

I wrote to Blanche yesterday and had a letter from Uncle William today.

Friday 22nd July 1870, Tyntesfield.

Charles, Alban and I came down here for the sad ceremony of burying poor dear Georgey and Stanley. We took in George Heberden at Didcot and found at the church George Louis and Antony who went with Martin by the 6 a.m. from London, picking up at Didcot Sidney Harrison, Willy and Alfred Pott. George Henry came over from Weston, and Uncle William and Blanche from Malvern. Hardie had come before to make the preparations. All went off as well as could be expected – with much pain at the time, but they seem composed and comfortable now. After dinner George and Alban and Heberden went back to town, Willy to Abingdon and Henry to Weston. This evening I sketched a letter for Uncle William to write to Mr Chalk (Ecclesiastical Commissioner) about the proposed division of Wraxall, and building a church at Failand and a chapel here.

Saturday 22nd July 1870, The Myth Malvern.

Charles and John went away this morning, the former to Stowe, the latter to Clifton (*Hampden*). We came away by the 3.15 train and arrived (an hour late) at 6.40. This is a very pretty and comfortable house. Dear Alice was lying out in the Garden, and looked, I thought, a very little better. Dolly, Albinia and Miss Townley are here.

I went up to Belmont while I was at Tyntesfield, and saw the progress they were making on its alteration. The house looks better outside than ever it did, the roof being now shewn; but the inside puzzles one considerably. One comes to some well known corner and finds oneself nowhere! However, the plan is a very good one, and though the number of rooms is much diminished, all that are left are good ones, and almost all that are taken are bad. The only one I regret is my dear Mother's room which was a very pleasant one. The windows only remain in the gallery of the Racket Court.

Sunday 24th July 1870, The Myth Malvern.

This morning dear Alice received the Holy Communion, and all of us with her according to the office for the sick. She has been pretty comfortable all day. I have had a baddish headache, but it is better this evening. Alfred and some of us went this evening to Newland College for old men and women. The College Chapel is the Parish Church. The reredos representing the crucifixion is particularly effective. The service was admirably done. Albinia and Martin had been there in the morning and said that the Warden preached a most striking sermon.

Monday 25th July 1870, The Myth Malvern.

Wrote to Louisa, and finally settled Uncle William's letter to Mr Chalk. He has now written it, and I am to get it pressed and posted tomorrow. We drove by Little Malvern where we saw the picturesque Manor House, and the not less picturesque ruined Priory Church, the remaining part of which serves as a Parish Church and from thence to the Wyche where Blanche, Antony and I had a beautiful walk over the crest of the hills, delicious in this sultry weather. The Hertfordshire side is lovely. Dear Alice has had a cold today but is better this evening. Uncle William is very low and uncomfortable tonight.

Thursday 22nd September 1870, Lowestoft

Blanche gives a very bad account of poor Alice, and I am sorry to say of Albinia. Uncle William told me in his last letter that they were very anxious about her, and thought of sending her to Australia for the voyage and to avoid the winter. I wrote to dissuade them and they have now consulted Dr Beddoe of Bristol about her, who, while he confirms the other doctor's account of the state of her lungs, objects to the long sea voyage, as I did, and suggests Egypt; and this I think they will do. It will be very painful for them but they will always be within hail. Louisa wrote to Blanche.

Monday 26th September 1870, Lowestoft.

Letters from Uncle William, Aunt Charlotte and Penny. Uncle William gives a deplorable account of poor Alice's weakness, but says she is quite resigned to death which she fully believes to be approaching.

Tuesday 27th September 1870, Lowestoft.

Wrote to Uncle William, Aunt Charlotte and Charles Crawley.

Wednesday 5th October 1870, Tyntesfield.

Letters from Uncle William, George Furnivall and Louisa. Wrote to George, Louisa and Augusta. Louisa's letter met me here after I had written. Poor Edith has had a bad tooth with much suffering notwithstanding nitrous oxide. I came here by the 4.33 train, having Edward Crawley Boevey as my companion, and we met Hardie at the station returning from London. Alice is more comfortable this day, and Uncle William and Blanche very cheerful considering the state of things in the house. Albinia looks thin.

Thursday 6th October 1870, Tyntesfield.

Heard from and wrote to Louisa. Blomfield came and I was much occupied with him, discussing Failand Church and Tyntesfield Chapel. I had a baddish headache all day. Antony dined at the Miles. Louisa's letter today told me poor Edith had another tooth taken out, with little less pain than the other. I saw Alice today – very thin and weak, but cheerful. She had while I was with her a rather alarming fit of exhaustion and breathlessness, which she soon got over, and tonight she has again been dreadfully exhausted; but without the struggle for breath.

Friday 7th October 1870, Tyntesfield.

We have had a beautiful day's shooting in the outlying covers at Charlton and here. Antony, Edward and I killed four pheasants and a few partridge and rabbits – my share being 20 pheasants, a brace of partridge and a rabbit (51 cartridges). I have just given my foot a severe blow against the stairs in running up and I fear it may bring on gout.

Wednesday 12th October 1870, Tyntesfield.

So it did; but happily not a bad attack; and only in the bruised foot and I am now downstairs again, but with a sock on. Dear Alice is, I am happy to say, much more comfortable, and Uncle William and Blanche, pleased with the good arrangements they have made for Albinia's journey, are more happy about her going. I have heard every day from Louisa. Our wretched well is not yet done. Antony went on Monday to shoot at Clifton (*Hampden*), and came back today.

Thursday 13th October 1870, Tyntesfield.

I am getting well fast as to the foot, but I have a small touch of lumbago to add to my discomfort. Blomfield came this evening. Wrote to Penny and to the Watford Highway Board, Harrison, George and Louisa answering letters from them. Wrote also to Joseph. Tyndall Bright came to shoot.

Friday 14th October 1870, Tyntesfield.

I am better this afternoon. Heard from Alban, Louisa, Clutterbuck and Hubbard. I wrote to the three latter. Also to Douglas Gibbs of Alexandria to introduce Hardie and Albinia. Much talk with Blomfield about the Failand Church and Tyntesfield Chapel. He went away today. I saw Alice again for a minute. She didn't seem worse than on the 5th when I saw her before.

Saturday 15th October 1870, Tyntesfield.

Dear Albinia went away under Hardie's care, Antony accompanying them to Liverpool. Now that the parting is over they are all better, including Alice, though she was much agitated and overcome at first. I find my foot so much better that I have even put on my shoes and taken a walk with Blanche, but I have a bad headache and have come to bed directly after dinner.

Sunday 16th October 1870, Tyntesfield.

A miserable rainy day and we had service in the Oratory. Heard from

Louisa and wrote to George Louis and her. I better – all but my back.
Monday 17th October 1870, Tyntesfield.
Fine day again and I much better. Walked round the hill with Blanche.
Alice who had been very comfortable yesterday morning had a sharp
attack of congestion of the lungs last evening, but has pretty well got
over it now. Heard from Paten about the well, and wrote to Louisa.
Antony came home tonight bringing a good account of the travellers.
Tuesday 18th October 1870, Tyntesfield.
Letters from George and Louisa. Wrote to her. A stormy, rainy day.
Blanche and I got caught in the rain on our way back from the new
Lodge. Medley went away and Frederick Gurney came. Alice is still
suffering.
Wednesday 19th October 1870, Tyntesfield.
She is much better today and I have sat with her about an hour this
evening. Letters from Hubbard, John, Harrison and Louisa. Wrote to the
last two.

**Figure 31. Harriett, George Gibbs' wife and William's sister, a miniature by
Sir William Charles Ross, 1840.**

Thursday 20th October 1870, Tyntesfield.

Most miserable weather – nevertheless I went to Weston to see the Hendys and they gave me a good silhouette of Aunt Harriett as a young woman, shewing the miniature I have of her not to be unlike her, though not a pleasing likeness. They promised me also the one by Leakey of Uncle George's first wife (Salvina Gibbs, née Hendy – Plate 5). Poor Susanna is quite blind, but very cheerful, and both of them much pleased to see me. I drew a codicil for them. While there I drove over to Hutton to see Henry and Mildred – both very well, and their house is a beautiful one. The Miss Cardales were staying with them. Antony came back from Wells wither he went on Tuesday to quarter sessions. Heard from Penny and Louisa. Wrote to her and to Hubbard about Blake sending a letter for the latter to sign – which he won't.

Friday 21st October 1870, Tyntesfield.

Letters from Louisa, George and Harrison. Wrote to them…Vicary I am sorry to say, has been sent home from Eton. I don't yet know what is the matter. Antony and I went out shooting, and killed 26 pheasants, a few rabbits, three hares and two pigeons. Antony had hardly any shooting, but he killed also a woodcock. I sat a while with Alice this evening. She said when I went away, I shall hope to see you again – I feel so much better.

Saturday 22nd October 1870, Clifton Hampden.

Left Bristol by the 10.10 train and went to Oxford where I called on the Master of University (*University College*) and the President of Corpus (*Corpus Christi College*), and put Vicary's name down at both colleges. He has been ill with jaundice, as I hear from Louisa's letter of today, and though he is better, it will no doubt keep us from going to Aldenham for another week.

Tuesday 31st January 1871, St Dunstan's.

Wrote to Harrison, Uncle William and Baring, answering letters from the two last.

Thursday 2nd February 1871, St Dunstan's.

Wrote to Uncle William. I sent him the Ecclesiastical Commission's Scheme re Failand.

Friday 3rd February 1871, St Dunstan's.

Letters from Uncle William and Charlotte Yonge

Monday 6th February 1871, St Dunstan's.

Heard from and wrote to Uncle William.

Tuesday 7th February 1871, St Dunstan's.

Wrote to Uncle William.

Friday 10th February 1871, St Dunstan's.

A letter from Joseph tells us of the best returns we have had in any month from the Mexico and Pueblo Line - $40,000 and more nett. It is now being worked at little more than 40%. If this state of things would but go on, and even improve, but we can hardly hope for that till we have opened to Fortin.

Wednesday 8th March 1871, St Dunstan's.

Uncle William writes with a very bad account of dear Alice.

Friday 10th March 1871, St Dunstan's.

Uncle William gives a still worse account of poor Alice, who cannot, they think, live many days.

Saturday 11th March 1871, St Dunstan's.

No letter from Tyntesfield today, but Augusta Pode had one from Kate of the same date as mine received yesterday with if possible a worse account.

Monday 13th March 1871, St Dunstan's.

She rallied a little yesterday morning, but just as Uncle William was closing his letter (4 o'clock) a change took place, and it seemed certain that she was sinking. A letter to Augusta from Kate said the same. In the morning when she was better she said – just as Aunt Anne had done a few hours before death – when they thought she was sinking, "I don't think I am dying yet".

Tuesday 14th March 1871, St Dunstan's.

Dear Alice died Sunday evening at half past nine, having received the Holy Communion just after Uncle William wrote – during which he says, "She was perfectly conscious and looking forward to her happy change with peace and tranquillity". I wrote to Uncle William.

Thursday 16th March 1871, St Dunstan's.

Letter from Uncle William.

Friday 17th March 1871, St Dunstan's.

I should have gone down to the funeral today, but I awoke with a bad headache, and finally decided not to go. Alban went, and I hear John and Charles were there. All the party were as composed and even cheerful as would have been expected or hoped. George Louis came back with Alban and sleeps here. Dear Alice had made a list of things to be given to us all. To us she has sent Gustave Doré's Elaine.

Saturday 18th March 1871, St Dunstan's.

I called on Boxall and had a long chat with him. Wrote to Uncle William.

Tuesday 21st March 1871, St Dunstan's.

Letters from Uncle William and Kate.

Thursday 23rd March 1871, St Dunstan's.

Heard from and wrote to Uncle William. George and Mary, and Sylvia went home. Mary's carriage bag was stolen out of her carriage – it contained Alice's locket which she had left her.

Friday 4th August 1871, Tyntesfield.

Herbert and I came down here by the two o'clock train, and find the

231

Bishop of Ely, Mrs Harold Browne and their daughter, Sir John Kennaway, Mr and Mrs Meyrick, Mr Henry and Lady Anna Maria Courtenay and their son Hugh staying here. Uncle William seems very uncomfortable.

Saturday 5th August 1871, Tyntesfield.

The Bishop and Mrs Browne, the Courtenays and Sir J. Kennaway went away, and Antony came home this evening. I heard from Alban and Obicini, and wrote to them and to Louisa. Took a walk with Blanche.

Sunday 6th August 1871, Tyntesfield.

The Organ, which I heard for the first time, is a very good one. Vaughan preached in his surplice, hating it no doubt in itself, but rejoicing in it inasmuch as each man who adopts it now seems to himself to clench the Purchas Judgement (*The Judgement given by the Judicial Committee of the Privy Council in 1871 against the Rev. John Purchas with regard to Eucharistic vestments*). Wrote to Louisa from whom I heard.

Monday 7th August 1871, Tyntesfield.

The Goulburns and their niece came also Mme de Milanges and Miss Martin. Wrote to George Louis and Louisa…..

Tuesday 8th August 1871, Tyntesfield.

Heard from Louisa and wrote to her, also to George (*Edward Adams*) to congratulate him on Mary's being safely delivered of a son (*Mary, Henry Hucks' sister*), as I hear by a letter of his to Blanche, and to Ellis and to John Merivale from whom I had a funny letter.

Wednesday 9th August 1871, Tyntesfield.

Antony, Herbert and I came up today by the 12.09 train and I brought with me a bad headache. John and Isabel and their three elder children came to Tyntesfield yesterday.

Monday 1st January 1872, Tyntesfield.

Alban and I came down here by the 9.15 and went to join Antony and the other shooters – John Merivale, Mr Edwards, Joe and Henry Martin at Charlton. It was blowing a hurricane so our sport was not good, but the bag was 69 pheasants and other sundry game. Mrs Daubeny is here with her two boys, Polly and her two, Rose Merivale and George, son of John Merivale, Douglas Page, and his two sisters and Kate Lowe. Uncle William seems pretty well… I had a letter from Elizabeth Mary Remmett, daughter of Henry and one from Aunt Eliza. Wrote to Louisa, George Louis and Barron.

Tuesday 2nd January 1872, Tyntesfield.

Letters from Isabel, George Louis, Obicini, Sheppard and Leslie of Moscow. Wrote to the three former, Aunt Elisa, Louisa and Arnold. Took a walk over the hill with Blanche, the others going out with the Beagles. All the Doynes came yesterday to tea.

Wednesday 3rd January 1872, Tyntesfield.

Letters from Louisa, R. Thode and Co., the Dresden Porcelain Depot, Mr Fisher, John, Beresford Hope, Bruce of Dundee, Clark and George. I wrote to Louisa, John, Fisher, Hope and Bruce. Talked to Mrs Daubeny and Henry Daubeny about admitting the latter into the Counting House. Rose and George Merivale went away, Joe and Polly to Clifton (*Hampden*) and Antony to Wells, so we are a reduced party.

John Merivale and I walked into Clifton and back over the bridge. Heard from Leslie the cost of the Moscow Brocade is £39.4s.3d besides the charges. The quantity is 165 yards.

Thursday 4th January 1872 Tyntesfield.

John Merivale went away, and Joe and Polly came back; the former not at all well with dysentery. Letter from Aunt Eliza very thankful for Uncle William's kindness in buying the House at Littlemore, so that she shall live in it rent free for her life. He gives "+m" for it, which is much more than it is said to be worth, but it is the sum at which Uncle Charles valued it in his will, and the sum for which it was mortgaged, so it gives him an excuse for giving so much. Letter also from George and Isabel. Wrote to Louisa, George and Aunt Eliza. Called with Blanche on the Doynes.

Friday 5th January 1872, Tyntesfield.

The Pages went away and Dr Budd came bringing Joe's Edward, a very pretty little boy. I heard from Louisa, Aunt Susan and McMurray (about the Library Company) and Mr Chanter of Ilfracombe sending me a very good account of Mrs Henry Remmett and her daughter. I wrote to all, except Mr Chanter, and also to Miss Remmett to whom we agree to allow £30 a year for five years (Uncle William £20 and I £10), and Uncle William sends her £20 besides for present need. I wrote also to George suggesting that the shares in our new concern in South America should be Hayne 12½, Henry and Combes 7 each, Böhl 6, and Harrison and Miller 4 each percent, which if our calculations are correct, *means* that in Valparaiso we ought to make 150, in Antofagasta 50, in Tarapaca 210, in Lima 40 and in Arequipa 50 (500 M$ in all) *which* will give them all a tolerable share.

Dr Budd has been very entertaining, and gave me some curious instances of typhoid infection.

Saturday 6th January 1872, Tyntesfield.

A very pleasant day's shooting in the woods. I had letters from George and Louisa, Grenfell, Morrell and Son, and Huntingford, and I wrote to Willy, George, Henry, Morrell and Arnold. Sheppard came.

Sunday 7th January 1872, Tyntesfield.

Dr Budd went away and so did Alban this evening. I had letters from Louisa, Stubbs and Penny, and wrote to Louisa and George.

Monday 8th January 1872, Tyntesfield.

Letters from C.M. Remmett, and wrote to Louisa (from whom I had a telegram), Aunt Eliza and Upton, also drafted two letters to be sent to the Bishop about Failand. Shot some of the outside covers at Charlton.

Tuesday 9th January 1872, Tyntesfield.

A pleasant day's shooting at Charlton. All five of us shot each a woodcock. Heard from and wrote to Louisa and George. Wrote to Harrison.

Wednesday 10th January 1872, Tyntesfield.

Hard at work all day writing to Hayne and George and settling various matters with Uncle William. Joe went to town this morning and Pollie to Clifton (*Hampden*) this afternoon. Heard from and wrote to Louisa, also to Rosalie Pickering.

Friday 12th January 1872, Littlemore.

Came into Bristol yesterday evening with Antony, Kate and Harry and Daubeny, and enjoyed hearing the Madrigals at the Victoria Rooms very much.

Tuesday 16th January 1872, St Dunstan's.

Wrote to Uncle William.

Wednesday 17th January 1872, St Dunstan's.

Wrote to Sir John, Uncle William and Penny.

Thursday 18th January 1872, St Dunstan's.

Wrote to Uncle William.

Friday 19th January 1872, St Dunstan's.

Letter from Uncle William (not very well).

Wednesday 24th January 1872, Norman Court.

I had very disquieting letters from Blanche this morning about Uncle William, who has been ill with a slight attack of bronchitis complicated with an indication of Bright's disease, but a telegram which I received from Louisa brought much comfort, though at the cost of a fright saying the danger was past. I wrote to Blanche and Louisa.

Thursday 25th January 1872, St Dunstan's.

Letter from Louisa enclosing two from Blanche, the first of the same purport as yesterday's telegram, and the second saying that Uncle William was going on fairly well, but was very low and wanted me to come; so I intend to go tomorrow afternoon. Alban and I came up by the 8.15 train; and we have been most of the day discussing the question of a sale of the Lima Railway shares.

Friday 26th January 1872, Tyntesfield.

Went up the City this morning, and then came down by the two o'clock train, and find dear Uncle William a good deal better, but of course very weak and still in his room. Charles Pode is here, having come from Oxford to attend him (under Dr Budd), but he goes tomorrow. Miss

Courtenay is here and Willy Cobham, also Miss Drury, a cousin of the Merivales, as companion for Dorothea. Both Dorothea and Albinia are rather poorly. Henry Martin is tolerably well.

Saturday 27th January 1872, Tyntesfield.

Willy went away to Abingdon – and this evening came Janet and Catherine Merivale to stay a week. Uncle William had but a bad night, but he is certainly better this evening. I wrote to Tommy Sheppard and Vicary. Antony and I went out shooting and killed nine cock pheasants, a rabbit, a jack sniper, of which my share was the two last, and four of the cock pheasants.

Sunday 28th January 1872, Tyntesfield.

Uncle William came downstairs while we were at church and received the Holy Communion with us all in the Oratory. I hear from and wrote to George Louis, and Louisa. Letter also from Penny.

Monday 29th January 1872, Tyntesfield.

A wretched day, meant to have been devoted to coursing, but though the farmers and dogs came, nobody went out with them but Antony.

I walked after luncheon to call on the Vaughans, propounded my scheme for their new chapel and small district including only the park, Uncle William building also and endowing a chapel for Failand to belong to the mother parish.

Tuesday 30th January 1872, St Dunstan's.

Came up by the 12.09 train having Edward Kendall as my travelling companion from Bath.

Thursday 6th February 1872, St Dunstan's.

Wrote to Uncle William about Vaughan, who after all refuses his assent to the new proposal about Wraxall.

Wednesday 7th February 1872, St Dunstan's.

Letter from Uncle William and wrote to him.

Thursday 8th February 1872, St Dunstan's.

Letter from William Barron. We had a small saloon dance and the people are just going away. Antony came up to stay for a few days.

Saturday 10th February 1872, St Dunstan's.

Antony dined at the Merivales.

Sunday 11th February 1872, St Dunstan's.

I went to church at All Saints, Norfolk Square, and had luncheon with John Merivale. His sister Louisa was there whom I was glad to see again after many years. I went with him by train to Hammersmith and thence walked to Putney – called on Mary – walked to Battersea and home by train.

Tuesday 13th February 1872, St Dunstan's.

Much worried all day by Barron's recalcitrance in Mexican Railway matters. Went to the Pantomime with Antony, Lee Warner and Janet

and Katy Merivale at Drury Lane. Wrote and heard from Uncle William.
Saturday 17th February 1872, St Dunstan's.
I gave my foot a blow on Monday evening, and it went on getting very slowly worse till Tuesday night, when I had a night of pain and sleeplessness, which followed a bad night of worry on Barron and the Mexican Railway account. So I thought I was in for a bad bout. It seems however to be departing and I am down stairs again today. Wrote to Uncle William from whom I have heard lately.
Monday 19th February 1872, St Dunstan's.
Heard from Uncle William and wrote to him.
Tuesday 20th February 1872, St Dunstan's.
Wrote to Uncle William.
Wednesday 21st February 1872, St Dunstan's.
Heard from and wrote to Uncle William, and telegraphed to Antony re a message from Blanche about the tickets for the function in St Paul's.
Thursday 7th March 1872, St Dunstan's.
Uncle William came back to town yesterday, but I have not been able to go and see him yet.
Friday 8th March 1872, St Dunstan's.
Rather bad news from Mexico, both as to the progress of the Revolution, and as to the impediments placed in our way by the officials preventing us from getting our subventions.
Saturday 9th March 1872, St Dunstan's.
George and I called on Uncle William.
Sunday 10th March 1872, St Dunstan's.
Edith and I went to church at St Michael's and to luncheon at Hyde Park Gardens......Wrote to the Secretary of the St Paul's Completion Fund offering for Uncle William that he would give £1000 if nine other people would do the same, and if that was successful to repeat the operation.
Friday 15th March 1872, St Dunstan's.
Antony dined here.
Thursday 21st March 1872, St Dunstan's.
We dined at Hyde Park Gardens.
Sunday 24th March 1872, St Dunstan's.
The last two days passed much as usual – a visit to Uncle William who I am sorry to find today has caught a cold in this snowy weather, and church at St Michael's.
Saturday 13th April 1872, St Dunstan's.
Today we heard the good news that Antony is engaged to Janet Merivale. She has bound him to secrecy till she goes down to Barton Place (Wednesday) which is foolish, and hard on Antony who of course wants to tell his own friends. Blanche however told us, and we dined there (Louisa, Edith and I) today. The boys all went to Aldenham, and Alban

and Antony are gone to the Opera.

Sunday 14th April 1872, St Dunstan's.

St Michael's as usual – after which Vicary and I had luncheon in Hyde Park Gardens. I went to Norfolk Square and had a chat with J. Merivale and Rose in the Garden.

Sunday 16th June 1872, St Dunstan's.

St Michael's with Herbert. Had luncheon at Hyde Park Gardens.

Thursday 20th June 1872, St Dunstan's.

A sitting from Watts this morning. Edith, John and I went to see Pygmalion. Miss Robertson's acting is excellent.

Friday 21st June 1872, St Dunstan's.

Talked a long while with Tomasich about Uncle William's miniatures. This evening we have all been to tea at Hyde Park Gardens where we found John Merivale, Janet and her Aunts Fanny Rose and Caroline, and her cousin Louisa Buckingham. Louisa, Alban and Edith are gone on to a Ball at the David Powells in Grosvenor Square.

Saturday 22nd June 1872, St Dunstan's.

The wedding at St Michael's Paddington went off very well, and Antony and Janet are gone off to Oxford. Alban and I went to Aldenham, and all the party except myself dined in Hyde Park Gardens.

Sunday 23rd June 1872, St Dunstan's.

John and I went to St Michael's, and I had luncheon in Hyde Park Gardens. Afterwards we called on…..Mrs Herman Merivale. Then to the Albert Hall, and with Charles whom we found there to call on the Molesworths (43, Kensington Square). Borlase and Charles dined here.

Monday 24th June 1872, St Dunstan's.

Letter from J. Merivale about the Molesworths.

Wednesday 26th June 1872, St Dunstan's.

We all dined at Hyde Park Gardens, where were George and Mary, and John.

Thursday 27th June 1872, St Dunstan's.

Mr Molesworth called yesterday with his daughter Imogen and Charles. Louisa, Edith and Alban are gone to the Inns of Court Ball. Herman Merivale the younger called today, a pleasant young man.

Friday 28th June 1872, St Dunstan's.

Edith and I dined at Hyde Park Gardens. Boxall there.

Sunday 30th June 1872, St Dunstan's.

Hyde Park Gardens as usual, and after Church I wrote an answer for Uncle William to the Bishop of Bath and Wells.

Tuesday 2nd July 1872, St Dunstan's.

Spent the morning chatting to Uncle William while Tomasich was giving him the last sitting for the two miniatures, one as our wedding present to Antony, and one for ourselves – also in finally settling the letter to the

Bishop of Bath and Wells. Went to see "Money" at the Prince of Wales with Edith and Herbert.

Wednesday 3rd July 1872, St Dunstan's.

I sat to Watts this morning. Alban dined at Greenwich, but we others in Hyde Park Gardens to meet the H. Mallets.

Thursday 4th July 1872, St Dunstan's.

I went to St Albans to be sworn in as a J. P. and sat on the bench while a case was being tried…Then to Aldenham, where Blanche joined me after a while and went all over the house and gardens much to her satisfaction.

Saturday 6th July 1872, St Dunstan's.

Edith, Herbert and I heard a beautiful concert at the Albert Hall this afternoon.

Monday 8th July 1872, St Dunstan's.

Another sitting with Watts this morning, after which I stayed in Hyde Park Gardens till it was time for the William Gibbses to go away which they did by the 2 o'clock train.

Thursday 11th July 1872, St Dunstan's.

Wrote to Butterfield about Keble College Chapel which Uncle William is going to build. Also to Antony sending him his father's miniature by Tomasich.

Friday 12th July 1872, St Dunstan's.

Heard from and wrote to Uncle William who had sent me up a most pleasing letter from Sir John Colerdidge about Keble College. Shaw-Stewart showed me one of Sir John's which Butterfield had sent him on the same subject as the Duke of Wellington's the other night.

Saturday 13th July 1872, St Dunstan's.

I had a very long talk with Butterfield, and find him a most satisfactory man to have to do with. After luncheon I went to Lords.

Monday 15th July 1872, St Dunstan's.

Heard from and wrote to Antony.

Tuesday 16th July 1872, St Dunstan's.

Wrote to Uncle William…and I dined with John Merivale and met Mr Molesworth and his daughter Cordelia, Miss Clare Drury and Herman Merivale the younger.

Wednesday 17th July 1872, St Dunstan's.

Heard from and wrote to Uncle William, and to Sir John Coleridge, after paying a short visit to Butterfield.

Thursday 5th September 1872, Tyntesfield.

Edith and I came down by the 11.45 train with Butterfield picking up old Sir John Coleridge on our way at Bristol. Here we found Talbot (Warden of Keble), Charlotte Yonge, Madame de Milanges, Albinia, Blanche and Catherine Daubeny, and Kate Lowe and Alfred Gurney. The latter's children are away, little Willy being far from well. Uncle William, Sir

John Coleridge, Talbot, Butterfield, Hardie and I held a conclave about Keble Chapel and settled all preliminary matters about size and general form.

Friday 6th September 1872, Tyntesfield.

Sir John Coleridge, Butterfield and Talbot went away, going first with Uncle William and me to Charlton and Wraxall.

Saturday 7th September 1872, Tyntesfield.

Heard from Louisa and wrote to Davy, Arnold and John. George Bright came over to shoot. The birds are scarce and wild and we only shot 9½ brace. Mrs à Court Repington, and Dean and Mrs Goulburn came. Charlotte Yonge went away.

Sunday 8th September 1872, Tyntesfield.

Wrote to Charles, Mary Gibbs, Furnivall and Louisa answering her letter to me and one yesterday to Edith.

Monday 9th September 1872, Tyntesfield.

Took a long walk with Goulburn, calling on Vaughan, and going to Clapton Church. George and Beatrice came – also Alfred Pott, Mrs Lambert, Janet and Kate Lowe.

Tuesday 10th September 1872, Tyntesfield.

Heard from and wrote to Louisa. Walked to Backwell Church which they are restoring (with Uncle William's help) with Goulburn and Pott. Madame de Milanges went away.

Wednesday 11th September 1872, Tyntesfield.

A rainy morning. Uncle William, Blanche and the Dean went to Bristol to see the restoration of the Cathedral and I stayed in till 4 o'clock and read to the ladies. Then I went out shooting with George; shot few but missed none.

Thursday 12th September 1872, Tyntesfield.

Walked with Dean Goulburn to Cadbury Camp, and home by Tickenham, where the farmer's daughters showed us over the old Court House and Church. Antony and Janet came.

Friday 13th September 1872, Tyntesfield.

Mrs à Court went away this morning; and the Lamberts at noon. George and Antony and I went shooting and picked up a few brace. No letter from Louisa. I wrote to her today and to her and Edith yesterday.

Saturday 14th September 1872, Tyntesfield.

George and Beatrice and the three Daubenys went to their respective homes, and Antony, Janet and Edith to Bath – 21, St James Square. A foggy, muggy, rainy day – the Dean and I walked round the hill. John and Johnnie came, also Alfred and Ellen Gurney and Rose and Catty Merivale. I wrote to Louisa.

Sunday 15th September 1872, Tyntesfield.

Heard from and wrote to Louisa – also from Tyndall, and to Vicary.

Monday 16th September 1872, Tyntesfield.

Took a delightful country walk with the Dean to Easton in Gordano and home through Prior's Wood and Charlton. We called on the Walkers at Easton, and Mrs Walker, who was at home, gave us some tea and took us down to the Church – a beautiful new church with a fine old tower.

Charles Merivale, Dean of Ely, with his wife and youngest daughter came today. (*Charles Merivale was Janet Gibbs' uncle, her father John Lewis Merivale's second eldest brother.*)

Dean Charles Merivale of Ely went to Harrow School with Bishop Charles Wordsworth of St Andrews who was the nephew of the poet. The two boys were very keen on rowing. Charles Merivale went on to St John's College Cambridge and Charles Wordsworth to Christ Church College, Oxford. One day Charles Merivale wrote a letter to Charles Wordsworth challenging Oxford to a boat race with Cambridge. We do not have Charles Merivale's letter, but this is the first paragraph of Charles Wordsworth's reply.

My dear Merivale,

I thank you very much for your letter – its impudence was unparalleled. I do not know which to admire most, its direct assertions or its occult insinuations. The very supposition of my being in our boat has quite delighted you – allow me to assure you of the truth of the report. But this is not the only bone I have to pick with you: the sufficiently candid manner in which you talk of 'lasting us out' amuses me so much that I am ready to die with laughter whenever I think of it. My dear fellow, you cannot possibly know our crew, or you would not write in such an indiscreet manner. Allow me to enlighten you!

Charles Wordsworth.

The first Boat Race took place in March 1829 at Henley-on-Thames in Oxfordshire and contemporary newspapers report that crowds of twenty thousand travelled to watch. Charles Merivale rowed with the eight in the Cambridge boat and Charles Wordsworth rowed for Oxford. Oxford won by six lengths. The race was stopped soon after the start and, following the restart, the Oxford eight were clear winners. The event was such a resounding success that the townspeople later decided to organise a regatta of their own which duly became Henley Royal Regatta. After the first year, the early Boat Races took place at Westminster in London, but by 1845, when Westminster had become too crowded, the Boat Race moved six miles up-stream to the then country village of Putney. In 1856 the race became an annual event, (except in the war years).

Tuesday 17th September 1872, Tyntesfield.

Heard from and wrote to Louisa – also to Vicary and Stubbs…Called on the Vaughans with Dean Goulburn. Janet and Edith came to spend the day and went back after dinner.

Wednesday 18th September 1872, Tyntesfield.

The Goulburns went away this morning and the Merivales this afternoon. I walked to Charlton with John.

Thursday 19th September 1872, Clifton Hampden.

John and I came away from Tyntesfield by the Bourton train 9.38 and got here at half past one.

Monday 30th December 1872, Aldenham.

Heard from Rose Merivale and wrote to her. I had a letter from Barron saying he had travelled by rail the whole way from Vera Cruz to Mexico City except 5 miles on horse back.

Wednesday 1st January 1873, Bedgebury.

Yesterday I called in at Hyde Park Gardens, and attended also the Mexican Railway Meeting which was rather enthusiastic. I had a letter from Joseph B. Crawley which as well as Barron's said the line would certainly be opened throughout today. Ojala!

Tuesday 21st January 1873. 16, Hyde Park Gardens.

Letter to Alban from Albinia Gibbs[xvi].

My dear Alban,

I was so glad to hear of your engagement yesterday and I write to wish you every possible happiness. Father spoke to me about being one of the bridesmaids and seemed to think it out of the question as it could not be settled for certain; it is very kind of Lady Mildred and Miss Hope to have thought of me, will you thank them for me? Cousin Henry was dining here last night and told me he did not think they could mind its being left uncertain as of course it must depend on the weather and how I am, but if they don't mind I should like to be one very much. Will you ask them what they really feel about it and let me know?

With love from us all

Believe me

Your affectionate cousin

Albinia A. Gibbs.

(Alban was to marry Bridget, the daughter of Alexander Beresford Hope M.P., whose family had been merchant bankers in Amsterdam. He also

inherited the vast estates of his step father, Viscount Beresford. His wife Lady Mildred was the first daughter of the 2nd Marquess of Salisbury.)

Saturday 1st February 1873, St Dunstan's.

Edith has gone with Herbert to dine at Hyde Park Gardens and go to the Albert Hall. She is to sleep at Hyde Park Gardens.

Monday 4th February 1873, St Dunstan's.

Lady Mildred and Bride (*Bridget*) dined here after having had lunch at Hyde Park Gardens. Bride had a bad headache and so had I.

Tuesday 5th February 1873, St Dunstan's.

Called in Hyde Park Gardens this evening and talked with Uncle William about further diminution of the legacies in his will by giving Henry Martin his portion and completing the portions of his daughters.

Wednesday 6th February 1873, St Dunstan's.

A very long talk with him and Blanche on the same subject.

Sunday 9th February 1873, St Dunstan's.

A wretched day. Alban and Edith went to St Michael's and Hyde Park Gardens.

Monday 17th February 1873, Bedgebury Park.

Shoals of guests have been arriving all day – Blanche and Albinia, George and Mary, George and Beatrice, Charles and John, our four boys and Miss Ellaby, and Antony and Janet, Lord and Lady Salisbury and three of their children (Lady Maud being one of the bridesmaids), Lord and Lady Eustace Cecil, Arthur and Eustace Balfour and their sister Alice, the Bishop of Winchester, Adrian Hope and Lady Ida, and Monsieur Martineau. We settled the settlements according to our wishes, and all signed them tonight – Lord E. Cecil and Captain Hayter being with George Louis and Antony, the Trustees, and Lord Salisbury and the Bishop being witnesses.

Tuesday 18th February 1873, Bedgebury Park.

Our wedding has gone off happily and well, and dear Alban and Bride (*Bridget*) have gone, man and wife, to Mrs Campbell's house in London, whence they go tomorrow to Devon. The Bishop and John did the Service excellently, Mr Harrison reading the exhortation. (*The wedding service was at Christ Church, Kilndown, Kent*). It was a very gay wedding and everybody as kind as possible. There were about two hundred people at the breakfast (*at Bedgebury Park*) and, happily, no speeches. After breakfast there was dancing till the pair went away... After a merry dinner we had more dancing until bed-time.

Wednesday 19th February 1873, St Dunstan's.

Blanche and her party went away by the 12.30 train, and we, Charles, Antony and Janet, by the 2.52, some of the party having left by the early morning, so that the house is nearly cleared.....Before luncheon Hope, Antony, Charles and I took a long walk about the grounds with great pleasure. We had a note this evening from Alban saying he was well and happy, and that they were going tomorrow into Devon.

Friday 21st February 1873, St Dunstan's.

Letter from Alban from Exeter. I wrote to him, and to Sidney Harrison and Upton. Called in Hyde Park Gardens.

Saturday 22nd February 1873, St Dunstan's.

Heard from Upton about Uncle William's affairs.

Sunday 23rd February 1873, St Dunstan's.

I spent all the afternoon in Hyde Park Gardens.

Monday 24th February 1873, St Dunstan's.

We all dined at Hyde Park Gardens in our wedding garments, George and Mary, Antony and Janet, and Miss Buckingham being there. John also and Charles. Uncle William gave Mary and John £10,000 a piece, and Charles, who has no family £8000. To Milly and Dolly he has given the same as to Mary, and to Joe and Willy the same as to Charles. He has also most kindly given £2000 to Edith, and other amounts to cousins and friends.

Thursday 27th February 1873, St Dunstan's.

Spent the afternoon at Hyde Park Gardens.

Sunday 2nd March 1873, St Dunstan's.

The usual walk to Hyde Park Gardens with Herbert. George and Beatrice there, Charles called there. Uncle William not very well.

Wednesday 5th March 1873, St Dunstan's.

Herbert dined in Hyde Park Gardens and went to the Albert Hall. We had a telegram on the 3rd from Mexico dated the 28th – the quickest we have ever had.

Thursday 6th March 1873, St Dunstan's.

Shocked to see the death of Mrs Cecil Hubbard announced in the papers – a young, strong, beautiful woman. She died on the 4th.

Friday 7th March 1873, St Dunstan's.

The death of Mrs Hubbard was happily altogether a mistake. She had had a daughter; and the announcement was put in the wrong place in the Times!

Saturday 8th March 1873, St Dunstan's.

Went with Edith and Herbert to the Old Masters; and then to the City for a hour, and then to luncheon in Hyde Park Gardens where Uncle William surprised me by giving me a present of £8000, of which one is for Alban, and the other seven for the younger boys who of course will need it more. This with the £2000 to Edith makes £10,000 which he has given me for my children, besides the £7000 his intended legacy to myself given beforehand. The letter which accompanied this gift is as kind as the gift itself. To George Louis for his children he also gives £5000. I apportion his gift where he leaves it to me, to Vicary £2050, Herbert

Figure 32. Blanche Gibbs photo by Valentine Blanchard, 1873.

£1950, Kenneth £1700 and Henry £1300 – so the two elder will have about £2150 when they come of age, and the two younger about £2050.
Monday 10th March 1873, St Dunstan's.
Alban and Bride came back from Oxford and dined with us.
Tuesday 11th March 1873, St Dunstan's.
Today they dined at Hyde Park Gardens and we all dined there to meet them – so did George, Beatrice, Polly, Kate Lowe. Georgina Hayley and Etta Hogg staying in the house, so we had a large party.
Thursday 13th March 1873, Littlemore.
I came down here by the 3.40 train from Paddington, my head being not quite well….Aunt Eliza much more feeble than when I was here in October because of her late illness. She is very much pleased with Uncle William's kind present to her. He has given her £5000, and has now

Figure 33. William Gibbs photo by Valentine Blanchard, 1873.

added £600 to enable her to make some provision for her nieces.Saturday 15th March 1873, Aldenham.

Had luncheon with Vicary in his pleasant rooms in the new building at Christ Church and calling with him on Rigaud, Richard Crawley, the Warden of Keble, Tom Crawley… I met also West, the Bursar of Keble. The papers say Disraeli will not take office, so I suppose Gladstone will come back.

Monday 21st April 1873, St Dunstan's.

George Crawley, who brings excellent accounts from Mexico, called at the Bank.

Thursday 24th April 1873, Keble College Oxford.

I came down here to stay at the Warden's lodgings. Uncle William and Blanche going by train before to Littlemore, and Antony, Janet, Albinia and Edith going with them as far as Oxford where they have rooms at the

Randolph. Vicary came to the train to meet me and we went to see them there. Lord Lyttleton is here, and Mrs Gladstone came in the evening. There is also a Mr Festing, a guest of Talbot's.

We have had a very full gathering in Hall, I sitting between the Warden and Dr Acland. The Rector of Exeter dined with us, also Canon King and several other familiar faces – Lord Beauchamp, Shaw-Stewart, C. Wood, Hubbard (who came with me), Bernard, Woolcombe, Dalton, Bright and others. Lord Caernarvon made a very good and eloquent speech to which Talbot made an excellent reply. Poor West, the Bursar, was not able to be here having been summoned curtly by the suicide of his brother Lord De La Warr. Mrs Talbot is something like her older sister, Mrs John Talbot, and a very charming person, as they all are. I found a letter here from John about the proposed Reredos at Clifton Hampden.

Friday 25th April 1873, St Mark's Day, Littlemore.

This was Keble's birthday, (also my Mother's, my Grandfather Crawley's and his sister my Aunt Yonge's). Our function has passed off exceedingly well notwithstanding the bleak cold wind, which did its best to discourage us. Uncle William was happily well sheltered under the wall from the cold blast which pierced us all through and through, and seems none the worse for his exertions – everybody was delighted with the way in which he said his short Latin speech, and Mrs Gladstone desired to be introduced, that she might talk to him of her old friendship with Uncle Joseph and Aunt Anne……

The programme of the day was early communion at 8; breakfast some in hall, but I and Mr Festing with Mrs Talbot and Mrs Gladstone and Charlotte Yonge, who had come up from New College where she was staying. Matins at 10, luncheon at 1 o'clock, and the ceremony at 2 o'clock. Edith and the rest went to luncheon with Vicary, and I fetched her from there to the Warden's lodgings, wither Antony and Janet and Albinia followed Uncle William and Blanche picking them up in the carriage. They all went away home by the 5 o'clock train, and we two with Vicary drove out here, where we find Eveline and Alice Sherard, and Margaret Crawley, a nice little girl. Aunt Eliza very tolerably well. Vicary of course went back to sleep.

Saturday 26th April 1873, The Randolph – Oxford.

Mr Green, the Vicar, came to breakfast today, and Edith and I called on him afterwards to see his nice house – also on May Crawley and her daughters. Vicary came out and joined us in our visit, and we then all drove into Oxford, Vicary going to Christchurch.

Sunday 27th April 1873, Oxford.

Among other things we saw the chapel at New College and when we asked the Porter whether it would not some day be restored, he said, "I hope so, Sir," (not of course knowing who we were) "we want another

Mr Gibbs. I wish they had restored the old chapel rather than build the new buildings."

Tuesday 22nd July 1873, St Dunstan's.

I wrote to Uncle William Yesterday and today. Alban and Bride (Bridget) came to stay for a few days.

Wednesday 23rd July 1873, St Dunstan's.

I had letters from Uncle William and Kingdom.

Monday 28th July 1873, St Dunstan's.

Alban and Bride went to Tyntesfield.

Thursday 31st July 1873, St Dunstan's.

I was glad to hear from Escandon, who called at the Counting House, that W. Barron is coming home in October.

Friday 1st August 1873, Tyntesfield.

Edith was to have come down here with me, but a slight swelling of the glands, of yesterday, has declared itself for mumps this morning, so she must stay at home. This is Uncle William's Wedding Day, the 34th anniversary, and very well he looks on it. There are here Mrs Hogg, Etta and Margaret, Sally and Blanche and George Daubeny (*junior*), Mr Kingdom and Sanderson, a friend of Martin's – also Alban and Bride. Antony dined here.

Figure 34. Janet Gibbs with baby George Abraham.

247

Saturday 2nd August 1873, Tyntesfield.

Bridget makes great friends of the people here I am glad to say. We all went up to afternoon tea at Charlton, which place Antony has very greatly improved. Louisa, Rose, and Caroline and Catty Merivale are there, and John and Reginald came today.

Louisa Merivale tells me her brother Herman wrote the article in the Edinburgh Review about "Mrs H. Coleridge's Life" lately published by E.C. Janet's baby is a nice little creature (Figure 34).

Sunday 3rd August 1873, Tyntesfield.

Letters from Louisa and from Baker and Son. Edith is not much worse as yet and I hope she may have the disorder lightly. Vicary went yesterday to Antwerp with the Keatings on their way to Engadine. I wrote to Louisa and Harrison. Blanche wrote to Lady Mildred (who is at the Northcotes) to ask them to come here tomorrow.

Monday 4th August 1873, Tyntesfield.

A very pleasant but tiring day. I forgot to mention that the baby (*George Abraham*) was christened yesterday evening, and today we had a great luncheon in the hall at Charlton in commemoration thereof. Before that we had the function of laying the first stone of the chapel here, Vaughan reading the special service and Uncle William the words of action. We have heard nothing of the Hopes, and I think their scheme must be connected with the dreadful accident on the North Western, in which our poor friend, Sir John Anson has met his death. Very likely Lady Mildred has gone to Lady Anson's. I wrote to Louisa…. Two Miss Courtenays, John and Augusta Pode, and Polly and her two children came this evening. The three Daubenys went away.

Tuesday 5th August 1873, St Dunstan's.

Came up by the "Flying Dutchman" at 12.09.

Wednesday 31st December 1873, Tyntesfield.

From a letter written by William Gibbs to Sir John Coleridge[xvii],

"My dear friend let me thank you particularly for the affectionate manner in which you express yourself towards my beloved child Albinia, who I can say without any partiality is worthy of the affectionate interest you take in her. I can truly say I have never been angry with her in my life for with an extraordinary sweetness of temper and disposition, her mind seems naturally inclined to everything that is good. May God in his infinite goodness and mercy preserve to us so great a treasure. I wish I could say that we felt quite easy about her, for though better in may respects, she does not regain her strength, but as you say God is all good, and will be sure to order for her what is best".

Friday 2nd January 1874, Tyntesfield.

Vicary and I came down here by the 11.45 train and find John and Isabel with Johnny and the two girls here. Uncle William not very well;

his New Year's Eve disputation having tired him. I wrote to Louisa.

Saturday 3rd January 1874, Tyntesfield.

I brought a cold with me from my Railway journey and have had to stay in all day. I had a long course with Blanche in her sitting room de omnibus rebus et quibusdam alliis (*about almost everything and some more besides*). Antony and Janet, John Merivale, George and Catty, Rose and Caroline, and Tommy Sheppard all came to dinner.

Sunday 4th January 1874, Tyntesfield.

Cold rather worse so I still stay in. I had letters from Louisa, Monroe, Kenneth, Sparey, Baker and Son… Wrote to Bakers, Harrison, George Crawley…Butterfield and Louisa.

Monday 5th January 1874, Tyntesfield.

Still resfriado (*got a cold - Spanish*). I wrote to Louisa. Catty and Constance Bright dined here.

Tuesday 6th January 1874, Tyntesfield.

I went up the Midge with Blanche to call at Charlton and have luncheon there. My cold is no better and its presence has made my foot a little worse, nevertheless at the Servants' Ball tonight, which they enjoyed to the utmost and to which we all went in, I danced in Roger de Covereley with Jones. Antony and Janet came over on purpose and danced in the same set. I heard from and wrote to Louisa.

Wednesday 7th January 1874, Tyntesfield.

The servants did not get to bed till about five, and the housemaids not at all I believe. I feared for my toe but find myself little the worse, and better than at dinner time yesterday. I had a walk with Kate half way round the hill, calling on Susan Thomas; and if I am not worse tomorrow I shall expect to be better. John and Isabel and their children went to Clevedon today. I heard from Bateman, George Low and Louisa and wrote to them and Henry Crawley. Vicary went out to a coursing meeting with George Merivale.

Saturday 10th January 1874, Tyntesfield.

But I was worse on the morrow, and passed Thursday and yesterday in bed instead of going on the first day to the Charlton Ball, which everybody else enjoyed very much. However it has been a very light attack and I am up today in my room, and my trouble has been much lightened by everybody's coming to sit with me and write letters for me. Adams has given me a very good liniment for my toe, being Liquor Potasser two drams, Laudanum ½oz, and oil fill a 2oz bottle. Edith and Herbert came to Charlton on Wednesday, and so did Vicary's friend Maxwell here. Butterfield came last night.

Sunday 11th January 1874, Tyntesfield.

Day spent still in my room though I continue to improve not without fear that my right foot may be following next. I have written to Louisa (and

heard from her each day) either by my own or somebody else's fingers.
Monday 12th January 1874, Tyntesfield.
Today Butterfield went away in the early morning, and Rose, Caroline and Catty Merivale after breakfast, and George Merivale this evening. John and Johnny rode over from Clevedon. Vicary dined at Charlton. I came down stairs after breakfast and Kate wrote for me a long arrears of letters. M. Field and Annie Hogg came.
Tuesday 13th January 1874, Tyntesfield.
I seem to be getting better and drove to Charlton with Uncle William and Annie. Louisa tells me (and Bride tells Edith) that Audrey Hope is going to be married to Mr Marwood Tucker…..General De Gaja and Atkinson came – also Alfred Gurney. Janet and Edith went to spend the evening at Clevedon, and Antony and Herbert came to dine here.
Wednesday 14th January 1874, Tyntesfield.
Edith and Herbert went home. Emily and May Gurney came here and took away Annie Hogg with them.
Thursday 15th January 1874, Tyntesfield.
I had a head ache all day and though I am better as to my foot, I am condemned to have a blister on it. We drove out to Charlton.
Friday 16th January 1874, Tyntesfield.
A stormy day: Vicary went home. Mr Field , General Gaja and Atkinson and his daughter went away. I have been teaching Kate and Dora Ambre, and find the latter an able pupil. Heard from Louisa, Alban, Henry Louis, Greene and Sayer and wrote to them (all but H.L.). Herbert writes speaking of some people he does not like in an allusion to Euclid's definition of a point – "X has neither health nor wealth nor principles but has a position."
Saturday 17th January 1874, Tyntesfield.
A beautiful frosty day. Heard from and wrote to John Harrison and George – also from Louisa and Greene. Drove with Uncle William through Ashton Court Park.
Sunday 18th January 1874, Tyntesfield.
Blanche blistered my little toe last night, as the great toe had been so successful, but it did not rise in the least, owing no doubt to the thickness of the skin, but it did good for I was able to run briskly up stairs for the first time, but at about 11 the blister began to rise, and to judge by the present I feel has done its work thoroughly. Blanche and Dora went this morning with Alfred to hear him preach at All Saints.
I heard from Louisa, and wrote a long letter to her, and a short one to Greene. Antony and Janet came down to dinner.
Monday 19th January 1874, Tyntesfield.
Herbert came and brought me a letter from Louisa, and one from the Warden of Keble. I wrote to Louisa and Tom and Henry Crawley. Mr

Prescott and Blanche and Jenny Page came to stay.

Tuesday 20th January 1874, Tyntesfield.

Uncle William, Prescott, Herbert and I drove up to Charlton, and we two walked back. I wrote to Butterfield with a draft of my answers to Talbot, also to Louisa.

Wednesday 21st January 1874, Tyntesfield.

Letters from Louisa, Greene, and Gibson which I answered, and from George. Wrote also to Harrison and sent the conveyance of Basham Park to Messrs Hesp, Owen and Co, Robinson's solicitor. Herbert and I went to Charlton to shoot with Antony and George Henry who had driven over. I shot one woodcock, but performed very ill on the whole.

Thursday 22nd January 1874, Tyntesfield.

Heard from Louisa, and Greene, and a Mr Coombs and Gibson. Wrote to them and to Harrison…Charles Bright came over to shoot, and we shot in the woods here, a very pleasant day. Mr and Mrs Tracy came to dine and sleep. Also Emily Gurney, and Janet and Antony came to dinner.

Friday 23rd January 1874, Tyntesfield.

The Tracies went away. I wrote to Louisa but had no letter from her till this evening. Kenneth went back to school yesterday and Vicary goes to Oxford today. I had a letter from George and wrote both to him and at much length to Barron. John and Johnny rode over and stayed an hour.

Saturday 24th January 1874, Tyntesfield.

Blanche and I meant to have driven over to Clevedon today to dinner, but the weather looked so unpromising and we had besides a letter from John saying that Isabel was still but poorly and had to keep to her bed, so we put off our trip. Alfred and Emily Gurney went away. I heard from Louisa and Greene, and wrote another note to Barron saying his hesitation causing us to postpone bringing out our Jalapa loan might be fatal to its success, as it was we here were told very likely now or never, and even while I was writing, the chance might probably be passing away; and so it was for this evening has come the startling news of the Dissolution, which will probably paralyze business for a while. Wrote to Harrison, Gibson and George Cokayne.

Sunday 25th January 1874, Tyntesfield.

I had a little cold so have not been out for fear of gout, but we had an early celebration in the Oratory, and Evening Services. Heard from Lyall, Louisa, Harrison and Butterfield, the latter letter enclosing a letter of Talbot's to him and my draft letter to Talbot; I have written it out fair with some alterations and won't send it till I hear again from Butterfield. I wrote also to Louisa and George. Antony and Janet came to dinner.

Monday 26th January 1874, Tyntesfield.

Heard from Harrison and wrote to him, Louisa…and Tom Crawley. Blanche and I drove over to Clevedon to luncheon. John's house very ugly, but good and comfortable. Prescott went away.

Tuesday 27th January 1874, St Dunstan's.

Herbert and I came up by the 1.40 train, and find all well here. Bride much better.

Wednesday 28th January 1874, St Dunstan's.

Very busy all day, discussing Barron's stupid conduct about the Jalaja Loan with Sandars, Escandon and Crawley.

Thursday 29th January 1874, St Dunstan's.

And again today, but this time without Crawley, and with Fergusson as Barron's representative; and I think we shall come to an agreement. I wrote to Uncle William, and heard from Butterfield.

Tuesday 14th April 1874, St Dunstan's.

Blanche could not come down to dinner.

Wednesday 15th April 1874, St Dunstan's.

Albinia a little better, but the illness is necessarily very grave.

Thursday 16th April 1874, St Dunstan's.

Albinia much the same.

Friday 17th April 1874, Bromley.

I called in at Hyde Park Gardens this morning and found Uncle William a little more cheerful about Albinia, but this afternoon she became worse, Edith tells me, and is in a very alarming state. Weak as she is, a relapse or return of the inflammation must be more than she can bear up against.

Saturday 18th April 1874, St Dunstan's.

This morning Louisa sent us down a messenger with the dreadful news that she had passed away. The fresh acuteness of illness began at half past two, and she died at five o'clock, having suffered in that short time very much pain. She sent a message to me and Louisa, and Alban and Bride, always thoughtful and affectionate to the last. If there ever was a Saint on earth, she was one. I never remember her to have failed in temper, to have said an unkind word, or to have needed any correction all her life. We came up of course (from Bromley) immediately after breakfast, and Louisa and I have both been to Hyde Park Gardens to see her poor dear bereaved father and mother. I saw her too, poor darling – her face already greatly and I think unusually altered by death. They will go to Tyntesfield on Tuesday. None of her brothers were there. Antony was at Charlton, Martin at Juniper, and Dolly (*Dorothea*) also away. She arrived early this morning, and so did Antony.

Sunday 19th April 1874, St Dunstan's.

Edith and I went to St Michael's in the morning and she had luncheon with Kate and I in Hyde Park Gardens. I went to church with them in the afternoon and also called on Kate.

Tuesday 21st April 1874, St Dunstan's.

The William Gibbses and Antony Gibbses went away into Somerset in a sad party. I went in the morning to wish them good bye. Blanche was a little better but Uncle William very wretched. Kate Lowe goes with them.

Friday 24th April 1874, Tyntesfield.

Alban, Edith and I came here by the 7.50 train to Bristol. George going on to Clevedon. George Henry, Willy and John are here – also Kate and the two Daubeny girls and Miss Courtenay. Dear Uncle William is certainly more comfortable and calm than he was, and both he and Blanche have slept better since they came here, but Blanche looks very sad and worn.

Saturday 25th April 1874, Tyntesfield.

Our sad day is over, and Uncle William and Blanche have gone through their heavy trial as composedly as I could hope. Dear Blanche broke down thoroughly once when the coffin was being taken out of the Oratory; but it was better that she should let her tears flow than restrain them as she has done. It is not restraining them indeed, but some sorrow is too great for tears. George Louis and Beatrice came over from Clevedon, and John returned with them. Alfred Pott came from Abingdon, and returned, and so did Elizabeth Crawley Boevey and Tom from Flaxley, and Emily and May Gurney from Clifton. The Doynes also were there, and a large number of Parishioners. George Henry and Willy went back to Hutton after the service.

The funeral was at 3 p.m. At 9 in the morning, Hardie celebrated the Holy Communion in the Oratory wearing for the first time a plain linen chasuble and alb. There was a large congregation, many of the servants communicating. After breakfast matins were said; and just before our procession began, a few short prayers in the oratory. At the Grave, hymn No 378 (Ancient & Modern) was very well sung. Before service I took a long walk with John, and after service Edith and I had a pleasant walk around the "West Hill".

Sunday 26th April 1874, Tyntesfield.

Holy Communion again this morning in the Oratory. The rest of the party went to matins at Wraxall but I being not very well, stayed at home. At evensong Alfred gave a long impassioned and powerful address as a sort of funeral oration on our dear Albinia. No text except that of the 23rd Psalm was woven into his sermon, and that he cited also in the last chapter of St John's gospel and the last of Revelations. He spoke of four spiritual exercises which she applied herself each day. The study of Holy Scripture, self examination, meditation, and intercessory prayer. It was not however as is too often the case, fulsome praise of herself. He rather took her for his text, and showed us what a holy life should be. It was very beautiful and though it lasted more than an hour, it did not seem half the time. Yet to her father and mother it was I think painful, so much being said about one who was so unaffectedly humble herself – Nothing that he said was too good for her, but it seemed that it might be poignant to them to have it all said so plainly.

Monday 27th April 1874, Tyntesfield.

Blanche tells me she did feel as I thought. The servants tell us that they never heard anything so beautiful and that they would like to have listened another hour. The Daubenys went away before breakfast. I heard from and wrote to Louisa yesterday, and heard from her again this afternoon from St Leonard's – also from Sydney.

John came over from Clevedon, and drove with Uncle William, Blanche and me to Charlton. The Hall is hugely improved by its restoration to its original condition by the removal of the modern porch. They are building a new one where the older one must have been.

Tuesday 28th April 1874, St Dunstan's.

Alban, Edith and I came up by the 12.09 train, leaving Uncle William but poorly.

Thursday 30th April 1874, St Dunstan's.

A very busy day. The Majorca Land Company finally disposed of and its debts paid, the New Majorca Land Company adopting half its debts…. The Indian Council opening the tenders for their loan convene the Governor and myself (*The Governor and a Director of the Bank of England*), but I escaped and went to the Mexican Railway Office, where the Creditors had a meeting for the arrangement of their debts, and I have some hope that we have come to a real agreement.

Wednesday 20th May 1874, St Dunstan's.

Wrote to Uncle William about Otty and about Davy's Will.

Friday 22nd May 1874, St Dunstan's.

Heard from Uncle William and Aunt Eliza, and wrote to the latter.

Thursday 23rd July 1874, Tyntesfield.

After Bank, Edith and I came down here, and find all tolerably well – Mrs Armstrong, the widow of the South African Bishop, is staying here. Antony and Janet are away.

Friday 24th July 1874, Tyntesfield.

Wrote to Louisa, Stubbs and Ellacombe. Drove with Uncle William, Blanche and Edith to Charlton, and walked back with Blanche. Mrs Armstrong went away and Basonet de Milanges came.

Saturday 25th July 1874, Tyntesfield.

Letters from Louisa, Alban, Harrison, Greene and G.B. Crawley, the latter asking me, much to my disgust, to go up to London on Monday. Wrote to him, Greene, Harrison, Alban and to Childs and Son. This afternoon we all drove into Clifton. The Dykes called.

Sunday 26th July 1874, Tyntesfield.

Holy Communion this morning in the Oratory; and after breakfast,

Edith and I drove over to Service at Backwell. I heard from Greene and Louisa and wrote to the latter…Blanche and I took a walk before dinner.
Monday 27th July 1874, Tyntesfield.
I came up by the 12.09 train and went to Bishopsgate Street.
Saturday 19th December 1874, Tyntesfield.
Herbert and I came down here by the 1.50 – a tedious, cold journey – we did not arrive till 7 p.m.. All pretty well here. Aunt Charlotte and her two daughters are with them – also Alba and Blanche Daubeny, George Crawley and Inez, and John. Antony and Janet dined here.
Sunday 20th December 1874, Tyntesfield.
A cold, damp, foggy day on the turn between frost and thaw. Some of us went to Church, but we had a service in the Oratory. Letters from Sandars and G.J. Harrison. Wrote to George Cokayne, Louisa and Vicary.
Monday 21st December 1874, Tyntesfield.
A beautiful day, and capital shooting – considering it was the sixth time the covers had been shot – or whether or no, for I never met more slaughter. Four guns, Antony, G.B.C. (George Crawley), Herbert and I, and we killed 106 pheasants besides hares and rabbits. George killed 24, I killed 23 and Antony and Herbert divided the rest about equally, I suppose. Janet came to luncheon with us, and Antony and Janet came to dinner. I wrote to George Louis and to Louisa. The foreman to the Builder has had an accident at the Chapel, a pole fell and struck him on the head causing concussion of the brain, it seems.
Tuesday 22nd December 1874, Tyntesfield.
It was a much worse case than we thought! The skull was fractured and the poor man died this morning! He leaves a widow and two children and another expected. Strange that at Keble also the Clerk of the Works fell and was killed.
George and Inez and their little Ernest went away today. I heard from Greene and Harrison, and wrote to the latter and to Louisa.
Wednesday 23rd December 1874, Tyntesfield.
Antony and I drove through the snow to Wrington, where we had a capital day's shooting with Mr Edwards, beginning at Barleywood where Hannah More used to live. Two letters from Louisa. Blomfield came.
Thursday 24th December 1874, Tyntesfield.
A capital day's shooting at Charlton 165 head. 8 woodcocks of which 4 fell to my share, and two more ought to have done so. We had luncheon at the house, which is now beautiful internally, the hall which was spoilt before being now excellent. The porch too is very good; but I wish they had followed my plan and carried it up to the top of the front breaking the ugly line of the roof. Blomfield went away and Butterfield came.
Letters from Louisa and I wrote to her, also to Harry Norris from whom I

255

heard yesterday.

Christmas Day – Friday 25th December 1874, Tyntesfield.

The new Altar and Retable came for the Chapel and have been put in the Oratory meanwhile. The Altar is of Cedar enriched with white wood carvings by Forsyth, and with ivory and coral in the Retable. Heard from and wrote to George, Alban, Louisa, Dufane and Greene.

Antony and Janet, John Merivale and Catty came to dinner.

Saturday 26th December 1874, Tyntesfield.

Letter from Louisa. Wrote to George Crawley. I had also a telegram from Charles consulting me about his leave. He has paid for the return message, but they have sent me the wrong form from the office, and I hear by wire from Vicary that he sends me the right one by this post.

Sunday 27th December 1874, Tyntesfield.

Letter from Louisa and also from Vicary. I meant to have gone to Clevedon this afternoon to see John and Butterfield. Herbert and I went to church at Backwell, stayed awhile at the parsonage (Mr Burbridge's), walked through the Coombe and over the Common, the roads linked to it being a sheet of ice, as far as Barrow Court; the occupier thereof, Mr Miller, showed us all over the beautiful old house. To think Uncle William might have bought it and couldn't!! The consequence was that it was too late to go to Clevedon.

Monday 28th December 1874, St Dunstan's.

Herbert and I came up by the early express, and find all pretty well here. Alban arrived from Bedgebury.

Thursday 31st December 1874, St Dunstan's.

Stayed in bed most of the day…….Letter from Blanche …..Wrote to Aunt Eliza, Aunt George….and Butterfield.

Tuesday 2nd February 1875, St Dunstan's.

Letter from and to Uncle William.

Saturday 6th February 1875, St Dunstan's.

A letter from Uncle William tells me G.W. Daubeny is going into partnership with Mr Popplewell, a tea merchant in Tower Street, and is to be married on the strength of it on Tuesday next to his (I fear penniless) love Miss Annie Hamilton.

Thursday 11th February 1875, St Dunstan's.

Heard from Uncle William.

Friday 12th February 1875, St Dunstan's.

Wrote to Uncle William.

Monday 15th February 1875, St Dunstan's.

Have written tonight to Blanche.

Tuesday 16th February 1875, St Dunstan's.

A letter from Blanche crossed mine, and gives of course much the same account, but she said there had been no particular illness. This evening however Joe has come up, principally with a view to tell me that yesterday after dinner he (Uncle William) had a very violent attack of irritation of the bladder, and was unable himself to pass the catheter, and suffered therefore till 11 when Adams came. Adams said he did not think it could last many days – yet as Blanche tells Joe that she does not apprehend any immediate danger, I shan't go down till Thursday – unless indeed I should hear any worse account tomorrow.

Wednesday 17th February 1875, St Dunstan's.

No news this morning, though John had a letter from Hardie, and one from Isabel enclosing a letter from Janet, both speaking from the same time as Joe's report; for they were written about the time at which he left. Heard from and wrote to poor Blanche.

Thursday 18th February 1875, St Dunstan's.

I meant to have gone down to Tyntesfield today. I excused myself from Lyall's in consequence; but I had a telegram from Antony saying there was no cause for immediate anxiety and so I postponed my going until tomorrow. Edith went down to the Lyall's.

Friday 19th February 1875, Tyntesfield.

I came down by the 11.45 train and find poor Uncle William in a very precarious state. Sometimes pretty comfortable, but sometimes not quite himself. He sits down in his study as usual, and in between the intervals of sleep occupies himself feebly with his papers. At dinner to which he comes in as usual, no one would have found out that he was ill. He eats well, and joins as much as he has done of later years, in the conversation – but shortly after dinner he began to wander a little, and began to tear his clothes open, not knowing where he was. But Blanche got him to bed soon and they were both I believe asleep when we came to bed.

I wrote to Harrison, Louisa and George Louis.

Saturday 20th February 1875, Tyntesfield.

Uncle William slept pretty well, and has been tolerably well all day, but tonight he was so weak that he could not get into bed, and Blanche was not strong enough to lift him, and it was all Antony could do. I hope I have persuaded Blanche to allow a nurse to be called for, and I am writing to Sir Henry Thompson to send one.

Sunday 21st February 1875, Tyntesfield.

The snow is deep, so that I neither went to Clevedon as I had intended, nor could we go to Church. I heard from Harrison, Greene, Butterfield and Louisa, and wrote to them; also Tyndall Bright, Mrs H. Merivale, Charles G. Crawley, John and Alban, and finished my letter to Sir Henry Thompson. Uncle William seems much the same.

Monday 22nd February 1875, Tyntesfield.

I went by train to Clevedon and had luncheon with John and Isabel. They have made a very comfortable house of it. John afterwards drove me part of the way home, and we then walked the rest of the way over the hill by Naish. John is sleeping here. I heard from George Louis and wrote to Louisa and Sir Henry Thompson.

Tuesday 23rd February 1875, St Dunstan's.

Uncle William was really better this morning, and read all the packet letters before I went away, which I did by the 12.45 train.

Wednesday 24th February 1875, St Dunstan's.

I went and ordered a chair for Uncle William, and wrote to Blanche about it.

The Death of William Gibbs

Thursday 25th February 1875, St Dunstan's.

Wrote to Blanche, who sends me but a poor account of dear Uncle William.

Monday 1st March 1875, St Dunstan's.

Edith had a letter from Martin, just packing up for the return to Lima.

Friday 5th March 1875, St Dunstan's.

Wrote to Blanche.

Monday 8th March 1875, St Dunstan's.

Blanche's account of Uncle William is very bad, weakness of body very much increased, but his memory better, irritability less. Adams thinks his life cannot now last long and that he may very probably pass away painlessly in sleep. I wrote to her and also to John Merivale, who had written to me about his son George.

Wednesday 10th March 1875, St Dunstan's.

A letter from John this morning gives a very bad account of poor, dear Uncle William, who seems now to have taken to his bed… I wrote to Blanche and John, and to Henry Adams with his account.

Thursday 11th March 1875, St Dunstan's.

A telegram from Blanche saying that he was too bad for my going to be of any comfort to him; so of course I stay.

Friday 12th March 1875, St Dunstan's.

Antony's report of his father is as bad as possible.

Saturday 13th March 1875, St Dunstan's.

I have a letter from Blanche saying he is a little better, and got up next morning, but of course he is still most dangerously ill.

Monday 15th March 1875, St Dunstan's.

No news from Tyntesfield.

Thursday 18th March 1875, Tyntesfield.

I came down here by the 1.50 train and find dear Uncle William very much changed in the last 3 or 4 weeks. His voice is very feeble and his memory also, and himself very helpless. He has fallen almost into second

258

childhood, except that when he speaks or is spoken to he is nearly himself. In short there is no imbecility, but great feebleness. Blanche seems better than she was.

Friday 19th March 1875, Tyntesfield.

He has had a much more comfortable day and has been able to busy himself with his letters. I wrote to Louisa and Hubbard, and George Louis and George Crawley. John came over for luncheon and took a walk with me over the hill.

Saturday 20th March 1875, Tyntesfield.

It has been a very bad day with poor Uncle William – his mind has wandered much, so that he has scarcely ever been able to continue a sentence right through.

Sunday 21st March 1875, Tyntesfield.

Uncle William's condition alternates very much and today he is a little better. I went to Clevedon in the morning, and to church with John (*Lomax Gibbs*) and his two girls at the pretty little Church at Walton. His boy Robert and Ernest Crawley sang in the choir; also Edmund Elton. I went to lunch afterwards with them and found Isabel better. John came back with me to dine and sleep. Charles will be down on Tuesday.

Monday 22nd March 1875, Tyntesfield.

John and I went to Weston this morning and I came back to luncheon. We saw Margaret Hendy and her niece Mrs Menzies and sat half an hour with them. Margaret was very glad to see me and seems to have recovered herself after poor Susanna's death. I had a note from Harrison and wrote to West, Aunt Susan, Louisa, Charles Bright and Charles. Bride, and Mary Hope got into a ridiculous muddle in the Drawing Room. Lady Mildred was to have presented them, but was too ill, and they understood from Lord Nutford that as a special favour Mr Hope might take them, but when they got to the Palace, they found it could not be, and the Queen sent down word that Lady Abercrombie was to present them. But they had seen Mrs Knatchbull-Huguesson and asked her to do so. When they got to the throne room they saw Lady Abercrombie. She also bowed to them, and they thought she was their godmother for the occasion; but in the newspapers they appear as presented "by their mother, Mrs Knatchbull-Huguesson"! Hope will have had it corrected in the papers. It has been very bad day with Uncle William today.

Tuesday 23rd March 1875, St Dunstan's.

I came up by the 12.09 train leaving Uncle William in much the same state, but having had a good night.

Friday 2nd April 1875, St Dunstan's.

Letter from Antony gives a lamentable account of his dear father. I wrote to him.

Friday 2nd April 1875 – Letter from Rev. Hardie, Tyntesfield. ^{xviii}

My dear Gibbs,
I enclose a letter received this morning from the Dean of Norwich. You will see from it that he cheerfully undertakes to write a short memoir for the Guardian. The facts he asks for you can supply so much more easily and correctly than I, so that I have ventured to write to him today and tell him that you will do so. We all met at your dear Uncle's bedside believing that the end had come. But a couple of hours later he had strength enough to throw off a quantity of phlegm, which had oppressed him very much, and he has been slightly better since. I fear that the relief will only last a few hours, though it is a sign of something like a rally that he asked for some tea this morning and drank a cupful. He had taken no nourishment during the previous 36 hours but a little beef tea which I got him to swallow yesterday after much persuasion. He is quite conscious and answers though not always articulately to any questions put to him, and he sometimes smiles most sweetly on those near him. He is able to listen for a little while to comforting passages from scripture and to share our intercession. He suffers no pain unless the oppression of his breathing can be counted as such. It is sad to witness the gradual parting of soul and body, yet the transition to another life could hardly be gentler, and I pray that on the spiritual side my last end may be like his. With very kind regards to Mrs Gibbs as well as to yourself,

Yours most sincerely,

John Hardie

Saturday 3rd April 1875, St Dunstan's.
I had a letter from Hardie this morning enclosing one from Goulbourn saying that he will write a short Memoir of Uncle William for the Guardian, and asking for dates and particulars which I am to send him. We went to Aldenham and were followed by a telegram from Hardie saying the dear good man breathed his last breath this morning between 12 and 1, and I had a letter from Antony tonight saying that his death was apparently without pain. Hardie's letter said that they thought the night before that the end had come. I wrote to Hardie.

Saturday 3rd April 1875, Tyntesfield – Letter from Antony Gibbs. ^{xix}

My Dear Henry,
The end has come and my dear father has gone to his rest. I am thankful to say that it was very peaceable. There seemed to be no struggle. He

simply ceased to breathe. There had been a great deal of rattling in his throat for 24 hours or more, but when asked he said he was in no pain. He died in the middle of the night at half past twelve. This must go to Bristol immediately or you will not get it this evening.

Your affectionate cousin

Antony Gibbs

Sunday 4th April 1875, St Dunstan's.
I wrote to Hardie and Antony sending the two letters by Rail so as to be posted on the way to reach Tyntesfield tomorrow. Wrote also to Dean Goulbourn and Sidney Harrison.
Monday 5th April 1875, St Dunstan's.
A telegram from Hardie tells me the funeral will be on Friday. I wrote to Charles and Kate to tell them.
Tuesday 6th April 1875, St Dunstan's.
A foolish notice of Uncle William in the Times with as many errors as lines. Letter from Antony. I was elected and sworn in today Governor of the Bank of England.

A <u>BRISTOL</u> MERCHANT – Yesterday the death was announced, at the patriarchal age of 84, of Mr. William Gibbs of Tyntesfield, near Bristol, who has been spoken of – probably erroneously – as the richest commoner in England, he having amassed <u>immense</u> wealth as head of the <u>shipping </u>houses of Antony Gibbs and <u>Co </u>of London, <u>and Gibbs, Bright and Co., of Liverpool and Bristol engaged in the West Indian and Australian trade.</u> Mr Gibbs married the daughter of Sir Thomas <u>Martin </u>Crawley-Boe<u>vey,</u> of Gloucestershire, and is succeeded by his eldest son, Mr Antony Gibbs, J.P. The deceased gentleman is known for his many princely acts of munificence in connection with Keble College, Oxford, Bristol Cathedral restoration, Weston-super-Mare sanatorium, and other undertakings. Several churches have been entirely built or restored at his expense, and towards the restoration of Ivybridge Church in Devon, which has just been completed, he contributed £5000. Mr Gibbs never filled any public office <u>except that of High Sheriff of Somersetshire</u>.

(The errors are as underlined by Henry Hucks Gibbs.)

Wednesday 7th April 1875, St Dunstan's.
That foolish thing was corrected as annexed in today's paper.

THE LATE MR. WILLIAM GIBBS. – With reference to a paragraph which appeared in our issue of yesterday, we are informed that Mr Gibbs whose death was announced at the age of 84, was not a Bristol merchant, as stated. The deceased gentleman was a member of the firm of Messrs. Antony Gibbs and Sons, which firm however is distinct from the highly respected house of Gibbs, Bright and Co., of Liverpool and Bristol, referred to. We understand that Mr Gibbs never filled the office of High Sheriff of Somersetshire. Mr Gibbs married a daughter of Sir Thomas Crawley-Boevey.

I did my first duties as Governor (*of the Bank of England*) swearing in the New Directors as I did the Deputy Governor yesterday. I heard from and wrote to Hardie.

Friday 9th April 1875, Tyntesfield.

I came down here with Alban, Charles, Harry Daubeny, Stubbs and Sir Thomas Waller, Alfred Pott and Sidney Harrison joining us at Didcot, to pay our last sad duty to dear Uncle William. It was a bad day, and rained a good deal, with a sharp North Wind. Dean Goulbourn was here, Prescott, and Risley, John Daubeny, Henry Crawley, George and Beatrice, George Heberden and Dolly, Joseph, George Henry, and Willy, Douglas Page, Mr Courtenay of Mamhead; and many neighbours, lay and clerical, who followed him to the grave. The Church was as full as on Sunday. None have stayed behind tonight, except John Merivale and myself. Dearest Blanche is as composed as we could hope, but sadly exhausted by her long watching, which can only be made up for by months of rest. She talks of going out at the end of the month to meet Martin (Henry Martin Gibbs) in Bordeaux, but I doubt the prudence of it. She has many most sweet and touching letters from various friends – especially from Canon King, and Sir John Coleridge; poor dear Sir John being in a very failing state of body and not likely long to survive his old friend.

Saturday 10th April 1875, Tyntesfield.

Occupied all day in reading the Will and considering its contents – George also came over from Clevedon. I had a great deal of talk with Blanche and Hardie separately about the latter's position vis a vis to Antony, and I think I shall be able to aid in putting matters on a good footing.

Monday 11th April 1875, Tyntesfield.

I had a very satisfactory talk with Antony as we walked to the Church. Vaughan preached a very good sermon, making pleasing mention of Uncle William; and Hardie preached us an admirable one this evening in the Oratory on "There remaineth a rest for the people of God".

Monday 12th April 1875, St Dunstan's.

I meant to have come up by the 12 o'clock train with George and Beatrice, but I found so much to do that I stayed till 2.45 and came up then…. Blanche showed me a letter from old Sir John Coleridge written in June 1873, asking her if Uncle William would accept a peerage.

Tuesday 13th April 1875, St Dunstan's.

I always find plenty of arrears in the Governor's Room. I sent for Upton to talk about the probate of Uncle William's Will, and also about my Will, which must be altered now that I stand in Uncle William's place. Palmer and I went to the Chancellor of the Exchequer to talk about a feature in his budget – also about Exchequer Bonds, and about Public Balances. Wrote to Blanche.

Wednesday 14th April 1875, St Dunstan's.

Heard from and wrote to Antony.

Thursday 15th April 1875, St Dunstan's.

Heard from and wrote to Blanche, who gives a good account of herself.

Friday 16th April 1875, St Dunstan's.

Hardie sent me the "In Memoriam" for Uncle William to be sent to Rivingtons to get printed. Wrote to him and to James Hayne.

Saturday 17th April 1875, St Dunstan's.

Louisa had a letter from Blanche, and I wrote to her.

Sunday 18th April 1875, St Dunstan's.

Vicary and I went to Church at St Michael's, went to luncheon at the Beresford Hopes (where we found Lady Mildred was a little better) and called on Kate and on the Coleridges.

Monday 19th April 1875, St Dunstan's.

Answered letters from Antony and Hardie. Had a long talk with the two Georges and Sandars and finally settled the question of the Mexican Railway release.

Tuesday 20th April 1875, St Dunstan's.

Heard from and wrote to Blanche, Harrison, Mrs Remmett, Percy Doyle, and John Merivale. Alban came home.

Wednesday 21st April 1875, St Dunstan's.

I heard from Blanche and wrote to her thanking her for her sweet affectionate letter in which she gives me Ross's miniatures of Uncle George, Aunt Harriett and Aunt Anne.

Saturday 24th April 1875, Oxford.

They went away to France by the 10.15 train, and I came here by the 10 o'clock train and was met by Vicary at the station, and went straight to Keble, where we had a pretty full council, Dr Pusey being there. Afterwards Vicary and I drove to Littlemore – Aunt Eliza very well… I had luncheon with the Talbots, and met old Mrs Talbot there. Dinner with Kenneth and whist afterwards in Vicary's rooms. I have comfortable rooms myself in Keble, and so has Lord Beauchamp, opposite me.

Sunday 25th April 1875, Oxford.

Breakfast in Hall between early service 7.45 and matins 9.30. Dr Lowe was there, and also Mr Powell – M.P. for the North Riding. I went to luncheon with Kenneth, and Talbot came up to fetch me there and take me to call on Pusey, but the Doctor was out; and so he and I walked round Christchurch Meadows, and then to chapel at 4.30 where Illingworth preached a very remarkable sermon. The two boys came to our chapel. We dined in hall at 6 and went afterwards to the Common Room where we had much pleasant chat. They have Keble's writing table in the Common Room at which much of "The Christian Year" was written. Went to tea in West's rooms, and then back to Christ Church and spent an hour with the boys.

Monday 26th April 1875, St Dunstan's.

Breakfast in Hall after half past nine chapel, and then came up to town…

Tuesday 27th April 1875, St Dunstan's.

Heard from Rivington's with proofs of the "In Memoriam" for Uncle William. Telegram from Martin to say that he had arrived at Bordeaux but was in quarantine.

Thursday 29th April 1875, St Dunstan's.

Louisa and I both had letters from Blanche – mine about her will, which I have begun to answer.

Wednesday 12th May 1875, St Dunstan's.

Edith went to Oxford with Antony and Janet.

Saturday 15th May 1875, St Dunstan's.

I went to the Kensington Museum and to Hyde Park Gardens.

Monday 17th May 1875, St Dunstan's.

Edith and I, and Antony and Janet spent the day at Aldenham.

Tuesday 18th May 1875, St Dunstan's.

Today George and I distributed to the Clerks the £3000 of Uncle William's Legacy together with £2250 by which she (Blanche) and Antony had increased it following the analogy of what he said in his letter to her about the legacy to servants.

Wednesday 19th May 1875, St Dunstan's.

Had letters from Blanche today and yesterday.

Friday 21st May 1875, St Dunstan's.

Wrote to Blanche.

Saturday 22nd May 1875, St Dunstan's.

Wrote to Blanche (to Bourges, *in France*) after a long talk with Upton about her will and mine.

Wednesday 26th May 1875, St Dunstan's.

Wrote to Blanche.

Friday 28th May 1875, St Dunstan's.
Letter from Blanche in much trouble at my letter having missed her. I wrote her a line.
Saturday 22nd April 1876, St Dunstan's.
Dear Blanche came home last night. I went there today and was glad to find her looking very well. After luncheon she came back with me to see Louisa.
Sunday 23rd April 1876, St Dunstan's.
The boys and I went to St Michael's, and to luncheon at Hyde Park Gardens.
Monday 24th April 1876, Oxford.
Edith, Vicary, Herbert and I came down here by the 10 o'clock train and after luncheon at the Randolph where we are lodged, Edith and I went forth to call on the Aclands and then on Mrs Cosen and then on Cosen at the Bodleian, and then at the Deanery. Before luncheon I went to Keble and saw West and Beauchamp, and was much pleased to hear from the latter that all was practically settled with the Bishop, and on the terms of his last letter to me. Nevertheless at the Council which met at half past four to establish the Concordat we had considerable discussion about it. Dr Pusey and Dr Bright objecting to the word "deferred" as appearing to admit that the chapel would at some time be consecrated. "Well", said Lord Beauchamp, "I should be very loath to say it should not". Either all fear of disestablishment may have passed, or we may have been disestablished, and in either case no obstacle would remain to the rite of Consecration, from which no political dangers could then be expected to flow. Dr Liddon was not there or no doubt he would have voted with the above mentioned, who divided the Council, but of course in vain. Kenneth found me at Keble. I saw poor Mrs Talbot for a moment, and the Warden told me she would take Blanche over to the Chapel, but Blanche, coming tonight to Keble from the train, missed my note. She went to see Mrs Talbot after Church, and is to breakfast with her after Chapel tomorrow. I went after a pleasant dinner in Keble's temporary Hall to Lady Beauchamp's.
Tuesday 25th April 1876, Oxford.
A glorious but most tiring day. Holy Communion at 9.30 about 350 receiving. The Archbishop being Celebrant, and the Bishops of Rochester, Maritzburg, Ely, Tennessee, and Bishop Abraham assisting, besides two other priests. Afterwards I breakfasted at a quarter to ten with the Beauchamps, Edith and the boys going home instead between the services. At the 11.30 service, the Bishop of Oxford was there and at luncheon I sat next to him and told him I eat with the better appetite for his presence. We had the matter (*of consecration*) out together in the intervals of business. Blanche had luncheon with Lady Beauchamp, who

was also in mourning and did not come into Hall. The speeches were very good, both at the Luncheon (where Beauchamp presided) and at the laying of the first stone of the Library. At the evening service, I read the second lesson. We dined at the Randolph – Blanche, Antony, Dora, and I. Borlase and his Mary came, Charles, the three boys (Alban could not come by reason of Bride), Alfred Gurney, Fields, John and George Merivale, and John and Isabel who came in from New Inn Hall where they were staying with Chase, the Head, when we had nearly done dinner. Horribly tired all of us.

Wednesday 26th April 1876, St Dunstan's.

Herbert, Edith and I came up with Richmond and Alfred by the capital nine o'clock train. All well here and at Park Square.

Sunday 30th April 1876, St Dunstan's.

Kenneth and I went to St Michael's and Hyde Park Gardens and I called also on John Merivale and the Hopes. Alban and Sidney Harrison dined here.

Friday 2nd June 1876, Tyntesfield.

I came down here by the usual 1.50 train, travelling with a specimen of a North Country man, one Haggie, a rope maker of the neighbourhood of Newcastle – a right thinking intelligent man. Dear Blanche seems pretty well, and so are Antony, Janet and Martin. Edith too is I think better for her change of air. The little Gurneys are here and a Mr Kenrick, a friend of Martin's. Letter from Few yesterday about the Keble Scholarships.

Saturday 3rd June 1876, Tyntesfield.

A good deal of rain this afternoon, whereby I stayed in all day, helping Blanche with her accounts.

Sunday 4th June 1876, Tyntesfield.

Edith and I drove over in the Brougham to Clevedon and brought back John with us in the Box. Arthur Pott and Morton Cokayne came from Cornish's School with Bertie for luncheon, and I had an amusing conversation on our way home arising out of something Cyril said one day at luncheon in the character of an Enfant Terrible.

Monday 5th June 1876, Tyntesfield.

Isabel and Blanche, Isabel, Mary and Bertie came over this afternoon and stayed to dinner going back with John in the evening. Some of us walked to Charlton. Heard from and wrote to Louisa and also to Henry Bright.

Wednesday 7th June 1876, St Dunstan's.

Wrote to Blanche.

Friday 9th June 1876, St Dunstan's.

Heard from and wrote to Blanche also to Tom Crawley offering his son Charles an uncovenanted clerkship in the Bank.

Thursday 26th September 1876, Tyntesfield.

Went to town as usual, and came straight away from the Indemnity to

Paddington and there I found Dora awaiting my escort by the 1.00 p.m. train. I find John and Isabel and their children here. She not very well; also Kate Lowe and a young Mr. Reid (a friend of Antony's). Janet also came to dinner.

Friday 27th September 1876, Tyntesfield.

A nasty misty day in which we could not go out much. John and I however walked round the hill. I had a great deal of talk with him and Blanche and Isabel about Exwick, and with Blanche about her Cheddar plans. I wrote to Louisa. Antony and Martin came home from Scotland and Willy came also to Charlton, he, Antony and Janet dining here. Charles came after dinner and George and Beatrice came today by the same train as we did yesterday.

Figure 35. St Michael's Home, Axebridge near Cheddar.

Saturday 28th September 1876, Tyntesfield.

We have had a most successful day at Cheddar, the weather favouring us and the ceremony passing off without a single hitch thanks in great measure to us having so good an organizer as Butterfield and so good a ceremoniarius (*religious master of ceremonies*) as Martin. The Chapel is most beautiful and the whole building is excellent. Hicks and Alethea, his wife, occupy the pretty little lodge till the Chaplain's House shall be ready. Mr and Mrs Brendon were there of course, very kind as usual and their daughters, Mrs à Court and Miss Brendon. I had not seen the former before and was much charmed with her. George Henry was there and we made a goodly family party. I had a letter from Louisa and one from Milnes, with a copy of a letter he had written to Mr Dumbleton – a proper dressing down!

267

Sunday 29th September 1876, Tyntesfield.

With Butterfield's help for the description part, I wrote a letter to the Guardian describing yesterday's proceedings. It is to go also to the local paper, and Charles has copied it that Mr Beadon may send it him.

Antony has offered John the living at Exwick.

Tuesday 1st October 1876, Tyntesfield.

John and I went down to Exeter by the 12.10 train, and had a good look at Exwick with Willy's help (*the Rev. William Cobham Gibbs*), who gave us the most complete account of the place, its virtues and vices. The house in an excellent one with a pretty little Oratory (the old Clifton Hampden window in it) in which Willy read evensong. We dined and slept at Tom Snow's at Clear House. Both he and his wife were most kind to us. He said he had been expecting me for 35 years.

We came up today, John only as far as Bristol where Beatrice joined me.

Wednesday 6th December 1876, St Dunstan's.

Heard from and wrote to Antony. George and I finished Uncle William's Residency Account. He and Beatrice went to Charlton.

Thursday 7th December 1876, Tyntesfield.

Came down here by the 1.50 train in a most wretched day. Albinia and Blanche Daubeny are here, Milly and her Mary, Charles, John and Isabel. John is very much better than I expected to see him, too fat, indeed, and very weak, but his flesh has come again to him like the flesh of a little child, and the skin of his face is as softy as a baby's.

Friday 8th December 1876, Tyntesfield.

A beautiful day. After luncheon we went out and shot a few hares and pheasants in the valley. Lambert, George Louis, Antony and Dick Bright coming over from Charlton. I dined there and met besides these the Charles Caves, the Tylers, and Catty and Constance.

Saturday 9th December 1876, Tyntesfield.

We had a great shoot today at Charlton, George Bright joining the party. We all shot well and slew 312 pheasants. I heard from Louisa that both of the boys had done well at Oxford, and that Herbert seemed satisfied with his paper work at Cambridge so far as it had gone. Milly went away today.

Sunday 10th December 1876, Tyntesfield.

Letters from Louisa and Coleridge and I wrote to her….I, surpliced, read the lesson in Chapel. John walked with me as far as Belmont, by far the longest walk he has taken, and he seems none the worse for it.

Monday 11th December 1876, Tyntesfield.

Blanche and I had an amusing jaunt today. We meant to have gone to Cheddar to see how her St Michael's Home was going on, but we overshot our station and went to Weston instead, where we saw the excellent sanatorium (to which she has given free beds), and called on

Margaret Hendy. Antony and Janet, George and Beatrice dined here, and we went through the Executors' accounts with Antony.

Tuesday 12th December 1876, Littlemore.

I came here by the 12.09 (Flying Dutchman) to Swindon where I had to wait 20 minutes; but at Didcot where one changes again the Oxford train was ready on the same platform. I found the Warden of Keble fled, but fortunately both West and Shaw-Stewart were there, so we had a good talk over scholarship matters. Then I came out here and find Aunt Eliza pretty well. Wrote to Talbot.

Thursday 14th December 1876, St Dunstan's.

Blanche has come up to see Kate who is dangerously ill.

Wednesday 23rd May 1877, St Dunstan's.

Heard from and wrote to Blanche with her accounts.

Saturday 26th May 1877, Tyntesfield.

Edith and I came here by the 1.50 train and found Antony here who had come by an earlier.

Sunday 27th May 1877, Tyntesfield.

I wrote to Louisa and the Warden of Keble.

Monday 28th May 1877, Tyntesfield.

Edith and I walked to Charlton. Antony thinks he'll be in the house in 3 weeks! Not in two months if they are to clean the paint from the hall and paint what needs painting in the house. Kate and Charlotte Doyne came to dine.

Tuesday 29th May 1877, Tyntesfield.

Edith and I went to Weston super Mare, walked to the Sanatorium, and enquired how Blanche's beds were working, and had a satisfactory answer. Edith liked the building and its arrangements much. Then we walked all through the town, and having been refreshed by a hard shower (taking refuge in the Post Office where I despatched to Rowbotham his Majorca Report) we had a beef luncheon at a Pastrycooks, made a pleasant visit to Margaret Hendy and came home. The Superior of St. Peters came to stay. I like her very much. She is a Miss Oldfield. Catty and Constance Bright and Mrs Hamilton (Lord Dufferin's mother in law) came to call. I heard from Louisa.

Wednesday 30th May 1877, Tyntesfield.

Letter from Louisa… Blanche went with us to Axbridge Station whence we walked to see St Michael's Home for incurables, a handsome house very well arranged and with a pretty chapel. Thence through the Cheddar Cliffs, which I had not seen since 1845, and home from the Cheddar Station, getting a ducking as we neared the station.

Thursday 31st May 1877, Tyntesfield.

Blanche, the Mother Superior, Edith and I went to Clevedon Court and saw Sir Arthur and the new Lady Elton – no beauty but a very pleasing

Figure 36. Henry Hucks Gibbs photo by Valentine Blanchard, 1877.

looking person. Called also on Edith and Agnes Elton, but didn't see them – also Mrs Burrowes whom we did see. Heard from and wrote to Louisa. Alfred Gurney came.

Friday 1st June 1877, Oxford.

Blanche and the Mother Superior brought us into Bristol in time for the three o'clock train. Kenneth had taken us rooms at the Randolph. He dined with us.

Saturday 2nd June 1877, Oxford.

Called on Morrell, Shaw-Stewart and the Warden in the morning and settled with the latter the corrections to the deed. Then we called on Cosen at the Bodleian, went to luncheon with Kenneth, called at the Deanery – not at home – and went to Mrs Talbot's Garden Party, where was Prince Leopold, a pleasant looking young man. Then we drove to Clifton (*Hampden*) and dined with Sidney Harrison.

270

Tuesday 8ᵗʰ January 1878, Tyntesfield.

I came down here by the 1.50 and find Antony and Janet, and Martin and Dora, and Hardie here.

Wednesday 9ᵗʰ January 1878, Tyntesfield.

I wrote to Louisa and Catty Bright, and heard from Vicary. Blanche and Martin and I went to Cheddar to see the hospital where we met Butterfield who came back to dine and sleep. We went to luncheon with Mr Beadon, the Vicar, Mr à Court's nephew, and I met his wife and daughter. Miss McCorky and two young Doynes dined here.

Thursday 10ᵗʰ January 1878, Tyntesfield.

Butterfield, Blanche and I drove to Cleeve Hill, picking up Catty at Abbots Leigh, and I spent a pleasant morning with the Stephen Caves. The Barwick Bakers were there, and the Lawrence Caves, and Mr and Mrs Murray of Shrivenham. Charles, John and Johnny came to dinner, and the latter stayed. George and Beatrice also came with Mabel and Arthur, Tommy Sheppard, George Davy and Dick Payne. I heard from and wrote to Louisa and Alban.

Friday 11ᵗʰ January 1878, Tyntesfield.

Heard from Vicary and Louisa, and wrote to the latter. We had a fine days shooting at Charlton. Edward came over to shoot and dine and sleep. John also, and Bertie came to luncheon at Charlton and dinner here, and went back tonight with Johnny.

Saturday 12ᵗʰ January 1878, Tyntesfield.

Letter from Louisa. George, Beatrice and I went to Weston to see Margaret Hendy. George stayed there about some business, and we took a fly and went to Hutton to see George Henry and Mildred, but he had started for Exeter on a visit to Baildy half an hour before we arrived. He is very poorly and she also, but her lungs seem dormant; she is as fragile as possible however. It is a melancholy thing: both ill, and all the children and nice little girls having the seed of her complaint. The Charlton party went home and Sheppard and Davy with them.

Sunday 13ᵗʰ January 1878, Tyntesfield.

Antony, Davy and Sheppard came down to service. I went with Blanche and others to see Ellen Heap and Mark.....Heard from and wrote to Louisa, and to John, whom I meant to have gone to see today, but I was a little gouty all yesterday, and it has not yet quite departed. Heard also from Stephen Coleridge.

Monday 14ᵗʰ January 1878, St Dunstan's.

I went out shooting this morning, but left at 2, Blanche and Beatrice taking me in the carriage to the 3 o'clock train. We were delayed at Goring by the breaking down of some trucks in front of us, and so were an hour and 17 minutes late.

Figure 37. Antony Gibbs at Charlton with his son George Abraham.

Wednesday 16th January 1878, St Dunstan's.
I wrote to Blanche about Gerald Young taking the management of her
Paddington property.
Wednesday 24th April 1878, Oxford (Keble College).
Kenneth and I came down by the 10 o'clock train, and I was at work till
dinner time, first at the Financial Committee, then the Advowson
Committee and then the Council. Edith came with Blanche and Martin
by a later train, they, two of the Wardens and she to join me here at
Shaw-Stewarts in Norham Gardens. We all dined in hall at the Gandy's
and I sat between Professor Smith, candidate for Gathorne Hardy's
succession and my old friend Copeland. They put Smith between me and
Mowbray – two Tories – to neutralize him. I found him a very agreeable
neighbour. In the evening we went to the Wardens and had a pleasant
hour or two. The Pascoe Glyns are here and R.J. West. The Hall and the
Library are both beautiful.

Thursday 25th April 1878, Oxford.
A very tiring day. Holy Communion at eight. Matins half past eleven,
then the benediction of the Hall and Library, luncheon at 1.30. Evensong
at 5 o'clock. The speeches were all good, especially Gladstone's,
Hardy's and the Bishops of Oxford and Salisbury. Antony spoke well –
'with modest brevity' as the Daily News has it. The foolish reporter of
the Times suppresses all mention of him and Martin, and omitting my
speech leaves the names of the donors unknown to its readers. The
Oxford Chronicle gives the speeches best but rather muddles mine.
Unless I find a better report in the Guardian, I will paste the Chronicle's
report on the other side. Wrote to Louisa. George and Mary were there,
George Gibbs and his daughter Mabel, Alban and Bride, and Kenneth
and Charles. I find a good report in the Standard, which I corrected in
the margins, to what I really said.

Henry Hucks Gibbs said:
"Mr. Warden, the health of the anonymous donors has been proposed in
very kind terms. It is right that I should speak to answer the toast,
inasmuch that I have been the channel through which their good deeds
have been done to the College. I do it the more easily and with less
embarrassment because as one of the Council of the College, I am a
receiver and not a giver. I have therefore a right to take this opportunity
of adding my meed of praise to those of my kinsmen who have so
munificently cared for us, and who have added their names to the long
roll of benefactors through whose beneficence this College, to use the
phrase of the old benefactors, has been brought up in godliness and good
learning. I think, however, that those old benefactors stand on a different
footing as regards us from the benefactors of modern days. The old
founders of colleges, givers of quadrangles, and founders of scholarships
and fellowships are dead and gone these hundreds of years; and we owe
them our gratitude and veneration. They are the shadows of great names
to us, but we cannot have the same personal feeling of affection and
thankfulness to them that we have to the benefactors of later days. The
benefactors of later days are our own contemporaries. We have stood
face to face with them. Their good works have grown up under our own
eyes. We have taken daily interest in them ourselves, and to them,
therefore, we feel affection and thankfulness more real and more
personal. It is from them that we, the members of this college, received
these buildings, from them that we received large provision for the
encouragement of scholarships, and now that we have passed the
experimental stage, from them that we have this noble hall for our
common life, that beautiful library for your studies, and on the other side
of the quadrangle that glorious chapel in which you give thanks for those

things, and in which you are taught that all those good gifts must be used for the glory of God, in whose honour they were given. It is a great pride and pleasure to me that my family have had their part in those good gifts. For myself I have taken the greatest possible interest in this college, from the first conception of the building of the chapel, in every plan that has been made, in every stone that has been laid, from the first stone of the chapel till the last that was laid in this noble hall, and I cannot but think you will agree with me that we owe great thanks and congratulations to our architect, Mr. Butterfield, on the completion of this group of buildings, the like of which for beauty and for originality of design has not been exceeded, if equalled, for nearly four hundred years (cheers). Now with regard to the subject of the toast – the donors of these buildings. I thought I should have in my speech to make some dark allusion to the anonymous donors, their possible presence with us, and to the satisfaction which they would feel with your applause, and in their possible absence that I should have to convey your appreciation to them; but I am happy to tell you that I have obtained from my cousins, though not without great difficulty, permission to disclose that which they in their modesty would have kept unknown, and to tell you their names. They are Mr. Antony Gibbs and Mr. Henry Martin Gibbs, the sons of my late uncle, Mr William Gibbs (loud and protracted applause). I think you will agree with me that they are worthily following in their father's footsteps (renewed cheers). I congratulate them and you heartily on the successful and happy completion of the work. I feel proud of the possession by the college of those buildings, proud of the kinship of those who have given them, proud of the friendship of the great architect who designed them, and whose loving labour has brought them to completion, and proud that they now have your applause (cheers).

The Warden said that, as the names of the donors had now been formally announced, he felt it his duty to call upon the company to drink the health of Mr. Antony Gibbs and Mr. Henry Martin Gibbs as an acknowledgement of the admirable way in which they had followed in the footsteps of their excellent father.

Mr Antony Gibbs said,
"I rise to return you, in my brother's name as well as my own, our sincere thanks for the honour you have done us. When we first contemplated erecting this hall and library as a fitting conclusion to our dear father's gift of the chapel, we thought it desirable that our names should not appear as the donors; but as time went on it became almost impossible to prevent its becoming known, and as various reports were spread about as to who were the actual donors we at last gave permission

for our names to be mentioned. It only remains for me now to say how gratified we are at the successful manner in which Mr Butterfield has carried out his design (hear, hear), and we sincerely hope that this work, which has today been committed to your hands, may prove to be a lasting benefit to the college, and strengthen its hands in prosecuting that true and earnest work of the Church of England, which it has so successfully carried on ever since its first foundation. (loud cheers)

Friday 26th April 1878, Oxford.
Edith and I drove to Littlemore to lunch with Aunt Eliza where we found John Daubeny. I called also on Mr Green and Mrs Crawley and her two daughters. Kenneth dined with us in Norham Gardens and went with Edith and Miss Shaw-Stewart to some private theatricals, where they saw "A Scrap of Paper" well acted.
Saturday 27th April 1878, St Dunstan's.
Called on the Talbots, met the Sedgwicks there and came up by the 2.15.
Tuesday 28th January 1879, St Dunstan's.
I called on Robert, now Baron Heath, to console him on his father's death. He says Fanny Rose will go on living with her brother Henry. I hope she and John Merivale may come together again.
Wednesday 29th January 1879, Keble College.
I came down here with Kenneth by the 10 o'clock train, Bernard being in the carriage with us. I to stay at the Warden's and Kenneth with Charles Shaw-Stewart. Bernard and I did our auditing alone, the Bursar aiding us. We dined in Hall. Miss Lyttleton is here and Mrs John Talbot.
Thursday 30th January 1879, Keble College.
Occupied most of the day in the Council; then Kenneth and I and Johnnie walked out to Littlemore and back. Aunt Eliza very well.
Friday 31st January 1879, Tyntesfield.
Called on Mrs Liddell, the Rigauds, Sheppard, Coxe and C. Shaw-Stewart, finding all at home but Sheppard, whom I now find here....
Kenneth and I came away by the 2.30 train and came here in time for dinner. The George Brights are here with their daughters Ethel and Amy very dissimilar twins but both very nice girls. Amy the eldest is to be married in June to Herbert Alleyne, a brother of Foster Alleyne whom I know. The Heberdens also are here and their dear Sissy – i.e. Josephine. Mrs Burrows is here and the Charlton folk with Tommy Sheppard who is staying with them, and a Miss Denny dined here.
Saturday 1st February 1879, Tyntesfield.
We were to have shot in Priory Wood today, and after a while Antony, Sheppard and George Bright did go out but there was so much snow that I thought myself better indoors so I gave the lasses a lesson in Billiards. The Brights all went away before dinner and so did John. I wrote to the

Warden.

Sunday 2nd February 1879, Tyntesfield.

A complete thaw. Kenneth and I, Heberden and Sissy walked to Charlton and back. I heard from and wrote to Louisa.

Monday 3rd February 1879, Tyntesfield.

Mrs Burrows went away, Blanche and the Heberdens taking her into Bristol. Kenneth and Sissy and I walked to see old Betsy.

Tuesday 4th February 1879, Tyntesfield.

Heard from and wrote to Butterfield, Sidney Harrison…and Louisa. George, Kenneth and I walked up to Charlton to luncheon, and I afterwards walked down with Blanche to the "Home".

Wednesday 5th February 1879, St Dunstan's.

We all, except Martin, came into Bristol after luncheon, the others (with Charles, Beatrice and William whom we found at the station) going down to Exeter to Willie's Wedding, and Kenneth and I coming home.

Friday 7th February 1879, St Dunstan's.

I went in the evening to the Philological Society where the question was decided of making a contract with the Delegates of the Clarendon Press for the publication of our dictionary….The speakers were very complimentary to me.

Monday 23rd April 1879, Keble College.

Luncheon with Kenneth at which young Alexander joined us. Then we walked to Littlemore and back, spending an hour with Aunt Eliza, and meeting Aunt Susan on the road. I wrote to Louisa and afterwards we dined with the Coxes where we met the Warden of Wadham (Griffiths) and his daughter Maud, a very pleasant evening.

Tuesday 24th April 1879, Keble College.

After Chapel I went to breakfast with Shaw-Stewart; and then to the accounts – spent half an hour before noon when the Finance Committee met, in calling on my old master Bonanny Price who seemed to like the visit as much as I did….The Finance Committee from 12 to 4 with an interval for luncheon, a walk with Kenneth, who is in high feather at being elected without his knowledge and unanimously to Bullingdon. (The Bullingdon Dining Club). We have had a pleasant dinner at Shaw-Stewarts, Antony and Janet, Lord Beauchamp, Bernard, the Warden and Mrs Talbot and Miss Gladstone, Sir R. Wilbraham, Martin and Kenneth. Poor Blanche has an attack of jaundice and could not come.

Wednesday 25th April 1879, Keble College.

Early Service at 8, Breakfast in Hall, Matins at 10; Advowson Committee at 11; Council at 12. At half past one I went to luncheon with Kenneth, and there I found Mr and Mrs Coxe, Antony, Janet, Martin, Miss Shaw-Stewart, George Merivale, young Gordon, Aunt Susan and Selina. Shaw-Stewart followed me. I heard from and wrote to Louisa (who had been out for a drive)… Evensong at half past four; then tea at the Warden's, a long confab with him about Blanche's Scholarships, and a great and pleasant dinner in Hall at half past seven; I sat at the end of the High Table – Coxe and Bain on one side of me and Edwin Palmer and Bright on the other, a most lively quintile we made. Kenneth dined there, the only undergraduate in the Hall.

Thursday 26th April 1879, St Dunstan's.

Came up by the 9 o'clock train and find all well.

Saturday 28th April 1879, St Dunstan's.

Blanche has been very poorly with a kind of jaundice. I saw her yesterday and again today. She is now better and able to come out (as she did to see Louisa) but she looks very poorly. I had much talk with her and Martin about his affairs. I had a horrible bad night of tooth ache. I had the offender taken out. Heard from and wrote to Kenneth.

Friday 23rd January 1880, Tyntesfield.

We drove to Didcot, calling on the Clutterbucks on our way. They were very glad to see us, and as friendly as always. He had dined with us one day, and carried his eighty years well. On St Benedict's day next year is their golden wedding. Lucy Hannersby was there and a pretty little child of Ellen's. We changed at Swindon for the fast train. Blanche very well except for her eyes. Letter from Tyndall Bright and wrote to him; also Vicary and Louisa. The Mother Superior of St Peter's is here.

Saturday 24th January 1880, Tyntesfield.

Letters from Alban and Louisa, Sidney and Antony. Wrote to them… also to Charles and John about gifts. Mr Doyne dined and sleeps here.

Sunday 25th January 1880, Tyntesfield.

Letters from Mrs Herbert and Sir Henry Rawlinson, Sidney Harrison, Louisa and Alban and wrote to the three last; also to Kenneth, and to George Cokayne about my gift to him.

Monday 26th January 1880, Tyntesfield.

Charles Cave and Philip Mordant came to shoot; a Mr Long was to have come, but didn't. Martin stayed in bed with a cold. Antony came from London and joined about noon. John and the two Isabels came.

Tuesday 27th January 1880, Tyntesfield.

Letters from George, Mary and Charles, about the gifts, also from Elkington of the House of Charity, Louisa, Vicary and Alban. Mr and Mrs George Bright and Ethel and Amy came yesterday to dine and sleep and went away today, as did Antony also.

Said George and Antony, Fenton Miles and young Edwards shot with us at Charlton. 93 pheasants and sundry rabbits and hares yesterday; here we shot 70 pheasants, 50 rabbits and three hares. In the evening we went to a penny reading at Wraxall School. Blanche played the harp, and I read Gabriel Grub, and Barham's "Cynotaph", and Martin sang.

Wednesday 28th January 1880, Tyntesfield.

A very foggy day, but in London they have been having Egyptian darkness. Letter from Annie Pott. Wrote to Louisa. Elkington, Bedford, Gibson, Alban and Sidney. Catty and Constance Bright came to luncheon. I read aloud an amusing paper of Sophia Palmer's on "Dustyards"

Thursday 29th January 1880, Tyntesfield.

Letters from Remmett, and Stephen Coleridge. Wrote to the former, and to Burrell Hayley who had written to Louisa giving her Ashwell's "Wilberforce", and me Liddon's "Bampton Lectures". John, Edith and I walked to the Charlton Dairy.

Friday 30th January 1880, Tyntesfield.

Martin, Roger Ford and I went out shooting in the Woods, John being with us for two hours but putting in under stress of lumbago. We spared scores of hen, but killed six, 10 cocks, 43 rabbits and 2 hares. Letters from Alban, Bedford and Sidney, and wrote to the latter.

Saturday 31st January 1880, Tyntesfield.

Letters from Alban, George Louis and Shaw-Stewart. Wrote to the two latter and to Annie Pott, and a long letter to Sidney about repairs at Clifton Hampden. Catty and Emma Bright dined here.

Sunday 1st February 1880, Tyntesfield.

Letters from Louisa and Sidney, and a wrong headed one from Charles Daubeny. I wrote to them. Some of the party went to Wraxall as their wont is on the 1st Sunday in the month, but John being unable to go celebrated before breakfast in Chapel, and gave us viz. Mother Superior, Edith, young Isabel and me and some servants matins in the Oratory. Isabel (mère) had a bad night and is poorly today.

Monday 2nd February 1880, St Dunstan's.

Edith and I left at half past ten, the Mother Superior going to Bristol with us, where we saw her off to Bournemouth and waited for our 12.09 train.

Saturday 5th June 1880, St Dunstan's.

Vicary, Butterfield and I spent the day at Aldenham. I came back just in time for me to go with Edith to dine with Blanche and meet the Goulburns and Wallers. Then we went on to the Cranbrooks and met many friends.

Wednesday 9th June 1880, St Dunstan's.

Heard from and wrote to Edward Talbot about Chalmers who persecutes him to sign a memorial asking for a Baronetcy for Antony on the ground that his father founded Keble!! I wrote to Antony who I am sure will be indignant at being dragged through the dirt by this idiot.

Monday 12th July 1880, Tyntesfield.

Came here by the 12.50 driving over from Bristol over the bridge. Madame de Milanges is here, and the Beadons (3) and Courtenays (2) came soon after we did. Wrote to Louisa; also to Beresford Hope with my draft of the St Albans Chapter Bill, and to Upton with his draft of my will corrected.

Tuesday 13th July 1880, Tyntesfield.

Harry came here today and brought me letters from Alfred Gurney, Archdeacon Gaunt to whom I wrote, as also to the Lord Chancellor, and Mrs Menzies, and Louisa from whom I had two letters. All the party except me walked to a Garden Party at Backwell. I went to meet Harry and took a walk with him round the hill. Mrs Somerset (whom I used to meet at Colonel Fraser's) came today, and her daughter whom I met at Kate's. Young Woodland also came.

Wednesday 14th July 1880, Tyntesfield.

Sundry lawyers' letters in re Bath and Stevens. Letters from Ellacombe which I answered, and from Mrs Smith. Edith, Miss L. Woodard and I walked to Charlton.

Thursday 15th July 1880, St Dunstan's.

Came up by the 12.09 train.

Monday 23rd August 1880, Black Mount.

Davy insisted on considering us his guests till we crossed back into Argyleshire, and this morning about ten we left him and came with horses provided by McCourie of the Southern Hotel, as far as King's House and thence with fresh horses to this place. It was a most lovely journey through the pass at Glencoe, especially the first part of it. The grounds here are lovely and the grounds comfortable, and we have all been to have a row on the loch, and tea on the further shore not far from the fragment of an old castle. John and Isabel with Johnny and Blanche are here. Antony and Janet as well – the former discontented as I am that stalking by the rules of this place (St Breadalbane's I suppose) does not begin till the 1st September, and we go away on the 28th.

Wrote to George Davy and the landlords at Dalmally and Inverary for horses and beds for that day.

Tuesday 24th August 1880, Black Mount.

Antony, John, Johnny and I went out on the hill about 9 miles off, dismounting from our ponies when we came to a beautiful wood of birch and Scots fir. We had a most enjoyable day. Any two of us would have bagged as much as we did 12 brace and 9 hares, four guns are useless unless in separate parties. Heard from Selby and Louisa and wrote to her and Harrison.

Wednesday 25th August 1880, Black Mount.

Our brisk ride home – 10 miles in an hour and a quarter, has shaken up my liver and given me a little headache, but I have had a pleasant afternoon. Janet and Blanche rode to Loch Bar, and Antony, John, Edith and I drove to the turn from the high road and walked to the loch. Fished there a little and caught a few trout. Had tea and came home John, Edith and I walking to within two miles of home when Antony overtook us using a dogcart.

Thursday 26th August 1880, Black Mount.

A quiet day. John and I fished in the loch and caught three pike.

Friday 27th August 1880, Black Mount.

Antony, Johnny and I went over the same ground as on Tuesday. All three shot very badly, but we brought home 17 brace and five blue hares. We reached home at eight.

Saturday 28th August 1880, Black Mount.

Reginald Merivale came. We basked in a boat on the water while I read "The Legend of Montrose" to the ladies. We finished by chasing a brood of young birds and Johnny shot two with the gun Antony gave him this morning.

Sunday 29th August 1880, Black Mount.

John gave us service morning and evening in the drawing room. He and Johnny and Rooper and I walked up Ben Berrick (*Beinn Bhreacliath*) after luncheon. A most lovely view: about 3½ hours ascent and descent.

Monday 30th August 1880, Inverary.

John and Isabel went away at half past nine to Spean Lodge and we a few minutes later to Dalmally.

Friday 16th September 1881, Tyntesfield.

I came here by the 3 o'clock train and find the Goulbourns, Beadows, and Alfred Gurney here, also Kate.

Saturday 17th September 1881, Tyntesfield.

The Beadows went away and Mrs Atkinson (Geraldine de Gaja) came with her nieces, two Miss Bradstreets, nice girls who sing well. I walked up to Charlton and had luncheon with Antony. Wrote to Louisa and Mrs Rhode Hawkins.

Sunday 18th September 1881, Tyntesfield.

Letters from Louisa and Beatrice, and from and to Herbert and Upton. Alfred preached this morning, and the Dean this evening, excellent sermons.

Monday 19th September 1881, Tyntesfield.

Wrote to Louisa. John and all his tribe (but Johnnie and Bertie) came today. I played many sets at tennis with Miss Bradstreet.

Tuesday 20th September 1881, Tyntesfield.

I took a walk with Goulburn to Bourton, and saw the beautiful little church which Antony has lately restored. Such a pigstye as it used to be when I knew it. John and I went in the morning to Barrow Court and were charmed with that most picturesque house and much interested in Antony's plans for its restoration.

Wednesday 21st September 1881, St Dunstan's.

Mr Hicks and his Alethea came. I left after luncheon and came here by the half past six train.

Friday 18th November 1881, Aldenham.

After breakfast this morning I went to Norfolk Square, where Antony, Martin and Blanche slept last night (in Charlie's Absence). I had a chat with Antony about Amby Downs and St James's, and then went to Sant's (*James Sant R.A., official portrait painter to Queen Victoria from 1872*) where Blanche was, and stayed helping to bring about alterations in her picture till it was time to come back here. It is not a good likeness, but it is much better.

Wednesday 25th January 1882, Tyntesfield.

Edith and I came here by the 10.18 from Didcot. Charles and John are here with Bertie and Reggie, and Etta Hogg and Fanny Patteson.

Thursday 26th January 1882, Tyntesfield.

Fanny Patteson went away. Charles and I walked to luncheon at Charlton and Antony and Janet walked back with us. Mrs Drury, her two daughters and son, and Mr Hodgson dined here.

Friday 27th January 1882, Tyntesfield.

John and Etta and I walked to Barrow and back. Wrote to Louisa, George Cokayne, and Sidney. Poor Joe has I fear lost his eldest boy in some pony accident. Edith went to stay at Charlton.

Saturday 28th January 1882, Tyntesfield.

Antony, Martin and I shot Prior's Wood. 12 rabbits, 41 pheasant, and 1 woodcock (which I saw). George Bright and his wife, Grace, Tyndall, Catty and Constance dined here.

Sunday 29th January 1882, Tyntesfield.

After lunch, Martin, Charles, Etta and I walked to Barrow Court and found the house shut up and no one in. We remembered that we had opened a window upstairs on Friday and guessed it would not have been shut: nor was it. We found a cut off branch of a tree, and Charles and I held it against the wall while Martin climbed up and got in, and went round and opened the front door; and thus burglariously we entered the house, and I pointed out the alteration I suggested with a view of showing the staircase ceiling. Wrote to the Warden about Dr Thomas Aquinas's chapter on Affinity.

Monday 30th January 1882, Tyntesfield.

Antony and Janet are dining out, so Edith dined here – also Robert Neville (eldest son of Ralph N.G.) who is staying at Charlton. Louisa sends me a long and pleasant letter from Vicary, posted at St Thomas on the 15th.

Tuesday 31st January 1882, Tyntesfield.

Letter from Alban from Dunedin. I wrote to Vicary, and Fach, Coghill and Wheeler. Poor little Leonard is a little better, and I heard yesterday that there were some hopes of saving his life. He was run away with (*on a horse*), thrown and dragged some 300 yards, but there was no concussion of the brain nor fracture of the skull. His arm was broken and his leg also, the latter a compound fracture, and a large portion of the scalp was torn. John and Charles went away to their several homes. Blanche and I, and Edmund and Agnes Elton (from Clevedon) went to Cheddar, and Elton read, sang and acted, and I read to amuse the patients.

Wednesday 1ˢᵗ February 1882, St Dunstan's.
Edith and I left Tyntesfield and came up by the 12.09 train.

Monday 19ᵗʰ November 1883, Tyntesfield.
Left home by the 11.45 and stopped at Bath, and sat an hour and a half with Kate Lowe, coming on by the 4.05 train with Tom Crawley-Boevey, and picking up James and Mary Daubeny at Bristol. All seem well here, Antony and Janet and all their children being of the party and also young Henry Crawley, who is temporary tutor to the boys and much tired.

Tuesday 20ᵗʰ November 1883, Tyntesfield.
A capital day's shooting. I didn't shoot very well, but the others did. We got 195 pheasants, 25 rabbits and 8 hares and 2 woodcocks. Miss Stephanoff came to dinner.

Wednesday 21ˢᵗ November 1883, Tyntesfield.
A rainy day. We went to Charlton to see Antony's improvements – new billiard room, and Mr and Mrs Drury dined here. Edith came from Longton.

Thursday 22ⁿᵈ November 1883, Tyntesfield.
Rain till about three. Martin drove me up to see Barrow Court. It will be a beautiful house. Admiral and Mrs and Miss Cave dined here.

Friday 23ʳᵈ November 1883, Tyntesfield.
A very good day's shooting in Priors Wood, 202 pheasants, 22 rabbits and 11 hares. George Bright with us.

Saturday 24ᵗʰ November 1883, Tyntesfield.
Tom Crawley Boevey, and James and Mary and Alban went away. The rest of us went in two carriages to Barrow. Heard from Murray (*Oxford English Dictionary*) that he had had satisfactory letters from the delegates.

Sunday 25ᵗʰ November 1883, Tyntesfield.
Catty Bright and her cousin Mrs Hinde came to luncheon yesterday.

Monday 26ᵗʰ November 1883, St Dunstan's.
Edith and I came to town by the 12.09 and found Louisa's eyes better.

Tuesday 2ⁿᵈ September 1884, Tintern.
A very pretty day, but heavy dashing storms now and then which did not hinder our enjoyment of it. We drove to Raglan in the morning. I

spent a long time there. My indignation rising high at the destruction of so grand a building, but higher still at the rascality of the Parliament in not ratifying Fairfax's terms of capitulation granted to the grand old Marquis, and at the ingratitude of Charles II to his son. After luncheon at Monmouth we drove on here, and have thoroughly examined and admired the beautiful abbey – finding food also for a little indignation here. We walked around it through the fields and by the side of the Wye, asking permission with sweet words from an old woman, owner of the said fields. Then we crossed the river and took a walk to a height on the other side, whence we had a birds eye view of the Abbey; and so home to dinner. Wrote to Louisa, from Monmouth, Lord Powis, Hope and Harris.

Wednesday 3rd September 1884, Tyntesfield.

We drove this morning to Chepstow and Porthskewit, walking up the beautiful Wynd Cliff on our way, and seeing also Chepstow Castle. Then we crossed at the New Passage – a long business, as we arrived too soon, but the business of crossing, loading and unloading was very rapidly done. We drove to Knole Park and spent some time in seeing the lovely old place, and continued our drive to this place (Tyntesfield). Dr and Mrs Daubeny and their son Hugh, Fanny Patteson, Miss Horsley, John, Isabel and Johnny, Martin and Antony, Mr Codrington, Mr Humphrey and Hardie make up the party, and I have omitted Annie Crawley-Boevey.

Thursday 4th September 1884, Tyntesfield.

James and Mary Daubeny and a son and daughter came to luncheon and Arthur came from Flaxley. I wrote a great many letters, and walked with Mr Codrington, John and Edith to Barrow, where Martin showed me over the house. Woodyer has certainly done his work very well.

Friday 5th September 1884, Tyntesfield.

Wrote many letters and played much tennis.

Saturday 6th September 1884, Tyntesfield.

Wrote to Hope concerning the Altar piece. John, Isabel and Johnny went away.

Sunday 7th September 1884, Tyntesfield.

Mrs Russell (Maria Daubeny) called here with Mr Drury. I wrote to Bone, and to Louisa about Charles.

Monday 8th September 1884, Tyntesfield.

Letters from Bennett, Mr Fowler of Hatfield Hall, Durham, and Louisa, and I wrote to them. Miss Horsley went away, also Hardie and Hugh Daubeny.

Tuesday 9th September 1884, Tyntesfield.

Called with Edith on Mrs Drury and Mrs Russell – also with Blanche and Mrs Daubeny, we called on the Brights, Mrs Robert Miles and Frank.

Wednesday 10th September 1884, Tyntesfield.

Arthur and I went to call on the Vaughans this morning, and in the afternoon we went with Blanche, Annie and Edith to Cheddar, where after seeing the Home, Edith and Annie walked to Axbridge to see the Church and Arthur and I to Cheddar to see that Church where we made acquaintance with Mr Coleman, the parson thereof, and then walked through the cliffs to the top of the pass, and back by train to Axebridge where the others joined us.

Thursday 11th September 1884, Harrogate.
We left Bristol by the 12.20 train and are in our old quarters at the Prospect.

Wednesday 1st April 1885, Tyntesfield.
Edith and I came down here by the three o'clock train, half an hour late as was natural on the Wednesday before Easter. Antony and Janet and their children and Catty Merivale are here.

Thursday 2nd April 1885, Tyntesfield.
Had much talk with Blanche about her accounts and the investments we sold for her. Talked also to her, Antony and Janet about preparing one of the children to come at sometime into the house: Billy probably as he is keen, a clever boy, and I should like another William Gibbs in it.

Friday 3rd April 1885, Tyntesfield.
Letter from Gibson with the conveyance of Amos Holmes's cottages, also from Louisa, and Dr Murray (*the Editor of the Oxford English Dictionary*)

Saturday 4th April 1885, Tyntesfield.
Edith and I walked to Barrow, the others, save Antony and Janet, driving. The house is admirably done in all points.

Monday 6th April 1885, Tyntesfield.
I had a long talk with Hardie and Antony about the investments for Blanche. We all, except Janet, dined at Barrow. The Otter Barrys and Mr. Whitmore are staying there. Catty Bright and the Eltons came to dinner.

Tuesday 7th April 1885, St Dunstan's.
We came here by the 12.09 train. Edward is staying here. Harry is gone off to Antwerp this evening.

Saturday 27th February 1886, Oxford.
Came down by the 2.15 train to stay with the Master of Balliol (Benjamin Jowett). Lord and Lady Russell and their daughter, Mr and Mrs Pember and their niece and adopted daughter are staying here, also Mr Phelps, the American Minister. The Dean, Mrs Liddell and Rhoda came to dinner, very pleasant. They trotted me out about bimetallism, and showed great intelligence. (*Bimetallism is the concept of using silver as well as gold as a central bank reserve.*)

Sunday 28th February 1886, Oxford.
Walked about Oxford with the Vice Chancellor and his guests, after the

University sermon. Bat Price and his wife and daughter came to dinner. Dr Murray also. In the evening we had a charming concert in the College Hall, where Jowett has set up a great Organ, and the musical talent of the college, together with Mr Farmer, the organist and his daughter, joined in giving us some excellent music.

Monday 1st March 1886, St Dunstan's.

Mr Phelps, Mr Pember and I came up by the 9 o'clock train.

Tuesday 2nd March 1886, St Dunstan's.

The Russells and Pembers came to see the Bank (*of England*) and had luncheon with me. Blanche came to us to stay till Friday.

Thursday 4th March 1886, St Dunstan's.

Edith, Blanche and Vicary and Hardie (who came today) went tonight to see Faust.

Friday 5th March 1886, St Dunstan's.

Blanche and Father John went away.

Sunday 2nd May 1886, St Dunstan's.

I had a very pleasant dinner at the Royal Academy last night, well placed in the care of Mr Horsley who sat immediately opposite the President, and I next to him, Dr William Smith and Mr Alma Tadema opposite me and John Evans by my side. Speeches excellent, especially Lord Roseberry's. Janet and Georgey dined here tonight, also Charles, John and his daughter Isabel.

Monday 3rd May 1886, St Dunstan's.

Martin came up to dine and sleep, and I took him to the Levee and presented him.

Tuesday 4th May 1886, St Dunstan's.

Edith and I went to the Albert Hall to see the Queen open the Exhibition. A magnificent ceremonial. Antony and Janet and Blanche there, also Mary Silva and Silvia and Isabel Alice. Afterwards Janet, Martin, Antony and I walked about with Lady Mallet and a nice niece of hers, all the others having been lost in the crowd. Vicary and Herbert came home this morning from Paris, and Herbert went away to Canons Whitham. Anna went a day or two ago. Louisa Derwent is going to marry John Trotter the youngest brother of Colonel Trotter of Dyrham Park, a very good fellow, I hear. The girls will have, it appears, from £2500 to £3000 a year a piece.

Thursday 20th May 1886, St Dunstan's.

Went to Hyde Park Gardens to see Blanche and Emmy in their finery after going to the Queen's Drawing Room. Found a telegram at home saying that poor little Mary died at noon today. It is just a month yesterday since she came here to luncheon. It is a dreadful grief to poor John and Isabel.

Sunday 20th June 1886, St Dunstan's.

Dear Blanche still very poorly, though better. I went and sat with her some time after luncheon. Fanny Patteson there taking care of her. Etta Hogg also came to luncheon. Also Herbert and Anna who dined with us. Charles also dined here.

Tuesday 22nd June 1886, St Dunstan's.

Blanche called here, still not at all well.

Thursday 24th June 1886, St Dunstan's.

Herbert and Anna dined here and I took her to a soiree at the Royal Academy. Blanche was there which was imprudent.

Friday 25th June 1886, St Dunstan's.

And Blanche is ill again accordingly. I left my last molar in my right hand upper jaw in the possession of Mr Frank Bennett, the dentist.

Saturday 26th June 1886, St Dunstan's.

Blanche better. Antony and Janet and Cyril Gurney came to dine.

Saturday 8th September 1886, Barrow Court.

We came here by the 1 o'clock from Paddington, Lila and Sylvia Cokayne meeting us in the carriage at Bristol. Mr and Mrs Otter were here and Mrs Doyne with a little grand daughter.

Sunday 9th September 1886, Barrow Court.

Service in the Big Barn, which Martin has restored (during his rebuilding of the church) and which is itself a fine well proportioned building. The church will be a beautiful one. (*Henry Woodyer was the architect*)

Wednesday 20th October 1886, Oxford.

I ought to have come here yesterday, but I had mislaid my paper, and remembering that Wednesday and Thursday used to be the days, and not remembering that they were changed, I let yesterday slip, and arrived just in time for the Council, Beauchamp, Shaw-Stewart and Medd having done yesterday's work without me. Called on Reggie and Arthur Pott. Reggie seems well and happy. The Warden is his tutor and happy with him. I called also on Dr Murray and had some Dictionary talk.

Thursday 21st October 1886, Oxford.

I dined and slept yesterday at the Talbots. Beauchamp, Shaw-Stewart and Halifax dined yesterday at the Pusey house, so that our party was only the Warden and Mrs Talbot and Mrs Shaw-Stewart. Today Beauchamp, Halifax, the Shaw-Stewarts and I got a carriage to ourselves in the 9 o'clock train, and had a pleasant journey

Thursday 4th November 1886, Aldenham.

I went to the City, and to the Mexican Railway Board. Mr and Mrs Hambro, and Antony and Janet came to stay.

Friday 5th November 1886, Aldenham.

A deluge, but went out nevertheless, Hibbert joining us, and Cokayne

Maunsell after luncheon. We killed 319 head – 263 pheasants, one partridge, 23 hares, 14 rabbits, one woodcock and one wood pigeon

Monday 8th November 1886, Aldenham.

Antony and Janet went away.

Tuesday 23rd November 1886, Tyntesfield.

Came down to Bristol by the 11.45, Kenneth joining me there from Oxford. Blanche well. Guests Mrs Hogg and Etta, Annie Gibbs and her little Beresford, and Blanche and May, daughters of George Henry Gibbs.

Wednesday 24th November 1886, Tyntesfield.

Wrote to Louisa, Grenfell, Lord Coleridge and Mrs Edward Stanley. Walked with Blanche, Mrs Hogg and Etta to Bourton House which Antony has been doing up very nicely for Miss Downalls. Martin and Emmy, Mr and Mrs Carter (sisters of Moreton Frewen), Catty and Constance Bright dined here. Antony and Arthur Crawley Boevey called.

Thursday 25th November 1886, Tyntesfield.

Kenneth and I called on the Vaughans. We and Blanche dined at Barrow Court. Catty and Constance were there and Mrs and Miss Randall, Mr and Mrs Carter, Roger Ford, Mr and Mrs Hanbury, Tracy and Colonel Something. Kenneth wrote to Louisa from whom I heard.

Friday 26th November 1886, Tyntesfield.

Kenneth had luncheon at Barrow. I walked to Failand with Mrs Hogg, and she, Kenneth and I dined at Charlton. Blanche and Annie going to Clifton to hear Berlioz's Faust. Arthur and Annie Crawley Boevey are at Charlton. Wrote to Louisa and Grenfell.

Saturday 27th November 1886, Tyntesfield.

Heard from Mrs Edward Stanley, also from Louisa.

Sunday 28th November 1886, Tyntesfield.

Wrote to Louisa, and John and Burnett. Kenneth in bed all this morning with a cold.

Monday 29th November 1886, Tyntesfield.

Antony and Janet came down to dine.

Tuesday 30th November 1886, Quantock Lodge.

Kenneth and I came away by the 3.14 train and arrived at Bridgewater at 5 (half an hour late), and here about 6 o'clock. A beautiful house full of pictures and statues, and infinite books in best condition; Stanley delighted to show them to an appreciative brother Roxburghe. Mrs. Stanley hospitable and amiable.

Thursday 14th April 1887, Tyntesfield.

Edith and I came here by the 3 o'clock train, Fanny Patteson by the following one. Maurice Powell and his daughter here. Hardie gouty and went to bed soon after dinner.

Friday 15th April 1887, Tyntesfield.

Janet's ninth born (*Janet Blanche*) came into the world, a little girl.
Martin came to dinner bringing Una Hanbury-Tracy, a very pretty girl. In
the morning I read the Litany in the Oratory, no parson being available
for chapel duty. This evening Mr and Mrs Master of Bourton Grange
came to stay till Monday, he taking the duty. Very nice people they are.
Wrote to Louisa from whom I had a very bad account of Alexander
Beresford Hope.

Saturday 16th April 1877, Tyntesfield.

James, Mary and Violet Daubeny came to spend the afternoon with us.
The Talbots came before dinner, he much better.

Sunday 17th April 1887, Tyntesfield.

Excellent sermons from Mr Master. Beresford Hope a little better, but
still very ill.

Monday 18th April 1887, Tyntesfield.

The Powells and Masters went away. A slightly better account of A.J.
Beresford Hope. I wrote to Philip. Blanche, Edith and I drove to Charlton
and I walked back. In the afternoon we went with the Talbots and Fanny
to Barrow Court, and saw the House. Temple Bright and Ethel called and
talked about her son Trevor coming into the Liverpool House. The Miss
Downalls dined with us.

Tuesday 19th April 1887, Tyntesfield.

Mrs Talbot, Blanche, Edith and I drove to Charlton and then to Bourton
to call on the Downalls, where we saw George Henry and his daughters
Blanche and Emily, and Jen Mordant. Then to tea with the Masters. The
tapestry there is very fine and he has some good pictures. Mrs Talbot and
I walked back.

Wednesday 20th April 1887, Tyntesfield.

The Talbots went away, so did Fanny and Dick Payne. Blanche and
Edith went to Cheddar and I walked to and from Charlton. Antony came
to dinner and Mr Ash the new chaplain arrived today.

Thursday 21st April 1887, St Dunstan's.

Edith and I came home by the 12.09 train; stopping at Carter's to order a
wheelchair for Hardie.

Wednesday 31st August 1887, Aldenham.

Dear Blanche is very far from well and I feel anxious about her.

Thursday 1st September 1887, Aldenham.

I wrote to Blanche yesterday and I am sorry to find, on my return from
the City, today's account no better. I have been elected one of the
Governors forming the Council of the Church House. The others are the
Duke of Westminster; the Dean of Windsor, George Spothistwoode (3
years); Lord Justice Cotton; the Bishop of Carlisle and George Cubitt (2
years); [myself]; Mr Blakiston and Mr Thesiger (1 year) and we shall

appear in that order on the Charter.

Friday 2nd September 1887, Aldenham.

Heavy rain and wind all day. Blanche still very ill.

Tuesday 6th September 1887, Aldenham.

Dear Blanche is still very ill.

Wednesday 7th September 1887, Aldenham.

Antony has gone home to Tyntesfield, having given his shooting to Herbert, 66 stags to kill.

The Death of Matilda Blanche Gibbs

Thursday 8th September 1887, Aldenham.

The report of the Doctors (a Dr John Williams from London had been called in) is quite hopeless as to dear Blanche's recovery, but today's letter says she is a little more comfortable.

Friday 9th September 1887, Aldenham.

Blanche passed a quiet night. Beatrice and Evelyn left her yesterday.

Monday 12th September 1887, Aldenham.

Edith came home leaving dear Blanche a little more comfortable.

Saturday 17th September 1887, Aldenham.

The accounts of dear Blanche are still very bad; the operation of tapping which was performed yesterday was quite successful, and she was relieved by it, but Janet's letter this morning says I ought to go there soon, and that must mean that they are very apprehensive.

Monday 19th September 1887, Aldenham.

And with great reason, for a few hours after the letter came a telegram desiring me to come at once, and I hardly expected to find her alive. She had been able to keep nothing down, and had been very faint and they had feared she would not rally. But I saw her that evening, and though very weak she was able to talk with me a little, and was somewhat brightened for the moment by my visit. I saw her again yesterday and today, and both times she was able to speak as cheerfully to me as possible in the case of very dear friends who were never to meet again in this world. This was my most melancholy visit to Tyntesfield, and we returned today by the train from Bristol, calling at Barrow on the way to see Mrs Henry Daubeny about her son Henry.

Wednesday 21st September 1887, Aldenham.

Telegram from Tyntesfield saying that dear Blanche was "gradually sinking".

Friday 23rd September 1887, Aldenham.

A telegram from Tyntesfield tells us that our dear Blanche died this morning. It will not be for us the same world without her. I wrote to Antony, Hardie and Charles.

289

Saturday 24th September 1887, Aldenham.

Edith had a letter from Janet telling of dearest Blanche's last hours. I wrote to Harry. It was Thursday evening she died.

Thursday 29th September 1887, Tyntesfield.

The sad day is over, and all has gone well, even the great difficulty of a walking funeral for so long a distance. There was a great congregation of relations, and many friends. Mr Ford and his son Roger were there (I am sure not the Pope himself would have kept them away) and others too many to recount, all I am sure really sorrowing for the loss of our dear friend. Alban went back to town but Edith, Vicary, Kenneth and I stay the night. Dear Blanche made a new will on the 15th, executors myself, Antony and Martin. I had seen her old will many years back, and she had to make many alterations chiefly in the way of additions. She had left £5000 to Louisa, and nothing to our children except Edith, and now she has left £1000 a piece to Louisa, me and our sons and £500 to Edith and £500 to Katy - £8000 in all. She has left John and Isabel £8000 between them in trust, £500 to Blanche and £150 to Isabel, £24,000 among the Crawley Boeveys, £14,000 among the Daubenys, £3,000 to Mary Cokayne in trust, £2,500 to Charles, £12,000 among Uncle Joseph's children and grand children, £2,000 to the Pages, £3,000 to Augusta Pode, £1,000 to Tom Crawley and many other legacies; in all including £21,000 to Alfred Gurney (£1,000) and his two boys (the latter in trust), £5,000 to Woking (*home for consumptives*), and £5000 to Cheddar (*home for consumptives*), and £1000 to Brixham (*Seamen's Orphanage*), the residue divisible between Antony and Martin, the former taking her land, and the latter the settlement money.

Friday 30th September 1887, Aldenham.

We came in by the 12.09 from Bristol, Vicary who had gone in to Bristol to close the House there, coming later.

Tuesday 18th October 1887, Oxford.

Edith and I came to the Warden's House by the 9.09 train to St Pancras, only catching the 10 a.m. at Paddington. We should have done better to have had a good cab to meet us at Kentish Town. Warden very well. Mrs Drew staying here. Full Finance Committee. £900 profit on year. Dinner in Hall.

Wednesday 19th October 1887, Oxford.

Council at 12.00. Standing Order that two years should elapse from the date of the death of any benefactor, before the name should be inscribed on the commemorative tablet, suspended on the motion of the Warden, who then moved that Blanche's name be inscribed at once. Carried unanimously. I called on Tommy Sheppard, but the porter tells me he is too ill to come up. Also on Sir Henry Acland and his daughter. Edith called with me on Cyril Gurney, who has capital rooms in Canterbury

Quad, on Frank Crawley-Boevey, and on Morton Cokayne who has very good rooms on the High Street over the Leaders Bank.

There we saw Arthur Gibbs, and he and Reggie and Morton dined with us tonight, I acting as host in the Warden's absence at the Pusey House Meeting. Miss Mary Talbot dined with us, and also Mrs Woods, daughter of Dean Bradley and wife of the President of Trinity, a very remarkable little person and very agreeable. She had written an extraordinarily clever book, which Mrs Talbot gave me, "A Village Tragedy". A young Webber also dined here and played admirably on the piano. Shaw-Stewart and I went to see the new buildings at the Pusey House, and saw Charles Gore, the Warden.

Thursday 20th October 1887, Manchester.

We came here by the 9.50 and are very well lodged at the Queen's. Went straightway to the Exhibition, and stayed till 5, seeing 3 rooms of pictures. I wrote to Louisa this morning sending her the Warden's sermon of last Sunday, in which he spoke very well about dear Blanche.

Saturday 3rd December 1887, Aldenham.

Antony came last night to the Vicarage, and he and C. Barnett, A. Hibbert and Mr Thomas shot Berry Grove and High Woods with Vicary and me. Sir Walter Phillimore also. He came with Lady Phillimore last night. Our bag was 132 pheasants, 79 rabbits and 22 hares.

Monday 5th December 1887, Aldenham.

Edith and I took Lady Phillimore, with Alice Phillips and Antony to St. Albans, and after seeing the Cathedral, drove her to the station.

Thursday 8th December 1887, Aldenham.

Antony went away this morning.

Thursday 23rd February 1888, St Dunstan's.

Antony and Janet came here for a few days. Also James Edwards came to dine and sleep.

Friday 24th February 1888, St Dunstan's.

Edwards went home having had a very satisfactory talk with Antony. Antony and Janet went to Eton.

Monday 27th February 1888, St Dunstan's.

Antony and Janet went away.

Friday 18th July 1890, Tyntesfield.

Left Exeter by the 12.50 and came out here in the Tyntesfield Carriage. Cyril Gurney here. John G. Medley, also the Chaplain, arrived in time for Vespers. He looks little altered from the time when he was a tutor to Alban; a little more fat, and a little less hair. He dined here. The improvements in the house are very great. It is a painful visit however, my first to the house since dear Blanche was taken from us.

Saturday 19th July 1890, Tyntesfield.

Edith and I went to Belmont to luncheon with the Edwardses. Dyke and his daughter there. Afterwards we went over the Engine House and Accumulator Room here with them. It is a most splendid installation. The new stables too are perfect. 14 loose boxes and 5 stalls. Martin came from Barrow to see us.

Sunday 20th July 1890, Tyntesfield.

Early celebration here and Matins at Wraxall. Alban and Bride and their two girls, and Martin came over. Alban and I called on Medley at the Chaplain's lodgings built adjoining the first Lodge on the way to Charlton, a very comfortable little house. Medley dined here.

Monday 21st July 1890, Aldenham.

We came up by the 12.09 and find all well here.

Tuesday 31st October 1893, Tyntesfield.

Edith and I drove to the 11.45 train, Paddington, and came down here, Willy joining us at Bristol. A large party here, Martin and Emmy, John and Isabel, Dolly Herbertson and Evelyn Prescott and his daughters, a pleasant looking man named Lee, a friend of Hughie's. Medley also came to dinner, and George, Temple and Grace Bright. 20 at table.

Wednesday 1st November 1893, Tyntesfield.

Two contretemps today. Rainy weather, and the Bishop missed his train, drove all the way from Wells, and arrived with Lady Arthur just as the service was over, and contented himself with joining the party at tea at the Rectory.

The Church is beautiful, though not yet finished; the Screens, the Altar and the Reredos being yet to awaken. There was a large congregation almost all Wraxall folk, all Henry Vaughan tells me, very much pleased with the alteration and proud of their restored church. Old Mr Vaughan and Hensman are not reconciled to the changes, the Colonel really angry saying he will never come here again! Henry Vaughan under the great difficulty of the Bishop's absence had to preach a short extempore sermon and did it admirably.

Thursday 2nd November 1893, Tyntesfield.

Edith's birthday. I had a line from Grenfell on Tuesday, hoping I should be there yesterday, one of our officers being in trouble, and today I had a message from the Governor to the same effect, hoping I should be there today or at least tomorrow. They have not told me enough to let me see any occasion for it. Read Jevons on the value of gold. Curious how his arguments showing the then depreciation of gold are precisely those, mutatis mutandis, which I use as to its now appreciation.

Friday 3rd November 1893, Tyntesfield.

Rain more or less all day. Blanche Page came and Miss Kington Oliphant, daughter of Kington who sold Charlton to Uncle William.

Saturday 4th November 1893, Plymouth.

Left Tyntesfield at one and arrived here at six – the Royal Hotel.

Reminiscences of John Lomax Gibbs

Figure 38. John Lomax Gibbs.

JOHN LOMAX GIBBS [xx] was born on March 28th 1832 at 11, Bedford Square, London. He was the 8th son of George Henry Gibbs and his wife Caroline. He was educated at Eton from 1843 to 1845 and Charterhouse from 1846 to 1847. Then he was taught by a tutor, the Rector of Poundswick in Cornwall. He joined Antony Gibbs and Sons in 1854 but left due to ill health in 1856. As a young man, he travelled much abroad particularly in Spain and Italy, the Nile Valley and in Palestine. He was a student at Wells Theological College in 1858, and ordained Deacon at Exeter in 1859 and Priest in Exeter Cathedral in

1860. He was Curate at St Mary's, Torwood, Torquay, when his health drove him abroad again to the Pyrenees. After a year at Bradenham in Buckinghamshire (1863 to 1864), he was appointed Perpetual Curate of Clifton Hampden in Oxfordshire where he remained from 1864 to 1874. He resigned due to ill health and resided from 1874 to 1878 in Clevedon, Somerset. He was Vicar of Exwick, Devon from 1878 to 1885 and then Rector of Clyst St George from 1885 to 1897.

He married Isabel Marianne, the second daughter of Robert Bright of Abbots Leigh, Somerset, and his wife Caroline, on 3rd January 1860. They had four sons – John Arthur, Robert, Reginald and Francis – and four daughters – Caroline, Isabel, Mary and Ethel. John and Isabel retired to Speen House in Berkshire in 1897. He died there on the 12th January 1914, and his wife died at Speen House on 22nd March 1920.

THE REMINISCENCES

In 1853, John Lomax Gibbs travelled to Italy and Spain with his brother William and two friends – Reginald Barnes and William Sackville West, youngest son of the Earl of Delaware. They visited France and Italy after which William Sackville West retuned to England. In March 1853, the three other young men took a ship from Naples to Gibraltar and then proceeded to Cadiz and Seville, where they remained some time lodging in a 'casa de pupilos' in Calle de la Sierpe.

John Lomax continues:-

We saw all the Holy Week ceremonies and processions – most quaint and interesting. We went to a Bull fight in the great Plaza de Toros. We took Spanish lessons – and on the 4th April we retuned to Gibraltar visiting Puerto Santa Maria and Jeres. Mr. Gordon and the Osbornes, father and son, wine merchants, shewed us over the Bodegas, where the wine is stored – and were very kind and civil – talking about old days, old friends, my Grandfather, Father and Mother and many others.

From Gibraltar we went by sea to Malaga and from thence took our journey to Grenada on horseback where we spent many days of great interest and eventually got to Madrid after a journey by diligence, not without many accidents and mishaps. First the pole of the diligence broke, which caused a delay of six hours, then near Val de Peñas the diligence upset – we were in the upper coupé and must have fallen ten or twelve feet – but fortunately we suffered no harm. Then in the night we ran up against a wall as we passed through some town, but again escaped injury. Such were the perils of the road in those days. At Madrid, William and Barnes could only stay for a fortnight. Then they started on their homeward journey – and left me alone to my own devices.

I had made acquaintances in Madrid – O'Shea the banker and his family, the two old brothers Achaval, friends of Don Guillermo (Uncle William) and a pleasant Spanish master – Cornellas. I had a nice room in the Hotel in the Puerta del Sol, the busiest part of the town, and I settled myself down to work at Spanish. I picked up the language pretty quickly and though I was alone, it was not dull. There were pleasant parties at O'Shea's and at other houses, and I met many agreeable people – amongst them the Countess de Montigo, the Empress Eugenie's mother. One night there was a big dinner at the Embassy – Lord Howden was then the Ambassador, and once again 'tertulias' (*social gatherings*) in one or other of the houses of my Spanish acquaintances where I had the opportunity of airing my newly acquired knowledge of Spanish. I stayed on for some time in Madrid and from thence visited Aranjuez and Toledo – returning to Madrid again.

At Toledo I made acquaintance with some Spanish clergy – for I travelled thither with the Bishop of Jaen and two of his chaplains, and in their company I went over the Cathedral and saw all that there was to be seen…..

My next move was to Valencia where the Trenor family made it very pleasant for me – and after a stay there I went to Barcelona and there I met an artillery officer with whom I visited the Baths of La Puda making from thence an expedition to the Monastery of Monserrat – a well known and picturesque place of pilgrimage. We rode there – a large party of us – on ponies and mules. The Monastery is perched on top of a high mountain.

After this expedition I returned to Barcelona and soon after to Madrid – a journey by 'correo' of three days and nights, not stopping except to change the team of mules….I had agreed to make a stay with Cornellas, my Spanish master, and his family, at the Escorial and this I now did, many families take refuge there from the heat of Madrid for some weeks in the summer. It was dull there and the accommodation bad, but there was much which was very interesting in the Palace of the Escorial which was built by Felipe Segundo (*Philip II*). The ground plan is in the form of a gridiron in honour of San Lorenzo (*St Lawrence*). I had by this time much improved in speaking Spanish and could get on well without the help of Cornellas, so after some weeks I left the Escorial early in September and began to think of my journey northwards as I had hopes that Henry and Uncle William might come out before long with their families, and that I might join them somewhere or other.

I travelled to Salamanca first, then on horseback to Leon – a weary journey, flat plains and excessive heat. Then to Valladolid and Burgos, Santander, Bilbao, Vitoria, Pamplona and so to Bayonne. At Bayonne, hearing that the home party were on their way out; I pushed on to Bordeaux, and there awaited their arrival. I had not long to wait for the same day or the next arrived Henry and Louisa and their three children, my sister Mary and my brother William. Uncle William and Aunt Blanche and all their children arrived on the day following and we had a delightful family gathering – all the more delightful for me after so long an absence from all. Thus the first portion of my trip came to an end to be followed by another trip to Spain in company with Henry and Uncle William.

Uncle William having settled his family at Villa Mont Fleury near Pau (a house and place, later on, to be of special interest to me and mine) and Henry having located his family at San Sebastian, then we were ready to start off on our journey through Spain. Uncle William had not visited Spain since the days of his youth – and looked forward immensely to seeing it all again. To Henry it was all quite new.

It was on the 24th October or thereabouts that our journey began. Uncle William had taken the diligence from Bayonne and when he arrived at San Sebastian we were waiting for him. We took our place with him in the 'diligencia' and thus our pleasant journey began. We had eight weeks or so before us, and were to return by Xmas time to those whom we had left behind us. We went straight through to Madrid, a journey of at least two days and nights. (I am not sure that it was not three). We had Uncle William's old servant with us, James. The travelling was made as comfortable as possible under the circumstances. Uncle William had taken extra places so that we might have more room to stretch our legs. By day we all three sat in the tupé, James in the interior. By night I retired to share the interior with James. We took a good supply of food with us, so that we might at the stopping places not take food at the inn, but take the opportunity of walking on and so getting some exercise. Uncle William was full of spirits and so were we all, but he especially. He made himself although about 70 years old, quite young (*actually he was 63*) – smoking his cigar with us and occasionally singing some of his old songs to us Spanish and English – and teaching me to sing them. We arrived at Madrid pretty fresh, in spite of the long journey – and the same night went to the theatre – hearing 'El Oro y el Oropel'. The next day we got into lodgings – Calle Carretas No. 14. Our stay was only for a few days (*actually 5 days*) and these were very busy days – visiting all the pictures which I was delighted to see again, going through a great deal of hospitality on the part of O'Shea, Lord Howden, the Achavals – and many others – old acquaintances of my Uncle's.

On the 3rd November, we went on to Seville, another three days journey – with many incidents, breaking down of the carriage etc. We spent a week in Seville, which place I was glad to see again, and I think my Uncle enjoyed being there especially, as he was so often there in his younger days. There was much to see of interest – the Cathedral, the Alcazar, the Plaza de Toros etc. We did it all very thoroughly. We made an acquaintance with one of the Canons of the Cathedral, who was Precentor, and a great performer on the organ. He played one day after Divine Service many pieces for our benefit. Under his guidance we went all over the Cathedral and saw all the beautiful pictures and treasures. When our visit to Seville came to an end we went on to Cadiz, where again were many old friends. It was so pleasant to see how they all welcomed my Uncle and us for his sake. On one occasion he paid a visit to an old friend, Osborne I think, and he would not have himself announced, and then only by degrees disclosed who he was, and then such exclamations! Amigo mio! etc. – and such embraces – and expressions of welcome, which it was very amusing for me and Henry to witness.

I must relate one visit which was particularly interesting. There is a place near Cadiz called Chiclana where lived Doña Frasquita (*Francisca*) de la Peña, who was an old flame of Uncle William's in his youthful days in Spain. It was a case of mutual attachment, but the match could not come off on account of the difference of religion. The lady remained 'soltera' (*single*). Uncle William proposed that we should accompany him on a visit to this lady, so we all drove out to Chiclana. When we arrived at the house – as on other occasions – he would not have himself announced, and when Doña Frasquita entered, my Uncle bowed, but there was no recognition on her part. "No me conoce señora (*Don't you know me, senora*)?" he said; and then with a puzzled look she answered, "Por la voz, si – me acuerdo de la voz' (*For the voice, yes – I remember the voice*), and then after a few moments more – with an excited voice, she cried out "no es Gibbs (*It's not Gibbs*)?" and then tears on her part and embraces, a most touching affair – but my Uncle took it astonishingly calmly – smiling benevolently at his 'novia del tiempo pasado' (*girl friend of former times*). After such a scene it took some time to begin ordinary conversation. Henry and I were introduced and she was most pleasant to us both. She took especially to me because, she said, my eyes were like those of Don Guillermo. Then I remember she played to us most brilliantly on the piano-forte some of the old songs and pieces which she had played in the old days, some of which I had often heard my Uncles William and Joseph sing together. She made a medley of these old airs bringing them in, one after another as she played. Our visit did not last much longer. She asked after Uncle William's wife and family, and could not refrain from a sarcastic cut at my Uncle – "Los veijos siempre se casan con las muchachas (*The old ones always marry young girls*)". I think Uncle William must have been glad when this visit was over, but it was all very amusing to Henry and me. On our return

297

home my Uncle sent her a beautiful Broadwood semi-grand piano as a consolation gift.

Our time in Andalusia too soon came to an end. We then returned to Madrid, stopping at Aranjuez and Toledo, and after a few days there we went by diligence to Valencia, for there were the Trenors to be seen, and other old friends – to say nothing of the pleasure of going to the place itself. The time soon passed pleasantly away and with regret we had to turn our faces northwards and begin to bring our trip to an end. So on the 19th December we found ourselves at Madrid again, and soon after we took our places in the diligence, and started on the last journey. When we arrived at Vitoria, Uncle William left us to rejoin his family at Pau, and we said Goodbye to him with great regret. Such a happy time we three had spent together, and one Henry and I still look back to with great pleasure. We went to Bilbao where Louisa was with her children and my brother and sister, William and Mary. Later on – after Christmas was past – we all went to Pau and on New Year's Day 1854, there was a large family gathering, 18 in number, at Villa Mont Fleury – Uncle William's temporary home. But this was not the last act of our time abroad, for we travelled homewards leisurely, stopping to see various places of interest on the road, finishing up with a few days in Paris. Early in February 1854, I arrived in London having been absent from England since December 1852……

My brother Robert died at Belmont aged 17 on 31st of July 1856, and in December my brother Antony died at Cheltenham aged 34. In the midst of all these sorrows there was one bright gleam of gladness – for my sister Mary had become engaged to be married to George Adams, my sister-in-law Louisa's younger brother. This was a pleasure for all the family. The date for the marriage was fixed for December 2nd and though my brother Antony was very ill at the time it was thought better that the marriage should not be delayed, so all arrangements were made for it to take place from Belmont at the Parish Church of Wraxall. We had left my brother under his wife's care – and most of us went down to Belmont for the wedding, but full of anxiety as to what might happen at Cheltenham. The wedding took place – my Uncle Joseph performing the ceremony – George and Mary left for their wedding tour – and on that very day we received a message that dear Antony had passed away. The death of these two brothers was a great blow….These two brothers were buried at Clifton Hampden in the Family Vault.

Early in January 1857 my dear brother Francis was called away – he had borne his long illness very sweetly and patiently and he met his death calmly and hopefully. We laid him to rest with our parents, with George, Antony and Robert in the churchyard at Clifton Hampden. Only

Henry and I of our immediate family could attend the funeral – but there were many others, who had known him, round the grave with us.

I went to Wells Theological College on September 24th 1858 – and a very happy and I hope useful time I had there. I had lodgings in the Vicar's Close – a most picturesque and secluded old set of buildings with its chapel at one end and its ancient portico at the other. As I drew on to the end of my residence at Wells, an offer of a position came from the Rev. Hogg of St Mark's Torquay where Reginald Barnes was the Curate. Here I was to be allowed gently and gradually to begin my new work, but I was to have no stipend. Mr Hogg lived in his own house – Mount Hermon – they also had a house at Berry Head which came to Mrs Hogg from her father.

I was ordained at Exeter by the aged and famous Bishop Philpotts. My Uncles William and Joseph both most kindly came to Exeter to be present at the ordination. I went at once to Torquay, and for a time Reginald Barnes and I lived at "Mount Hermon" while Mr and Mrs Hogg were at Berry Head. We afterwards took a small house together.

Figure 39. The Rev. Joseph Gibbs, William Gibbs's younger brother by F.S. Amy Richardson after Sir William Charles Ross, 1838.

There was really very little for me to do except to assist in the services at the two churches of St Mark and St Matthias and to attend to my small district of about 100 poor people. In the autumn…Uncle William and Aunt Blanche and family took Mrs Hogg's House at Berry Head with the intention of staying there for some months, and I was constantly with them, riding to and fro from Torquay. Among their guests there who should come but Isabel Bright? I suspect that this was arranged by my kind Uncle and Aunt with the hope of bringing into my life the happiness which soon came to me. I was free to come over to Berry Head whenever I liked and so it came to pass that Isabel Bright came to be my wife. It was on October 27th 1859 that we were walking on the Head, and then and there the deed was done. I think our engagement brought great pleasure to all my dear relations and friends, and it was welcomed too by Mr. Bright and all his family. Uncle William who guessed what would be the result of that walk on the Head, met us as we returned home, and I remember that I said to him in Spanish as he met us 'Pued William me la embozabuena". It was delightful to see and hear his kind and affectionate interest in our happiness.

On the 3rd January 1860 John Lomax Gibbs married Isabel Marianne Bright, the second daughter of Robert Bright of Abbots Leigh.

"The wedding was fixed for 3 January, and on the 2nd of that month I went to Belmont (always a home to us all). My brother Charles had just returned on leave from the Cape, and he was my best man.

Uncle Joseph was to perform the ceremony assisted by Graham Tyndall a cousin of Isabel's….

On the wedding morning I drove over from Belmont to Abbots Leigh in the Tyntesfield omnibus with a large contingent of them. The weather was most unpropitious, a drenching rain fell all day, but in spite of the weather, there was a large gathering of friends and relations. I like to think of my Uncle George and my Uncle William and Aunt Blanche being present at my marriage. My brother Henry *was there* too, and Charles – and three or four of my old college friends, John Daubeny and Bishop King among them.

The ceremony took place, as was always the rule in those days, in the morning, before mid-day, and there was a great breakfast afterwards, but I was glad to be allowed to escape this ordeal, and after a private luncheon Isabel and I went off in a carriage and four, driving to Bath, and from thence taking the train to London which was to be our first stage on our way to the continent, and so my married life began and God who joined us together on that happy day has mercifully spared us...through more than 47 years – for I am writing this on the 20th February 1907.

Figure 40. Lieutenant Colonel Charles Gibbs

Charles Gibbs *was born on 28th June 1829 at 11 Bedford Square. He was the 6th son of George Henry and Caroline Gibbs. He was educated at Charterhouse School from 1839 to 1843 and then at the Royal Military Academy at Woolwich. He went on to Exeter College, Oxford where he matriculated on May 11th 1848. He served in the Royal Regiment of Foot from 1849 to 1877 and retired with the rank of Lieutenant Colonel. He served overseas in the Cape Colony (1854 to 1856) and in Aden (1867 to 1869). He died at his residence at 14, Norfolk Square, London on March 18th 1890.*

The first years of our married life were marked by many events, some of them causing sadness and anxiety, and some much happiness. One of the sad things was the death of my brother William, aged 29. His health had for some years past been failing – but we had hoped that by the invigorating life on board his yacht "The Gondola", he might have been restored to health – but it was not to be. He came home in June accompanied by Mr Hardie who had been his companion on his last cruise, and it was evident that he was failing fast. After a short stay in London at Hyde Park Gardens and at St Dunstan's, he moved to Clevedon where Uncle George and Aunt Harriett were staying, and there Isabel and I went to be with him for a while. Later on he went to Belmont, never to leave it again. He died on August 27th 1860. Reginald Barnes, William's and my old friend, and now my fellow curate, was with him and ministered to him at the last. It was a peaceful and happy end after a life of much sadness and trial.

On 21st September 1860, I was ordained Priest by the Bishop of Exeter in the Cathedral. Many of my relations were present.

There was yet another trial during this year for my health broke down….and a warmer climate was recommended for the winter. The hindrance to my early departure was that my dear wife was expecting her confinement some time in October and till that was well over we had of course to rest quietly at home.

Well the happy event took place on October 27th, the anniversary of our engagement day, and a little son was born to us. Aunt Blanche who was with Uncle William and their family at Baxton House near-by for the winter months was with my wife at the birth of the child… Thank God all went well and in due time (on the 7th December 1860) the boy was christened in St Mark's Church Torquay, in Jordan water brought from the Holy Land. He was named John Arthur.

On 10th December we left Torquay, soon to take our departure for Pau where we were to pass the winter. Isabel's maid accompanied us and Ellen Lord, the nurse for the baby. It was before Xmas that we found ourselves at Pau. We very soon moved into comfortable quarters at 'Maison St. Crieq' where we stayed till Lady Day 1861. Then we moved to 'Mont Fleury', a nice country house on the Côteau about a mile and a half from Pau, where Uncle William and Aunt Blanche were a few years ago for a winter – and where I stayed with them. We took the house for a year and two months. The doctor had advised that I should make a good long stay abroad so as to give my delicate throat a good chance of being cured.

The house was near the village of Gelos – it was situated on the 'côteau' – it was a good climb to reach it, but when you did arrive….the view on both sides was beautiful, On the one side Pau with its picturesque Château de Henri IV situated on the Gave de Pau – and on the other side a glorious view of the Pyrenees, with the Dent du Midi rising up greatly in the midst of the other mountains (*See Figure 23*)….

We had many acquaintances in Pau who frequently came out to see us. Some of these were regular residents there, whom I had known when I had been at Pau before. One was General de Gaja with his daughter. He was an old French General who had fought against the English in early life and had been a prisoner in England somewhere in the Berkshire Downs – Wantage I think it was. He was quite familiar with the Spanish tongue and spoke to me in that language.

The trips to the mountains were most refreshing and we all enjoyed the beautiful scenery. It was a most delightful time for us all… In September we went to Biarritz. We had a pleasant time there. The place was very gay. The Emperor Napoleon III was there and the Empress Eugénie and her little son, the Prince Imperial. Crowds of fashionable Spaniards and French were enjoying the baths and other gaieties – not a house or Hotel which was not full. We had our pony carriage and this was a great pleasure. We returned to Mont Fleury in October. By this time people began to flock into Pau again and soon another season began.

My dear Isabel was confined on the 27th November and a little daughter, Caroline Blanche, was born to us. All went well for a few days, but then Isabel became most seriously ill…and hope was almost given up that her life would be spared. Dr Ottley remained with us doing all he could for her…. He sent for another doctor, Dr. Smythe…. who restored her so much that we began to have hope again. From that time she improved and by slow degrees recovered.

Caroline Blanche was baptized on 29th January 1862 at the English Church at Pau. (Pedigree of Gibbs)

We remained at Mont Fleury till the 9th April when we left our home on the Côteau with regret though glad to think that we should soon be in England again.

Our journey home was a leisurely one – our object was to meet Uncle William and his family in Paris – the time fixed for us to join them made it unnecessary for us to hurry so we made halts at Bordeaux and Tours, and reached Paris a day or two before Uncle William's arrival there. We put up at the Hotel Bristol in the Place Vendome – and there our very happy meeting took place. Not only were all our expenses paid by my Uncle but Isabel had a nice present from him and my Aunt that she might fit herself out with some Parisian clothes…..At length our happy stay with them all ended and we left for London where we arrived early in May.

While we were waiting to move into our new home, Isabel was expecting her confinement and owing to her delicate health she was advised not to settle in. We had a most kind offer from Uncle William and Aunt Blanche to make Tyntesfield our home until after the event should have taken place so on 13th October 1862 we settled in there, and after long waiting and expectations another daughter was born on 27th December christened in due time at Wraxall Church by the name of Isabel Alice. I had already begun to get into work to some extent while at Tyntesfield – for I had assisted the Chaplain at Flax Bourton workhouse chapel occasionally – and took the duty several times at Flax Bourton Parish Church.

During 1863 I remember a ….visit to Clifton Hampden and here most unfortunately my dear Isabel was one night taken suddenly ill – and there followed a time of great anxiety….It was many weeks before she was able to be moved. After my dear Isabel's recovery….we moved to Dawlish for a change of air to complete Isabel's recuperation. The Tyntesfield family were at Mamhead at the time, the beautiful place near Dawlish which they had taken for two years during the alterations at their house. To Mamhead we went after Dawlish and there we spent our Christmas, returning home after a visit to Abbots Leigh.

Dear Uncle Joseph died quite unexpectedly of pneumonia on the 22nd March 1864 at Clifton Hampden. My brother Henry appointed me to succeed my Uncle – and I left with many doubts and fears in my mind as to the responsibilities which awaited me…… There were anxieties about the expense to which we were put by the increase of our family. This would have been really serious if it had not been for the great kindness shewn to us by Isabel's father who paid for my curates salary during the last two or three years of our stay at Clifton Hampden, and by our good kind Uncle William who made a most generous gift of £10,000 (*on the 24th February 1873*) thereby putting us in a comfortable position as regards our means…. My Uncle William at the same time made gifts to a great many of his family besides this gift which he gave to me. It was one great object of his life to make others share in the blessings with which God had blessed him.

In September 1864, my brother who was staying at Mamhead in Devon (where our Uncle William was residing at the time while Tyntesfield was undergoing improvements and repairs) while out shooting met with a very serious accident. He was climbing one of the high earth hedges, so common in Devon, and, placing his loaded gun on top of the hedge, it went off and dangerously wounded his right hand. Some of the shot, glancing off, lodged in his head. He was carried to Mamhead in a cart and the doctor who was sent for found that the right hand must be amputated at once. This was done and all passed off satisfactorily. It was a mercy that the accident was no worse. He bore his trial most manfully and cheerfully and made a rapid recovery. He soon taught himself to use his left hand and never uttered a word of complaint at the loss he had sustained. The very next season he was out shooting again and soon was able to make the left hand as capable in every respect as his poor lost hand had always been.

I had a letter from him soon after the accident which I have kept. *He wrote*, "My Dear John. It is very hard to write on one's back, and particularly so with the left hand but I think you and dear Isabel will be glad to see from myself that I am so far improving. Most thankful am I that the calamity was no worse, for no man ever had a more narrow escape from death or blindness than that which by God's mercy I have lately made. The kind sympathy and affectionate letters and messages from my dear friends have been the greatest possible pleasure and comfort to me..... Never more I fear shall we have a days shooting together, dear John, but what I can't take in meat I must in malt, and I have always too many blessings left me to be willing 'to sit down on my little bundle of thorns'. With kind love to dear Isabel, I am your affectionate brother, Henry H. Gibbs."

Dear Mr. Bright of Abbots Leigh, my dear wife's father, died in 1869. All his children were devoted to him and his death was a severe blow to them. He was always most kind to me. Isabel and I were staying at Tyntesfield during his last illness. I took the Burial Service *on the 24th September 1869*. He lies in Abbots Leigh Church yard where his wife's body also rests.

Improvements had been made at different times during our time at Clifton Hampden – the latest was the improvement of the Reredos… The expense of all the alterations was for the most part provided from a Fund which my brother Henry and all the rest of the brothers and sisters had formed with the object of raising a memorial to our dead mother's memory – a brass on the north side of the church records the gift.

It was on St Michael's Day (*Saturday 29th September 1866*), the Day of our Festival, that there was a special service for the Dedication of the new Screen and the rest of the improvements. The Choir on that occasion was put into surpluses for the first time…. The Bishop and Archdeacon were not to arrive till the afternoon but there was a full morning service. There followed a luncheon at which about 40 guests sat down. We had our house full – Henry and his son Alban, Uncle William and Aunt Blanche – and Mr Hardie – where we put them all I can't imagine. The Bishop stayed too. He arrived for the afternoon service and preached, and in the evening we had a large dinner party….The Bishop stayed with us for the Sunday, preaching again, and he left us on the

Monday – when our party broke up. It was a great happiness to have had such a successful gathering.

In the winter of 1871, I had a second attack of inflammation of the lungs – from which, Thank God, I recovered – though I passed through a time of great danger….. We stayed at Clevedon later on in 1872 and began to think that our winters should be spent in some warmer part of England – and that we could do no better than fix upon Clevedon….We went on through 1873 – wintering that year at Clevedon and the rest of the time at Clifton Hampden. It was in 1874 that we came to our final decision and left our home at Clifton Hampden for good.

In 1873 we had bought a house, "Oaklands" at Clevedon – which we hoped would do as a winter home – but it now became our only home. I was able to buy it by Uncle William's generosity. In addition to his former very handsome gift of £10,000 – he gave me another gift of £5000 – and out of this sum I obtained the house for £3,750. It was nicely situated facing the Green Beach and the sea and it made a very comfortable home for us – and in time we got to like our quiet life there and we both became stronger in health. All my children will remember a substantial stone built house, looking upon the beach, facing the Bristol Channel, with the distant views of the Welsh Coast with Steep Holme and Flat Holme islands in the foreground. The garden was not large but big enough for our wants.

About this time dear Aunt Blanche had given us a beautiful Landau – so that my dear Isabel, still far from strong – might be able to drive about in comfort. We had two horses, which would go in single or double harness – and all was most comfortable.

St Mary's Walton was a pleasant neighbourhood and we had many kind friends around us – the Eltons at Clevedon Court and the Cornishes at Walton School and many others. Our nearness too to Tyntesfield, where we were always welcomed, was a great pleasure. There were frequent visits from Uncle William and Aunt Blanche to us and from us to them. Charlton too was near where Antony and Janet lived. Old Uncle William was now well past eighty and his strength was failing, but he was always glad to see us. Mr Hardie too, for many years their chaplain at Tyntesfield, was a very kind and affectionate friend… In 1875, in the month of April, Uncle William died and we lost one who had been as a father to us. His generosity to me and mine was wonderful, and the kind and loving way in which he made his gifts to us made them all the more acceptable. It was not only to us that his kindness abounded – but far and wide he bestowed his benefits – always searching out for opportunities of doing good – and his noble gifts to the Church will always be remembered. I can mention a few of them (but there were many others known and unknown to the world) – Keble College Chapel,

St Michael's Church Paddington, and St Michael's Church Exeter – also the Reredos in Exeter Cathedral. He was most keen and earnest in the great business which he and my father had built up so successfully, but all through his life – and increasingly so in his advanced years – his piety, humility and generosity – and his loving affection were most striking. Business and money making may sometimes make people unable to cherish the higher qualities but it was never so with him. I hope there may be many to follow in his steps.

In 1878 towards the end of the year, there came to me an offer of work which I felt I should do well to accept. Willy Gibbs, Vicar of Exwick, had accepted the living of Abingdon, and he expressed a desire that I should succeed him at Exwick… I consulted Mr Hardie on the matter, for I always relied on his judgement in difficulties, and his advice was that I ought to accept the responsibility – and he gave me much encouragement saying that he thought I should be quite able to carry on Willy's good work at Exwick. Willy had had no easy time there. It was with rather a fearful heart that I wrote to Antony Gibbs on the 29th September 1878 to accept the living.

"Oaklands" at Clevedon was sold. Exwick Vicarage was built by Uncle William when Exwick became a separate parish. Uncle William was much attached to the place, many of our relations having lived there or in the neighbourhood in my Uncle's early days. It was always his wish to benefit places he had known in his early days……

Exwick Chapel, as it used at first to be called, now St Andrew's Exwick, was built by Bishop Medley, the then first Vicar of St Thomas and afterwards Bishop of Fredericton (*New Brunswick, Canada*). His son, John Medley, was at Exeter College with me – and became Chaplain of Tyntesfield, succeeding our old friend Mr Hardie in that office. Exwick became a separate parish in course of time, and my Uncle William became the Patron of the Living, which he endowed, and my cousin William Cobham Gibbs was the first Vicar of Exwick. During my incumbency sundry improvements were made, chiefly at the expense of our dear and kind Aunt Blanche who took the same interest in Exwick and its church as Uncle William in his lifetime took.

It was in August 1880 that we had a very pleasant trip to Scotland – Isabel and myself, Johnny and Blanchie – Antony had taken a large place called "Black Mount". I forget to whom the place belonged – there was every attraction in the way of grouse shooting, fishing etc., and it was in the midst of beautiful scenery. After a day or two at Tyntesfield, where we were always welcome, we started one evening from Bristol travelling all night to Stirling and then the next morning to Tyndrum, to Loch Earne and by coach to Inverrolan where we were met by Antony and Janet and rowed across the lake to Blackmount. It was a fatiguing journey and I believe we spent a good part of the first day in bed. My brother Henry and Edith were also of the party staying in the house. It was a thoroughly enjoyable visit lasting ten days. The fatigue of the expeditions, shooting etc. was a little too much for me and I had more than once to take to my bed and have a quiet day of rest – but on the whole I got a great deal of pleasure and refreshment from it all. The grouse shooting I delighted in and although nothing of a fisherman, I managed to catch some trout. We were sorry when the visit came to an end – but our stay in Scotland was not ended – for George Davy invited Isabel and me to his place, Spean Lodge, near Ballchulish – I remember well the beautiful trip on the lake through Loch Leven to Fort William – and this was followed by a ten mile drive to Spean Lodge – and there we spent a most pleasant visit – drives and shooting and delightful expeditions made the time pass very quickly – and then back to Carlisle where we stayed a night – seeing the cathedral next day – and so to Bristol and, after a day or two at Abbots Leigh, home again to Exwick after nearly three weeks absence

We lived for seven years at Exwick. Then while on holiday in Switzerland as we returned by boat from Lucerne a letter was put into my hands which had just arrived by post. It told us of Mr Ellacombe's death at the age of 93. He was the Rector of Clyst St George. My Uncle William, who was patron of the living, had years before told me that he would present me to it at Mr Ellacombe's death, but now, my Uncle William having died and his son Antony being the present patron, there was the possibility that he would not have the same intention that his father had. In a few days I had a letter from Antony which confirmed my expectations.

Charlton, Near Nailsea, Somerset.
August 5th 1885

.My Dear John,

You will I suppose have heard that poor old Ellacombe died on Thursday last and that he was buried yesterday at Bitton where his son is the Rector… He will be very much missed as he has done an immense deal of good there.

I do not know whether you are of the same mind now about succeeding him, but we should all be very pleased to see you there: and I think you have told me you would like to go there, if it were only for the sake of the old family connection with the place.

We go down to Elm Grove, Dawlish, on Monday for 5 weeks where a letter will find me. With all kind love to Isabel,

Your affectionate cousin,
Antony Gibbs.

Figure 41. The Church and Rectory at Clyst St George.

I determined to run back to England and have a look round – and so in a few days – having travelled through without a break in the journey – I found myself at Clyst St George – and Antony met me there. I stayed over the Sunday and preached the Sunday Morning Service. Everyone was most kind and I soon came to the determination that I must accept the living. Antony promised to rebuild part of the Rectory which was in a very bad condition. I paid a hurried visit to Exwick to tell my parishioners I must leave them.

While I was at Exwick, I had a visit from General Gordon just before he started on the expedition to Egypt which ended in his heroic defence of Khartoum and his death at the hands of the fanatical Arabs. General Gordon was a great friend of my old friend Reginald Barnes. It was when the General was paying a farewell visit to Barnes at Heavitree that the two walked over to see me. General Gordon had more than once visited Palestine and, as I also had been there with Barnes in 1858, it was kindly planned by him that the General should come to see me and have a talk with me about our Holy Land experiences.

I have too, on the walls of our drawing room, the six water colour drawings by Edward Lear which he painted during our visit in 1858. He lodged in the same hotel as our party at Jerusalem. He had journeyed to Jerusalem by way of the desert, visiting Petra and Mount Sinai, the only one to pass that year, for the country was very dangerous to pass through owing to the disturbed state of the Bedouin tribes. He suffered severely from them and was glad to have escaped with his life.

The year ended for us all at Tyntesfield where we were all taken for a long visit. I noted in my diary for Thursday 31st December 1885. "In the evening Antony and his party dined here and Martin and his party – 27 to dinner – Service at 11.30 p.m. and after that we all assembled in the Hall to wish one another a Happy New Year – and for those who cared to risk indigestion, there was toasted cheese to eat and hot ale to drink. A year of many changes and very much to be thankful for."

The Rectory of Clyst St George was held by one of our name and family, William Gibbs, in the sixteenth century. In 1543 he was made Rector of Clyst St George appointed, I believe, by one of the Gibbses of Fenton from whom our family is supposed to descend.

I believe it was a real pleasure for my cousin Antony to bring about my appointment – not only from his kind affection towards me and mine – but also for the sake of keeping the family connection with the Rectory. Antony had a strong family feeling – and I recall that on his first visit to us at the Rectory he said 'what a pleasure it is to find oneself in the home of our ancestors'.

Figure 42. John Lomax's daughters, Ethel (left) and Mary, 1885.

At this time our dear child Mary gave us some anxiety about her health. She had been confirmed at St Paul's Cathedral early in April. Her last illness came on and rapidly became very serious and she was in great danger. Soon she became unconscious and after lingering on for a time she was taken from us on the 20th May 1885. Alfred Gurney took the funeral service when she was laid to rest in the peaceful churchyard at Clyst St George – on the 25th May.

Soon after we left London for Barrow Court which Martin and Emily so kindly lent us and there we spent some weeks of quiet rest – and then after visits to Abbots Leigh and to Tyntesfield (in both of which homes we found, as always, such affection and sympathy) we returned to Devonshire and took possession of our now completed Rectory.

Figure 43. Barrow Court, Barrow Gurney, Somerset.

The year 1887 brought us also great sorrow. Our dear Aunt Blanche whom we loved so much and whose life was as precious to us as to her own family, was taken from us. She paid us a visit at Clyst St George on her return from a trip to the South of France which she had made with Mr Hardie, and while she was with us told my dear wife that she was suffering from an incurable complaint. I was attending a Retreat at Lancing College. She was wonderfully calm and brave, submitting herself entirely to God's will, but we could not but be very sad to think that we must not look forward to having her again with us – or hope to visit her again at Tyntesfield where she had for so many years welcomed us. She died on the 22nd September – only a few weeks after her visit to us. Neither of us was able to attend her funeral, both being laid up. She left us both a most generous legacy. There never was anyone so thoughtful for others, and I think my dear wife and I and our children experienced her loving care almost more than any others, excepting her own immediate family. She was laid to rest in the family vault in Wraxall

311

Churchyard, where rest Uncle William and Alice Gurney and two of their sons, George and Willy.

It was a wonderful instance of dear Aunt Blanche's calmness and courage that on the 21st June, when she was quite aware of the fatal nature of her illness, she took great interest in the Queen's Jubilee and was present with me and others in Westminster Abbey when the wonderful commemoration took place. She was eager and full of anxiety to see and hear all that went on just as if she had no bodily trouble to distress her. It was a long service and there was long waiting before it began – but she forgot all her troubles in the pleasure of seeing and hearing it all.

I was invited to be present and to preach at the Dedication of the Organ which had been given to Flaxley Church in Gloucestershire in memory of our dear Aunt Blanche. The church at Flaxley is a comparatively new one, built by my Uncle William and Aunt Blanche. Flaxley Abbey was my Aunt's old home. It was at the Abbey when I was a boy that I first knew my Aunt who was then a girl. It was shortly before her engagement to my Uncle. She was about 20 years old when she married and my Uncle well over 40. The Crawley Boeveys of Flaxley were cousins of my mother. Aunt Blanche was therefore my second cousin and was at that time always called by us 'Cousin Blanche'. We were glad to accept this invitation to stay at Flaxley. We stayed at 'The Cottage', a house at the entrance to the Park, where our cousin the Dowager Lady Crawley Boevey (née Daubeny) lived, her husband Sir Martin having died – and her son Sir Thomas was at the Abbey and is still there (1907). Our boys Reginald and Francis were with us on this visit which we all enjoyed.

After this the boys and I had a most enjoyable time in Scotland – my dear wife returning home. We stayed a fortnight with the Davys at Spean Lodge. On one Sunday during our stay I went with the Davys to Fort William, a drive of ten miles starting very early. I took part in the service, preaching, and celebrating the Holy Communion according to the Liturgy of the Scottish Episcopal Church.

On July 6th 1894, Antony's eldest son George came of age and the day was observed with great demonstrations. Antony, Janet and George came to us for the occasion. There was a big dinner in the schoolroom for all the Tenants and Cottagers on the estate. The room was decked with flags and made as smart as possible. At the Upper Table were Antony, Janet and George – Willy and Annie Gibbs, Major Tracey, Farr, the curate, myself and two daughters, Reginald too come over from Ottery. There were about 70 or 80 at the speechifying and all went off well. The only drawback was that my dear Isabel had to be away at

Oxford owing to the illness of one of the grandchildren. After dinner came cricket and other games – a capital band playing in the afternoon.

In September 1894, I had a nice trip with my two boys, Reginald and Francis, to Cornwall. Soon after this we received the sad news of our dear old friend Mr. John Hardie's death at Belmont. He had reached a good old age, I think 83. I had known him for 35 years – he had returned from the Cape after serving as Archdeacon under Bishop Armstrong of Grahamstown. The Bishop had lately died (*May 16th 1856*) and Mr Hardie's health being delicate he returned to England, but was not taking up any active work. My brother William who was then in a very poor state of health, was very glad to have him as his companion for his winter's trip on his yacht 'Gondola' and it was on his return from that trip that I first made his acquaintance. My Uncle William needed a tutor for his sons at Tyntesfield and I remember driving out in a Hansom Cab with him to some place outside London where Mr Hardie was staying – and then and there my Uncle came to an arrangement with him, and from that time to the day of his death he was intimately connected with my Uncle's family, first as Tutor, then as Chaplain at the Chapel at Tyntesfield, and after the death of my Uncle and Aunt residing first at Barrow Court with Martin, and later at Belmont where he remained till he died. He was always most friendly and kind to me and mine, and his death was a great loss to us. He left me one or two books which I still have on my shelves.

At the end of 1894... we determined on another trip abroad. We went to Cannes and remained there till the end of the year. Early in 1895, Reggie left us at Mentone to take up the curacy at Clyst St George. We had had a pleasant time together and it was a great help to have him with us during the first weeks of our stay abroad. Our stay in Mentone was on the whole successful. In these places with beautiful scenery and uncertain climate we were constantly tempted to do rash things – too long walks or going out in bright weather when the cold wind blew – it was so difficult to be prudent.

Our next stopping place was San Remo. There we stayed in a hotel close to the English Church and we had a large gathering of friends and relations with us.... Our party at the hotel consisted of fourteen or fifteen persons. Antony and Janet of Tyntesfield and some of their family, the Heaton family, Sylvia Cokayne and ourselves. It was a very pleasant gathering which did not last long – for each party went their way after a week or two. We met however later in Rome, but each in different hotels.

We went on southwards after this – first to Genoa, then Pisa and so on to Rome. Our stay in Rome was of only three weeks duration. The young people were able to enjoy themselves thoroughly but I was under the doctor's care all the time. I was glad to have visited St Peter's before the doctor's prohibition was given. I took pleasure in strolling in the piazzas and looking at the fountains and listening to the talk of the people. Antony was constantly with us and in his kindness he made beautiful presents to our two girls and to Sylvia Cokayne of very costly necklaces bought at Castellani's…. On Easter Day I was able to assist at the early Communion, a very striking service, more than 300 communicants. We left Rome with regret and turned our faces northwards; a few days in Florence at Paoli's Hotel, then to Milan – Geneva – Dijon – Paris – Rouen and home to 14, Norfolk Square, London (*the house inherited from my brother Colonel Charles Gibbs in 1890*) by the end of May.

At the close of the year, my brother Henry was offered a Peerage, which gave him and all who knew and loved him great pleasure. He and his wife celebrated their Golden Wedding on the 5th May 1895. I bought him a suitable present while we were in Paris. What a happy and prosperous life his had been.

Figure 44. Rev. John Lomax and Isabel Gibbs and their children, 1905.

On the Third Sunday after Trinity, the 4th July 1897, I preached my last sermon at Clyst St George to a very full Church and service over, the congregation remained outside to say 'Goodbye' – it was very

314

touching and overwhelming. All were so affectionate in their farewell to me and it was sad to think that I had finished my work amongst them.

A month or two before we left our home at Clyst St George, my dear brother Henry lost his wife, Louisa, on Easter Eve – they had been married more than fifty years – the loss to him and to all his family was felt by them all most deeply. Her whole life had been given to them and she had been a most devoted wife and mother.

Another great loss came to us on the 13th September 1907 when my dear brother Henry was taken from us. He had reached the great age of 88 – keeping up to a year or so of his death his usual vigour of mind and body. He was my father's eldest son and was born in August 1819. He had the most active mind, and the most kindly and affectionate disposition shewn not only to his own family in his own home, but to all his relations and to me he was always a most loving brother – shewing great affection also to my dear Isabel and to all my sons and daughters. He died simply from old age gradually becoming weaker and weaker as the end drew nearer. I miss him sadly and am now left the last of my father and mother's fourteen children. It cannot be long before my turn comes to follow them all to the life beyond. It seems most wonderful that my life should have been so prolonged as it has been seeing that I was from a child always delicate....

There was very great grief at Aldenham House where my brother died and this was greatly added to, for Harry's youngest son, Henry Lloyd Gibbs, whose home was close to Aldenham, fell ill at the same time and died only one day after his father leaving his wife and children to mourn his loss. My brother and his son were buried on the same day in Aldenham Churchyard. There was a great gathering of relations and friends at the funeral on September 18th 1907.

We have had other sad losses in our family. Dear Antony of Tyntesfield died in 1907 at the age of 65 – one of the kindest and most gentle of men – always most good to us whom he looked upon more as a brother and sister than as cousins. In his father and mother's time Tyntesfield had always been a second home to us and the sons and daughters we had been most intimate with from their childhood. As far as he could, Antony always tried to let us feel that he would be the same affectionate friend and relation to us that his parents were. It was he who presented me to the living at Clyst St George because he knew that his father wished me to succeed the Rectory and I remember especially one instance of his great generosity to Blanche and Ethel when we were all together in Rome. He gave to each of them and to Sylvia Cokayne who was with us the most beautiful and valuable presents of jewellery from Castellanis. He seemed always to be thinking what he could do for his relations.

John Lomax Gibbs wrote an "In Memoriam" for Antony Gibbs in the Parish Magazine of Clyst St. George, for June 1907, from which the following is an extract.

"On Monday 29th April 1907, in the Parish Church of Wraxall, in the lovely Churchyard which surrounds one of the most beautiful Churches in England, a Church restored by his munificence in memory of his mother some twelve years ago, was laid to rest the body of Antony Gibbs of Tyntesfield, Somerset.

"Antony was the eldest son of William Gibbs of Tyntesfield. The Hall and Library were given to Keble College, Oxford, by him and by his brother Henry Martin Gibbs. In 1872 he married Janet Louisa, eldest daughter of John Lewis Merivale, Senior Registrar in Chancery, the eldest son of which marriage is George Abraham Gibbs the present Member of Parliament for Bristol West. As a strong Conservative, Antony Gibbs always took a wide view of the Imperial responsibilities of England, and was intensely keen for the growth of a truer patriotism throughout the country. In 1887, on the death of his mother, he succeeded to his father's estate of Tyntesfield, and two years later took up residence there, where he will long be remembered as one of the best, most generous, and considerate of landlords. Naturally artistic, and a man of refined taste, he delighted in pictures and other beautiful works of art, while nature's colouring in both gardens and woods were an ever increasing source of pleasure to him.

"A true lover of all that is best and healthiest in sport, he was a good rider and an excellent shot, but singularly free from any of those vices which alas too often are associated with certain kinds of sport, and which tend to degrade it into mere monetary transactions.

"But though as a large minded Conservative in politics, as a loyal Churchman and promoter of all good and useful work in the county of Somerset and elsewhere, he was greatly valued and will be sorely missed, yet it is not by any of these things, conspicuous through they were in him, that he will be chiefly remembered and mourned by those who knew and loved him most, but for that singular gentleness and meekness of character, which, in spite of large wealth, simply abhorred anything like display or self advertisement, and led him (unless to promote some good cause or help the advancement of some friend) to shrink from the public gaze. For instance, to make a speech was positive pain to him, yet, when on any public occasion it had to be done, he always spoke wisely and to the point, and delighted those who heard him. In a word, that title of gentleman, so often misapplied to the mere possessor of wealth, but which in its oldest and best meaning embraces all that is most loveable and worth striving for in man, was his by nature, and it was this that made him the tenderest of husbands, the gentlest of

316

fathers and the most loveable of men, and his home a centre of unbounded hospitality, presided over by the most courteous of hosts.

"Such was the man, who, at the comparatively early age of sixty five years, was laid to rest on that April afternoon amid a large gathering of relations and friends from far and near – universally mourned, respected, and loved by rich and poor alike. May he rest in peace, and may God's Light and Love rest upon him."

Tyntesfield at his death passed to his eldest son George, who is married to the daughter of Mr. Walter Long, and his widow went to live at Charlton. She too was taken from us in 1909, and with her death the large family of sons and daughters are bereft of a very loving mother and their home is broken up.

At the same time that Antony passed away, his chaplain John Medley also died. An old College friend of mine who succeeded to the Chaplaincy at Tyntesfield when our dear old friend John Hardie died – a most cheerful and bright disposition Medley had, and a most valuable man he was to Antony and Janet – and all his family.

I do not know whether the beautiful chapel will now continue to be used. It was for two generations a very delightful and helpful house of God – not only to the family but to all the neighbouring inhabitants. Daily prayers and on Sundays full service. Everything most perfect and beautiful in the way it was arranged and furnished. I always took great delight in it and many times I preached there or celebrated the Holy Communion. As I write I call to mind the old days when good Mr. Hardie and after him, John Medley, held the post of chaplain, and my dear Aunt Blanche and her family daily worshipping there. (My Good Uncle William died before the Chapel was completed). Before the Chapel was built at Tyntesfield there was an Oratory in the House leading out of the Hall which served as a Chapel, and where my dear Uncle always read the Lessons at morning and evening prayer. We can never forget his impressive and reverent reading. It is a beautiful thing to look back upon. It was most helpful at the time, and it is helpful still to remember it all.

317

Gibbs after Guano

As its prosperity grew, the House of Gibbs became a Merchant Bank. The firm moved into the risky business of Stock Exchange investment and speculation. They invested in domestic, imperial and foreign government bonds. Speculations were made in Indian, Turkish, Egyptian, Russian, Danish, Brazilian and Chilean stocks. To a lesser extent they invested in railways, especially in Indian, North American, Cuban and Mexican lines. The buying of government bonds netted a profit of £77,739 for the 1860s. Railways brought losses totalling £151,173 with the greatest loss of £122,236 in the Imperial Mexican Railway. It was through Don Pablo Escandon, son of an associate of Antony Gibbs, that the firm came to be shareholders and financial backers of the Railway from Vera Cruz to Mexico City. With the overthrow of Maximilian and his execution in June 1867, the firm had to negotiate a new contract with Benito Juàrez's government.[xxi]

Figure 45. Ships await nitrates for export, Iquique, Chile 1885.

Gibbs money found its way into the City of Moscow Gas Company, the Mexican Gas and Electric Light Company, the Atlantic Telegraph Company, the Majorca Land Company, the Metropolitan Sewage Company, the Essex Reclamation Company and the International Finance Company.

318

The collapse of the great discount house of Overend and Gurney on Black Friday, 11th May 1866, caused Gibbs to record a loss of £60,798 for 1866 and this was followed by a worse loss of £71,105 the following year. Average profits for the 1860s were £60,984 and for the 1870s £15,892.

In South America, Gibbs invested heavily in the largest nitrate mining company, the Antofagasta Nitrate and Railroad Company of Bolivia, a Chilean firm controlled by British capital. In 1879, new taxes on nitrates of 10 centavos per hundredweight were levied by the Bolivian government and resisted by British and Chilean investors. It is not clear what part was played by Gibbs in the politics of this incident, but the Chileans mobilized with the intention of seizing the desert. This led to the War of the Pacific 1879-1884, when Chile defeated an alliance of Peru and Bolivia and annexed the nitrate rich provinces of Southern Peru and coastal Bolivia. During this war, Antony Gibbs and Company exported and sold guano for Chile from the occupied islands off the coast of Bolivia and Peru.[xxii] After the war the Gibbs involvement in nitrate mining beneath the Atacama Desert in Chile increased, and they invested in the following nitrate producing companies:

Alianza Nitrate Company	Pan de Azuar Nitrate Company
Rosario Nitrate Company	Cia de Salitera de Junin
Oficina Cala Cala	Cia Salitrera El Boquete
Cia Salitrera El Penon	Fortuna Nitrate Company
Cia Salitrera Lastenia	Cia Salitrera Los Dones
Santuago Zanelli	Tamarugal Nitrate Company

In the long run diversification brought expansion and substantial success. In 1890 Gibbs was strong enough to be included by the Bank of England in a syndicate to support the money market during the Baring crisis. By 1900, they were engaged in a wide range of commission trading, and had become a major issuing house and an important source of acceptance credits. Antony Gibbs and Sons had also become a major participant both as a producer and a trader in the Chilean nitrate industry. The firm was also heavily involved in the production of iodine in Chile. Henry Hucks Gibbs who had served as a Director of the Bank of England since 1853 became its Governor between 1875 and 1877 and the Member of Parliament for the City of London from 1891 to 1892. In 1896, he was elevated to the peerage as Lord Aldenham. Antony Gibbs and Sons were issuers of Government Bonds both in Britain and for foreign governments, and they had their own Insurance Company, and were Underwriters at Lloyds.

In 1902, Great Britain acted as arbitrator in a frontier dispute between Chile and the Argentine. Both countries had purchased warships from the United Kingdom. Following the resolution of the problem, these warships were no longer needed and Antony Gibbs was given the task of selling them. Two were sold to Japan, our ally at that time. Japan's enemy, Russia, wished to purchase the other two vessels. The British Government objected and to resolve the issue bought the other two warships from Antony Gibbs. They became H.M.S. "Swiftsure" and H.M.S. "Triumph". Both were sunk in the Dardanelles during the First World War. In South America, the Resolution of the Frontier Dispute was celebrated by the erection of the Statue of the "Christ of the Andes" on the Uspallata Pass at the border between the two countries.

In the first half of the twentieth century, Gibbs had offices in London, New York, Sydney, Melbourne, Brisbane, Adelaide, Perth, Santiago, Valparaiso, Iquique, Lima, Guayaquil, La Paz, Rio de Janiero, Buenos Aires, Johannesburg, Salisbury (Southern Rhodesia) and several other cities.

One of the earliest naval battles of the First World War was fought off Chile. The German Admiral, Graf von Spee, with five battle cruisers sank the British flagship, HMS Good Hope and another cruiser, the Monmouth, at Coronel off the coast of Chile on November 1st 1914. Hearing the news in London, the First Lord of the Admiralty, Winston Churchill, and the First Sea Lord, Admiral Fisher, sent two fast new Dreadnought battle cruisers, the Invincible and the Inflexible, under Vice Admiral Sturdee to the Falklands to join a flotilla to intercept the German squadron. On December 7th, in the ensuing Battle of the Falklands, four of the German battle cruisers were sunk, including their flagship, the Scharnhorst, with Admiral Graf von Spee on board. One battle cruiser, the Dresden, escaped and was later located at Cumberland Bay on Robinson Crusoe Island in the Juan Fernandez Islands off Chile. The Captain rather than surrender scuttled his ship. One of the coal supply ships that served the Royal Navy at this time was the S.S. Great Britain, which had been owned by Antony Gibbs and Sons between 1881 and 1886, when the ship was decommissioned and sold to the Falkland Islands. The whole episode reveals the strategic importance of nitrates from Chile to the British armament industry in time of war.[xxiii]

Antony Gibbs and Sons was the major supplier of nitrates to the Allied Powers during the First World War. In Britain, the firm did not profit from this enterprise, but delivered the nitrates at cost. Antony Gibbs and Sons purchased nitrates for the French and other allies until December 1917, when a Nitrate of Soda Executive was set up. Antony Gibbs' iodine imported from Chile was also in great demand for medical purposes.

The tonnage of Nitrates, provided through Antony Gibbs and Sons, to the Allies in the First World War was as follows:-.

For:

The United kingdom	1,660,000 tons
The U.S.A and Canada	1,630,000 tons
France	460,000 tons
Other Allies	50,000 tons
TOTAL	3,800,000 tons

During the First World War, Germany developed a method of producing nitrates by extracting nitrogen and oxygen from the air. This turned out to be cheaper than the mining of nitrates. In 1920, Antony Gibbs and Sons was requested by European stock holders to form a Nitrate Pool to endeavour to control the price of nitrates exported from Chile. Herbert Gibbs, who had been elevated to the peerage as Lord Hunsdon in recognition of his work in the wartime supply of nitrates by Antony Gibbs, was Chairman of the Nitrate Pool. The German producers were bought off with £350,000 and induced to join the Pool. The Americans refused to join and off-loaded their surplus nitrates at reduced prices in Europe. Antony Gibbs had 350,000 tons of nitrates purchased for £20 million in the Pool. When they were sold, these stocks realised only £13 million. In October 1921, the Chilean producers agreed to compensate the Pool with £1,250,000. However Antony Gibbs and Sons suffered a loss of more than £6 million and the firm never recovered the prosperity it once enjoyed. From July 1st 1932, the Chilean Government terminated Antony Gibbs and Sons involvement in the production, export and sale of Chilean nitrates. The firm survived but the Wall Street Crash and financial crisis of 1929, followed by the Depression of the 1930s, reduced its prosperity and power.

In 1958, the House of Antony Gibbs and Sons celebrated one hundred and fifty years as a trading and merchant banking house. In 1972, the family held shares were made available for the public to buy. By June 1973, the Hong Kong and Shanghai Bank had purchased 20 per cent, and by 1974 the Bank had bought 40 per cent. On June 2nd 1980 the remaining 60 per cent of the shares were acquired at a cost of £10.6 million. Thus from 1980 the Hong Kong and Shanghai Bank owned the entire equity in the company, valued at some £17.5 million.[xxiv]

Biographical Note

General Chevalier Victor Marion de Gaja

Chevalier de Gaja, as he was called, was one of the bravest officers in the French army. He had an adventurous career, especially during the Napoleonic Wars. He was taken prisoner at Corunna in 1808, but was subsequently exchanged and rejoined Napoleon, taking part in the retreat from Moscow. He was at the Battle of Leipzig in October 1813 when Napoleon narrowly escaped capture, attributing his escape to the prowess of de Gaja. Later, de Gaja was a French prisoner of war at Wantage. In 1817, he married Matilda, eldest daughter of Lord Robert Stephen Fitzgerald and grand-daughter of the 1st Earl of Leinster. She died at Pau, in the south of France, on 11th March 1850, and the general subsequently resided there for many years. His daughter married the Rev. Peter Righton Atkinson, Rector of East Hendred in 1868, and de Gaja went to live with his daughter and son-in-law at Hendred, where he died on 31st January 1875.[xxv] He and his daughter, Geraldine, became close friends of William and Blanche Gibbs and their family.

Table of Coloured Plates

Table of Figures

Index

In this index William and Blanche Gibbs are only indexed up to page 53. Thereafter their names occur on virtually every page until their deaths in 1875 and 1887 respectively. Similarly Henry Hucks Gibbs is not indexed for the pages of his own diary (55 to 292), where each page is of course related to him. Likewise John Lomax Gibbs is not indexed for his Reminiscences (pages 293 to 317). Because there are so many names in the diaries, the less significant and some referred to as correspondents are omitted from the index.

Tours, 8, 14, 86, 87, 88, 140, 142, 143, 303
Townley Ward, Henry, 7, 19
Trenor, friend of William Gibbs in Valencia, 125, 127, 295, 298
Trollope Anthony, 214
Turner Seymour, The Rev., 27, 34, 38
Tyntesfield
    1845 conservatory, 40
    Chapel, 228
    completed, Sept. 1865, 191
    completion of purchase, 38
    money for rebuilding, 175
    offered to William Gibbs, 36
    purchase agreed, 37
    Tower, 182, 187, 188, 190
Upton, W. Gibbs' solicitor, 172, 197, 207, 263, 264
Uspallata Pass, 320
Valencia, 10, 11, 104, 121, 123, 124, 125, 127, 128, 295, 298
Vallarino, Antonio, 14, 15, 16, 17, 18
Valparaiso, 26, 28, 29, 44, 46, 47, 48, 197, 233, 320
Vaughan
    Charles, 61
    Edward, The Rev., 36, 61, 71, 81, 82, 127, 199, 204, 232, 235, 248, 262, 287
    Henry, 204, 292
Vaughan Baugh and Co. of Bristol, 9
Venice, 26, 35, 36, 62
Vera Cruz, 15, 19, 186, 241, 318
Vicary
    Anne, 6
    Anthony and Elizabeth, 6
Victor, Marshal, 18
Villafranca, 95

Vimiero, Battle of, 17
Vitoria, 14, 22, 94, 95, 132, 133, 295, 298
Vitoria, Battle of, 21
Wallace, Sir Thomas, 220
Waller, Sir Thomas, 262
Walton, 259, 306
War of the Pacific, 319
Warship sales by Antony Gibbs, 320
Watercress Farm, 38, 39, 40
Watts, George Frederick, 237, 238
Wellesley
    General Sir Arthur, 17, 18, 21
Wellington
    The Duke of, 52, 76, 238
Wells Theological College, 299
Westminster
    The Duke of, 288
William Taylor and Son, 9
Williams
    Don Julian, 104, 112
    Don Manuel, 105, 113
    Dr John, 289
    UK consul in Seville, 101
Winchester, Bishop of, 242
Windsor, the Dean of, 288
Woodyer, Henry, 283, 286
Wordsworth, Charles, 240
Wraxall, 6, 74, 127, 137, 192, 193, 196, 198, 200, 201, 203, 207, 213, 221, 226, 235, 239, 253, 277, 278, 292, 298, 304, 311, 316
yellow fever, 13, 25, 223
Yonge
    Charlotte, 47, 205, 215, 230, 238, 246
    John, 48, 180
    William, 47
Zaragossa, 10
Zurbaran, 102, 123

REFERENCES

[i] "The History of Antony and Dorothea Gibbs and their Contemporary Relatives including the History of the Origin and Early Years of the House of Antony Gibbs and Sons, John Arthur Gibbs. Saint Catherine Press, London, 1922.

[ii] "Fragile Fortunes", Elizabeth Neill. Halsgrove, Exeter, 2008. Page 195.

[iii] "Fragile Fortunes", Elizabeth Neill. Halsgrove, Exeter, 2008. Page 289.

[iv] "Fragile Fortunes", Elizabeth Neill. Halsgrove, Exeter, 2008. Page 105.

[v] "Fragile Fortunes", Elizabeth Neill. Halsgrove, Exeter, 2008. Page 213.

[vi] "Fragile Fortunes", Elizabeth Neill. Halsgrove, Exeter, 2008. Pages 226-232.

[vii] "Fragile Fortunes", Elizabeth Neill. Halsgrove, Exeter, 2008. Pages 276-279.

[viii] "Fragile Fortunes", Elizabeth Neill. Halsgrove, Exeter, 2008. Page 289.

[ix] "Pedigree of the Family of Gibbs". Fourth Edition. Rachel Gibbs. 1981. Kingprint, Richmond, Surrey. Page 18 (7) and Page 19 (18).

[x] "Pedigree of the Family of Gibbs". Fourth Edition. Rachel Gibbs. 1981. Kingprint, Richmond, Surrey. Page 25.

[xi] "Pedigree of the Family of Gibbs". Fourth Edition. Rachel Gibbs. 1981. Kingprint, Richmond, Surrey. Page 26.

[xii] "Pedigree of the Family of Gibbs". Fourth Edition. Rachel Gibbs. 1981. Kingprint, Richmond, Surrey. Page 31.
"The Oxford Dictionary of National Biography" – Martin Daunton, 'Gibbs, Henry Hucks, First Baron Aldenham (1819–1907)', first published Sept 2004. The Times. September 14th 1907. Page 6. Column C. Obituary for Lord Aldenham.

[xiii] This and all further letters are from the Aldenham Letter Collection in the Archive of Antony Gibbs and Sons, the Guildhall Library, City of London.

[xiv] "Pedigree of the Family of Gibbs". Fourth Edition. Rachel Gibbs. 1981. Kingprint, Richmond, Surrey. Page 32.

[xv] Autobiography of Anthony Trollope, Chapter 3. Blackwood. 1883.

[xvi] The Aldenham Letters, the Guildhall Library, City of London.

[xvii] Courtesy of Keble College Archives.

[xviii] The Aldenham Letters, the Guildhall Library, City of London.

[xix] The Aldenham Letters, the Guildhall Library, City of London.

[xx] "Pedigree of the Family of Gibbs". Fourth Edition. Rachel Gibbs. 1981. Kingprint, Richmond, Surrey. Page 63.

[xxi] "The House of Gibbs and the Peruvian Guano Monopoly", by W.M. Matthew published in the Studies in History Series by the Royal Historical Society in 1981. (ISBN 0 901050 61 X).
"Antony Gibbs and Sons Limited, Merchants and Bankers 1808-1958" published by Antony Gibbs & Sons in 1958.

[xxii] www.geology.ucdavis.edu/~cowen/~GEL115/115CH16fertilizer.html

[xxiii] Castles of Steel by Robert Massie, Jonathan Cape, London, 2003.

[xxiv] The History of the Hong Kong and Shanghai Banking Corporation. Volume IV, The Hong Kong Bank in the Period of Development and Nationalism, 1941 to 1984. Frank H.H. King. Cambridge University Press, 1991.

[xxv] Royal Berkshire History. David Nash Ford. 2004.